YOU'RE READING THE WRONG WAY!

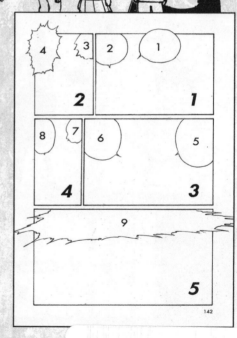

The Promised Neverland reads from right to left, starting in the upper-right corner. Japanese is read from right to left, meaning that action, sound effects and word-balloon order are completely reversed from English order.

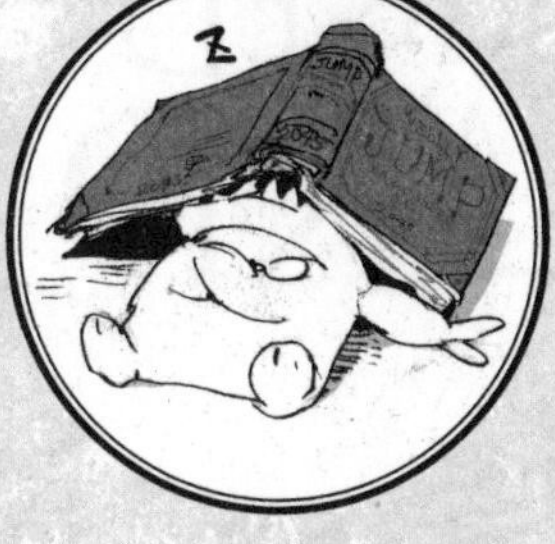

POSUKA DEMIZU

The library at Grace Field House has a vaulted ceiling, so the walls that continue to the roof are full of books!

I would love to live in a place like that, but I wouldn't want to be shipped out!

Please look forward to the reveal of a hidden room in volume 3. Grace Field House is still full of secrets.

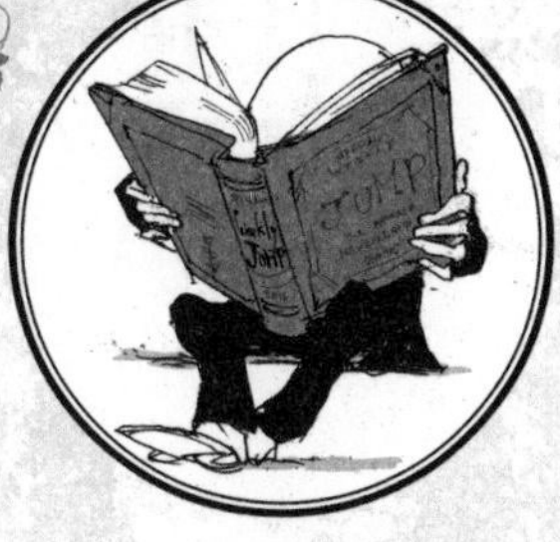

KAIU SHIRAI

Writer Shirai's personal highlights for *The Promised Neverland* fanatics, part 2:

1. The background characters (observing them is always fun—it's interesting how Demizu Sensei adds flair to each one)

2. The numbers on the characters' necks (do they have a system?)

I made a chart of the other characters (only some of them) with their corresponding numbers. (I wonder if they provide a hint of some sort?)

Okay, please enjoy the volume!

Posuka Demizu debuted as a manga artist with the 2013 *CoroCoro* series *Oreca Monster Bouken Retsuden*. A collection of illustrations, *The Art of Posuka Demizu,* was released in 2016 by PIE International.

Kaiu Shirai debuted in 2015 with *Ashley Gate no Yukue* on the *Shonen Jump+* website. Shirai first worked with Posuka Demizu on the two-shot *Poppy no Negai*, which was released in February 2016.

THE PROMISED NEVERLAND

VOLUME 2
SHONEN JUMP Manga Edition

STORY BY KAIU SHIRAI
ART BY POSUKA DEMIZU

Translation/Satsuki Yamashita
Touch-Up Art & Lettering/Mark McMurray
Design/Julian [JR] Robinson
Editor/Alexis Kirsch

Printed in Italy

Published by VIZ Media, LLC
P.O. Box 77010
San Francisco, CA 94107

10 9 8 7
First printing, February 2018
Seventh printing, April 2021

VIZ MEDIA
viz.com

SHONEN JUMP

THE PROMISED NEVERLAND

2

Control

STORY	KAIU SHIRAI
ART	POSUKA DEMIZU

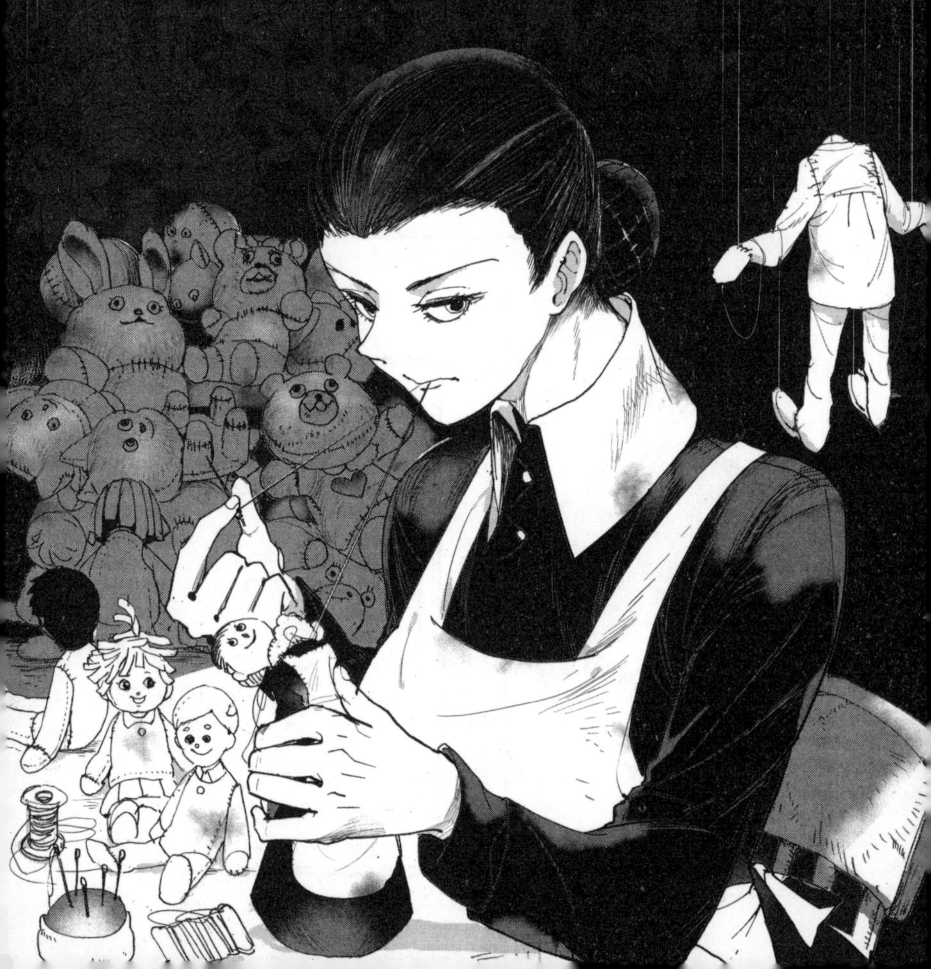

CHARACTERS

EMMA

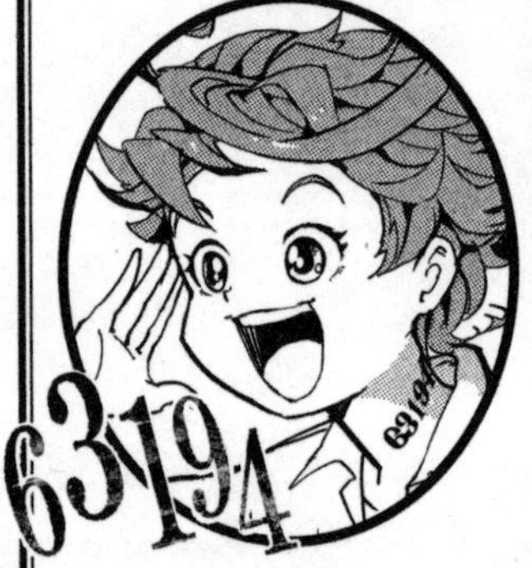
63194

An enthusiastic and optimistic girl with superb athletic and learning abilities.

RAY

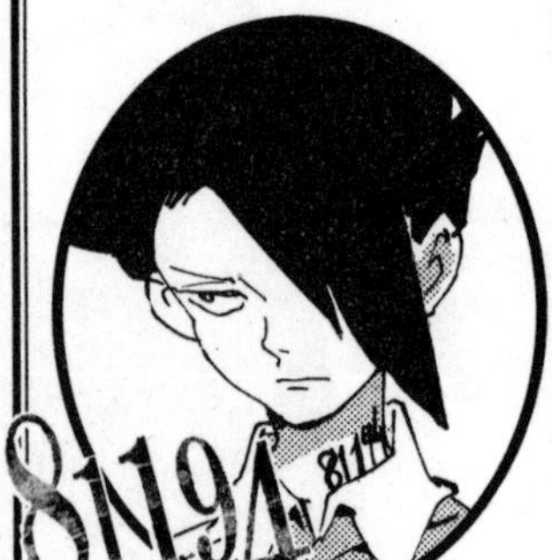
81194

The only one among the Grace Field House children who can match wits with Norman.

NORMAN

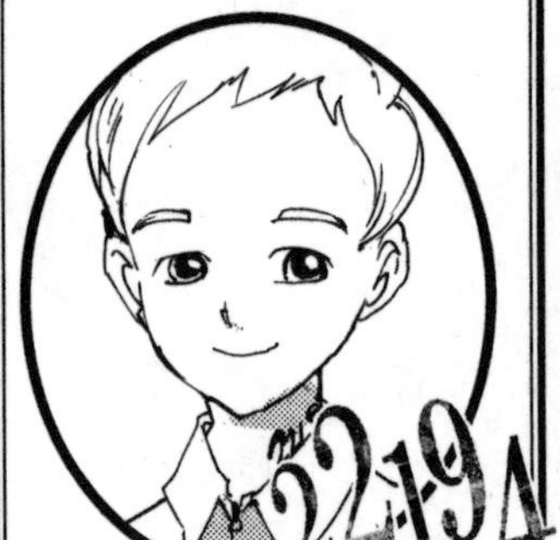
22194

A boy with excellent analytical and decision-making capabilities. He's the smartest child at Grace Field House.

KRONE

Isabella's assistant and a subordinate of the demons.

ISABELLA

The "Mom" of the children at Grace Field House.

DON

A carefree boy who is cheerful but competitive.

GILDA

A girl who is interested in fashion.

The Story So Far

The 38 children of Grace Field House orphanage are all living happily with their "Mom," Isabella, treating her as if she were their real mother. One day, one of the children leaves the orphanage to live with her new foster family. But when Emma and Norman go to the gate to deliver something she's left behind, they witness her lifeless body and some terrible monsters. In addition, they discover that Mom is raising them as food for the monsters. Emma swears that she'll never lose another family member and starts gathering information in order to survive. She and Norman figure out that the daily tests they take are to develop their brains, the monsters' favorite part to eat. They eventually get Ray to join their side, and the three start planning a way to escape.

THE PROMISED NEVERLAND 2

Control

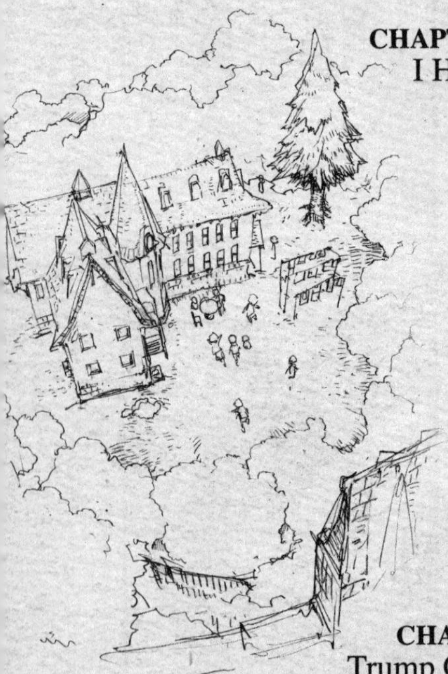

CHAPTER 8: I HAVE AN IDEA

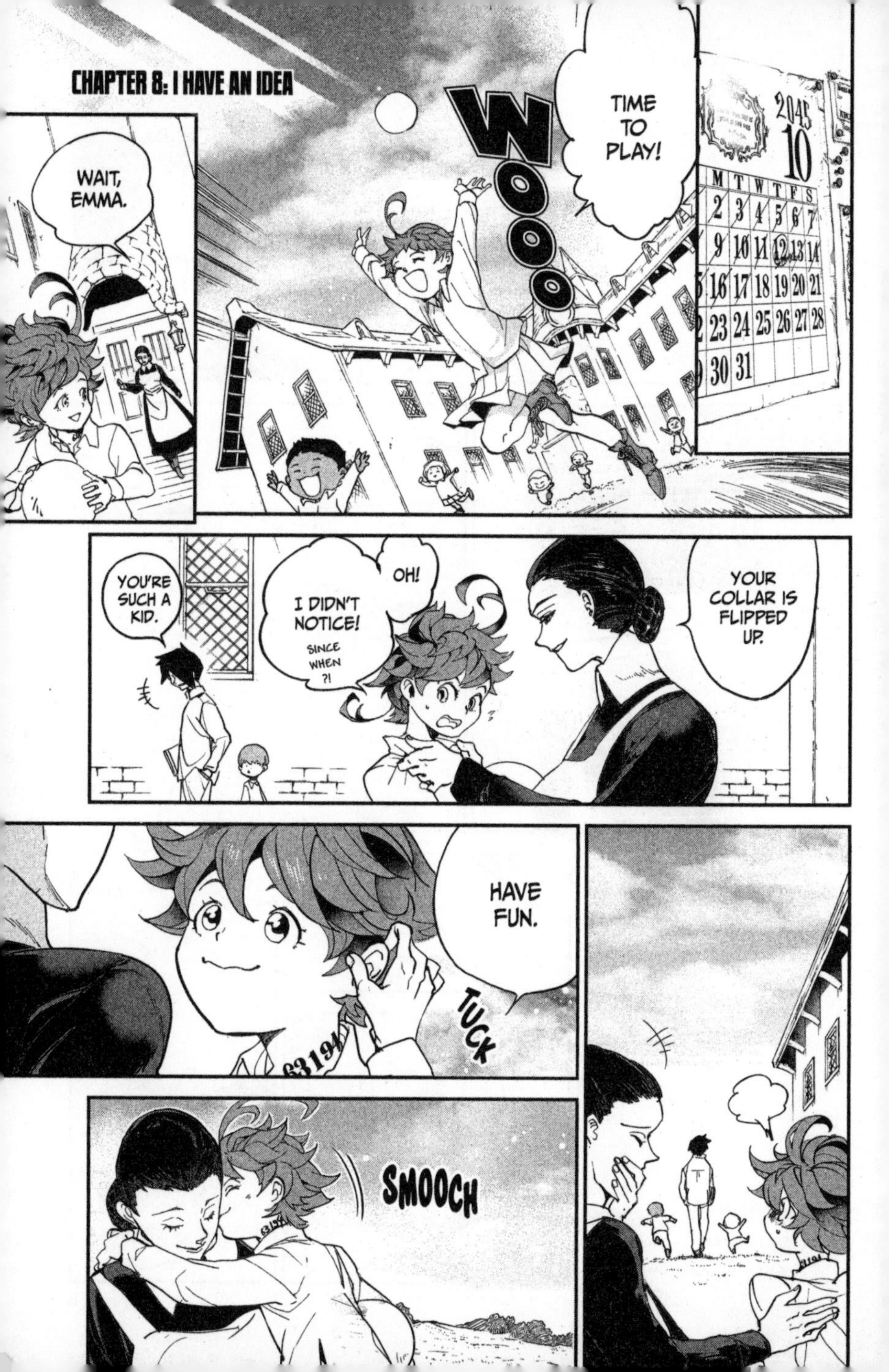
TIME TO PLAY!
WOOOO
2045
10
M T W T F S
WAIT, EMMA.
YOUR COLLAR IS FLIPPED UP.
OH!
I DIDN'T NOTICE!
SINCE WHEN?!
YOU'RE SUCH A KID.
HAVE FUN.
TUCK
63194
SMOOCH

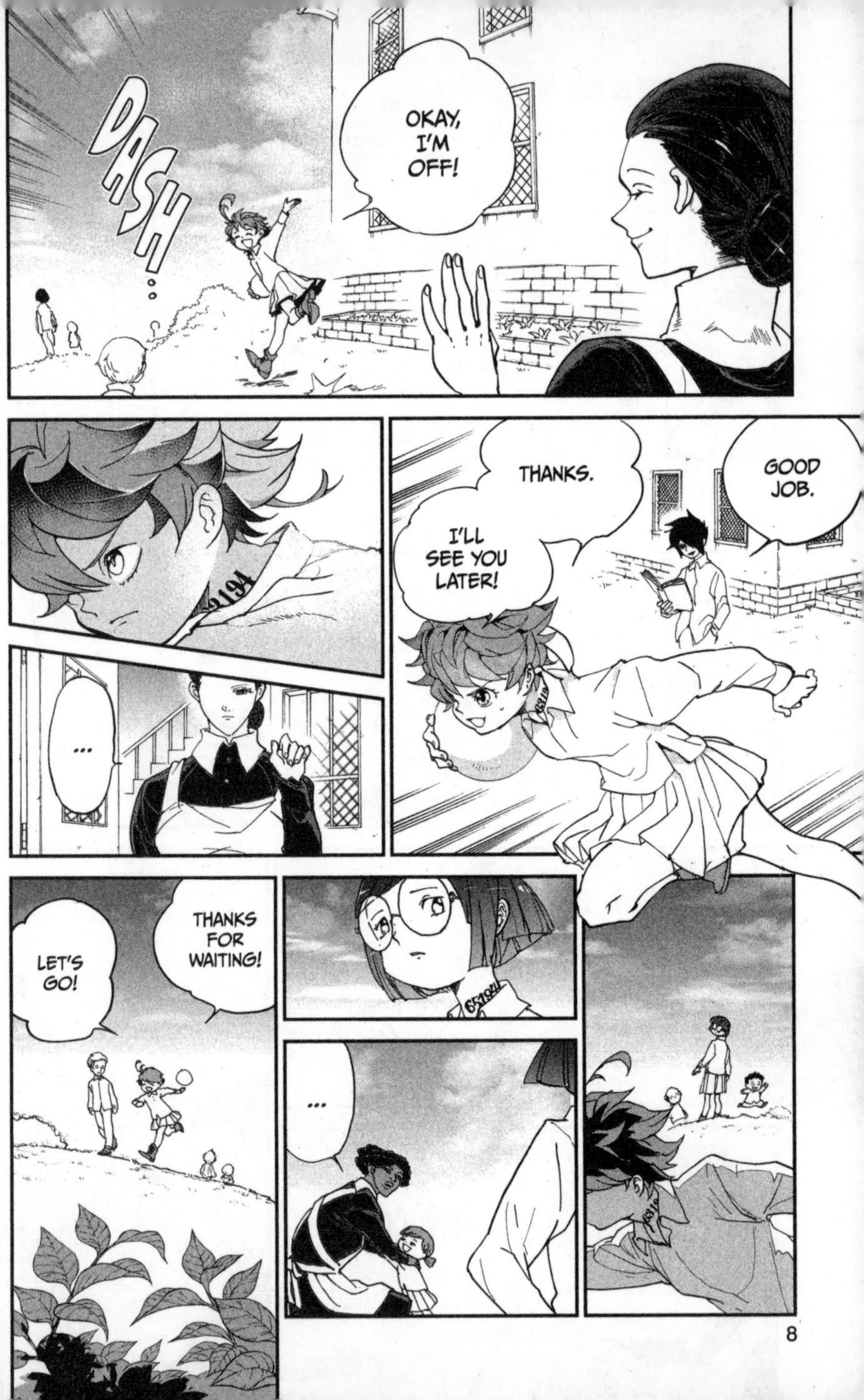
OKAY, I'M OFF!
DASH
GOOD JOB.
THANKS.
I'LL SEE YOU LATER!
...
...
THANKS FOR WAITING!
LET'S GO!

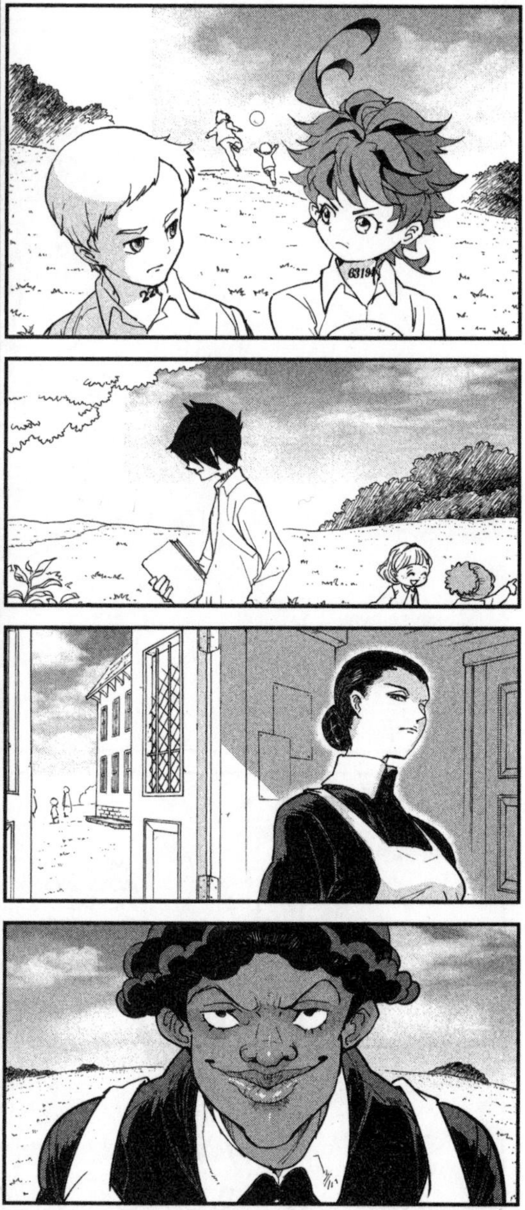
63194

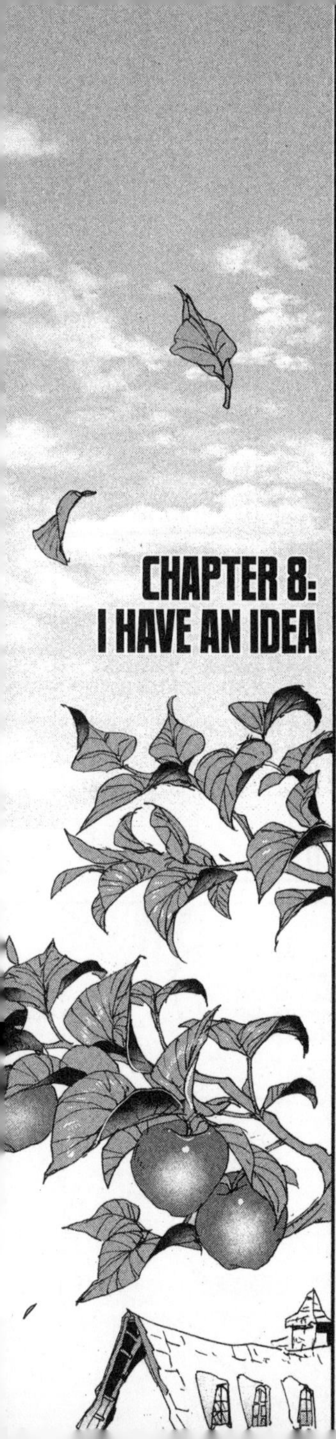
CHAPTER 8:
I HAVE AN IDEA

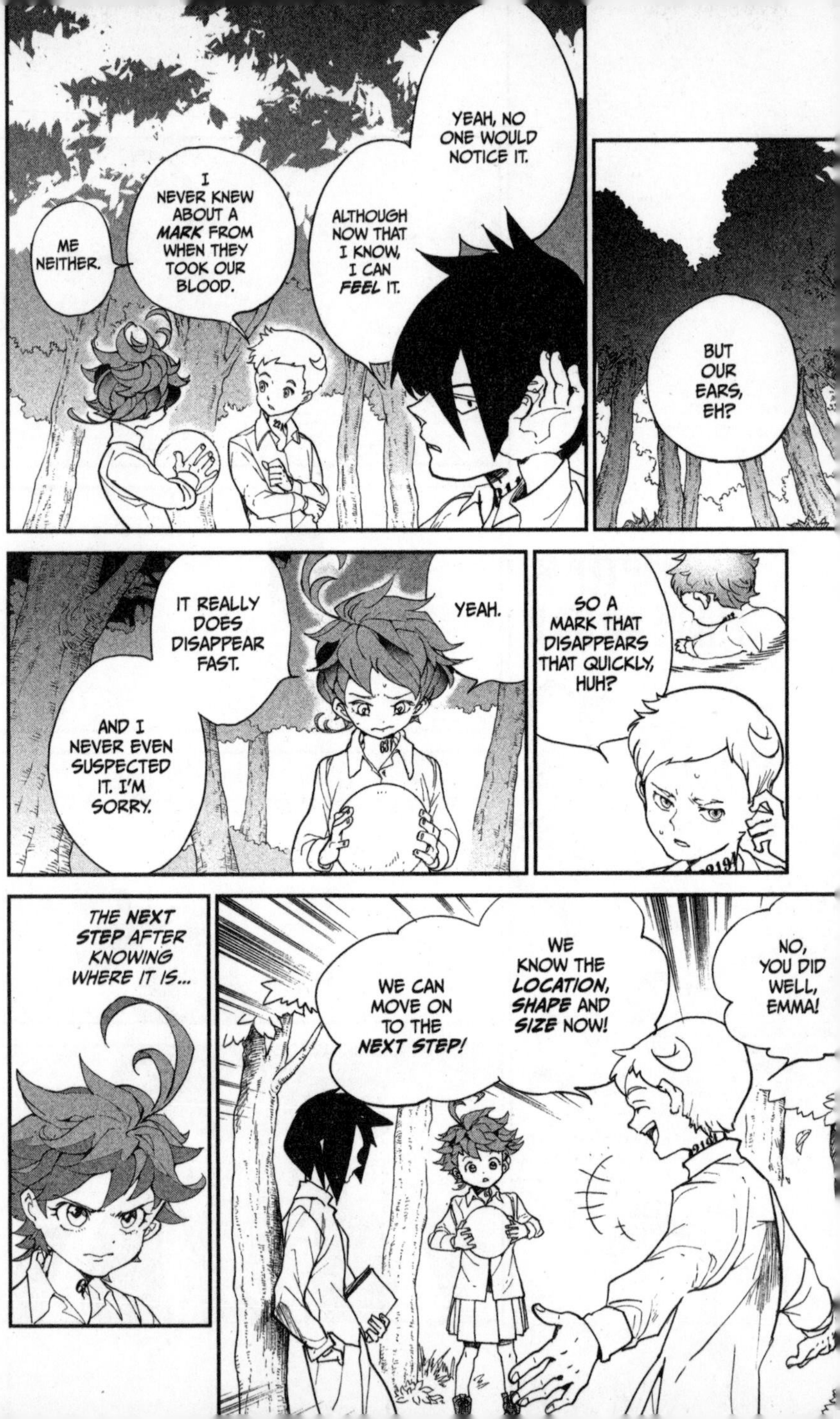
BUT OUR EARS, EH?
YEAH, NO ONE WOULD NOTICE IT.
ALTHOUGH NOW THAT I KNOW, I CAN FEEL IT.
I NEVER KNEW ABOUT A MARK FROM WHEN THEY TOOK OUR BLOOD.
ME NEITHER.
SO A MARK THAT DISAPPEARS THAT QUICKLY, HUH?
YEAH.
IT REALLY DOES DISAPPEAR FAST.
AND I NEVER EVEN SUSPECTED IT. I'M SORRY.
NO, YOU DID WELL, EMMA!
WE KNOW THE LOCATION, SHAPE AND SIZE NOW!
WE CAN MOVE ON TO THE NEXT STEP!
THE NEXT STEP AFTER KNOWING WHERE IT IS...

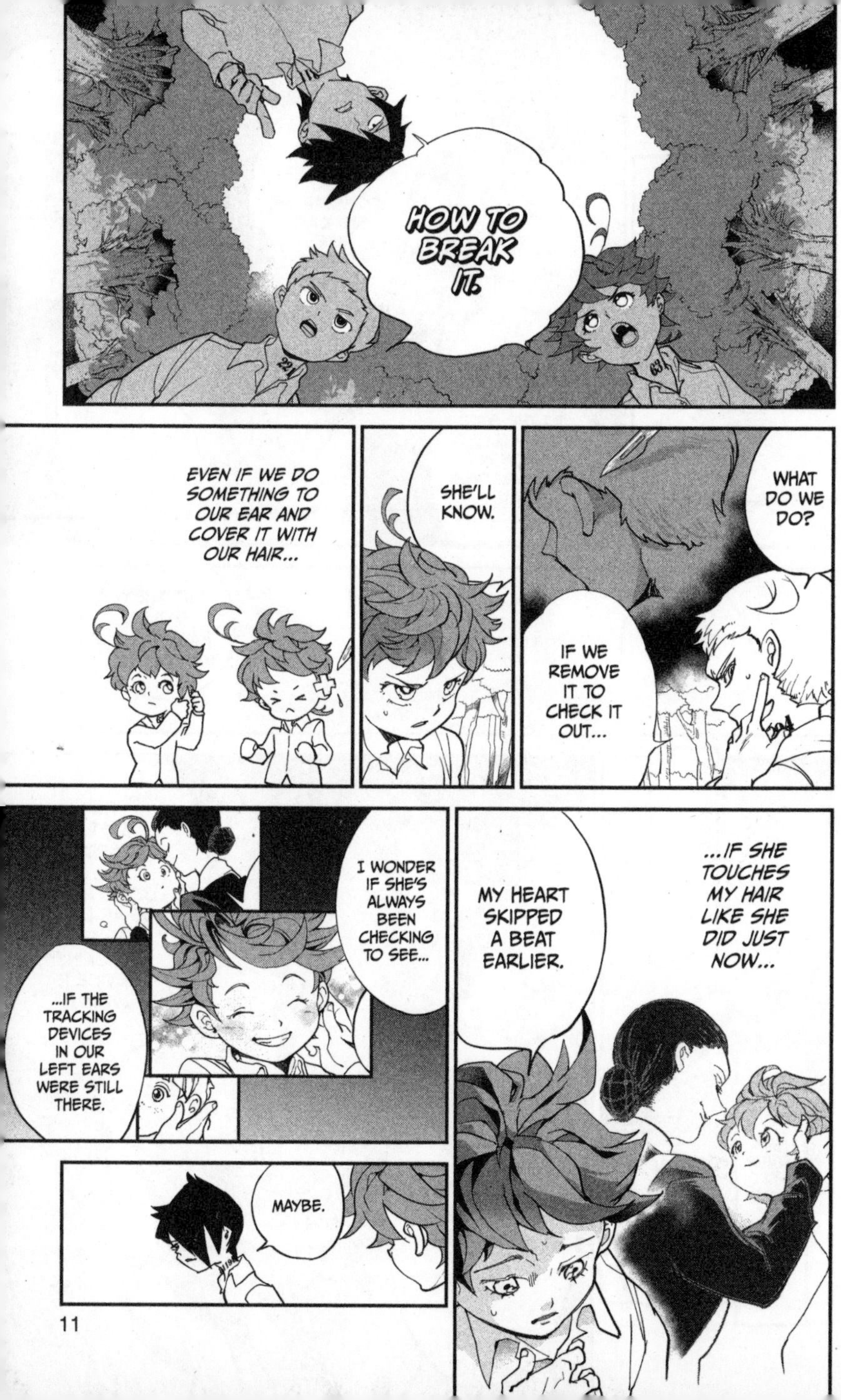
HOW TO BREAK IT.
WHAT DO WE DO?
IF WE REMOVE IT TO CHECK IT OUT...
SHE'LL KNOW.
EVEN IF WE DO SOMETHING TO OUR EAR AND COVER IT WITH OUR HAIR...
...IF SHE TOUCHES MY HAIR LIKE SHE DID JUST NOW...
MY HEART SKIPPED A BEAT EARLIER.
I WONDER IF SHE'S ALWAYS BEEN CHECKING TO SEE...
...IF THE TRACKING DEVICES IN OUR LEFT EARS WERE STILL THERE.
MAYBE.

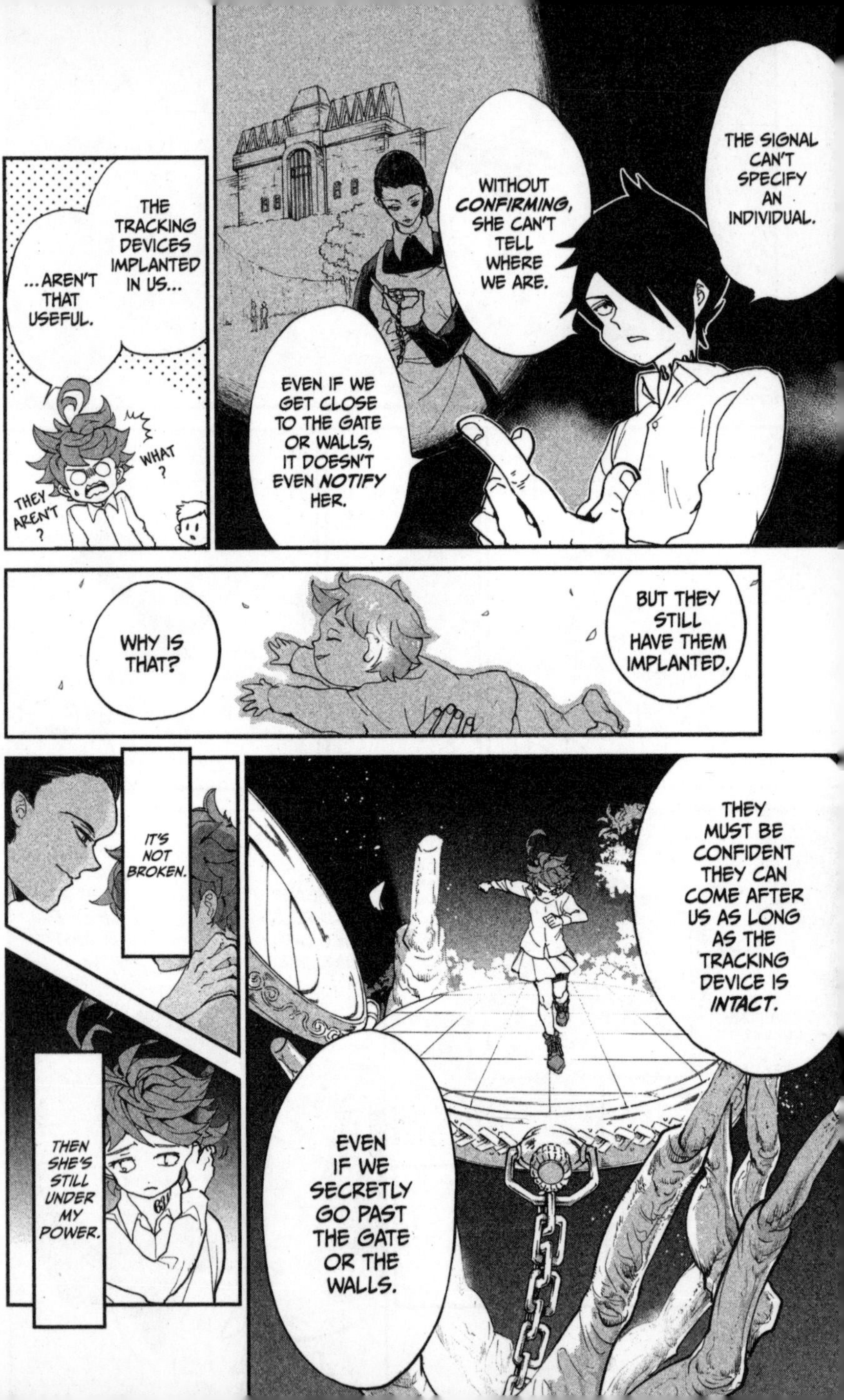
THE SIGNAL CAN'T SPECIFY AN INDIVIDUAL.
WITHOUT *CONFIRMING*, SHE CAN'T TELL WHERE WE ARE.
EVEN IF WE GET CLOSE TO THE GATE OR WALLS, IT DOESN'T EVEN *NOTIFY* HER.
THE TRACKING DEVICES IMPLANTED IN US...
...AREN'T THAT USEFUL.
WHAT?
THEY AREN'T?
BUT THEY STILL HAVE THEM IMPLANTED.
WHY IS THAT?
THEY MUST BE CONFIDENT THEY CAN COME AFTER US AS LONG AS THE TRACKING DEVICE IS *INTACT*.
EVEN IF WE SECRETLY GO PAST THE GATE OR THE WALLS.
IT'S NOT BROKEN.
THEN SHE'S STILL UNDER MY POWER.

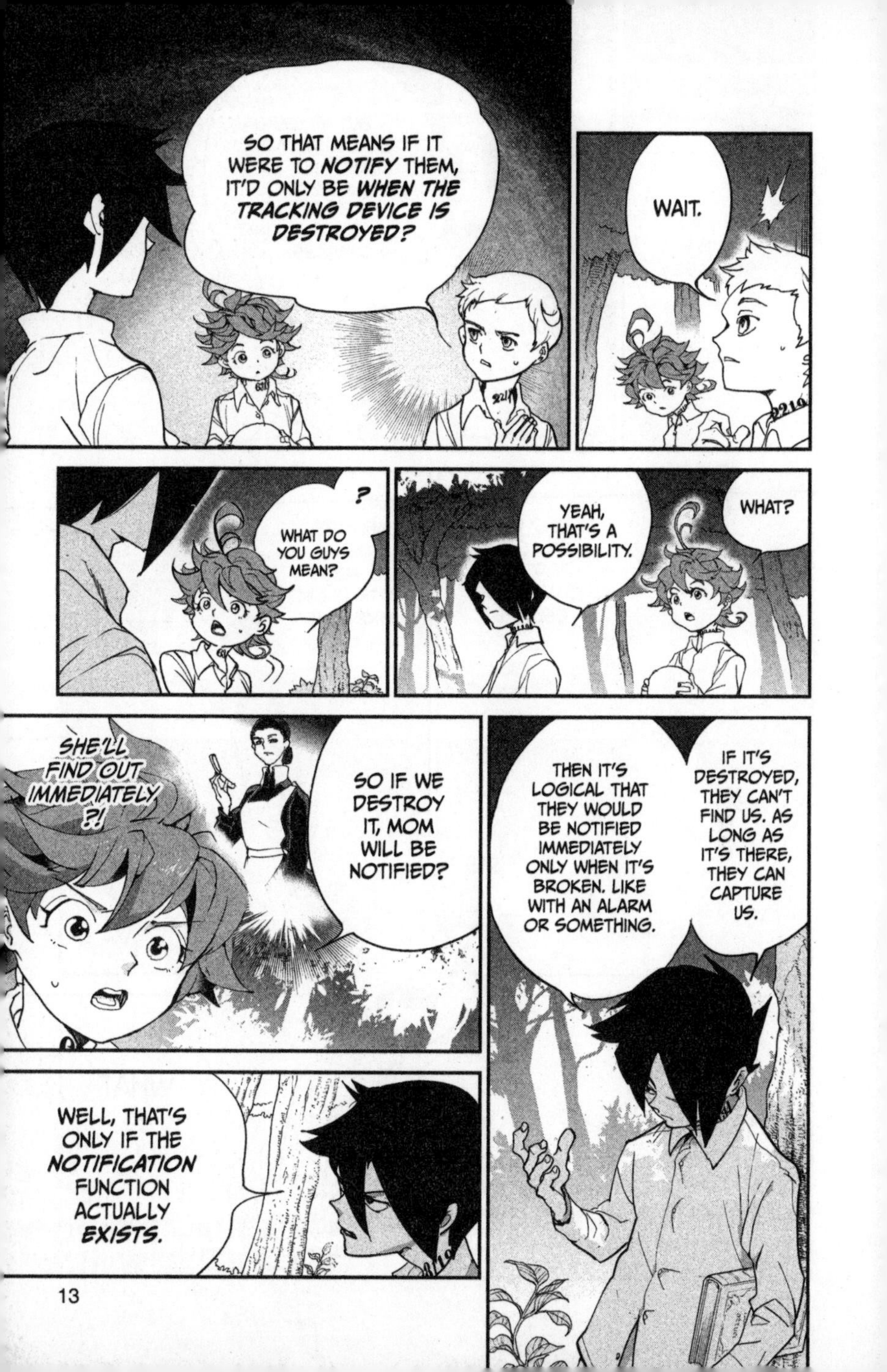
WAIT.
SO THAT MEANS IF IT WERE TO *NOTIFY* THEM, IT'D ONLY BE *WHEN THE TRACKING DEVICE IS DESTROYED?*
WHAT?
YEAH, THAT'S A POSSIBILITY.
?
WHAT DO YOU GUYS MEAN?
IF IT'S DESTROYED, THEY CAN'T FIND US. AS LONG AS IT'S THERE, THEY CAN CAPTURE US.
THEN IT'S LOGICAL THAT THEY WOULD BE NOTIFIED IMMEDIATELY ONLY WHEN IT'S BROKEN. LIKE WITH AN ALARM OR SOMETHING.
SO IF WE DESTROY IT, MOM WILL BE NOTIFIED?
SHE'LL FIND OUT IMMEDIATELY ?!
WELL, THAT'S ONLY IF THE *NOTIFICATION* FUNCTION ACTUALLY *EXISTS.*

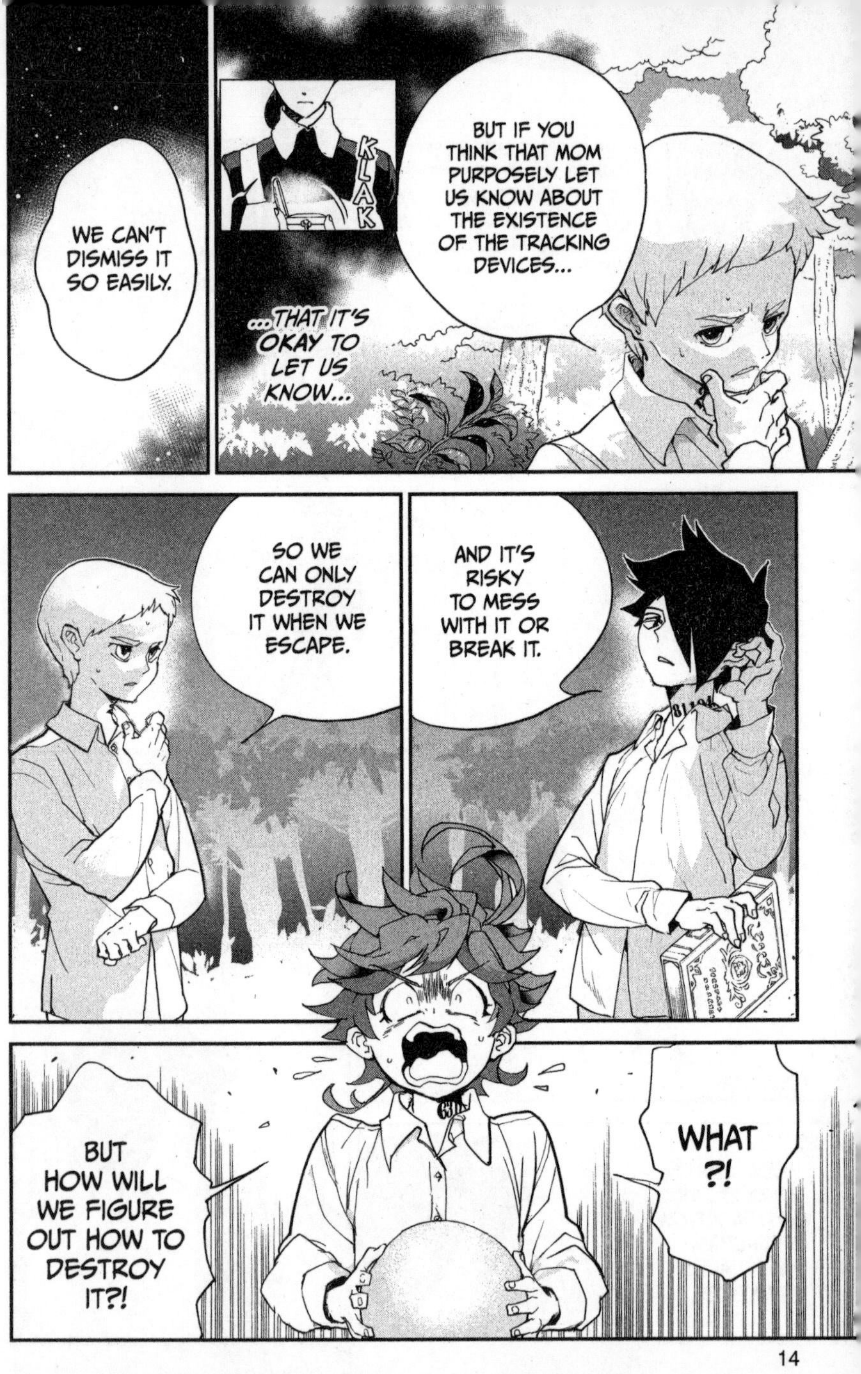
BUT IF YOU THINK THAT MOM PURPOSELY LET US KNOW ABOUT THE EXISTENCE OF THE TRACKING DEVICES...
KLAK
...THAT IT'S OKAY TO LET US KNOW...
WE CAN'T DISMISS IT SO EASILY.
AND IT'S RISKY TO MESS WITH IT OR BREAK IT.
SO WE CAN ONLY DESTROY IT WHEN WE ESCAPE.
WHAT?!
BUT HOW WILL WE FIGURE OUT HOW TO DESTROY IT?!

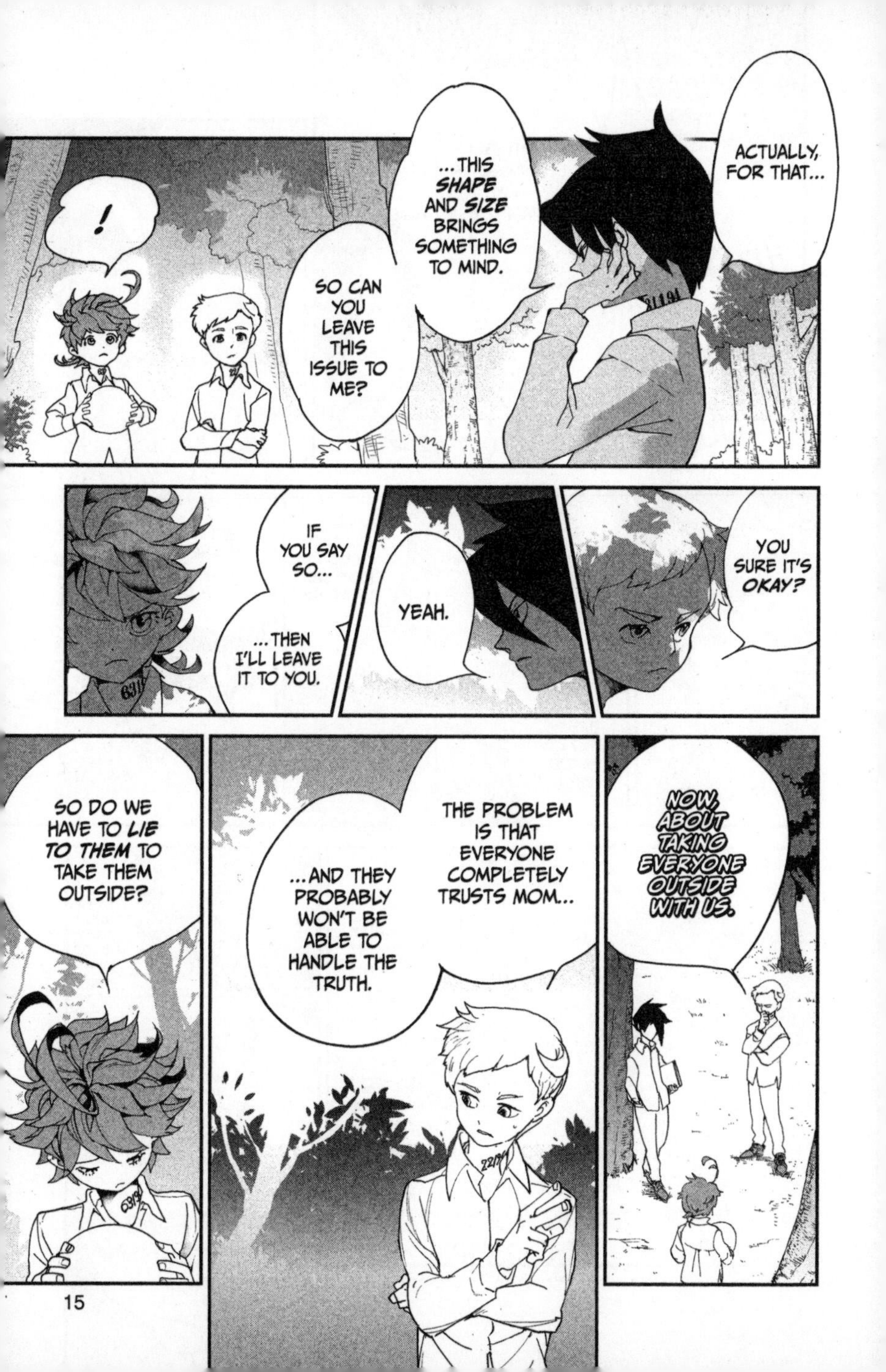
ACTUALLY, FOR THAT...
...THIS SHAPE AND SIZE BRINGS SOMETHING TO MIND.
SO CAN YOU LEAVE THIS ISSUE TO ME?
!
YOU SURE IT'S OKAY?
YEAH.
IF YOU SAY SO...
...THEN I'LL LEAVE IT TO YOU.
NOW, ABOUT TAKING EVERYONE OUTSIDE WITH US.
THE PROBLEM IS THAT EVERYONE COMPLETELY TRUSTS MOM...
...AND THEY PROBABLY WON'T BE ABLE TO HANDLE THE TRUTH.
SO DO WE HAVE TO LIE TO THEM TO TAKE THEM OUTSIDE?

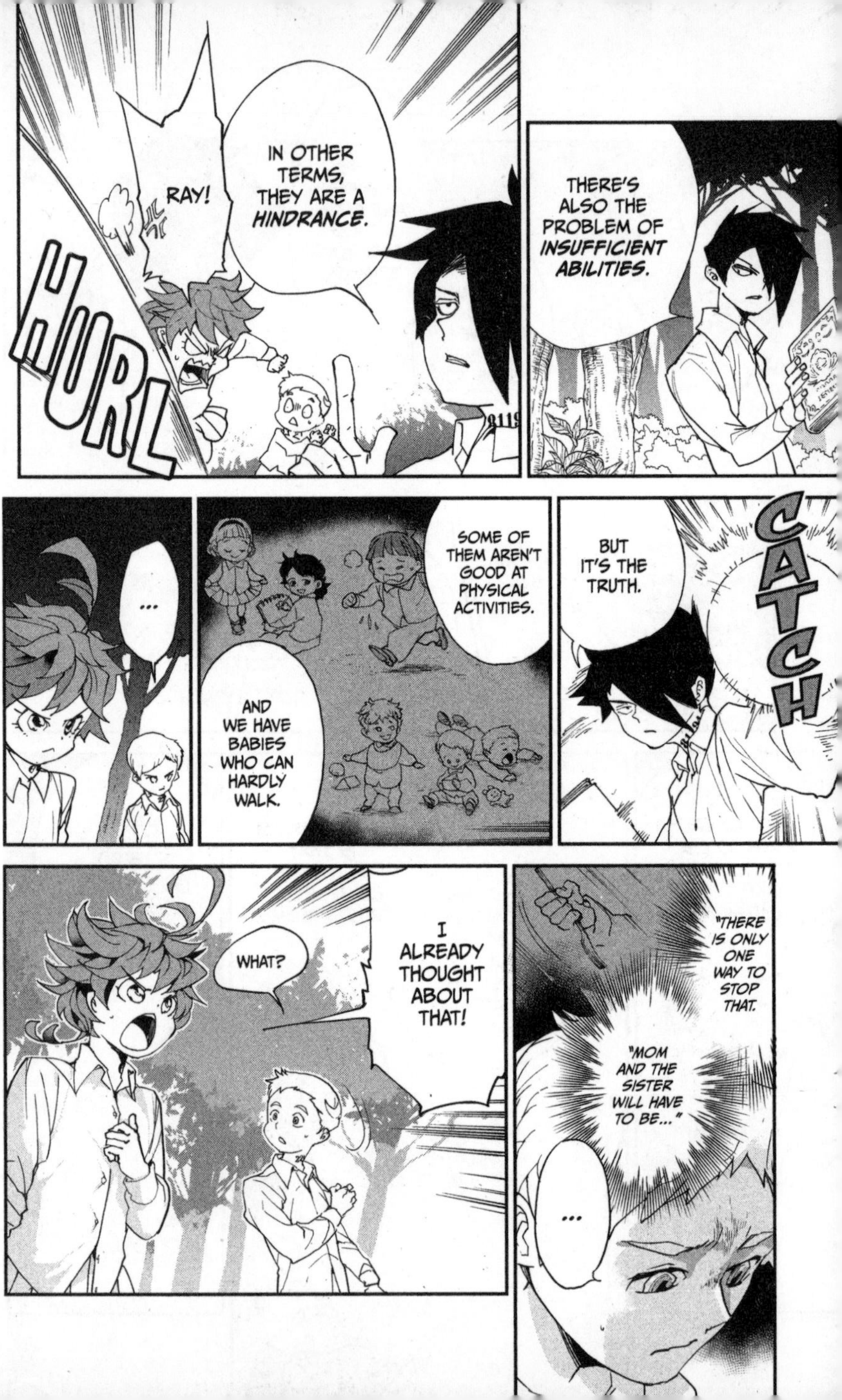
THERE'S ALSO THE PROBLEM OF INSUFFICIENT ABILITIES.
IN OTHER TERMS, THEY ARE A HINDRANCE.
RAY!
HURL
CATCH
BUT IT'S THE TRUTH.
SOME OF THEM AREN'T GOOD AT PHYSICAL ACTIVITIES.
AND WE HAVE BABIES WHO CAN HARDLY WALK.
...
"THERE IS ONLY ONE WAY TO STOP THAT.
"MOM AND THE SISTER WILL HAVE TO BE..."
...
I ALREADY THOUGHT ABOUT THAT!
WHAT?

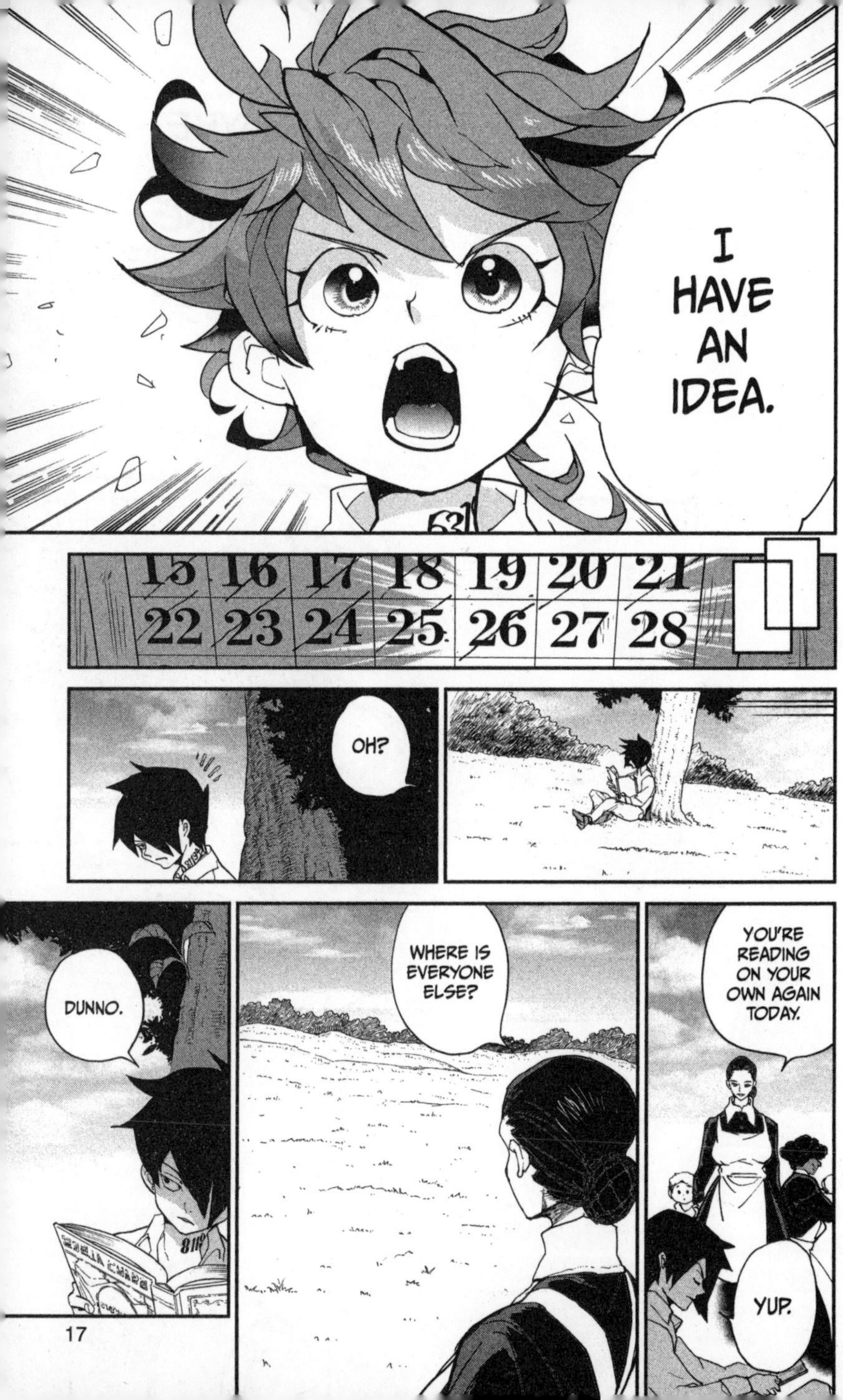
I HAVE AN IDEA.
15 16 17 18 19 20 21
22 23 24 25 26 27 28
OH?
YOU'RE READING ON YOUR OWN AGAIN TODAY.
YUP.
WHERE IS EVERYONE ELSE?
DUNNO.

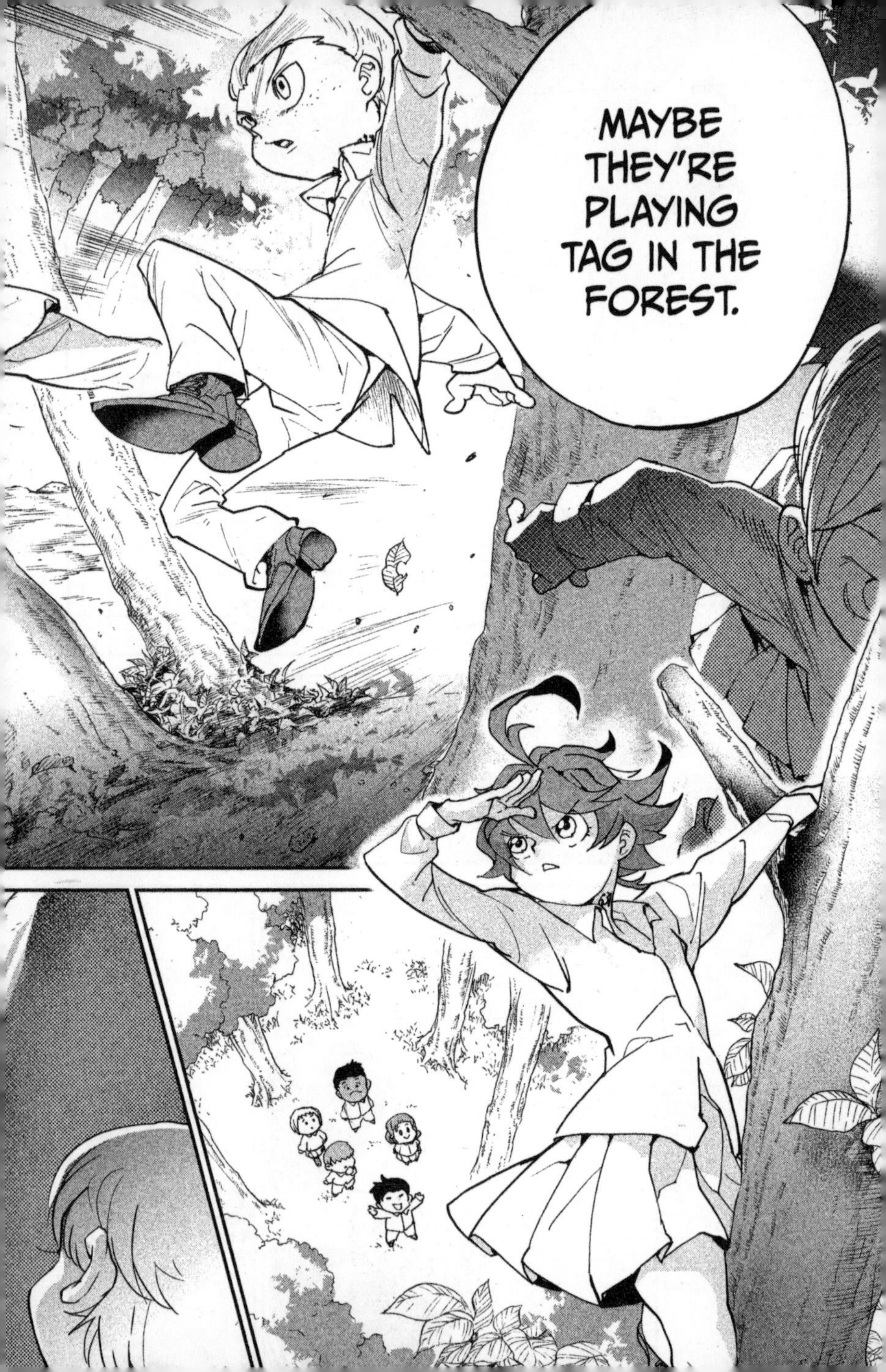
MAYBE THEY'RE PLAYING TAG IN THE FOREST.

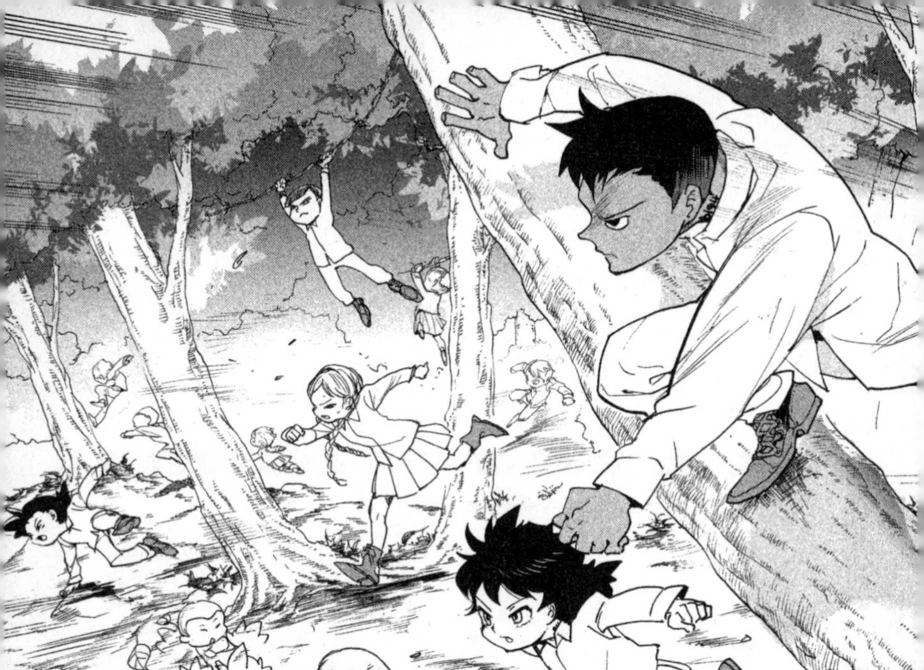

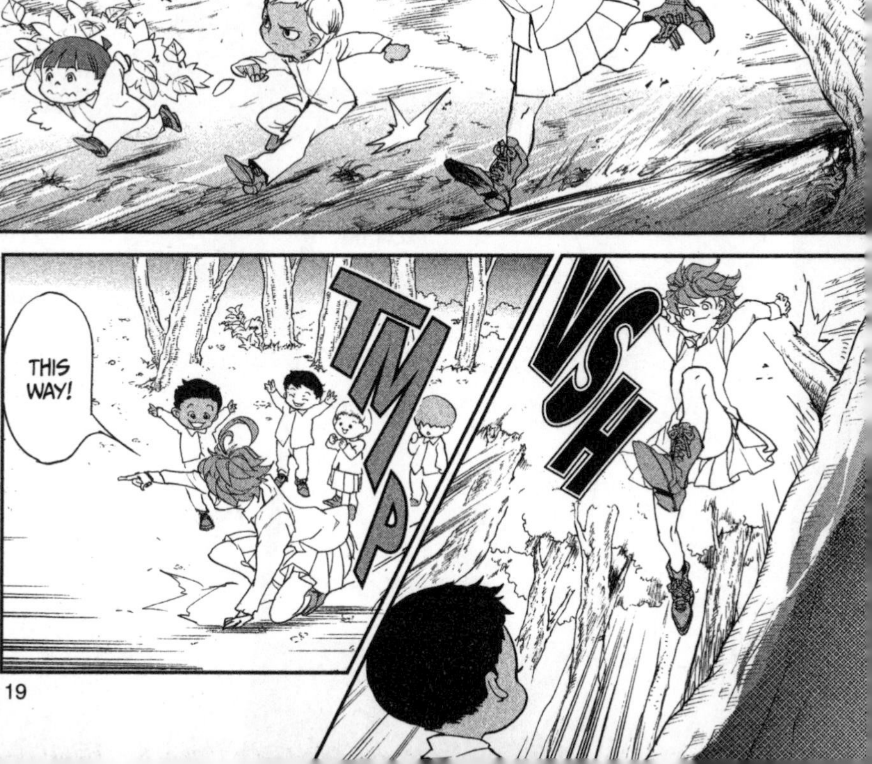
VSH
TMP
THIS WAY!

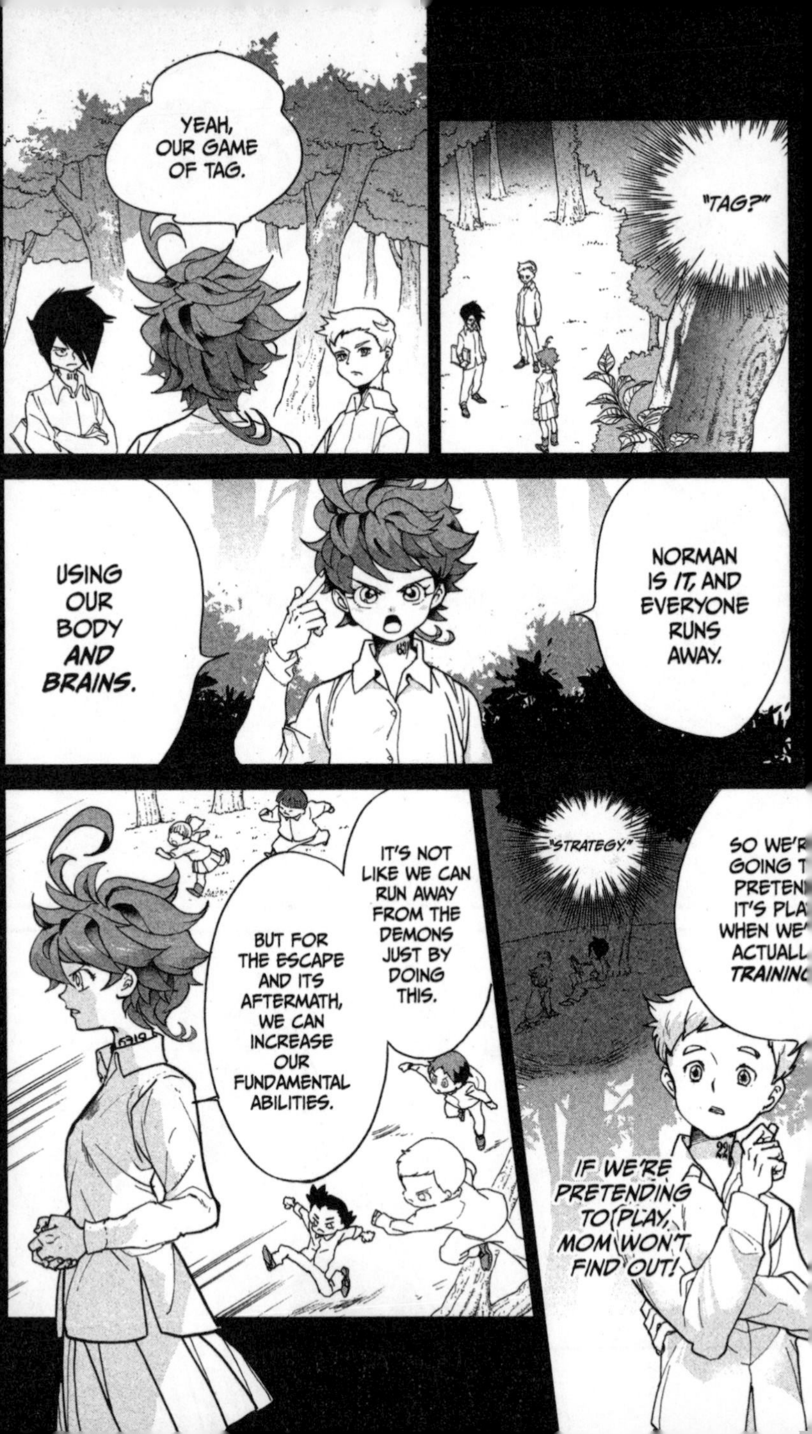
"TAG?"
YEAH, OUR GAME OF TAG.
NORMAN IS IT, AND EVERYONE RUNS AWAY.
USING OUR BODY AND BRAINS.
"STRATEGY."
SO WE'R GOING T PRETEN IT'S PLA WHEN WE' ACTUALL TRAININ
IF WE'RE PRETENDING TO PLAY, MOM WON'T FIND OUT!
IT'S NOT LIKE WE CAN RUN AWAY FROM THE DEMONS JUST BY DOING THIS.
BUT FOR THE ESCAPE AND ITS AFTERMATH, WE CAN INCREASE OUR FUNDAMENTAL ABILITIES.

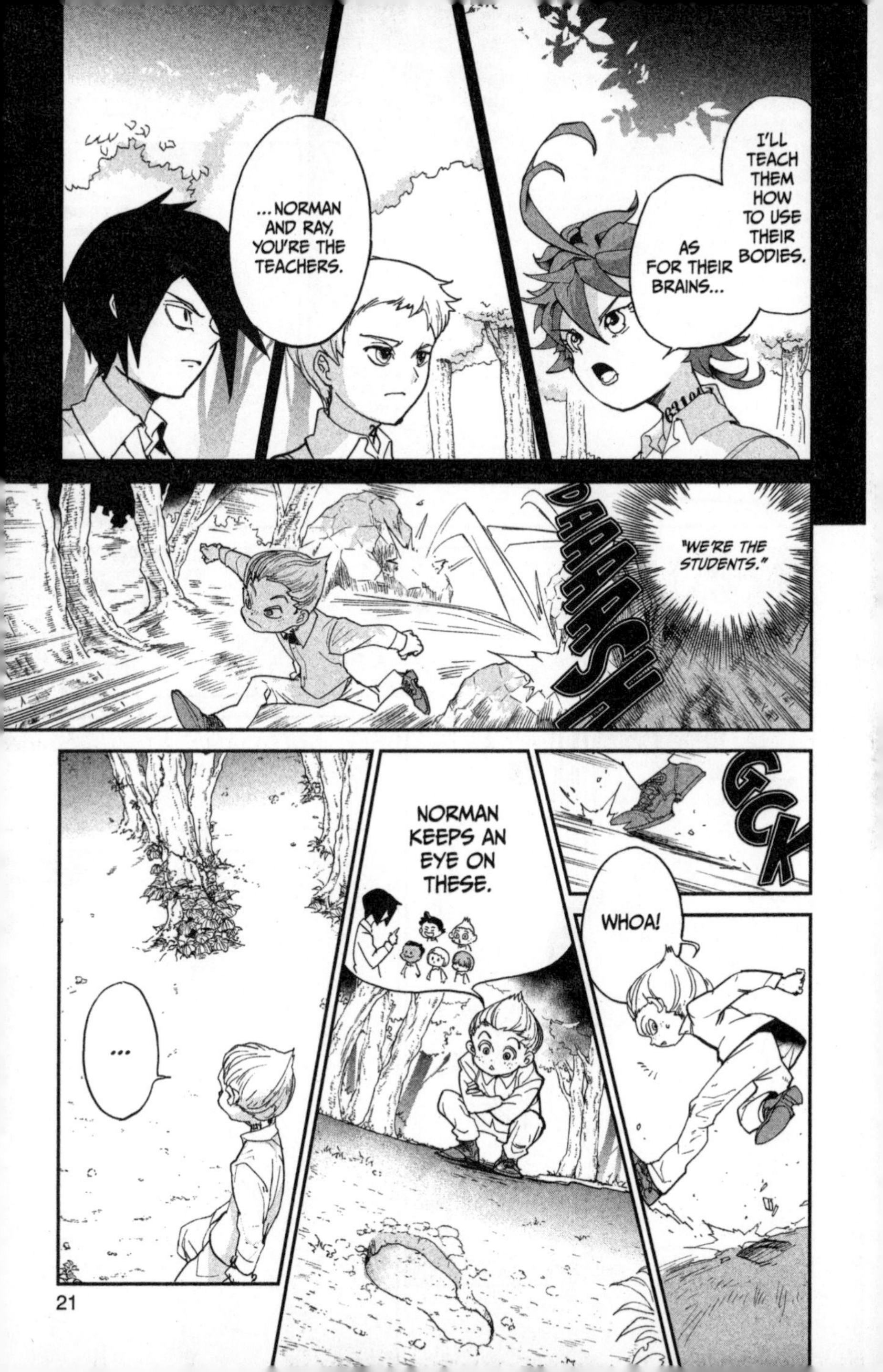

I'LL TEACH THEM HOW TO USE THEIR BODIES.
AS FOR THEIR BRAINS...
...NORMAN AND RAY, YOU'RE THE TEACHERS.
"WE'RE THE STUDENTS."
DAAAASH
GCK
WHOA!
NORMAN KEEPS AN EYE ON THESE.
...

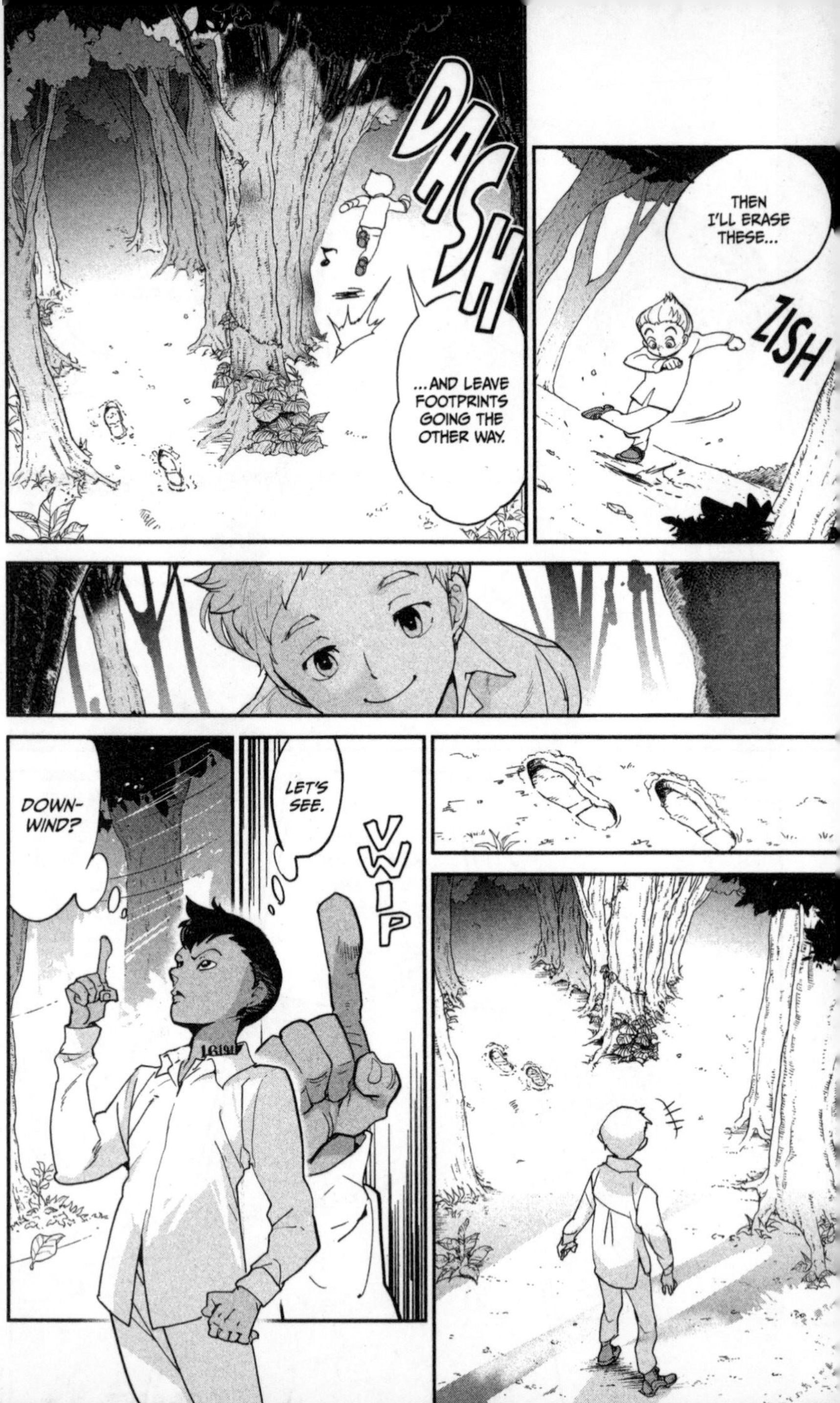
THEN I'LL ERASE THESE...
ZISH
DASH
...AND LEAVE FOOTPRINTS GOING THE OTHER WAY.
VWIP
LET'S SEE.
DOWN-WIND?

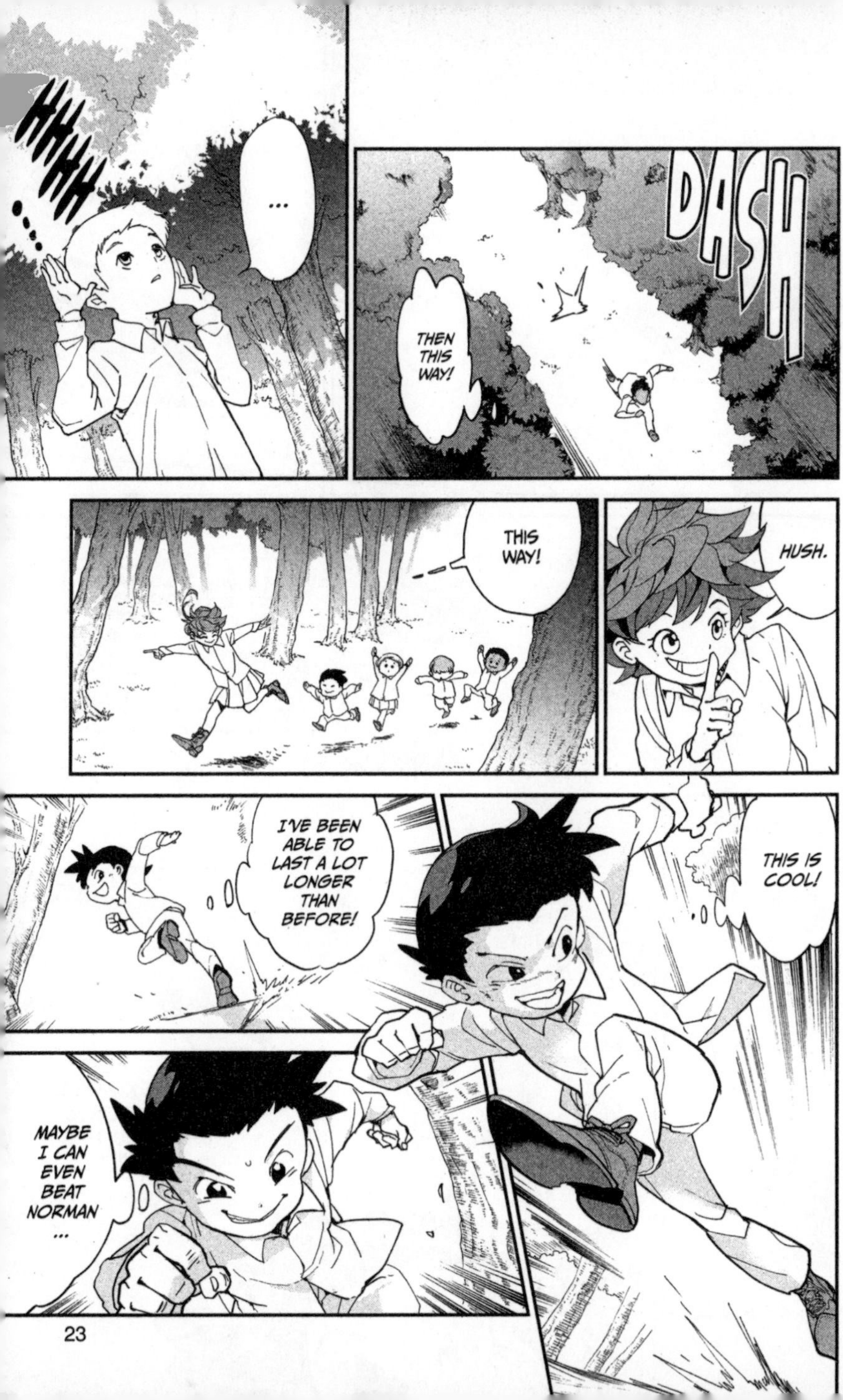
DASH
THEN THIS WAY!
HHHH...
...
HUSH.
THIS WAY!
THIS IS COOL!
I'VE BEEN ABLE TO LAST A LOT LONGER THAN BEFORE!
MAYBE I CAN EVEN BEAT NORMAN...

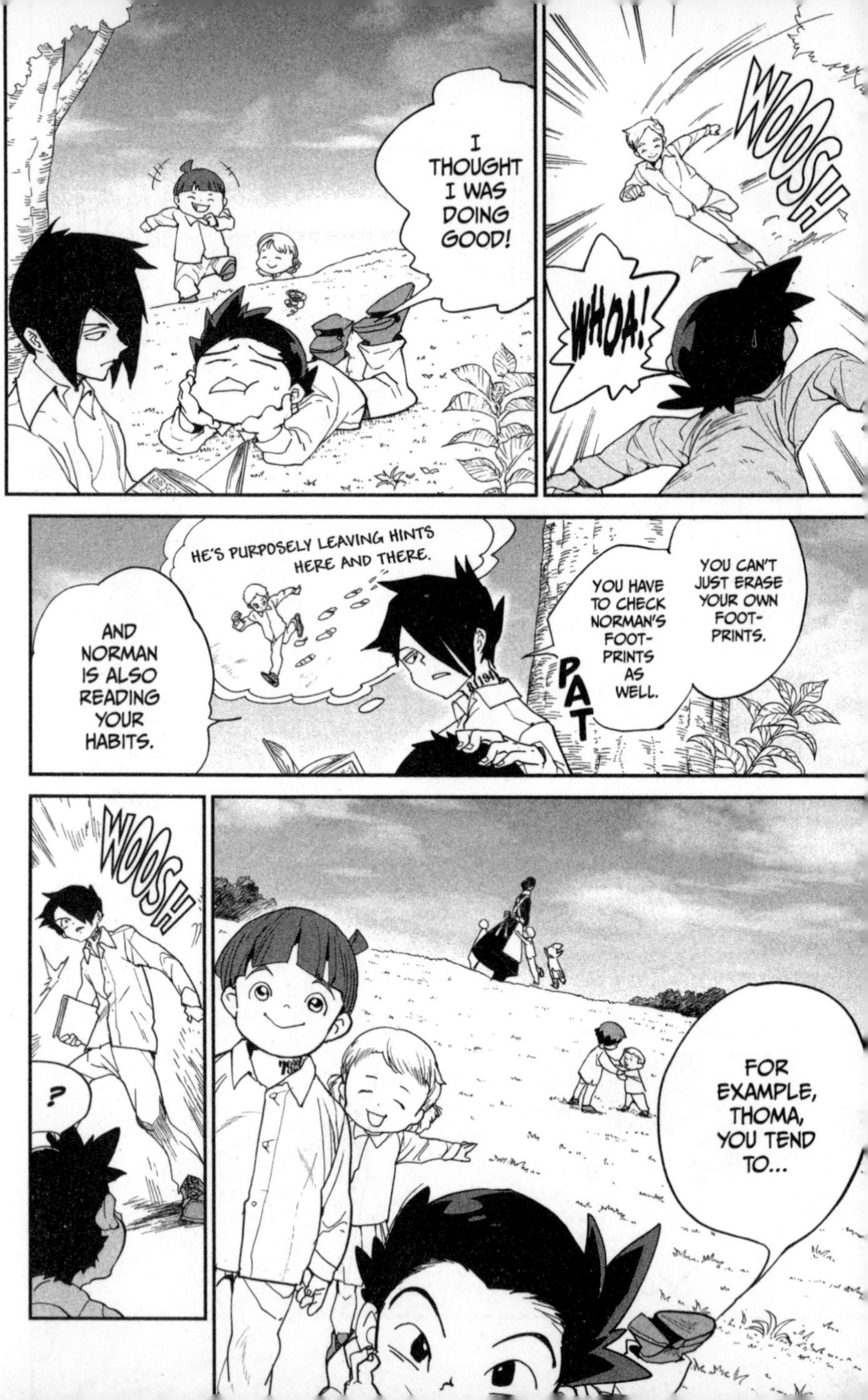
WOOSH
WHOA!
I THOUGHT I WAS DOING GOOD!
YOU CAN'T JUST ERASE YOUR OWN FOOT-PRINTS.
YOU HAVE TO CHECK NORMAN'S FOOT-PRINTS AS WELL.
PAT
HE'S PURPOSELY LEAVING HINTS HERE AND THERE.
AND NORMAN IS ALSO READING YOUR HABITS.
FOR EXAMPLE, THOMA, YOU TEND TO...
WOOSH
?

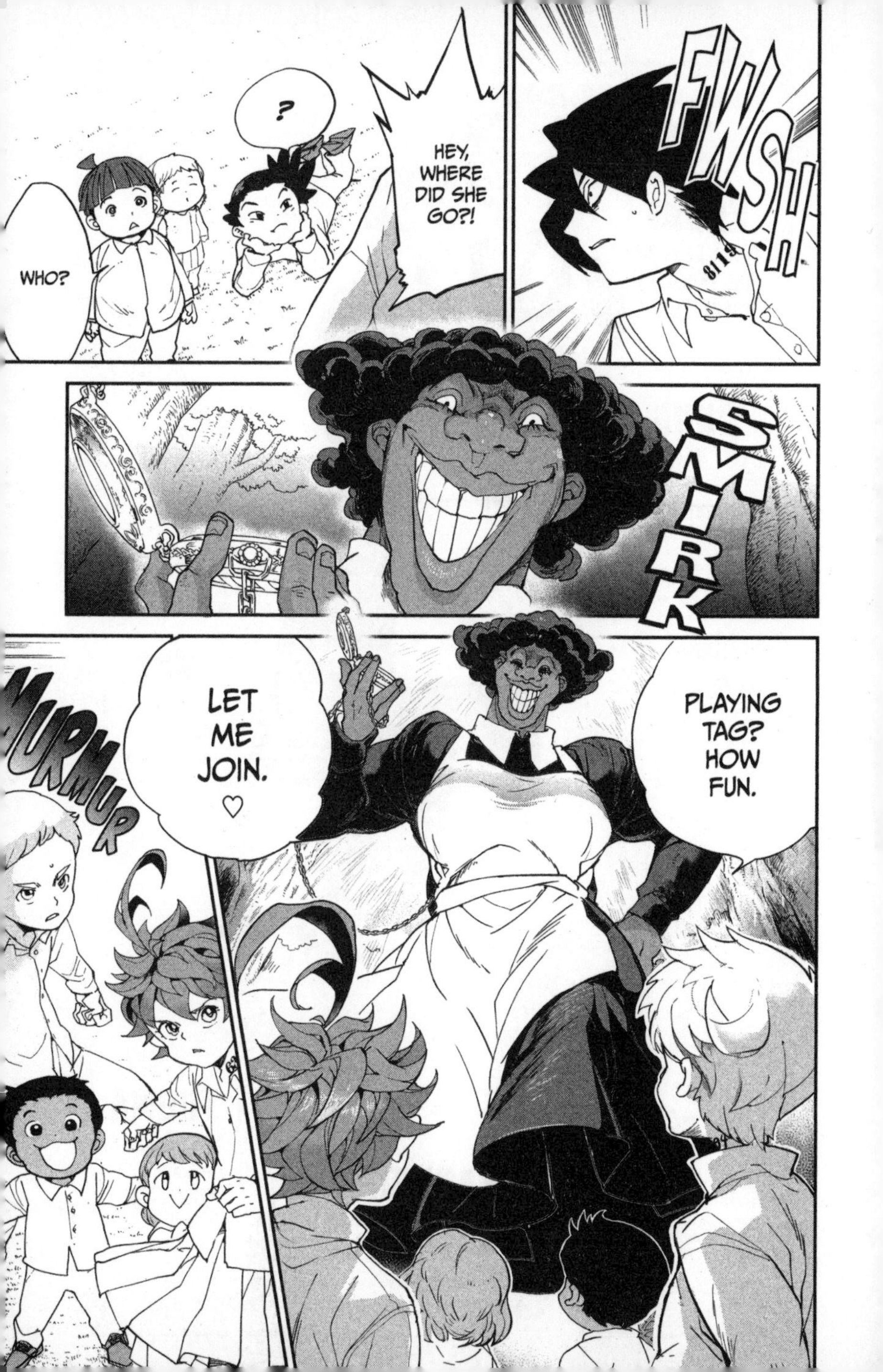
FWSH
HEY, WHERE DID SHE GO?!
?
WHO?
SMIRK
PLAYING TAG? HOW FUN.
LET ME JOIN. ♡
MURMUR

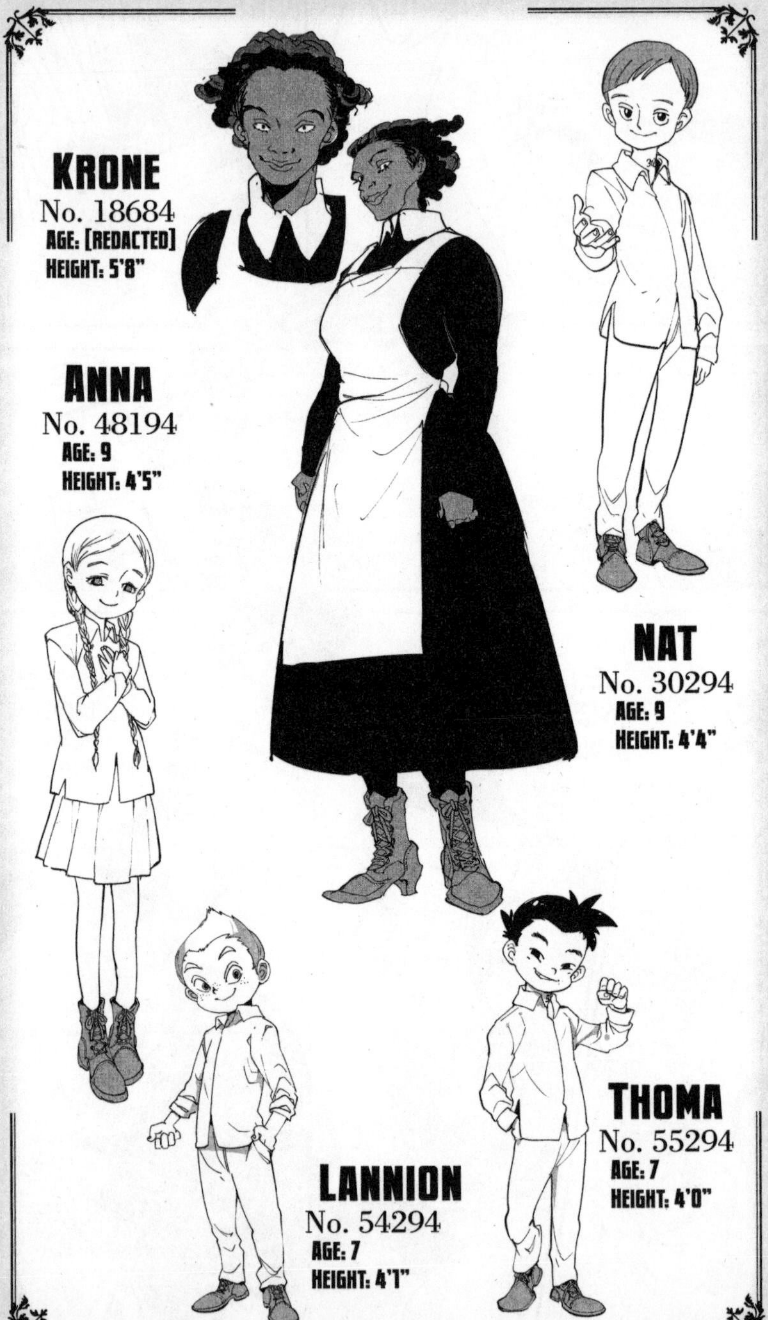
KRONE
No. 18684
AGE: [REDACTED]
HEIGHT: 5'8"
ANNA
No. 48194
AGE: 9
HEIGHT: 4'5"
NAT
No. 30294
AGE: 9
HEIGHT: 4'4"
THOMA
No. 55294
AGE: 7
HEIGHT: 4'0"
LANNION
No. 54294
AGE: 7
HEIGHT: 4'1"

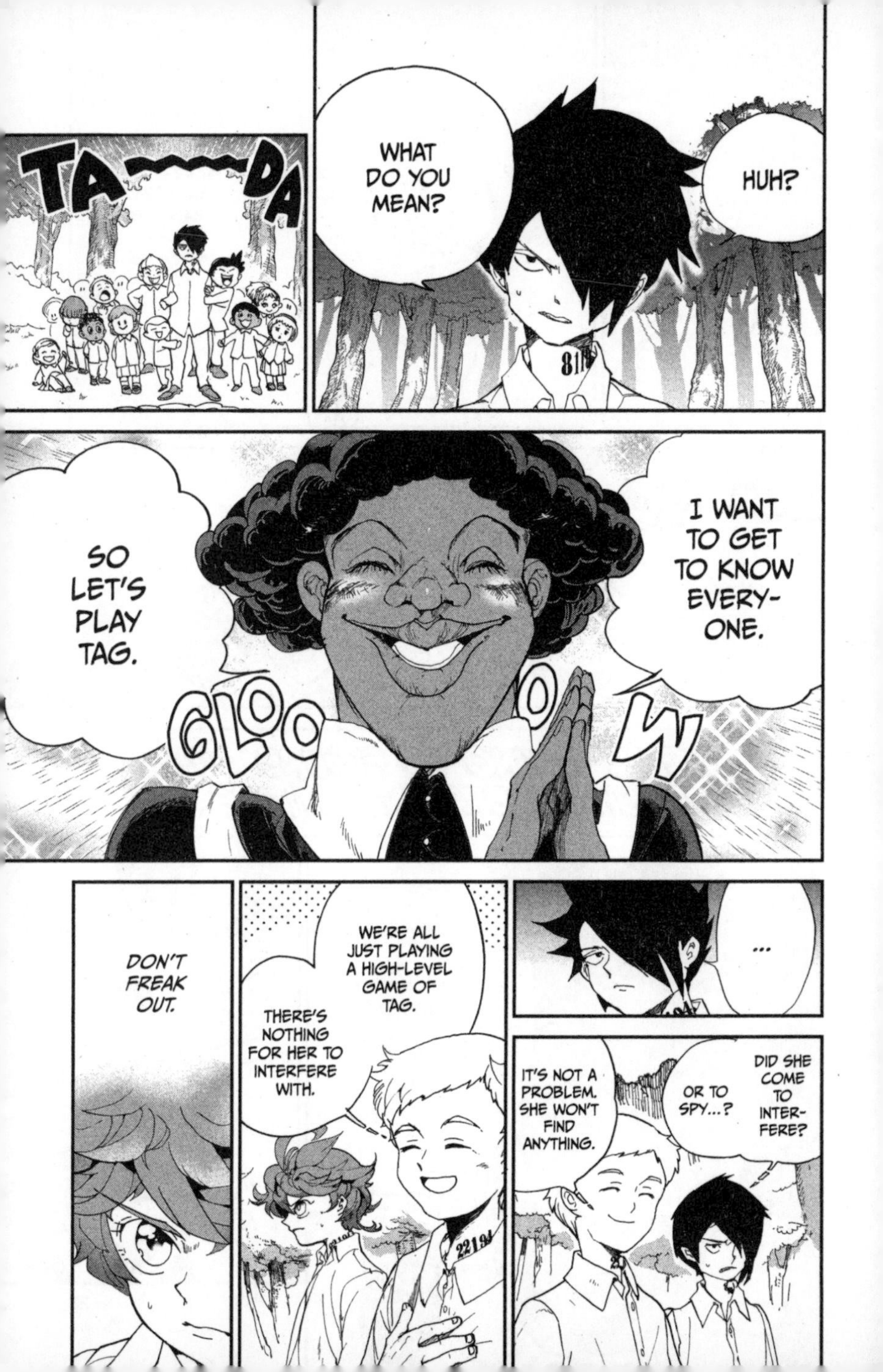
HUH?
WHAT DO YOU MEAN?
TA—DA
I WANT TO GET TO KNOW EVERY-ONE.
SO LET'S PLAY TAG.
GLOOOW
...
DID SHE COME TO INTER-FERE?
OR TO SPY...?
IT'S NOT A PROBLEM. SHE WON'T FIND ANYTHING.
WE'RE ALL JUST PLAYING A HIGH-LEVEL GAME OF TAG.
THERE'S NOTHING FOR HER TO INTERFERE WITH.
22194
DON'T FREAK OUT.

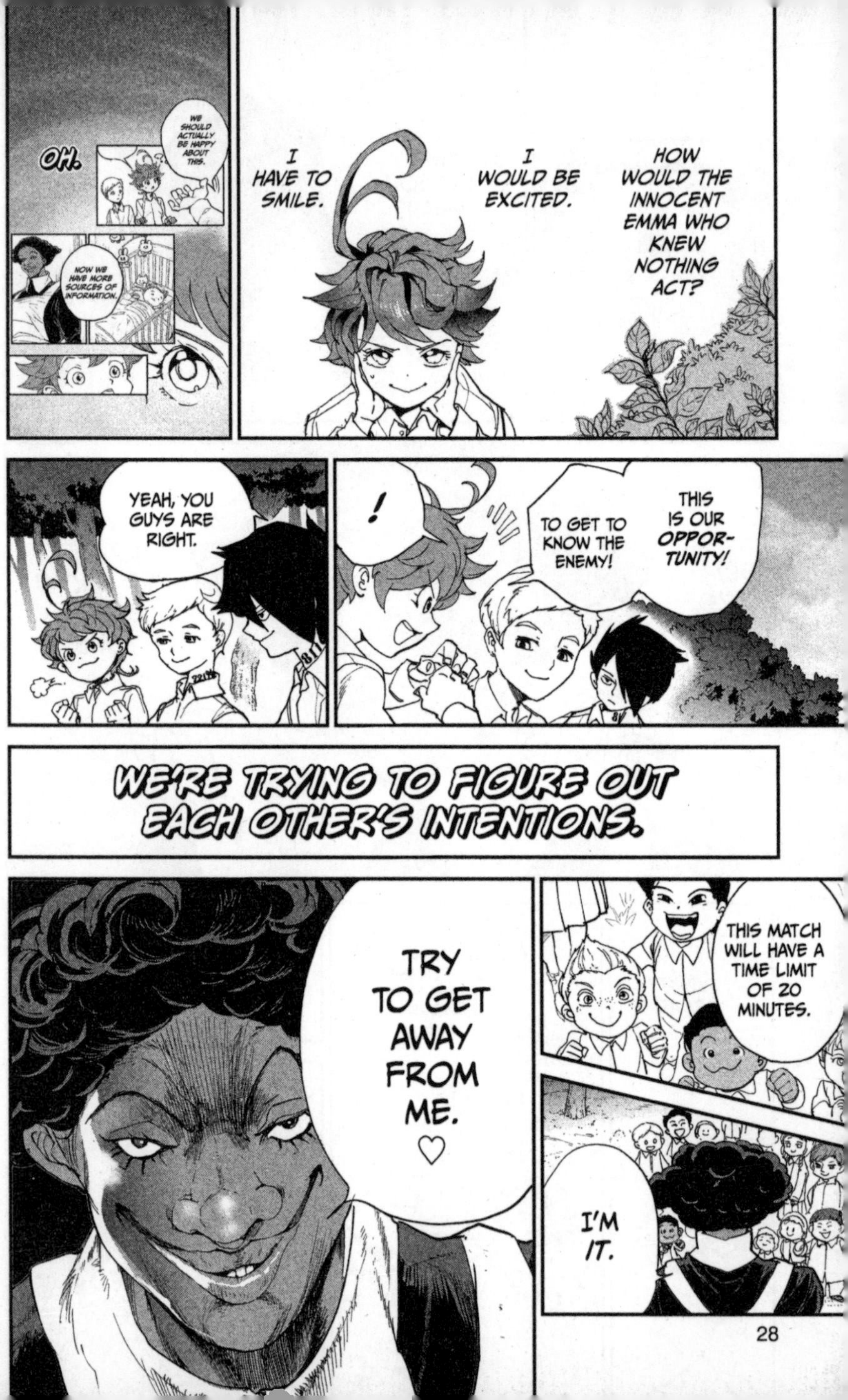

HOW WOULD THE INNOCENT EMMA WHO KNEW NOTHING ACT?
I WOULD BE EXCITED.
I HAVE TO SMILE.
OH.
WE SHOULD ACTUALLY BE HAPPY ABOUT THIS.
NOW WE HAVE MORE SOURCES OF INFORMATION.
THIS IS OUR OPPORTUNITY!
TO GET TO KNOW THE ENEMY!
!
YEAH, YOU GUYS ARE RIGHT.
WE'RE TRYING TO FIGURE OUT EACH OTHER'S INTENTIONS.
THIS MATCH WILL HAVE A TIME LIMIT OF 20 MINUTES.
I'M IT.
TRY TO GET AWAY FROM ME. ♡

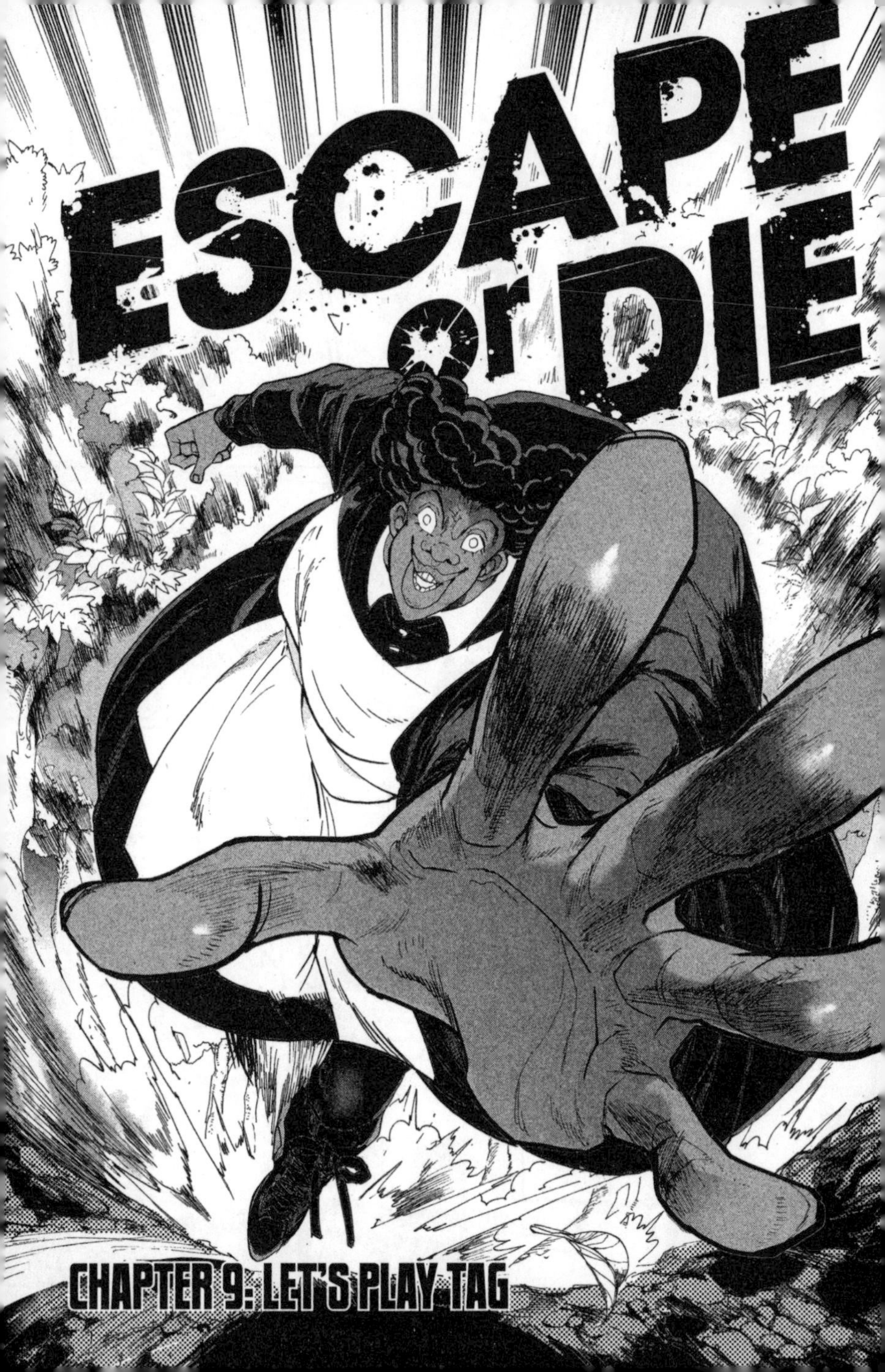
ESCAPE or DIE
CHAPTER 9: LET'S PLAY TAG

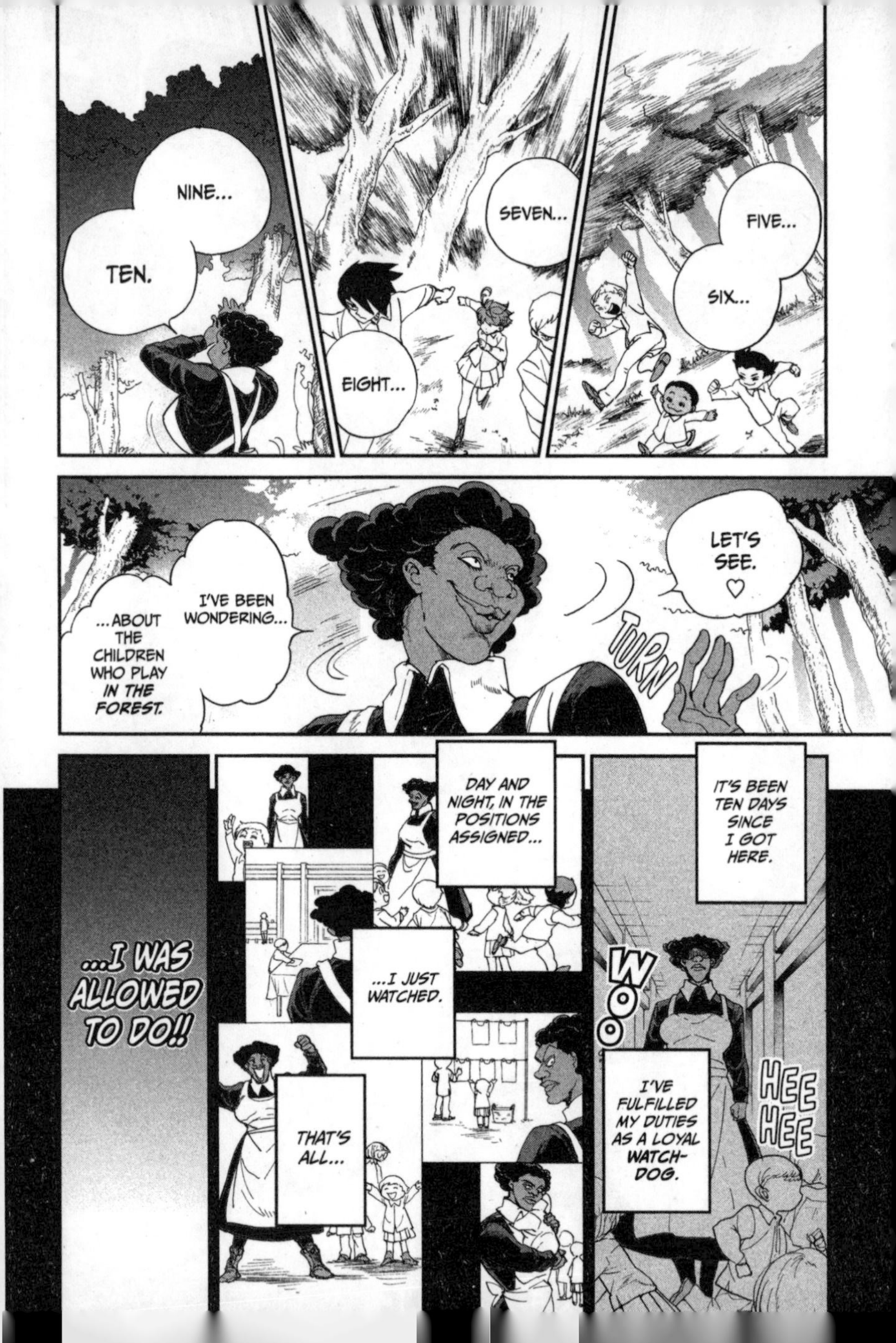
FIVE...
SIX...
SEVEN...
EIGHT...
NINE...
TEN.
LET'S SEE. ♡
TURN
I'VE BEEN WONDERING...
...ABOUT THE CHILDREN WHO PLAY IN THE FOREST.
IT'S BEEN TEN DAYS SINCE I GOT HERE.
WOO
HEE HEE
I'VE FULFILLED MY DUTIES AS A LOYAL WATCH-DOG.
DAY AND NIGHT, IN THE POSITIONS ASSIGNED...
...I JUST WATCHED.
THAT'S ALL...
...I WAS ALLOWED TO DO!!

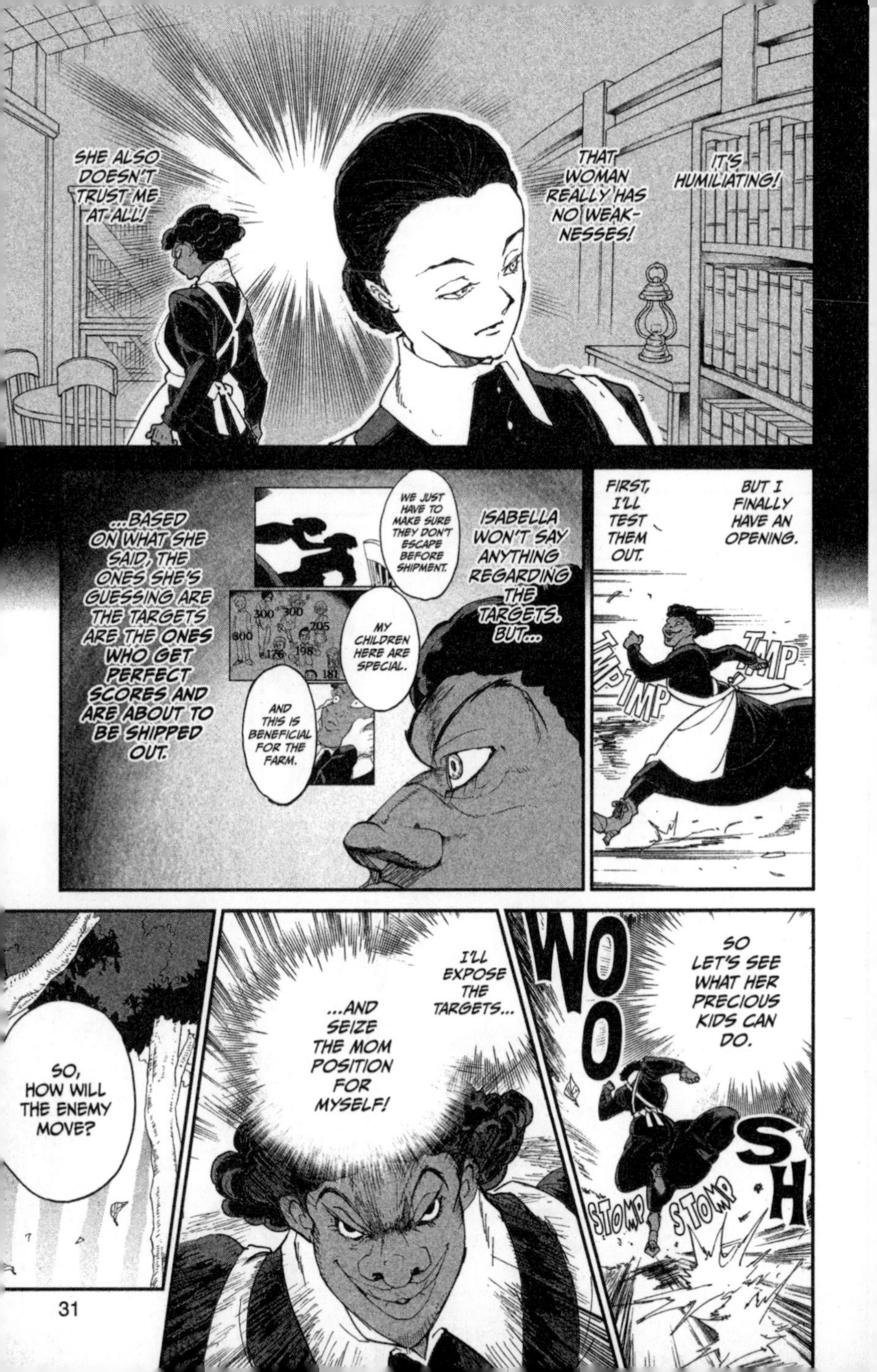
IT'S HUMILIATING!
THAT WOMAN REALLY HAS NO WEAK-NESSES!
SHE ALSO DOESN'T TRUST ME AT ALL!
BUT I FINALLY HAVE AN OPENING.
FIRST, I'LL TEST THEM OUT.
TMP TMP TMP TMP
ISABELLA WON'T SAY ANYTHING REGARDING THE TARGETS. BUT...
WE JUST HAVE TO MAKE SURE THEY DON'T ESCAPE BEFORE SHIPMENT.
MY CHILDREN HERE ARE SPECIAL.
AND THIS IS BENEFICIAL FOR THE FARM.
...BASED ON WHAT SHE SAID, THE ONES SHE'S GUESSING ARE THE TARGETS ARE THE ONES WHO GET PERFECT SCORES AND ARE ABOUT TO BE SHIPPED OUT.
SO LET'S SEE WHAT HER PRECIOUS KIDS CAN DO.
WOOSH
STOMP STOMP
I'LL EXPOSE THE TARGETS...
...AND SEIZE THE MOM POSITION FOR MYSELF!
SO, HOW WILL THE ENEMY MOVE?

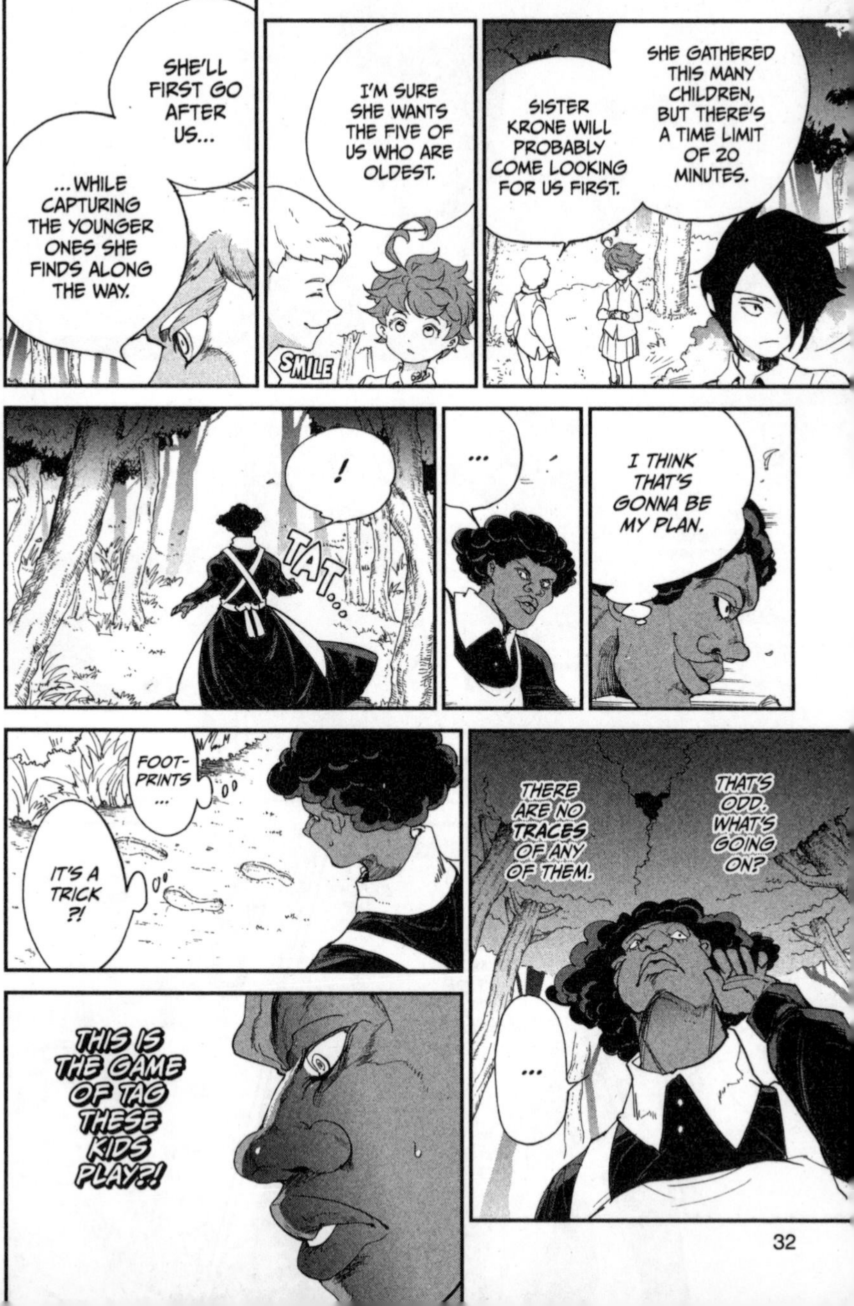
SHE GATHERED THIS MANY CHILDREN, BUT THERE'S A TIME LIMIT OF 20 MINUTES.
SISTER KRONE WILL PROBABLY COME LOOKING FOR US FIRST.
I'M SURE SHE WANTS THE FIVE OF US WHO ARE OLDEST.
SMILE
SHE'LL FIRST GO AFTER US...
...WHILE CAPTURING THE YOUNGER ONES SHE FINDS ALONG THE WAY.
I THINK THAT'S GONNA BE MY PLAN.
...
!
TAT...
THAT'S ODD. WHAT'S GOING ON?
THERE ARE NO TRACES OF ANY OF THEM.
...
FOOT-PRINTS...
IT'S A TRICK?!
THIS IS THE GAME OF TAG THESE KIDS PLAY?!

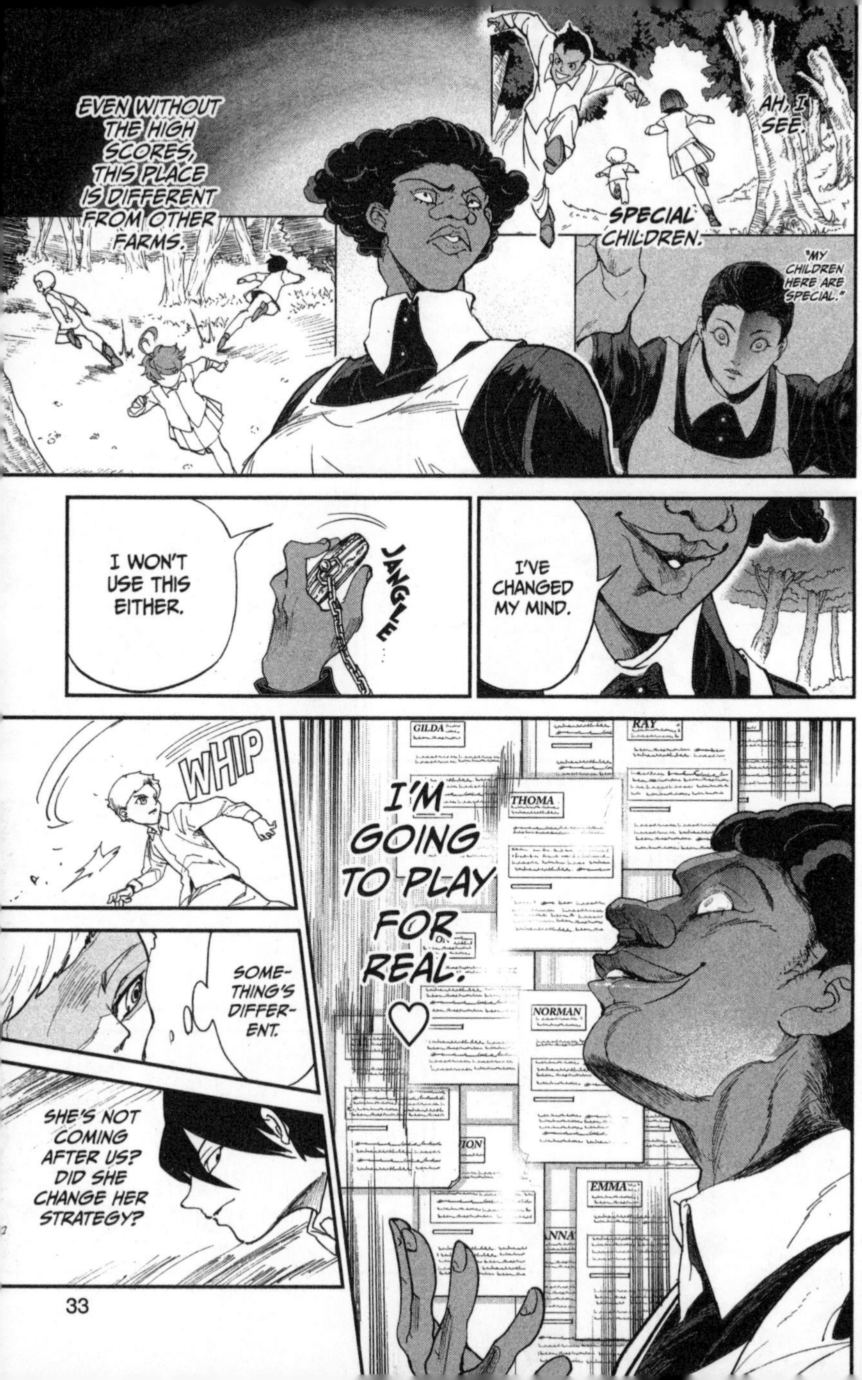
AH, I SEE.
SPECIAL CHILDREN.
"MY CHILDREN HERE ARE SPECIAL."
EVEN WITHOUT THE HIGH SCORES, THIS PLACE IS DIFFERENT FROM OTHER FARMS.
I'VE CHANGED MY MIND.
JANGLE...
I WON'T USE THIS EITHER.
GILDA
RAY
THOMA
NORMAN
EMMA
ANNA
I'M GOING TO PLAY FOR REAL. ♥
WHIP
SOME-THING'S DIFFER-ENT.
SHE'S NOT COMING AFTER US? DID SHE CHANGE HER STRATEGY?

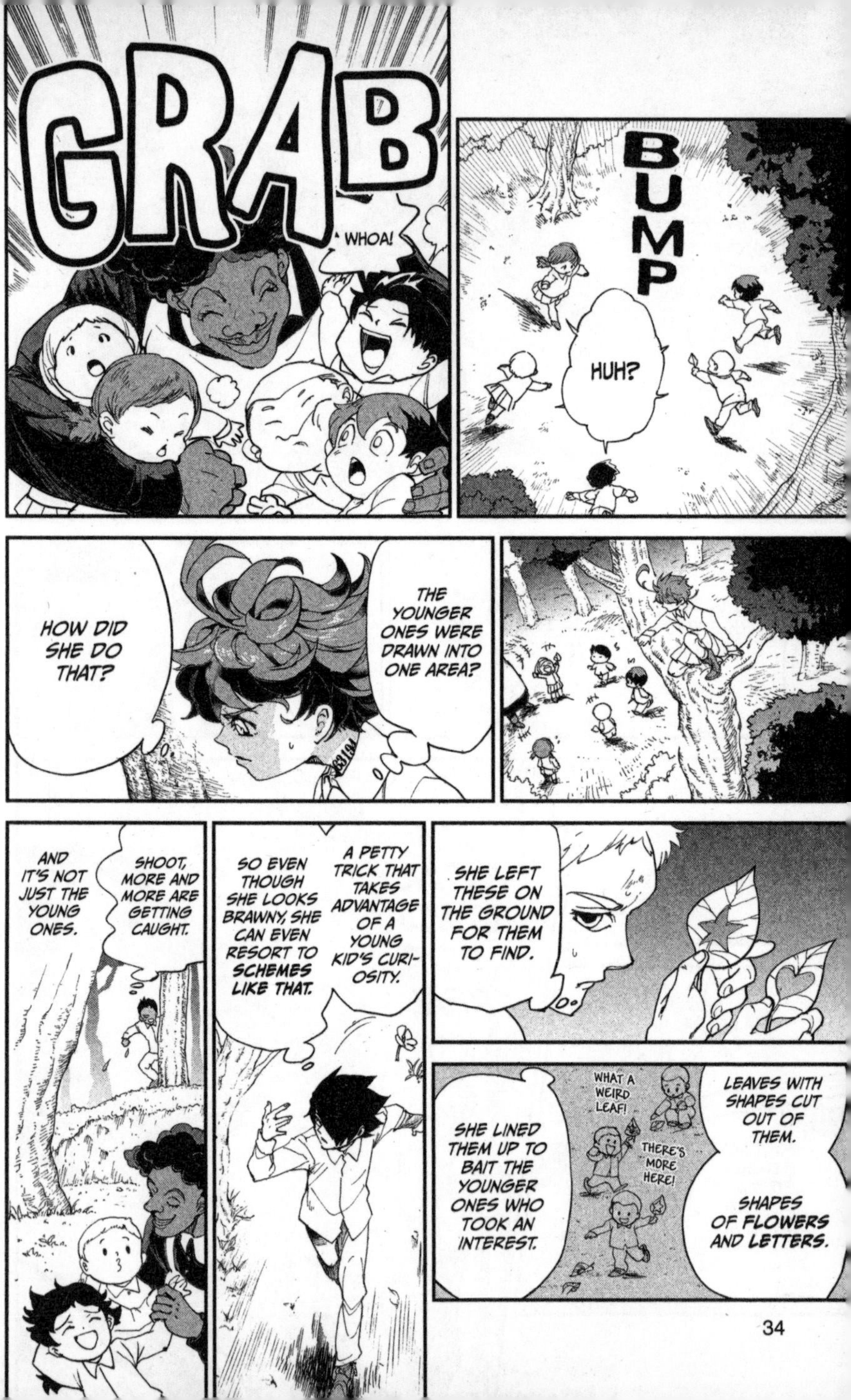
BUMP
HUH?
GRAB
WHOA!
THE YOUNGER ONES WERE DRAWN INTO ONE AREA?
HOW DID SHE DO THAT?
SHE LEFT THESE ON THE GROUND FOR THEM TO FIND.
LEAVES WITH SHAPES CUT OUT OF THEM.
SHAPES OF FLOWERS AND LETTERS.
WHAT A WEIRD LEAF!
THERE'S MORE HERE!
SHE LINED THEM UP TO BAIT THE YOUNGER ONES WHO TOOK AN INTEREST.
A PETTY TRICK THAT TAKES ADVANTAGE OF A YOUNG KID'S CURIOSITY.
SO EVEN THOUGH SHE LOOKS BRAWNY, SHE CAN EVEN RESORT TO SCHEMES LIKE THAT.
SHOOT, MORE AND MORE ARE GETTING CAUGHT.
AND IT'S NOT JUST THE YOUNG ONES.

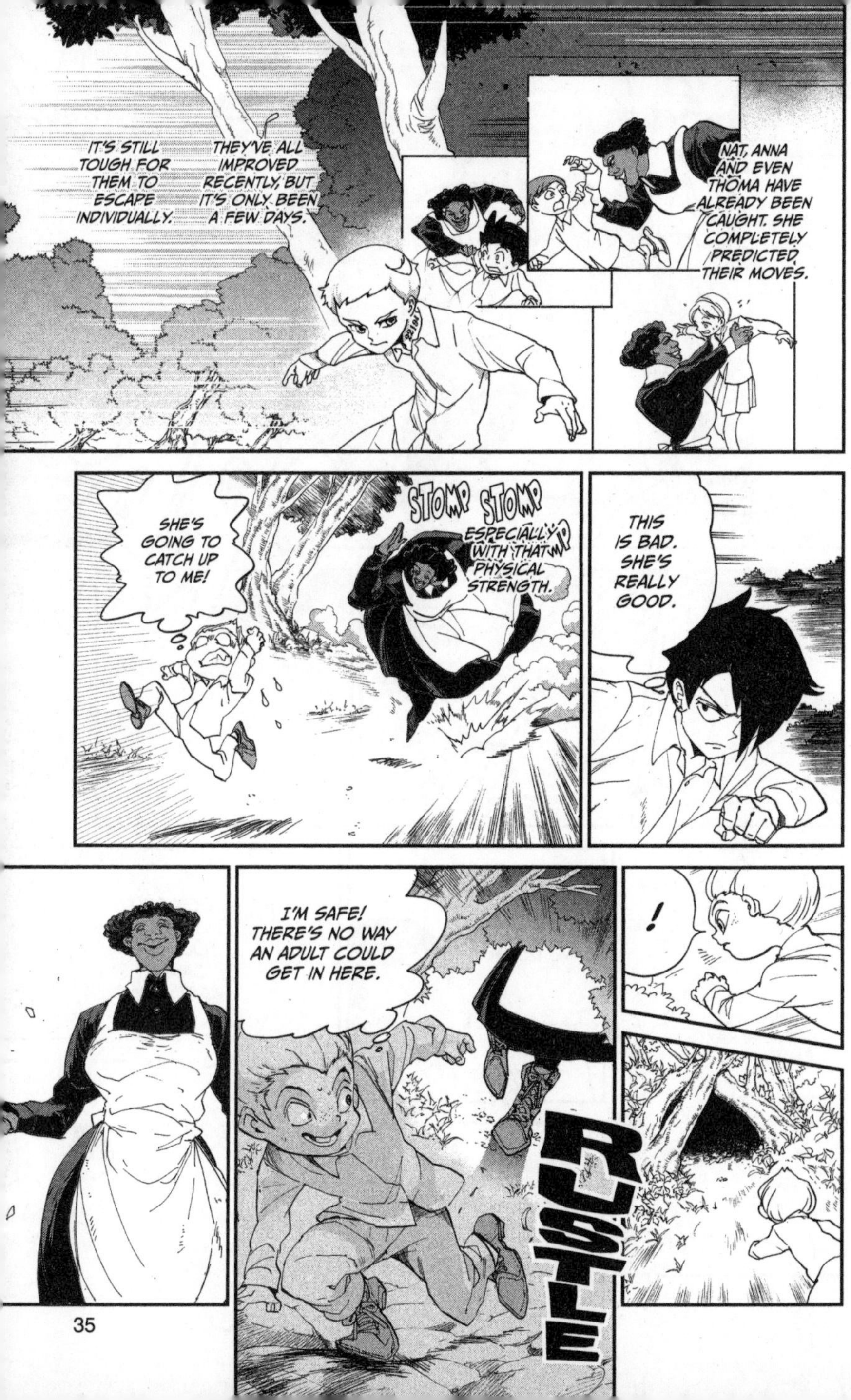
NAT, ANNA AND EVEN THOMA HAVE ALREADY BEEN CAUGHT. SHE COMPLETELY PREDICTED THEIR MOVES.
THEY'VE ALL IMPROVED RECENTLY, BUT IT'S ONLY BEEN A FEW DAYS.
IT'S STILL TOUGH FOR THEM TO ESCAPE INDIVIDUALLY.
THIS IS BAD. SHE'S REALLY GOOD.
STOMP STOMP
ESPECIALLY WITH THAT PHYSICAL STRENGTH.
SHE'S GOING TO CATCH UP TO ME!
!
I'M SAFE! THERE'S NO WAY AN ADULT COULD GET IN HERE.
RUSTLE

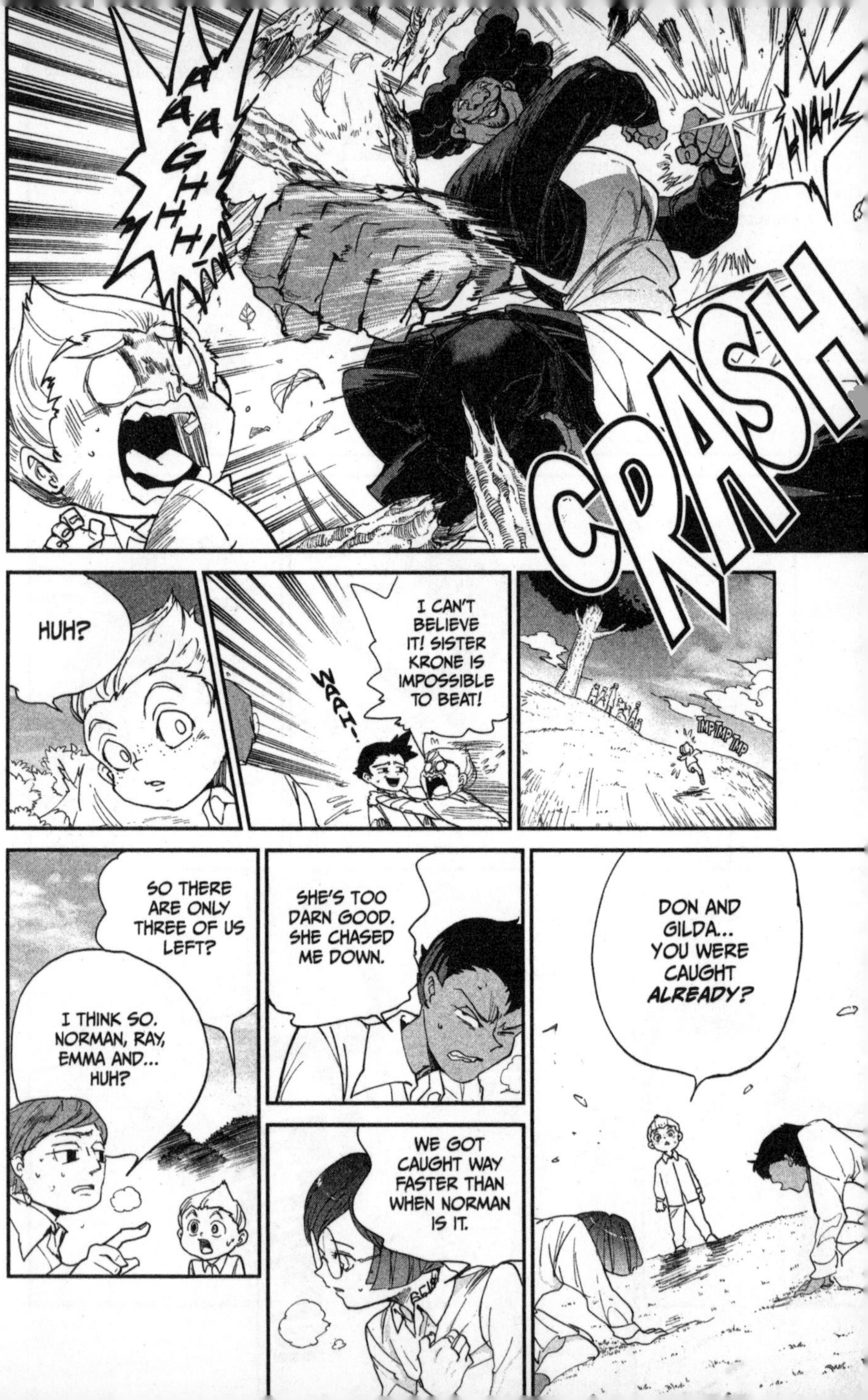
KYAH!
AAAGHHH!
CRASH
TMPTMPTMP
I CAN'T BELIEVE IT! SISTER KRONE IS IMPOSSIBLE TO BEAT!
WAAH!
HUH?
DON AND GILDA... YOU WERE CAUGHT ALREADY?
SHE'S TOO DARN GOOD. SHE CHASED ME DOWN.
WE GOT CAUGHT WAY FASTER THAN WHEN NORMAN IS IT.
SO THERE ARE ONLY THREE OF US LEFT?
I THINK SO. NORMAN, RAY, EMMA AND... HUH?

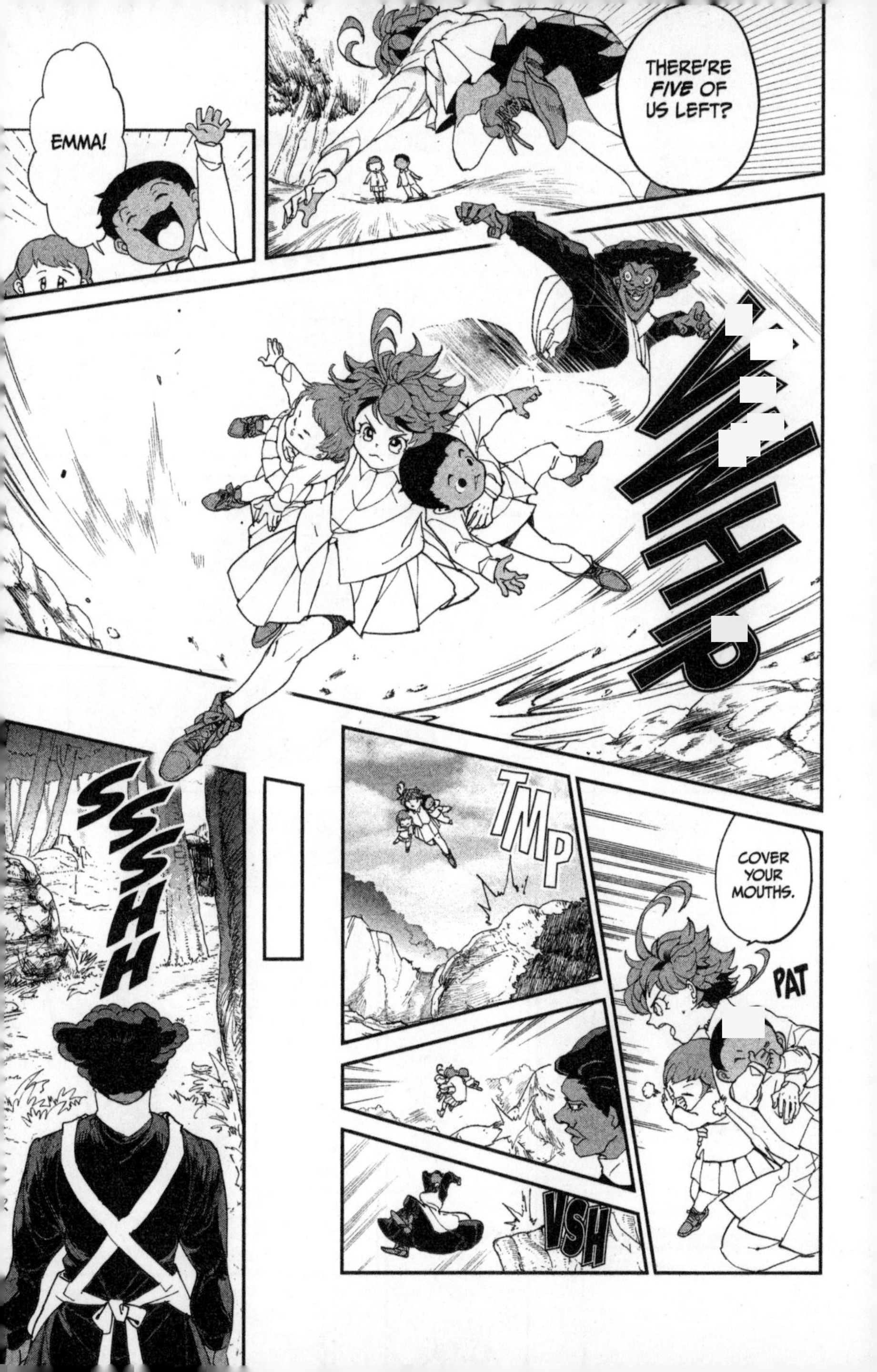
THERE'RE *FIVE* OF US LEFT?
EMMA!
WHHIP
COVER YOUR MOUTHS.
PAT
TMP
VSH
SSSHH

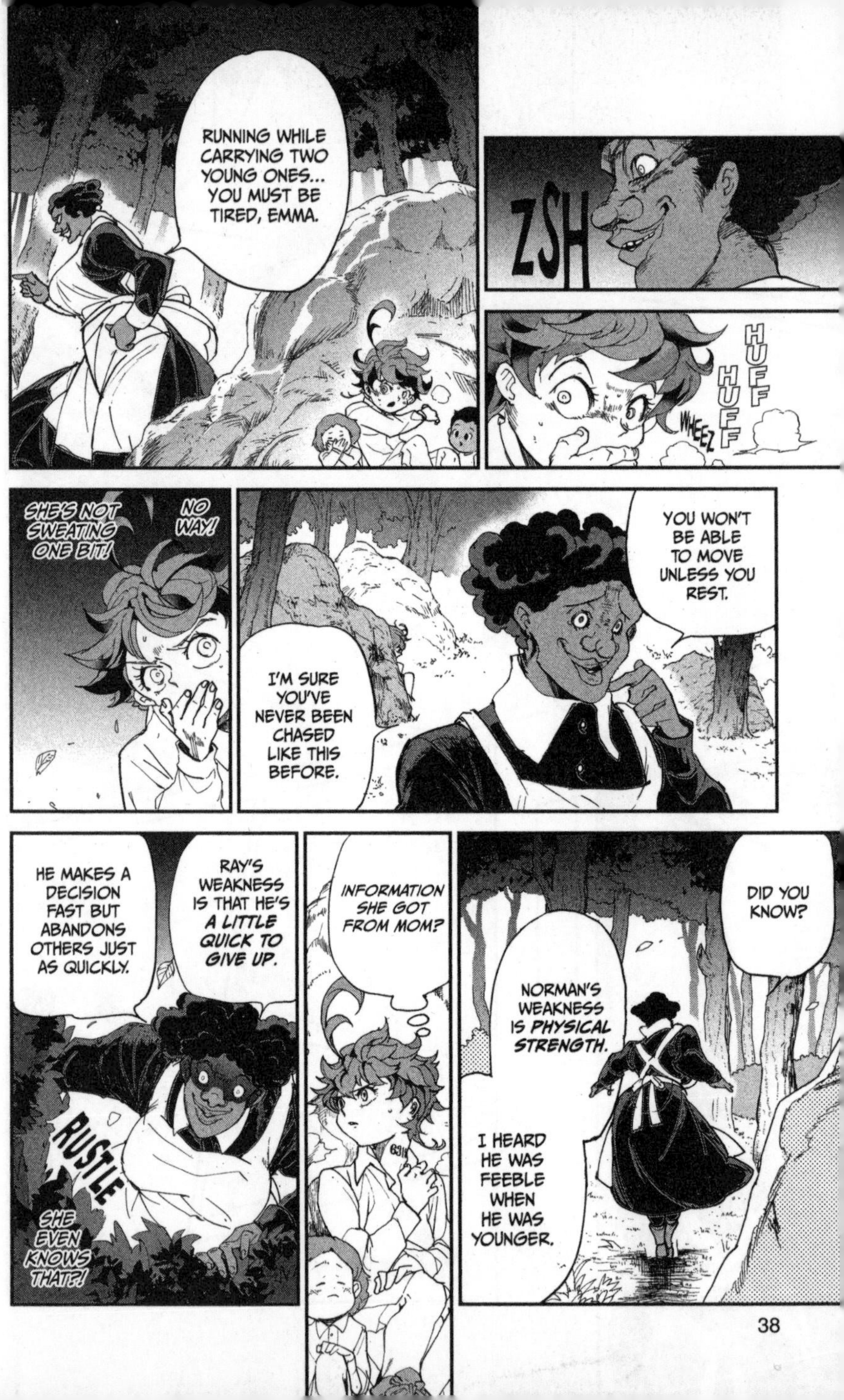
ZSH
HUFF HUFF WHEEZ HUFF
RUNNING WHILE CARRYING TWO YOUNG ONES... YOU MUST BE TIRED, EMMA.
YOU WON'T BE ABLE TO MOVE UNLESS YOU REST.
I'M SURE YOU'VE NEVER BEEN CHASED LIKE THIS BEFORE.
NO WAY!
SHE'S NOT SWEATING ONE BIT!
DID YOU KNOW?
NORMAN'S WEAKNESS IS *PHYSICAL STRENGTH.*
I HEARD HE WAS FEEBLE WHEN HE WAS YOUNGER.
INFORMATION SHE GOT FROM MOM?
RAY'S WEAKNESS IS THAT HE'S *A LITTLE QUICK TO GIVE UP.*
HE MAKES A DECISION FAST BUT ABANDONS OTHERS JUST AS QUICKLY.
RUSTLE
SHE EVEN KNOWS THAT?!

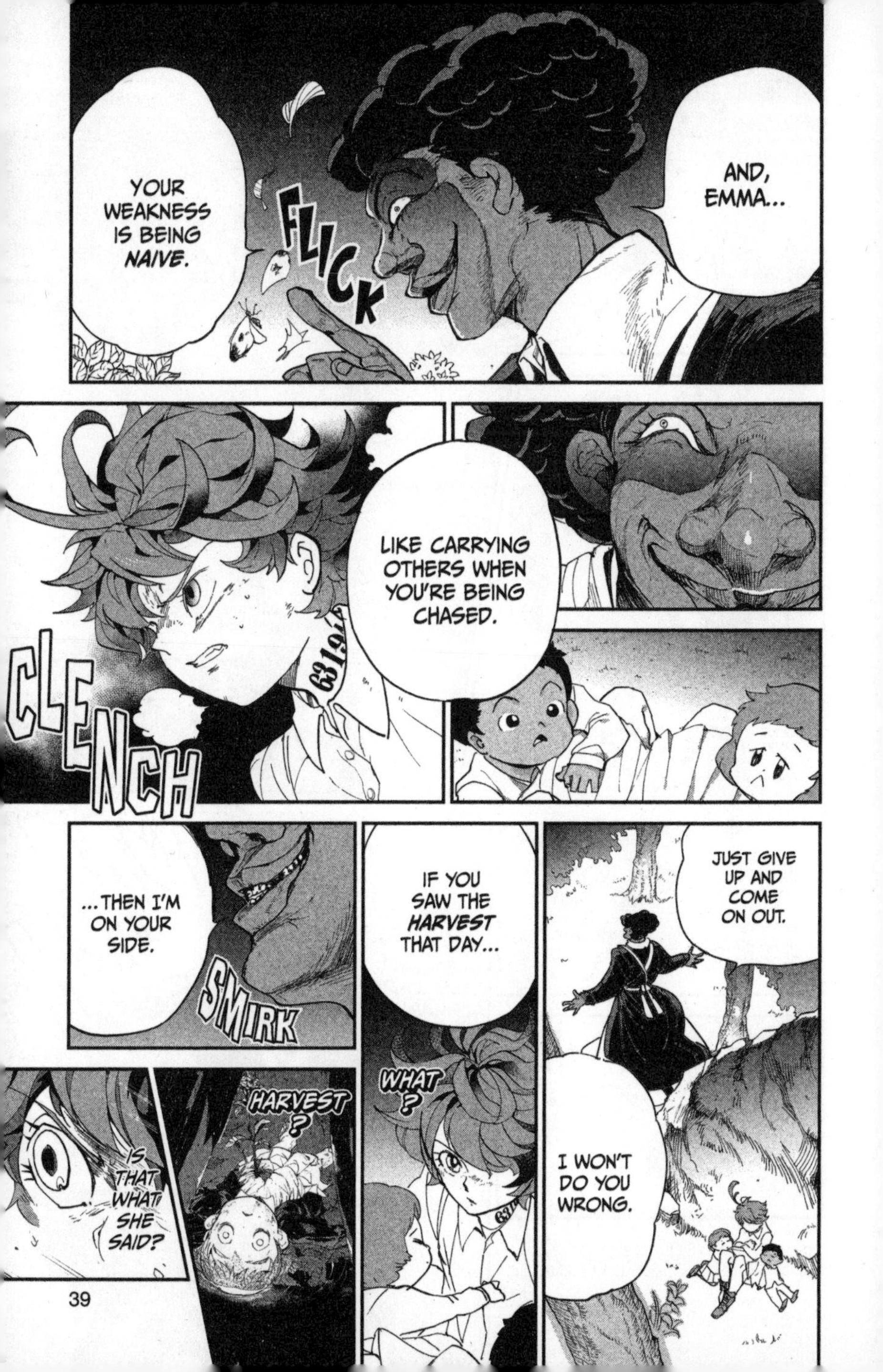

AND, EMMA...
FLICK
YOUR WEAKNESS IS BEING NAIVE.
LIKE CARRYING OTHERS WHEN YOU'RE BEING CHASED.
CLENCH
JUST GIVE UP AND COME ON OUT.
I WON'T DO YOU WRONG.
IF YOU SAW THE HARVEST THAT DAY...
WHAT?
...THEN I'M ON YOUR SIDE.
SMIRK
HARVEST?
IS THAT WHAT SHE SAID?

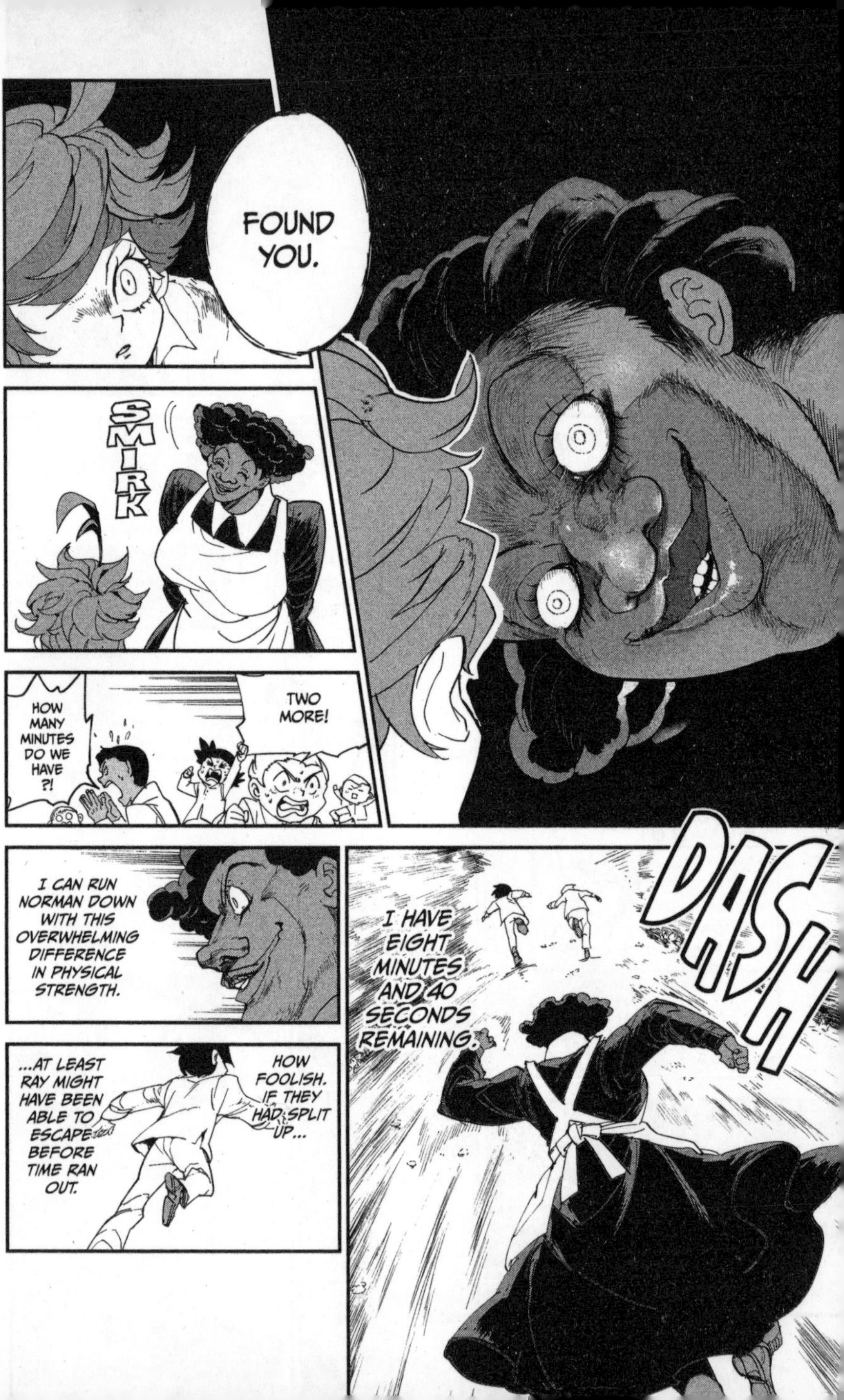
FOUND YOU.
SMIRK
HOW MANY MINUTES DO WE HAVE ?!
TWO MORE!
DASH
I HAVE EIGHT MINUTES AND 40 SECONDS REMAINING.
I CAN RUN NORMAN DOWN WITH THIS OVERWHELMING DIFFERENCE IN PHYSICAL STRENGTH.
HOW FOOLISH. IF THEY HAD SPLIT UP...
...AT LEAST RAY MIGHT HAVE BEEN ABLE TO ESCAPE BEFORE TIME RAN OUT.

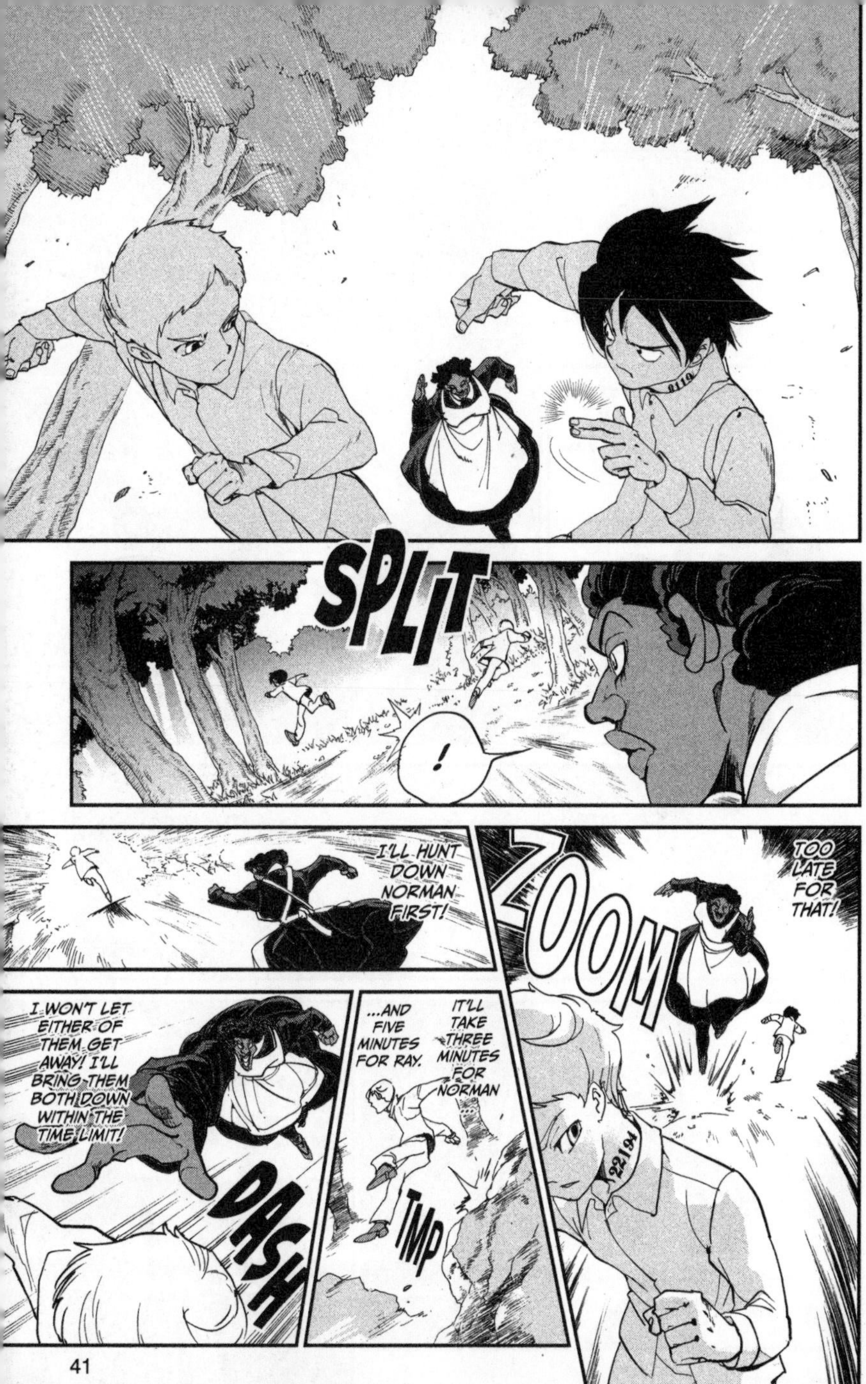
SPLIT
!
ZOOM
TOO LATE FOR THAT!
22194
I'LL HUNT DOWN NORMAN FIRST!
IT'LL TAKE THREE MINUTES FOR NORMAN
...AND FIVE MINUTES FOR RAY.
TMP
I WON'T LET EITHER OF THEM GET AWAY! I'LL BRING THEM BOTH DOWN WITHIN THE TIME LIMIT!
DASH

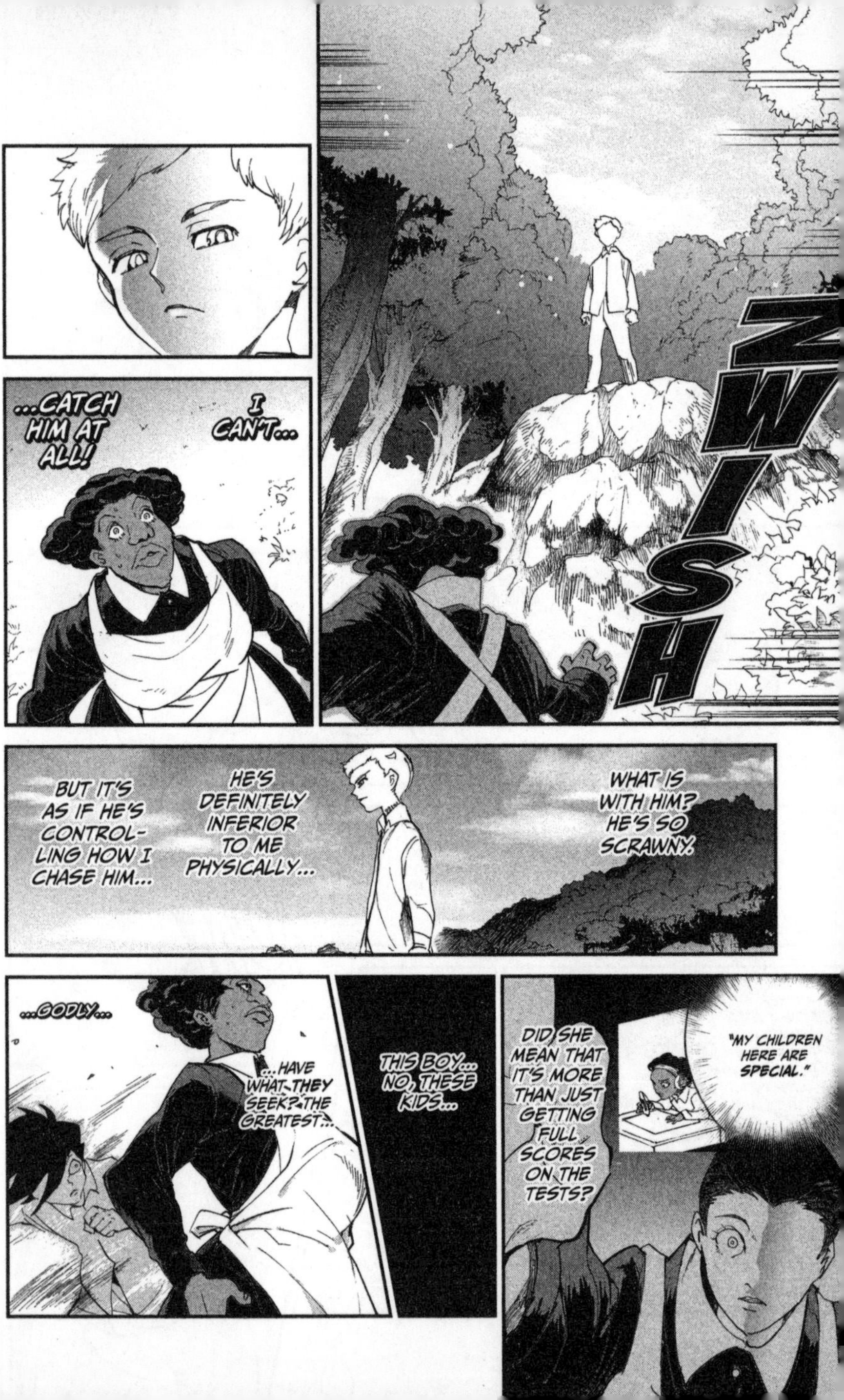
ZWISH
I CAN'T...
...CATCH HIM AT ALL!
WHAT IS WITH HIM? HE'S SO SCRAWNY.
HE'S DEFINITELY INFERIOR TO ME PHYSICALLY...
BUT IT'S AS IF HE'S CONTROL-LING HOW I CHASE HIM...
"MY CHILDREN HERE ARE SPECIAL."
DID SHE MEAN THAT IT'S MORE THAN JUST GETTING FULL SCORES ON THE TESTS?
THIS BOY... NO, THESE KIDS...
...HAVE WHAT THEY SEEK? THE GREATEST...
...GODLY...

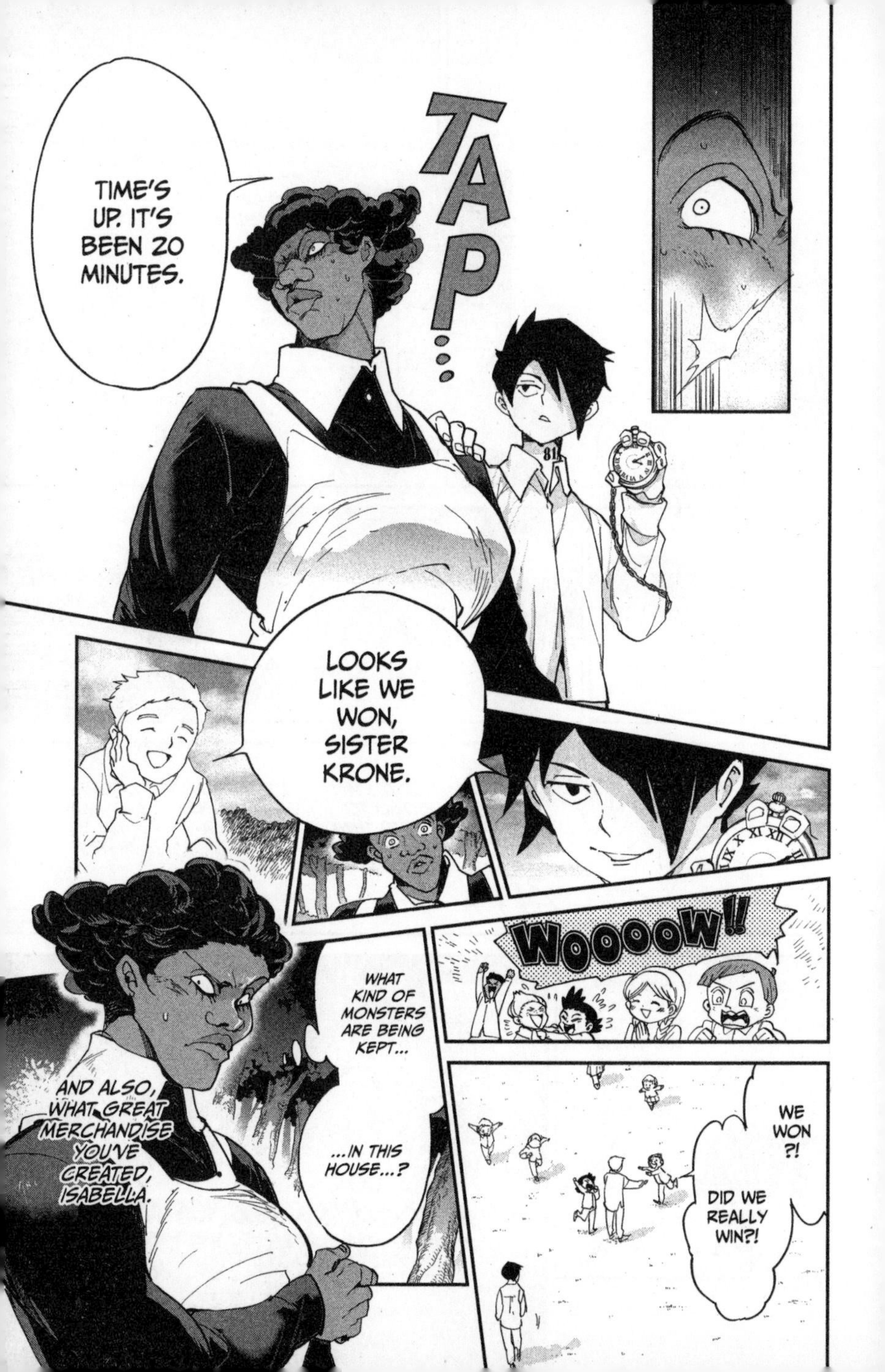
TAP...
TIME'S UP. IT'S BEEN 20 MINUTES.
LOOKS LIKE WE WON, SISTER KRONE.
WOOOOW!!
WE WON?!
DID WE REALLY WIN?!
WHAT KIND OF MONSTERS ARE BEING KEPT...
...IN THIS HOUSE...?
AND ALSO, WHAT GREAT MERCHANDISE YOU'VE CREATED, ISABELLA.

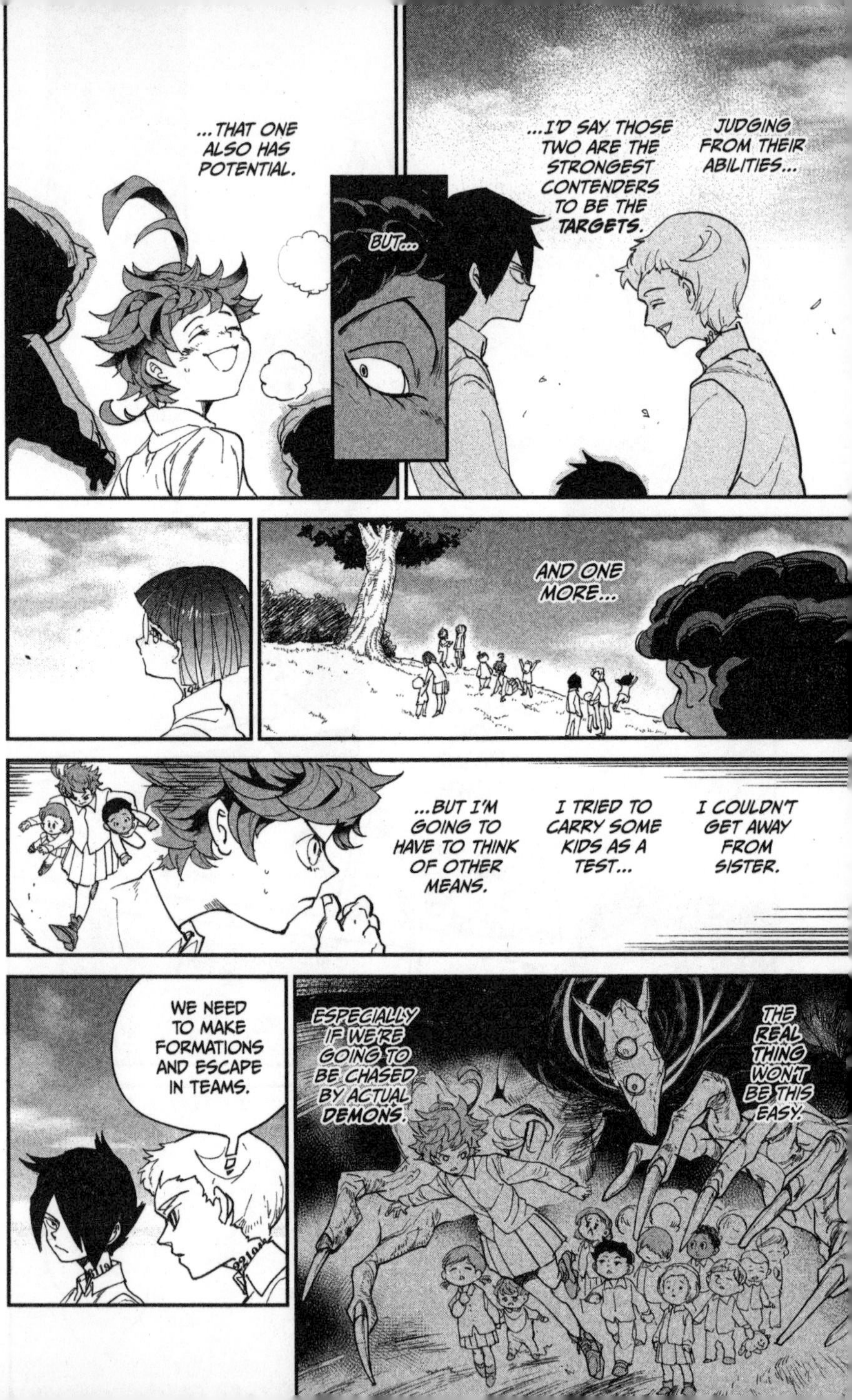
JUDGING FROM THEIR ABILITIES...
...I'D SAY THOSE TWO ARE THE STRONGEST CONTENDERS TO BE THE TARGETS.
BUT...
...THAT ONE ALSO HAS POTENTIAL.
AND ONE MORE...
I COULDN'T GET AWAY FROM SISTER.
I TRIED TO CARRY SOME KIDS AS A TEST...
...BUT I'M GOING TO HAVE TO THINK OF OTHER MEANS.
THE REAL THING WON'T BE THIS EASY.
ESPECIALLY IF WE'RE GOING TO BE CHASED BY ACTUAL DEMONS.
WE NEED TO MAKE FORMATIONS AND ESCAPE IN TEAMS.

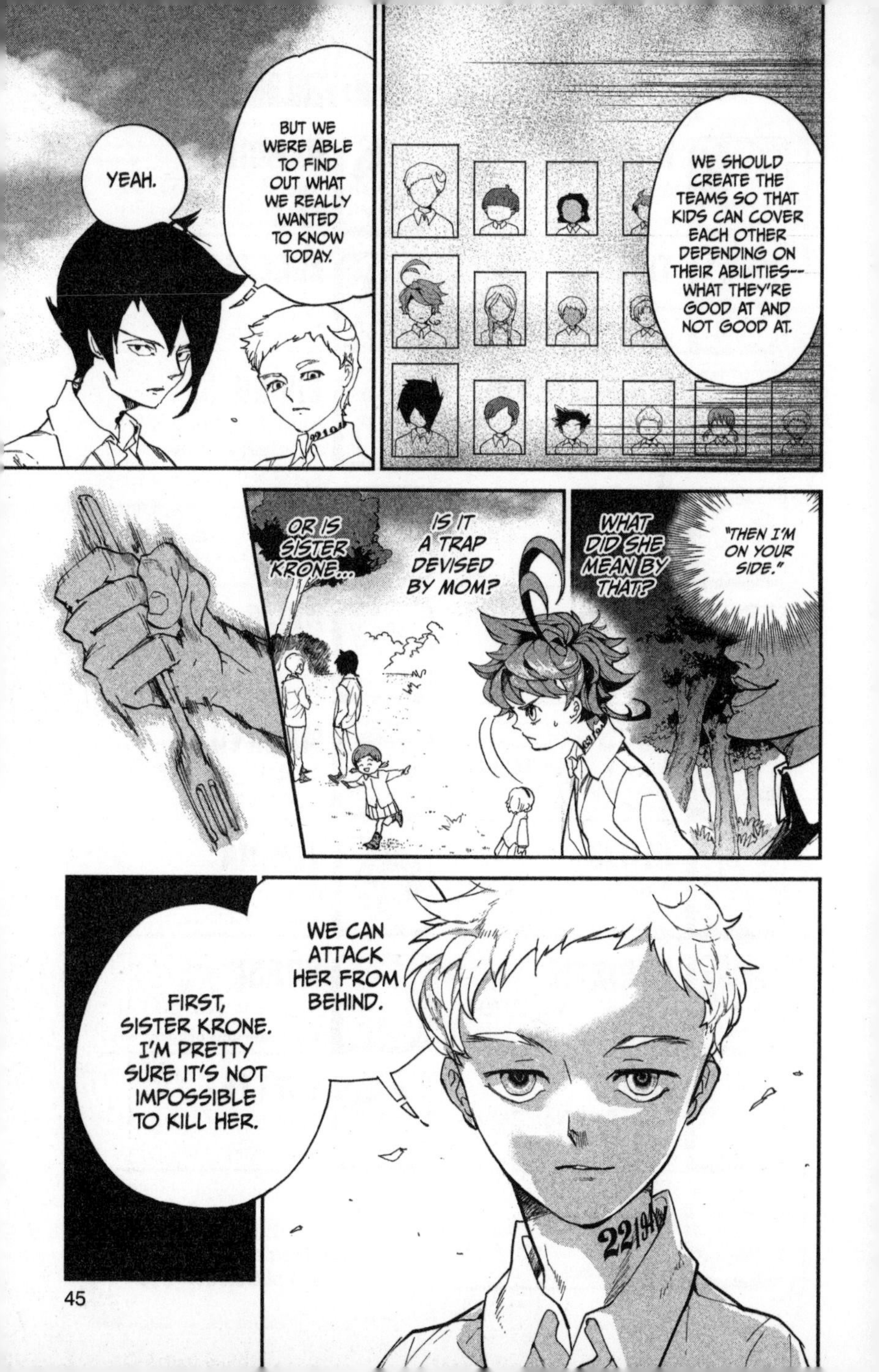
WE SHOULD CREATE THE TEAMS SO THAT KIDS CAN COVER EACH OTHER DEPENDING ON THEIR ABILITIES-- WHAT THEY'RE GOOD AT AND NOT GOOD AT.
BUT WE WERE ABLE TO FIND OUT WHAT WE REALLY WANTED TO KNOW TODAY.
YEAH.
"THEN I'M ON YOUR SIDE."
WHAT DID SHE MEAN BY THAT?
IS IT A TRAP DEVISED BY MOM?
OR IS SISTER KRONE...
FIRST, SISTER KRONE. I'M PRETTY SURE IT'S NOT IMPOSSIBLE TO KILL HER.
WE CAN ATTACK HER FROM BEHIND.

THE OTHER CHILDREN OF NEVERLAND

NINA
Age: 3 No. 77394

A determined girl.

YAWN

TOM
Age: 3 No. 66394

A boy from Emma's room.
His hair sticks up.

CHAMBERLAIN
Age: 3 No. 85394

A boy from Emma's room.
Often has flashes of wit.

SHERRY
Age: 4 No. 74394

A fashionable girl who
loves Norman.

JASPER
Age: 4 No. 04394

A sleepyhead.

HANS
Age: 4 No. 82394

A boy with a square face
and an upturned nose.

ALICIA
Age: 5 No. 71394

A tomboy who looks like
she could be a cheerleader.

CHRISTIE
Age: 5 No. 70394

Full of curiousity.

MARK
Age: 5 No. 79294

A boy who loves to eat.
He's good friends with Naila.

DOMINIC
Age: 6 No. 07294

An active boy.

DAMDIN
Age: 3 No. 57394

A boy with black hair
who wakes up early.

EUGENE
Age: 3 No. 46394

Thoughtful.

VIVIAN
Age: 3 No. 55394

A quiet girl with crossed eyes.

PHIL
Age: 4 No. 34394

A bighearted boy who
loves Emma.

NAILA
Age: 4 No. 53394

Goes at her own pace.
She's good friends with Mark.

MARNYA
Age: 4 No. 42394

A girl who loves Mom.

JEMIMA
Age: 5 No. 31394

A straight shooter.

ROSSI
Age: 5 No. 50394

A delicate and prudent boy.

YVETTE
Age: 5 No. 59294

An artist.

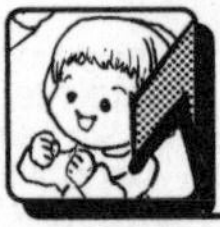

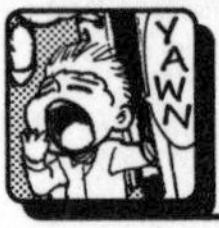

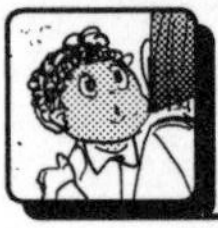

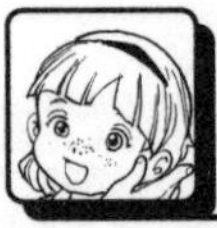

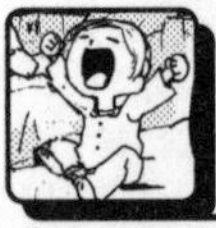

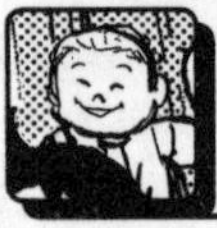

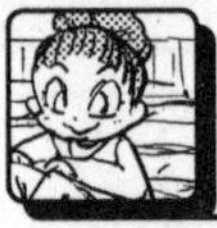

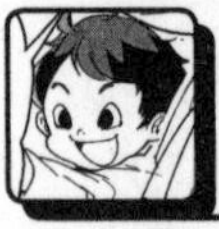

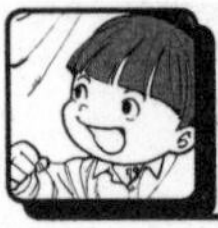

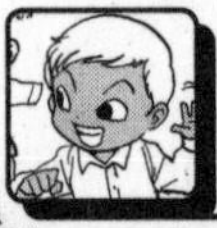

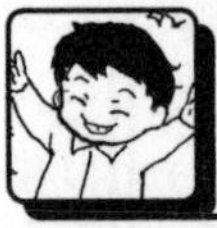

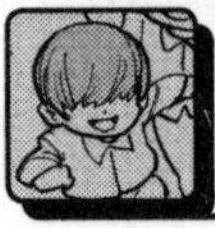

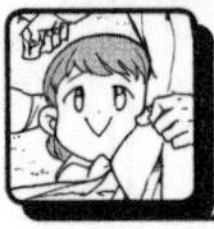

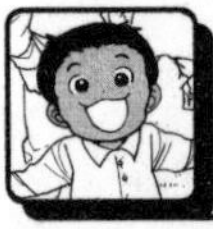

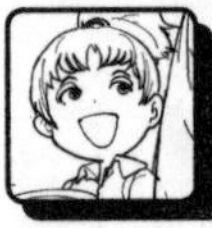

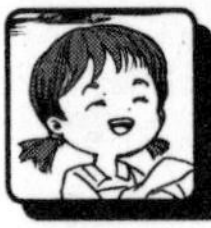

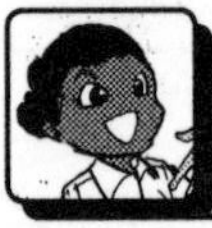

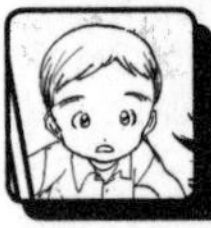

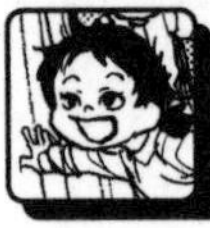

*Their ages at the
end of October 2045.

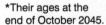

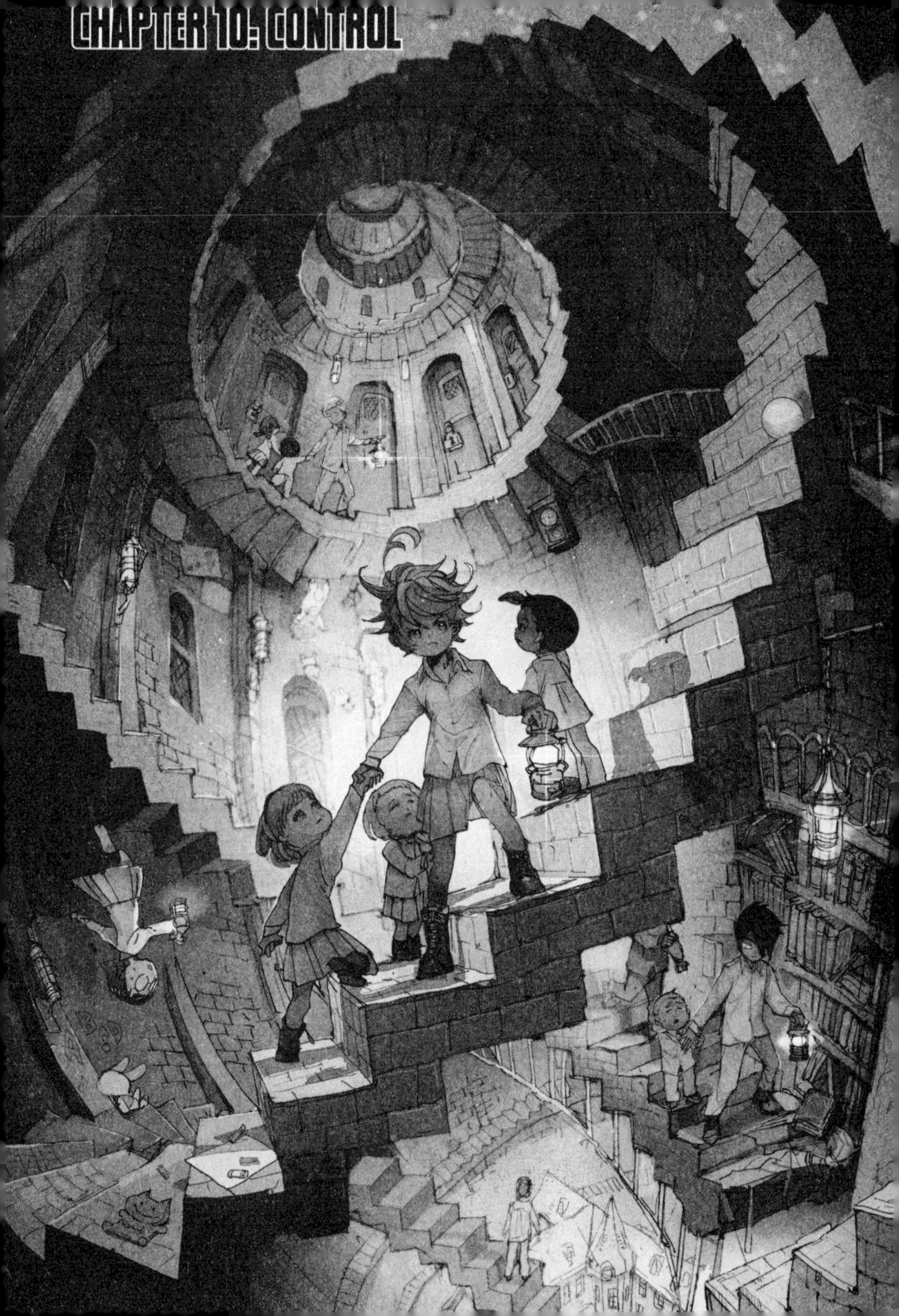
CHAPTER 10: CONTROL

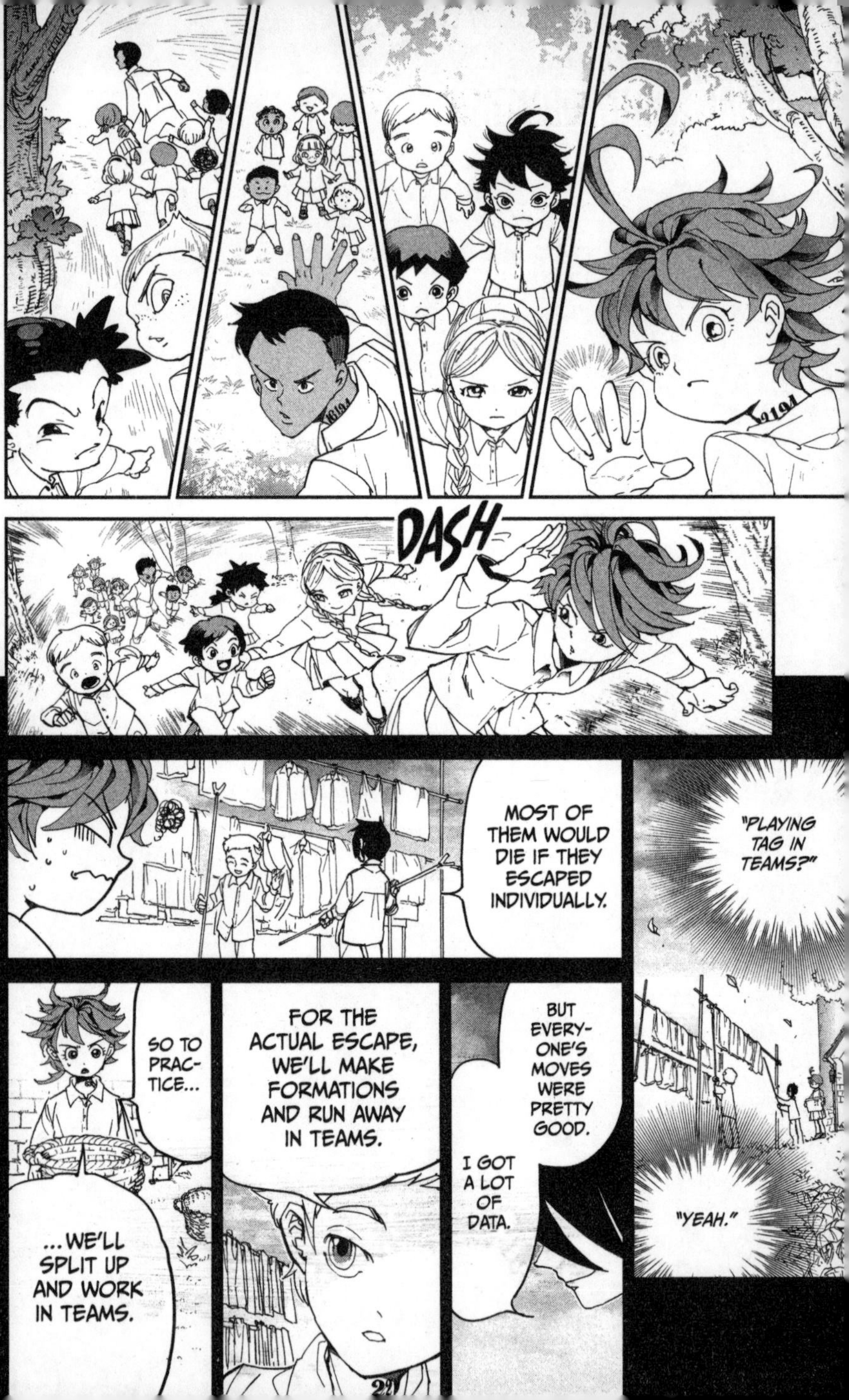
DASH
"PLAYING TAG IN TEAMS?"
"YEAH."
MOST OF THEM WOULD DIE IF THEY ESCAPED INDIVIDUALLY.
BUT EVERYONE'S MOVES WERE PRETTY GOOD.
I GOT A LOT OF DATA.
FOR THE ACTUAL ESCAPE, WE'LL MAKE FORMATIONS AND RUN AWAY IN TEAMS.
SO TO PRACTICE...
...WE'LL SPLIT UP AND WORK IN TEAMS.

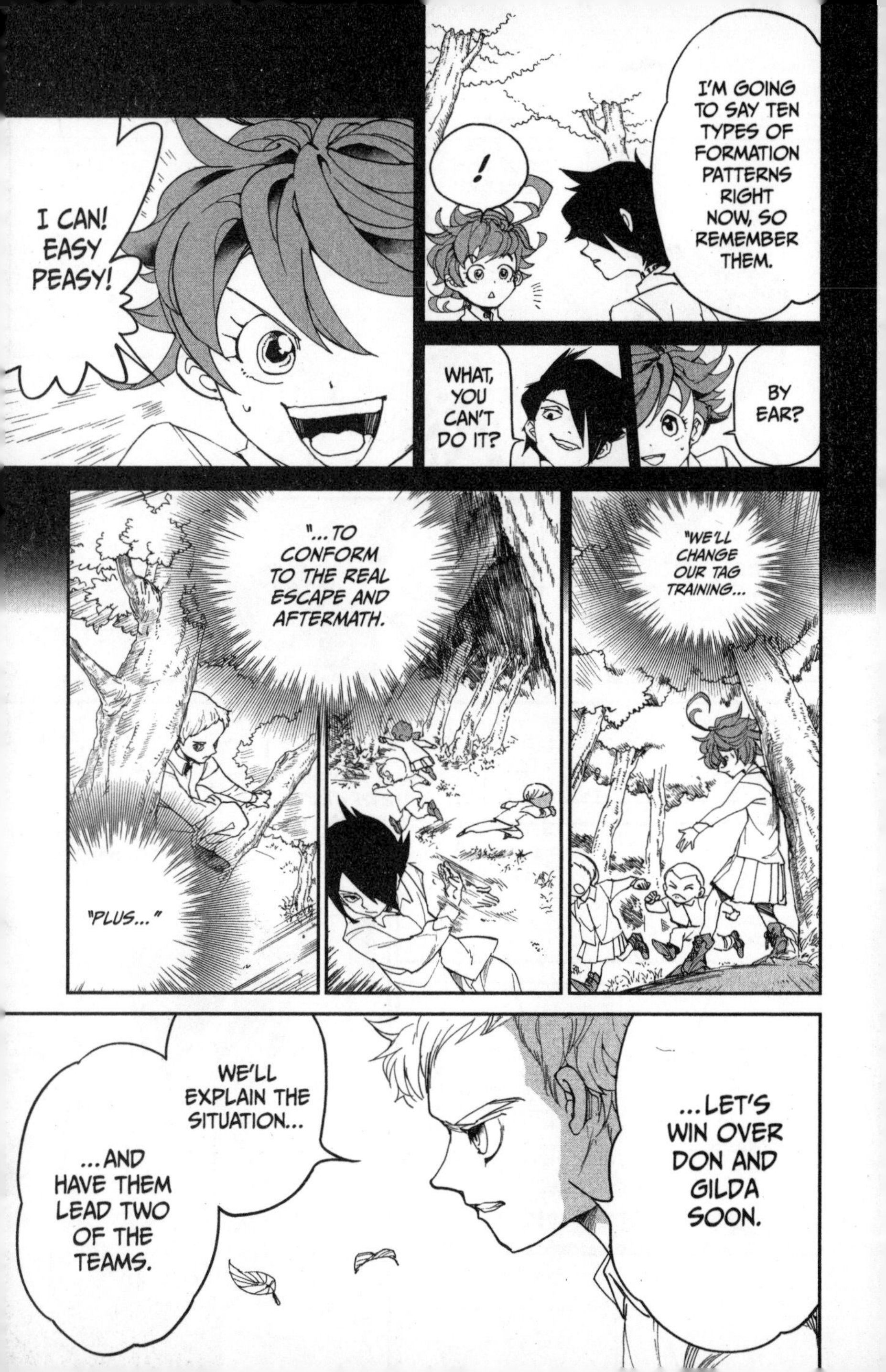
I'M GOING TO SAY TEN TYPES OF FORMATION PATTERNS RIGHT NOW, SO REMEMBER THEM.
!
BY EAR?
WHAT, YOU CAN'T DO IT?
I CAN! EASY PEASY!
"WE'LL CHANGE OUR TAG TRAINING...
"...TO CONFORM TO THE REAL ESCAPE AND AFTERMATH.
"PLUS..."
...LET'S WIN OVER DON AND GILDA SOON.
WE'LL EXPLAIN THE SITUATION...
...AND HAVE THEM LEAD TWO OF THE TEAMS.

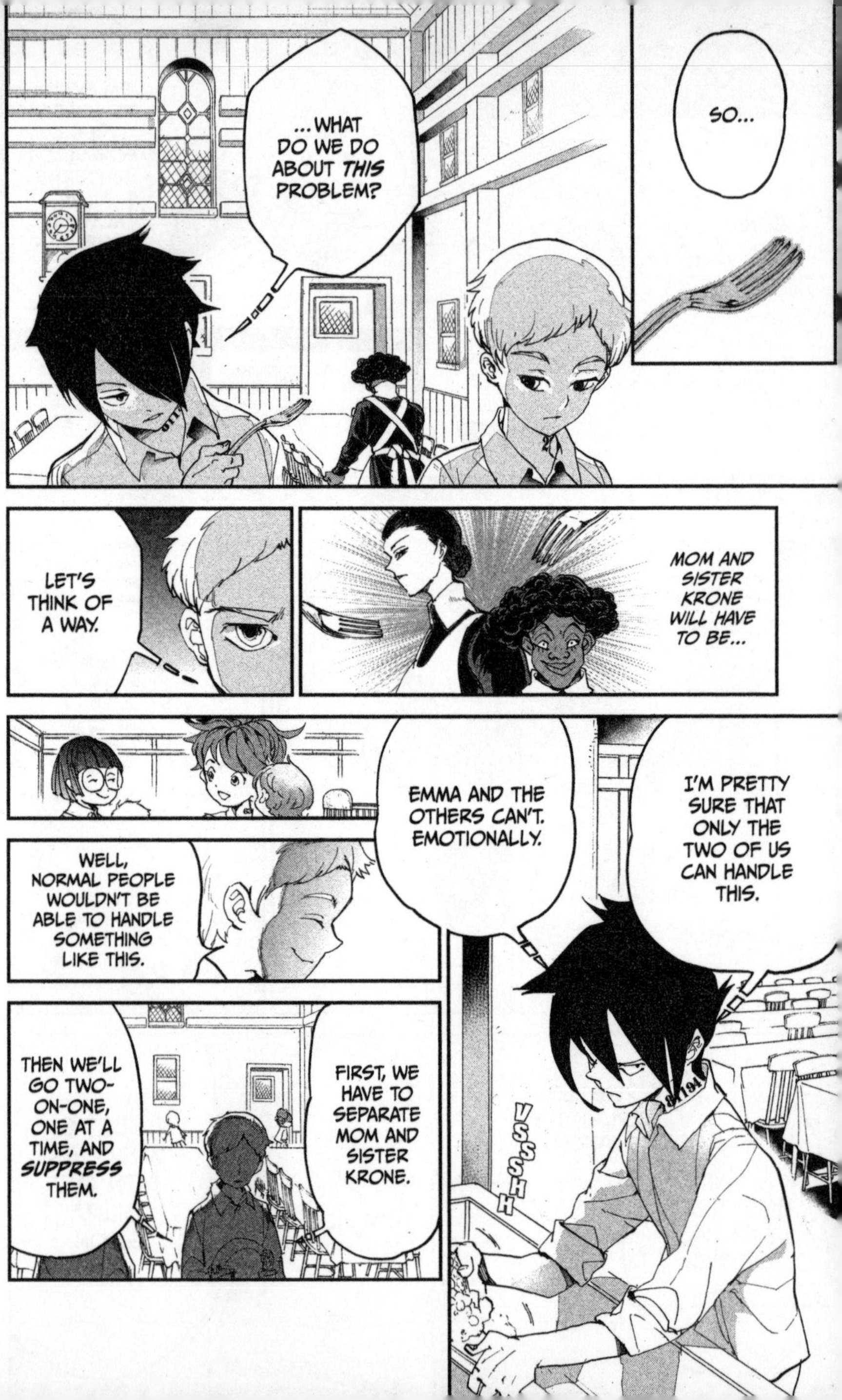
SO...
...WHAT DO WE DO ABOUT *THIS* PROBLEM?
MOM AND SISTER KRONE WILL HAVE TO BE...
LET'S THINK OF A WAY.
I'M PRETTY SURE THAT ONLY THE TWO OF US CAN HANDLE THIS.
EMMA AND THE OTHERS CAN'T. EMOTIONALLY.
VSSSHH
WELL, NORMAL PEOPLE WOULDN'T BE ABLE TO HANDLE SOMETHING LIKE THIS.
FIRST, WE HAVE TO SEPARATE MOM AND SISTER KRONE.
THEN WE'LL GO TWO-ON-ONE, ONE AT A TIME, AND ***SUPPRESS*** THEM.

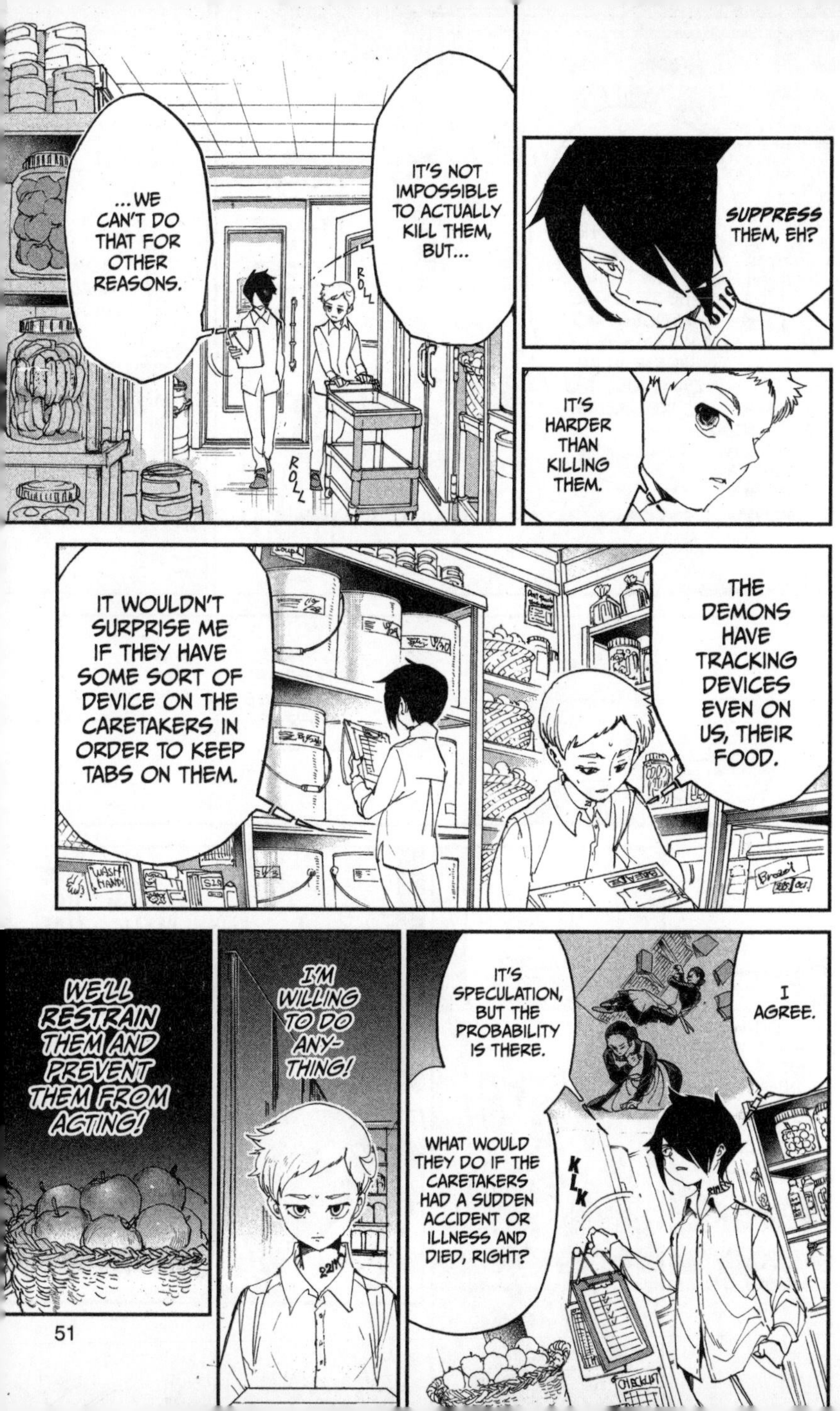
SUPPRESS THEM, EH?
IT'S HARDER THAN KILLING THEM.
IT'S NOT IMPOSSIBLE TO ACTUALLY KILL THEM, BUT...
...WE CAN'T DO THAT FOR OTHER REASONS.
ROLL
ROLL
THE DEMONS HAVE TRACKING DEVICES EVEN ON US, THEIR FOOD.
IT WOULDN'T SURPRISE ME IF THEY HAVE SOME SORT OF DEVICE ON THE CARETAKERS IN ORDER TO KEEP TABS ON THEM.
I AGREE.
IT'S SPECULATION, BUT THE PROBABILITY IS THERE.
WHAT WOULD THEY DO IF THE CARETAKERS HAD A SUDDEN ACCIDENT OR ILLNESS AND DIED, RIGHT?
KLK
I'M WILLING TO DO ANYTHING!
WE'LL RESTRAIN THEM AND PREVENT THEM FROM ACTING!

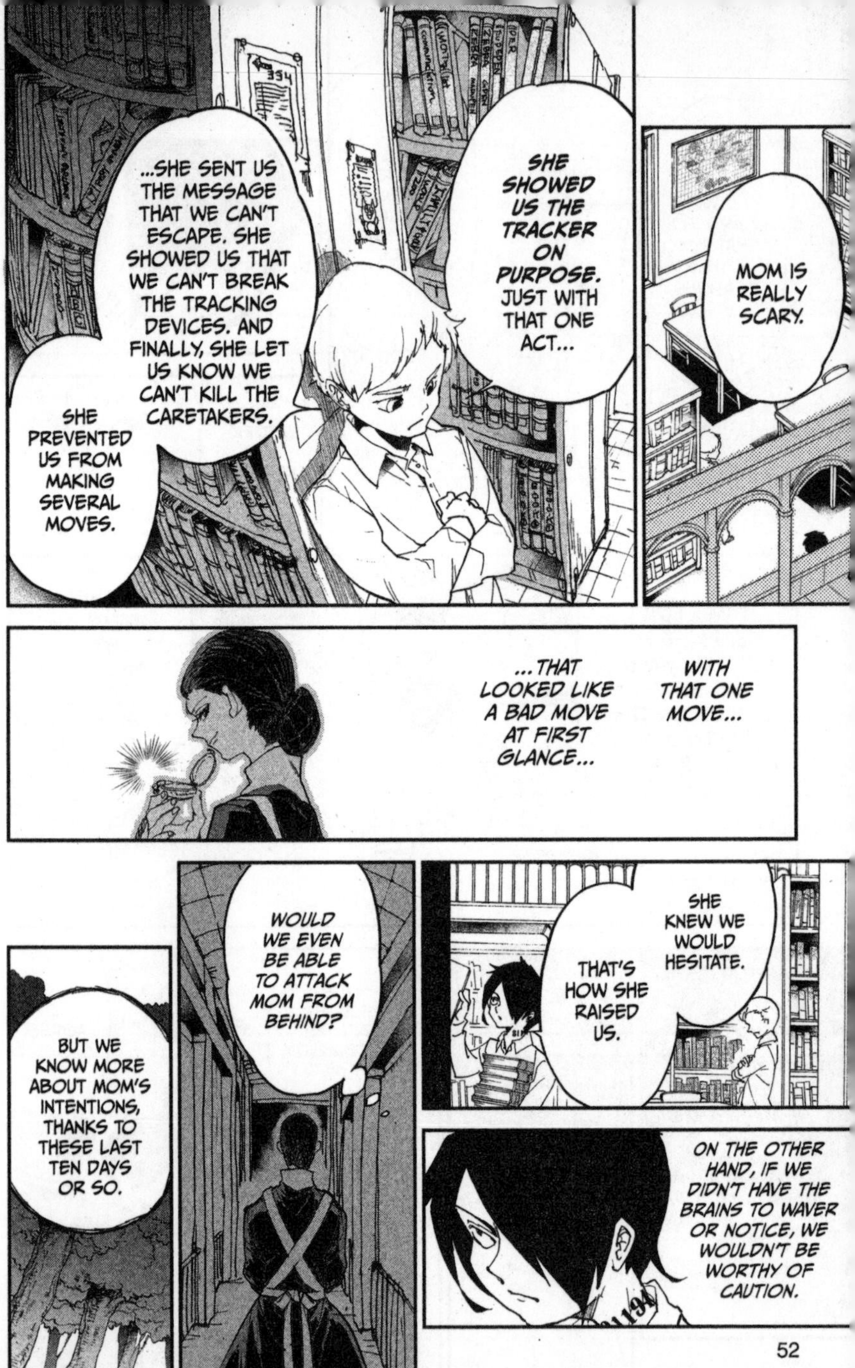
MOM IS REALLY SCARY.
SHE SHOWED US THE TRACKER ON PURPOSE. JUST WITH THAT ONE ACT...
...SHE SENT US THE MESSAGE THAT WE CAN'T ESCAPE. SHE SHOWED US THAT WE CAN'T BREAK THE TRACKING DEVICES. AND FINALLY, SHE LET US KNOW WE CAN'T KILL THE CARETAKERS.
SHE PREVENTED US FROM MAKING SEVERAL MOVES.
WITH THAT ONE MOVE...
...THAT LOOKED LIKE A BAD MOVE AT FIRST GLANCE...
SHE KNEW WE WOULD HESITATE.
THAT'S HOW SHE RAISED US.
ON THE OTHER HAND, IF WE DIDN'T HAVE THE BRAINS TO WAVER OR NOTICE, WE WOULDN'T BE WORTHY OF CAUTION.
WOULD WE EVEN BE ABLE TO ATTACK MOM FROM BEHIND?
BUT WE KNOW MORE ABOUT MOM'S INTENTIONS, THANKS TO THESE LAST TEN DAYS OR SO.

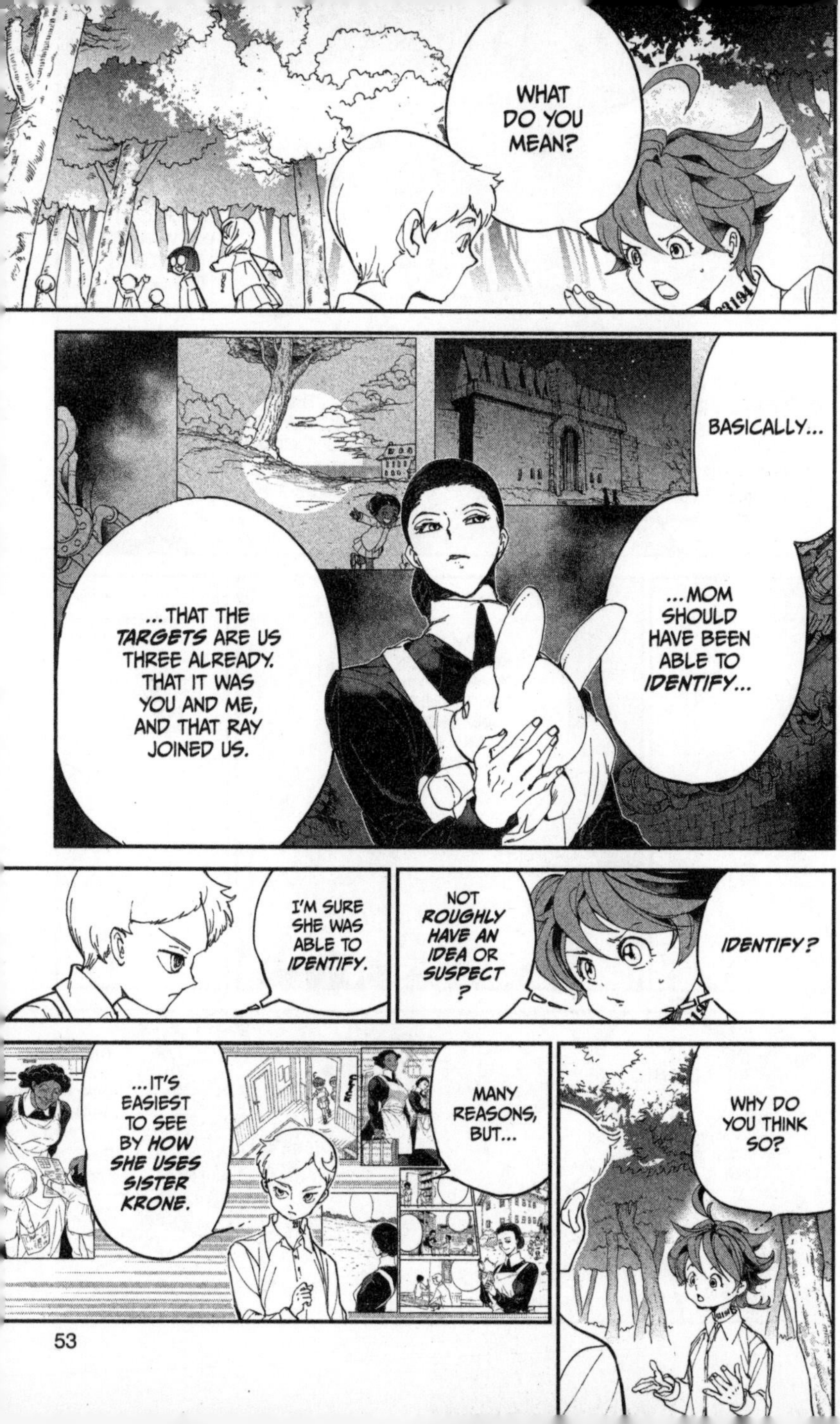
WHAT DO YOU MEAN?
BASICALLY...
...MOM SHOULD HAVE BEEN ABLE TO *IDENTIFY*...
...THAT THE *TARGETS* ARE US THREE ALREADY. THAT IT WAS YOU AND ME, AND THAT RAY JOINED US.
IDENTIFY?
NOT *ROUGHLY HAVE AN IDEA OR SUSPECT*?
I'M SURE SHE WAS ABLE TO *IDENTIFY*.
WHY DO YOU THINK SO?
MANY REASONS, BUT...
...IT'S EASIEST TO SEE BY *HOW SHE USES SISTER KRONE*.

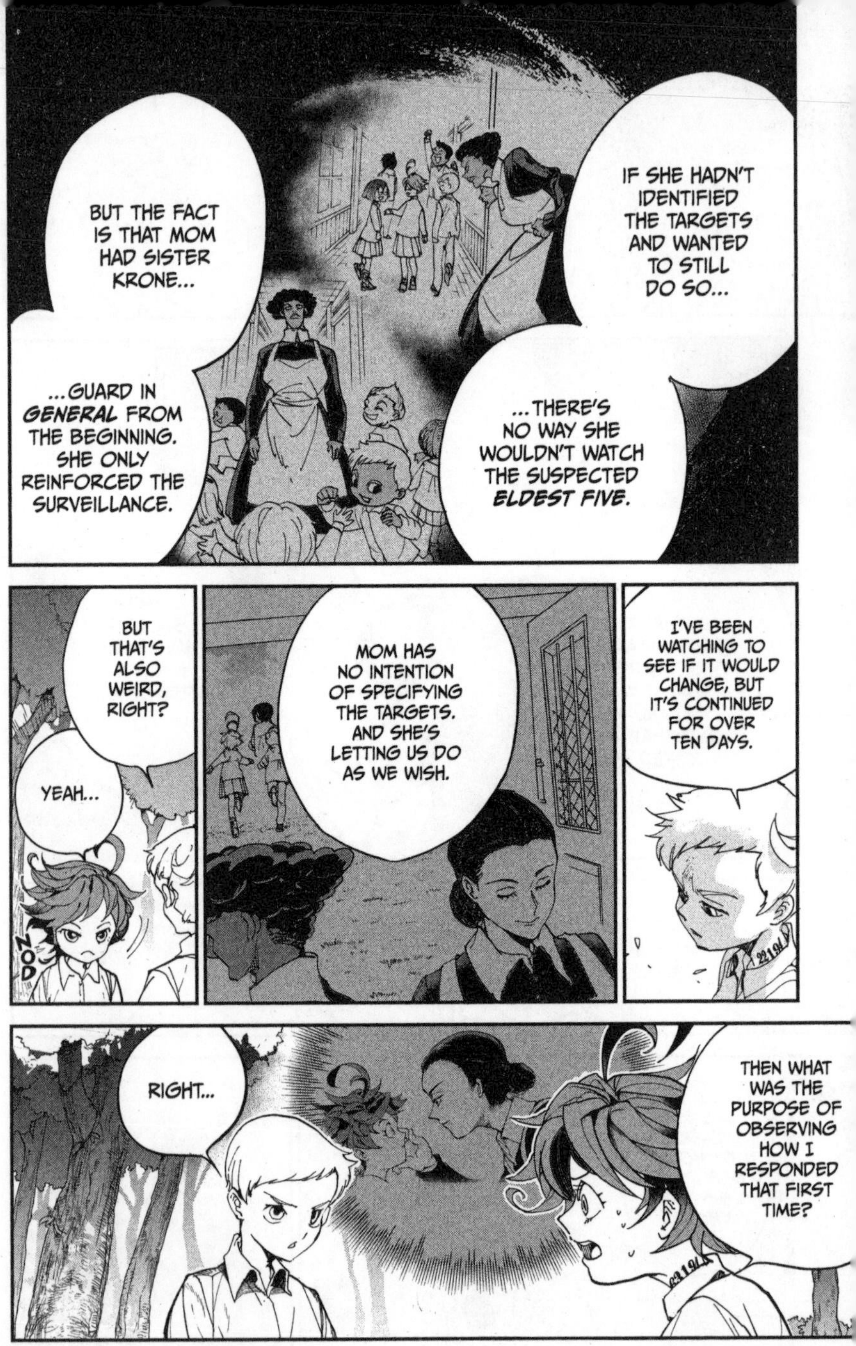
IF SHE HADN'T IDENTIFIED THE TARGETS AND WANTED TO STILL DO SO...
...THERE'S NO WAY SHE WOULDN'T WATCH THE SUSPECTED *ELDEST FIVE.*
BUT THE FACT IS THAT MOM HAD SISTER KRONE...
...GUARD IN *GENERAL* FROM THE BEGINNING. SHE ONLY REINFORCED THE SURVEILLANCE.
I'VE BEEN WATCHING TO SEE IF IT WOULD CHANGE, BUT IT'S CONTINUED FOR OVER TEN DAYS.
MOM HAS NO INTENTION OF SPECIFYING THE TARGETS. AND SHE'S LETTING US DO AS WE WISH.
BUT THAT'S ALSO WEIRD, RIGHT?
YEAH...
NOD
THEN WHAT WAS THE PURPOSE OF OBSERVING HOW I RESPONDED THAT FIRST TIME?
RIGHT...

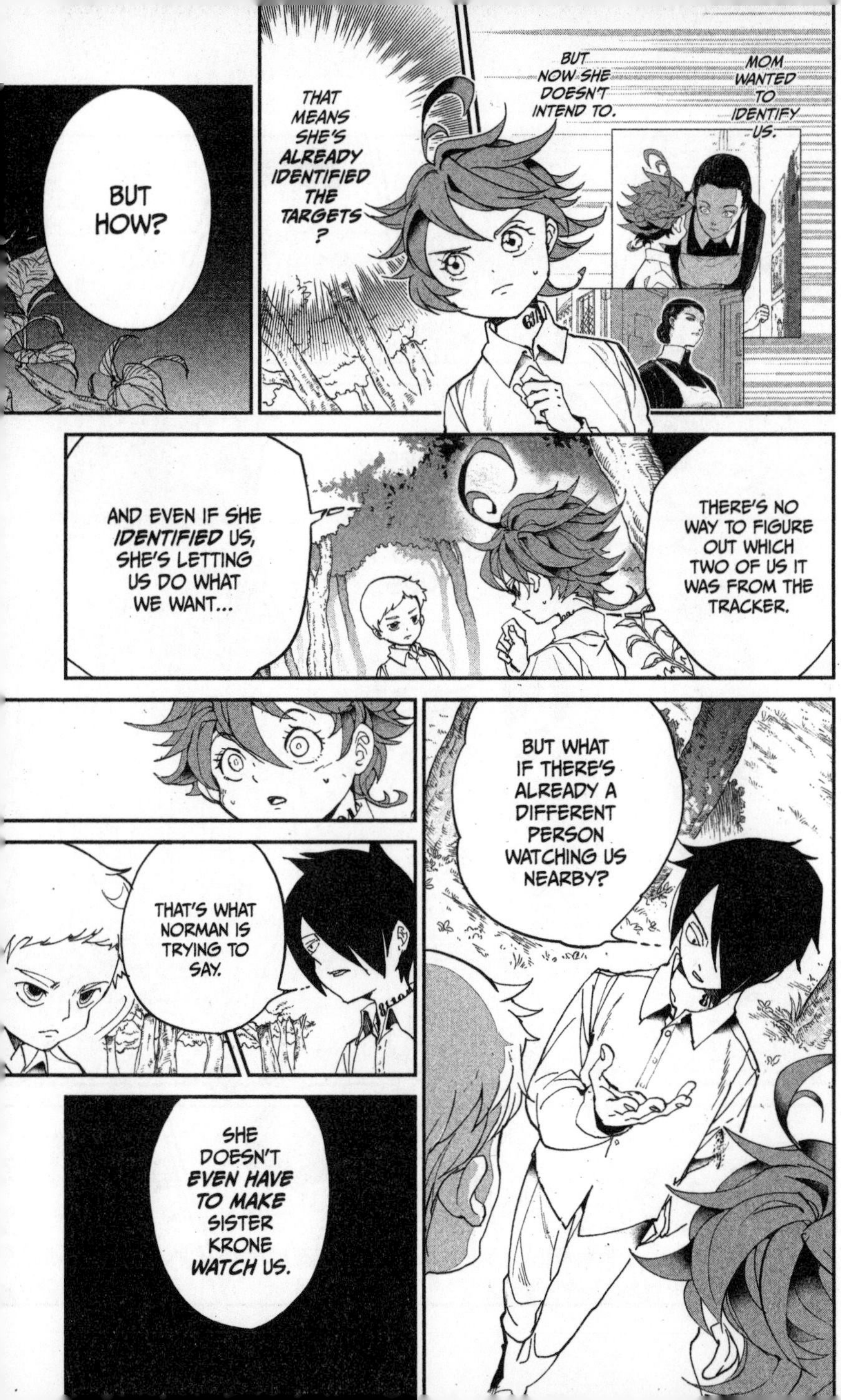
MOM WANTED TO IDENTIFY US.
BUT NOW SHE DOESN'T INTEND TO.
THAT MEANS SHE'S ALREADY IDENTIFIED THE TARGETS?
BUT HOW?
THERE'S NO WAY TO FIGURE OUT WHICH TWO OF US IT WAS FROM THE TRACKER.
AND EVEN IF SHE *IDENTIFIED* US, SHE'S LETTING US DO WHAT WE WANT...
BUT WHAT IF THERE'S ALREADY A DIFFERENT PERSON WATCHING US NEARBY?
THAT'S WHAT NORMAN IS TRYING TO SAY.
SHE DOESN'T ***EVEN HAVE TO MAKE*** SISTER KRONE ***WATCH*** US.

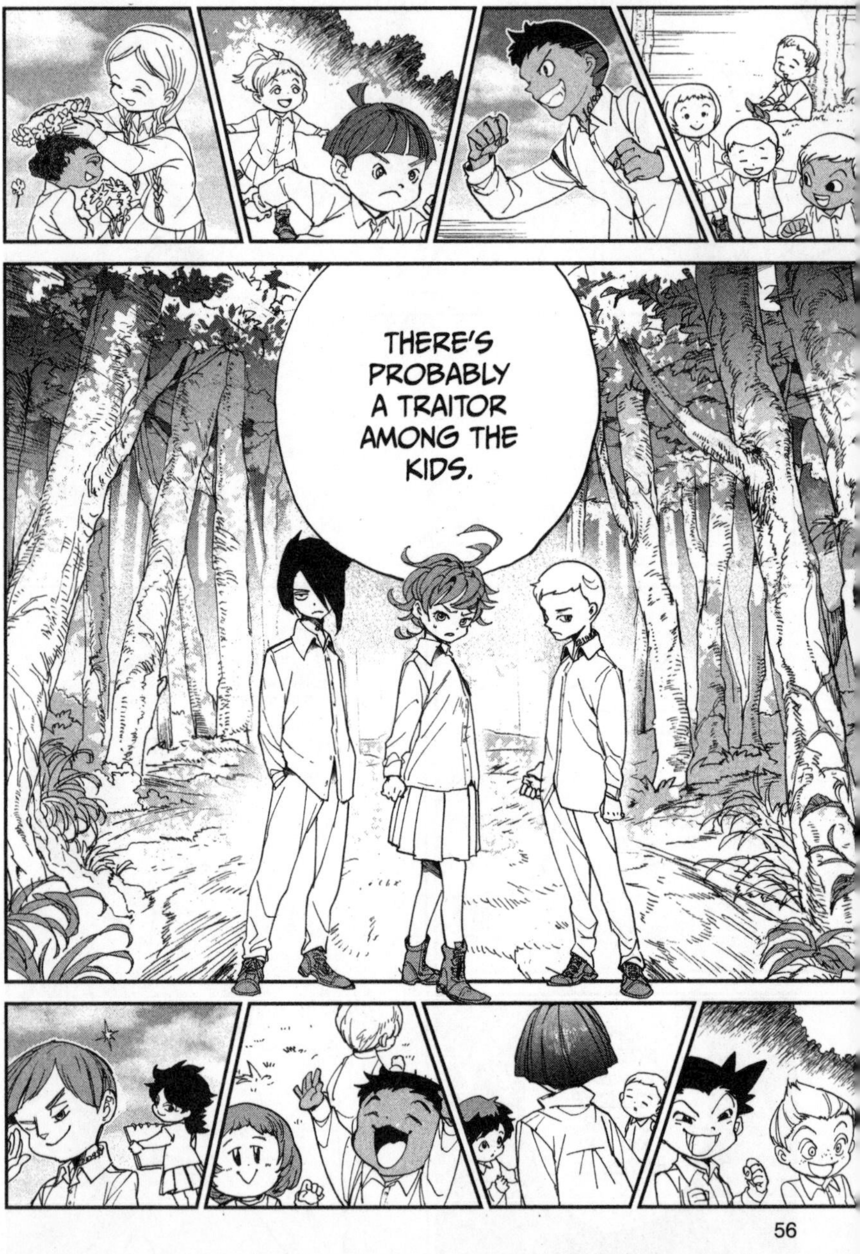
THERE'S PROBABLY A TRAITOR AMONG THE KIDS.

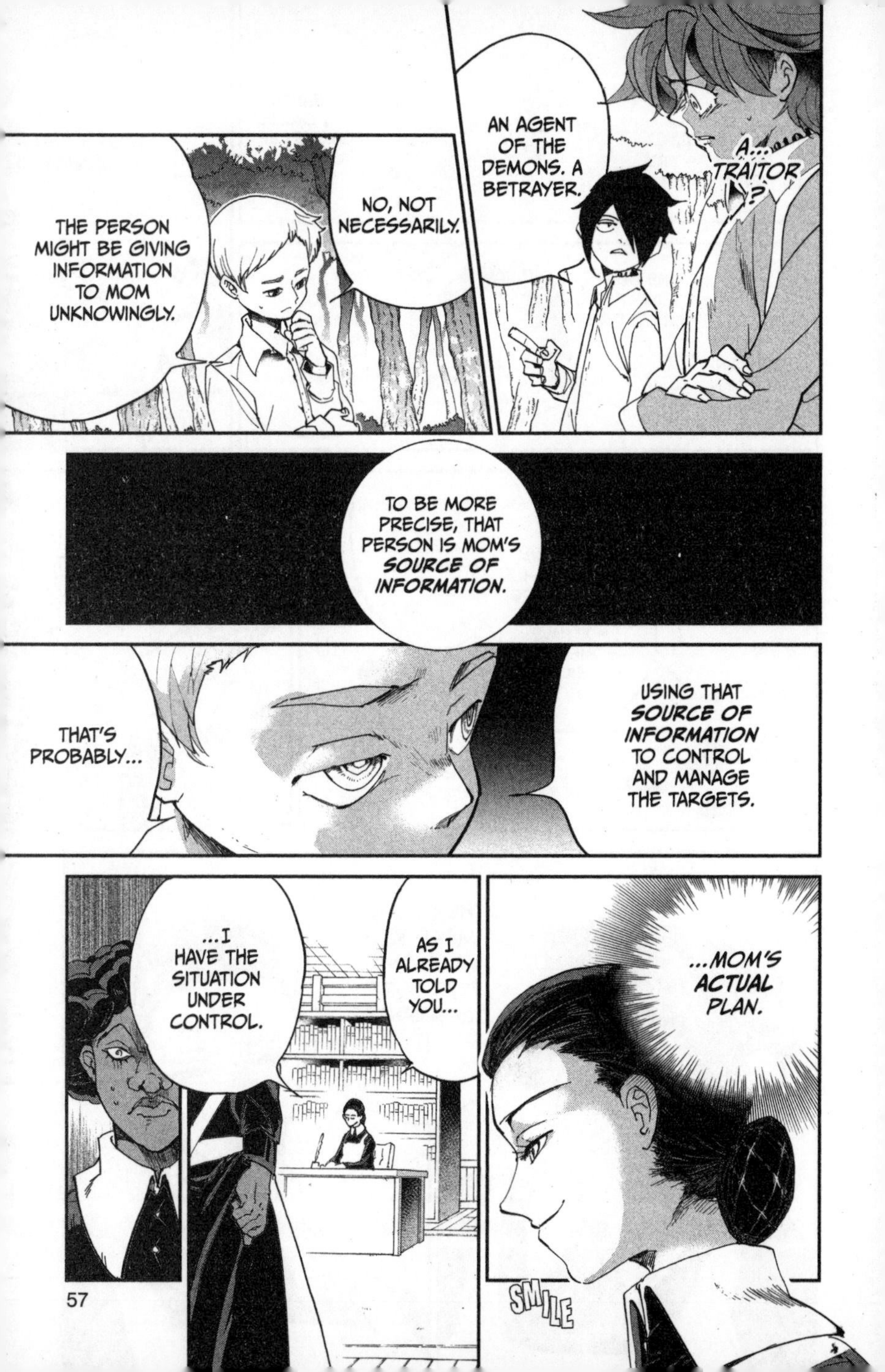
A... TRAITOR?
AN AGENT OF THE DEMONS. A BETRAYER.
NO, NOT NECESSARILY.
THE PERSON MIGHT BE GIVING INFORMATION TO MOM UNKNOWINGLY.
TO BE MORE PRECISE, THAT PERSON IS MOM'S *SOURCE OF INFORMATION.*
USING THAT *SOURCE OF INFORMATION* TO CONTROL AND MANAGE THE TARGETS.
THAT'S PROBABLY...
...MOM'S *ACTUAL* PLAN.
SMILE
AS I ALREADY TOLD YOU...
...I HAVE THE SITUATION UNDER CONTROL.

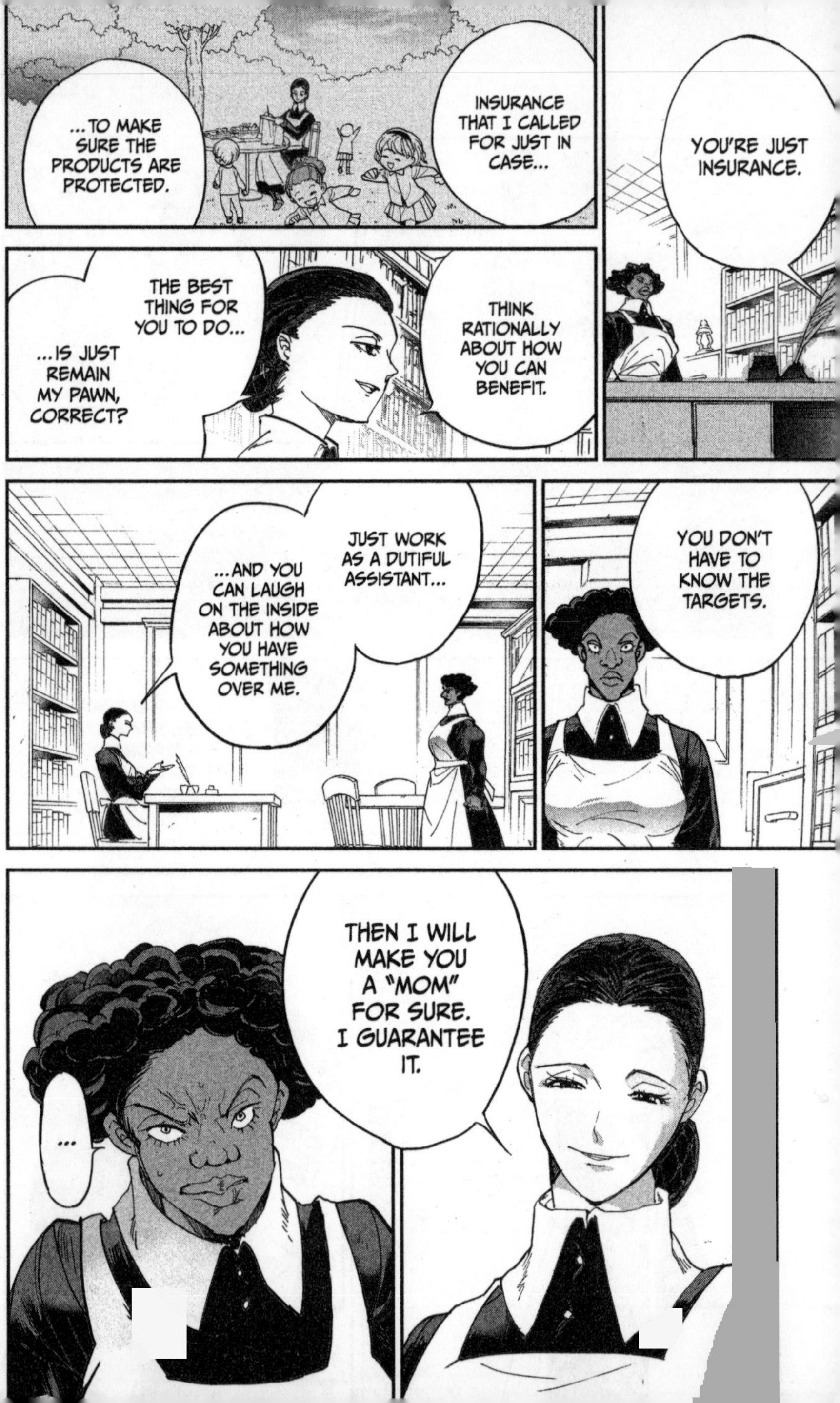
YOU'RE JUST INSURANCE.
INSURANCE THAT I CALLED FOR JUST IN CASE...
...TO MAKE SURE THE PRODUCTS ARE PROTECTED.
THINK RATIONALLY ABOUT HOW YOU CAN BENEFIT.
THE BEST THING FOR YOU TO DO...
...IS JUST REMAIN MY PAWN, CORRECT?
YOU DON'T HAVE TO KNOW THE TARGETS.
JUST WORK AS A DUTIFUL ASSISTANT...
...AND YOU CAN LAUGH ON THE INSIDE ABOUT HOW YOU HAVE SOMETHING OVER ME.
THEN I WILL MAKE YOU A "MOM" FOR SURE. I GUARANTEE IT.
...

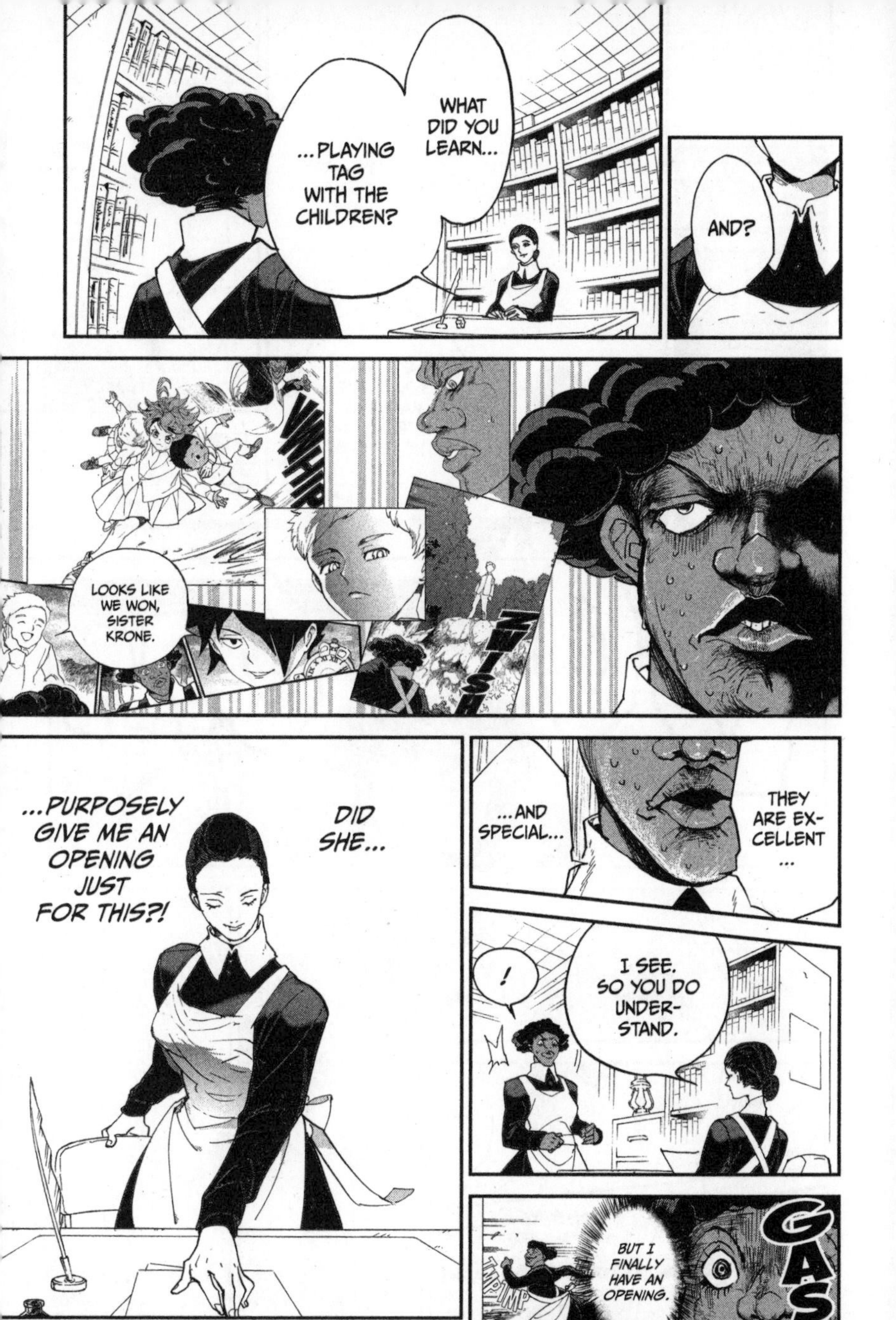
AND?
WHAT DID YOU LEARN...
...PLAYING TAG WITH THE CHILDREN?
WHIP
SWISH
LOOKS LIKE WE WON, SISTER KRONE.
THEY ARE EX-CELLENT...
...AND SPECIAL...
I SEE. SO YOU DO UNDER-STAND.
!
GASP
BUT I FINALLY HAVE AN OPENING.
TMP TMP
DID SHE...
...PURPOSELY GIVE ME AN OPENING JUST FOR THIS?!

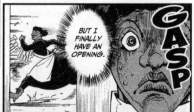

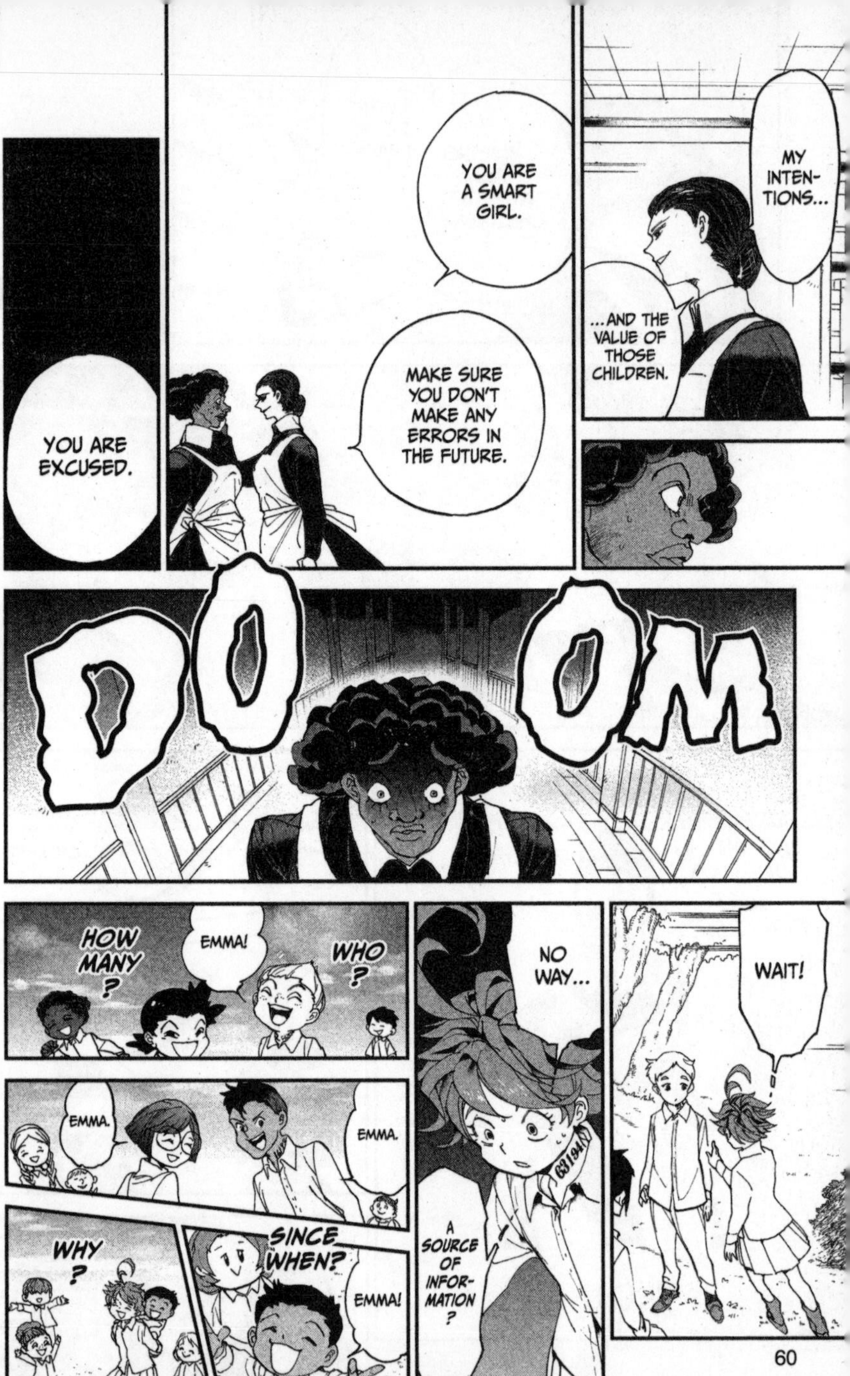
MY INTEN-TIONS...
...AND THE VALUE OF THOSE CHILDREN.
YOU ARE A SMART GIRL.
MAKE SURE YOU DON'T MAKE ANY ERRORS IN THE FUTURE.
YOU ARE EXCUSED.
DOOM
WAIT!
NO WAY...
A SOURCE OF INFOR-MATION ?
63194
WHO ?
EMMA!
HOW MANY ?
EMMA.
EMMA.
EMMA!
SINCE WHEN?
WHY ?

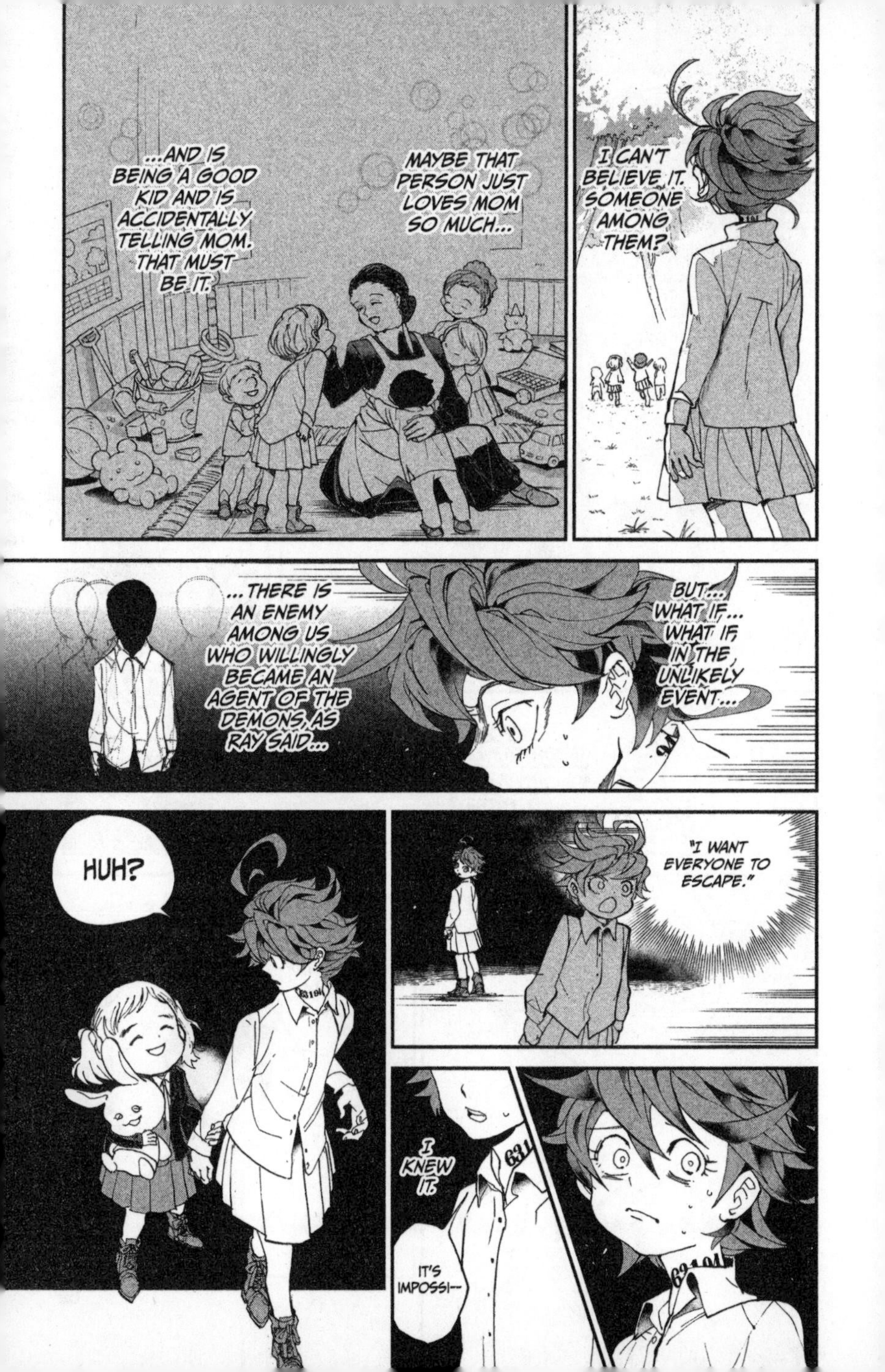
I CAN'T BELIEVE IT. SOMEONE AMONG THEM?
MAYBE THAT PERSON JUST LOVES MOM SO MUCH...
...AND IS BEING A GOOD KID AND IS ACCIDENTALLY TELLING MOM. THAT MUST BE IT.
BUT... WHAT IF... WHAT IF, IN THE UNLIKELY EVENT...
...THERE IS AN ENEMY AMONG US WHO WILLINGLY BECAME AN AGENT OF THE DEMONS, AS RAY SAID...
"I WANT EVERYONE TO ESCAPE."
I KNEW IT.
IT'S IMPOSSI--
HUH?

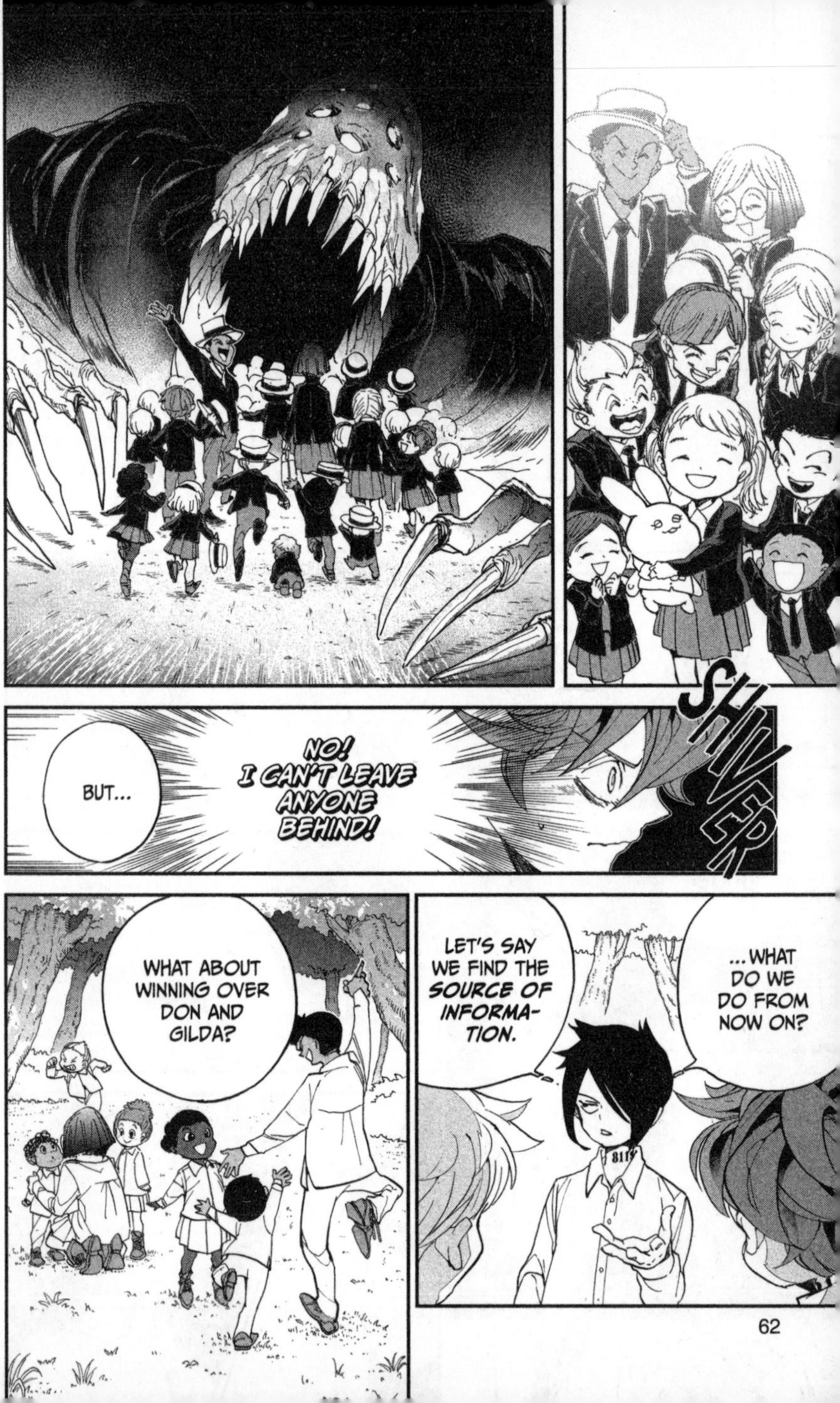
SHIVER
NO! I CAN'T LEAVE ANYONE BEHIND!
BUT...
...WHAT DO WE DO FROM NOW ON?
LET'S SAY WE FIND THE *SOURCE OF INFORMATION.*
WHAT ABOUT WINNING OVER DON AND GILDA?

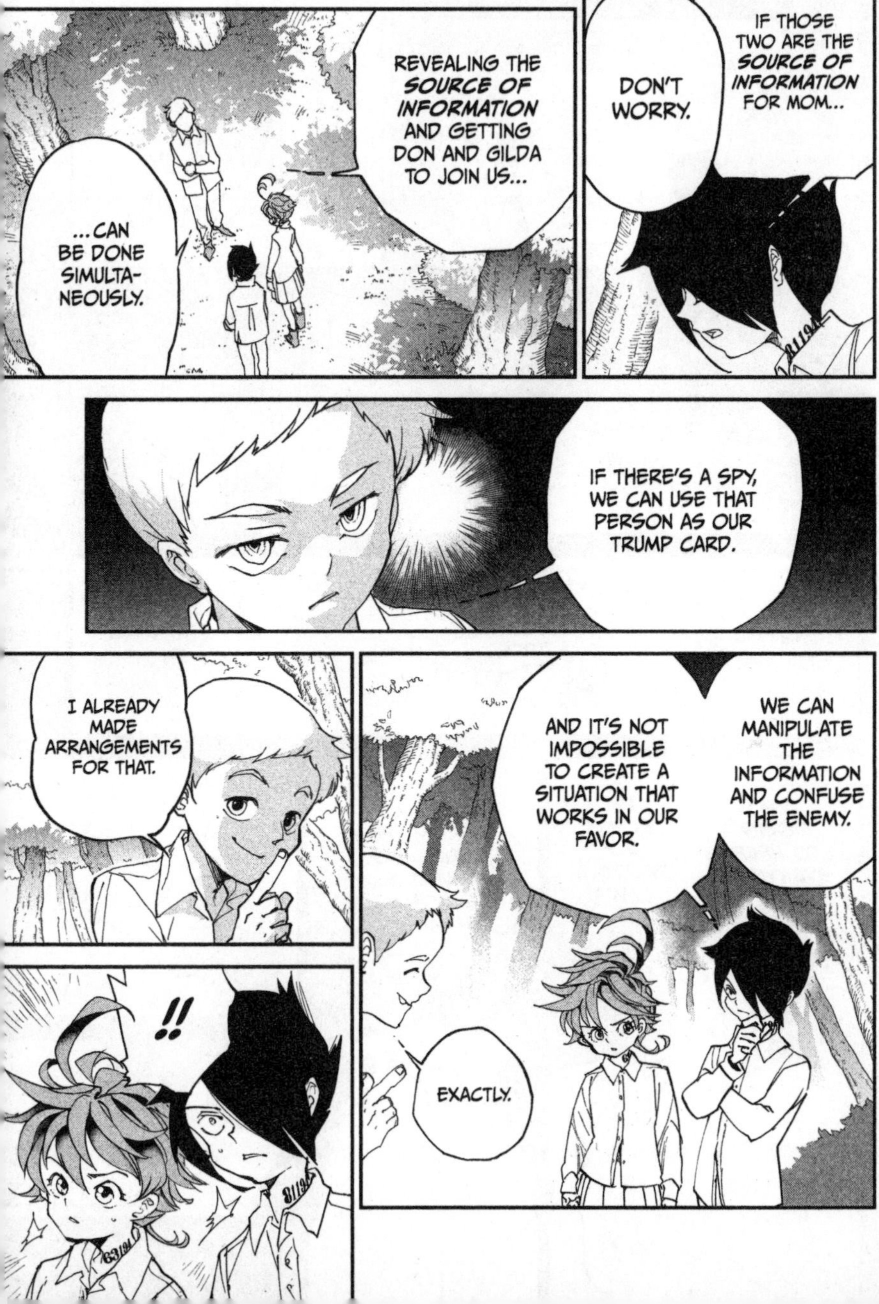
IF THOSE TWO ARE THE SOURCE OF INFORMATION FOR MOM...
DON'T WORRY.
REVEALING THE SOURCE OF INFORMATION AND GETTING DON AND GILDA TO JOIN US...
...CAN BE DONE SIMULTANEOUSLY.
IF THERE'S A SPY, WE CAN USE THAT PERSON AS OUR TRUMP CARD.
WE CAN MANIPULATE THE INFORMATION AND CONFUSE THE ENEMY.
AND IT'S NOT IMPOSSIBLE TO CREATE A SITUATION THAT WORKS IN OUR FAVOR.
EXACTLY.
I ALREADY MADE ARRANGEMENTS FOR THAT.
!!

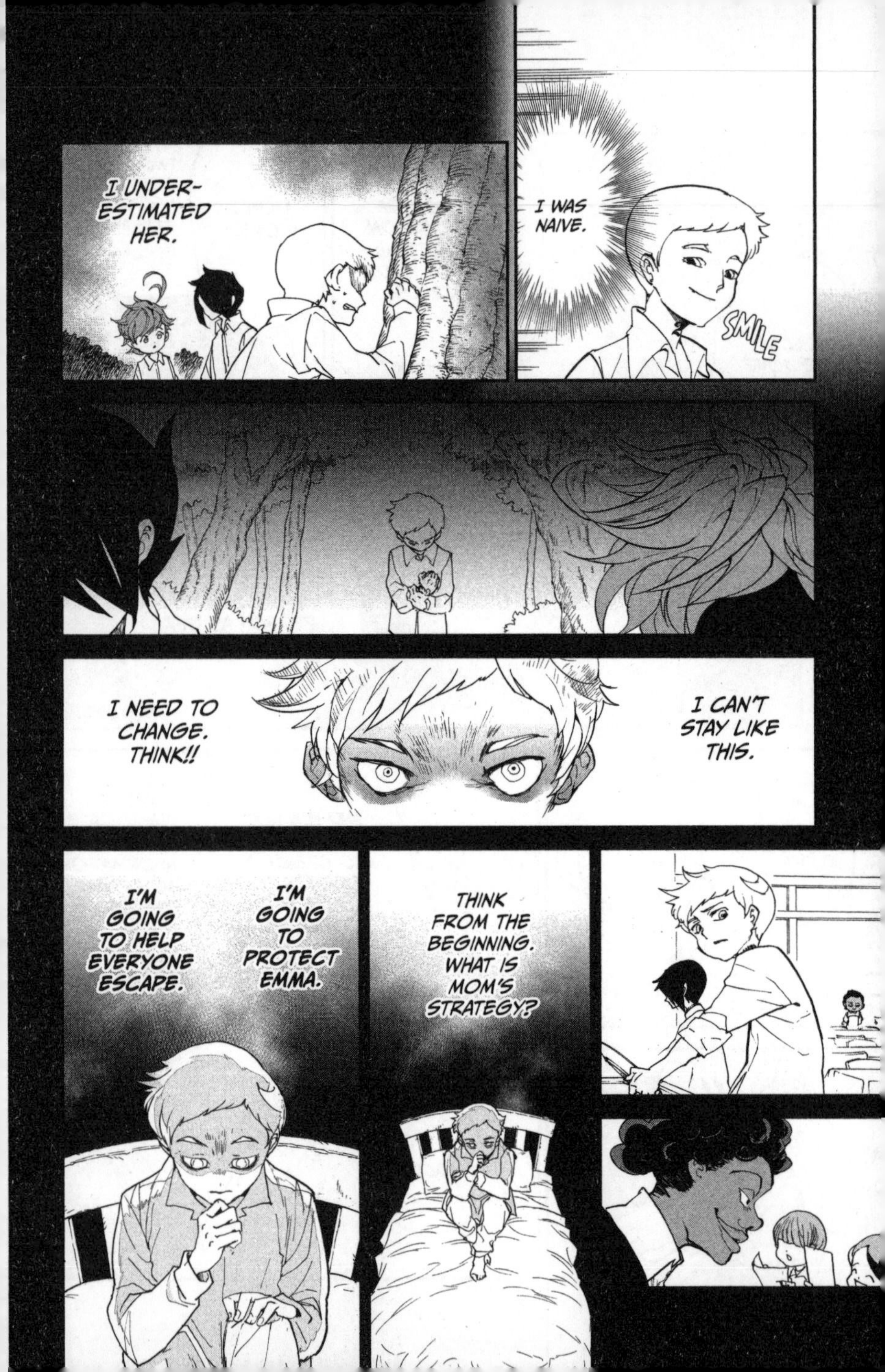
I WAS NAIVE.
SMILE
I UNDER-ESTIMATED HER.
I CAN'T STAY LIKE THIS.
I NEED TO CHANGE. THINK!!
THINK FROM THE BEGINNING. WHAT IS MOM'S STRATEGY?
I'M GOING TO PROTECT EMMA.
I'M GOING TO HELP EVERYONE ESCAPE.

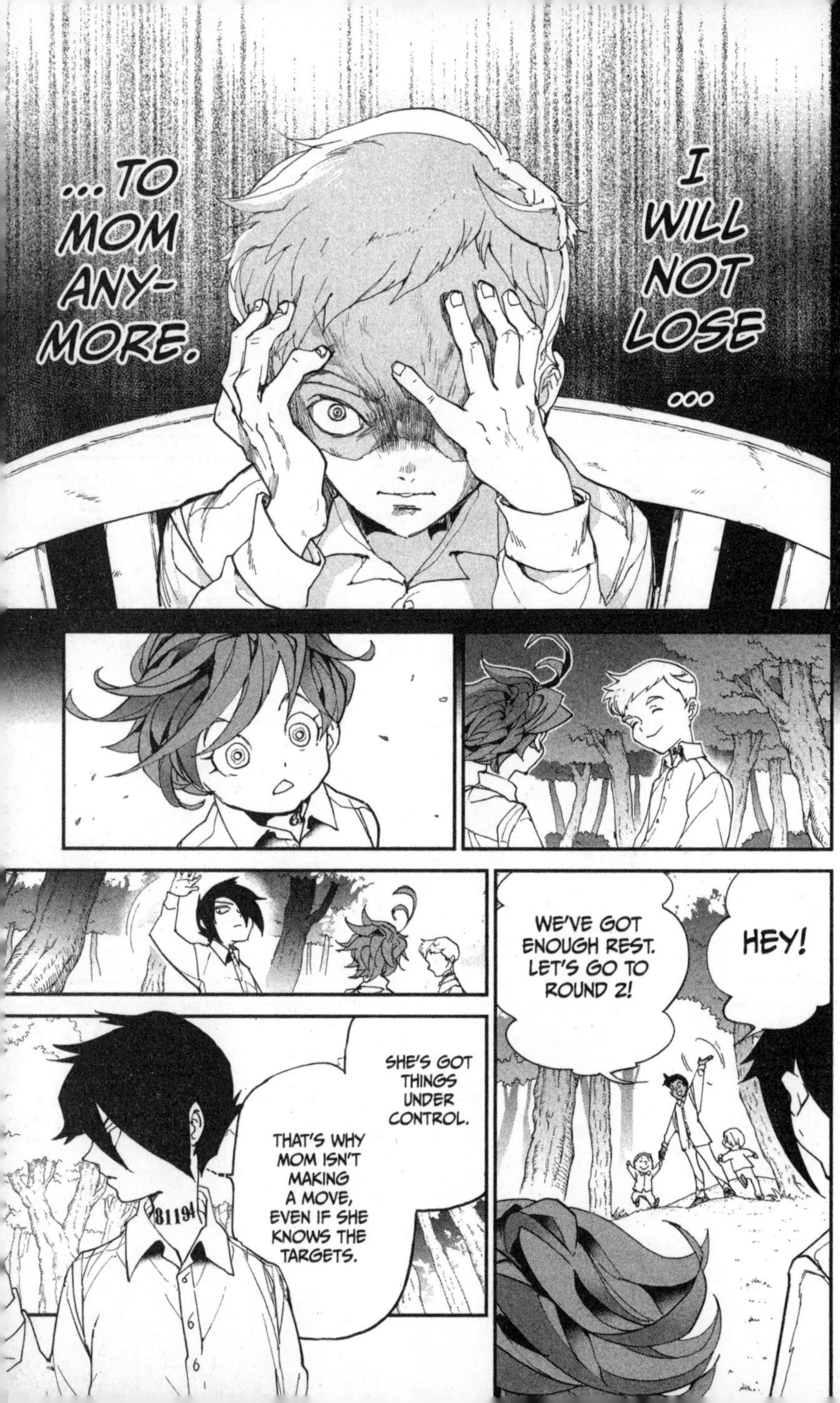
I WILL NOT LOSE ...
...TO MOM ANYMORE.
HEY!
WE'VE GOT ENOUGH REST. LET'S GO TO ROUND 2!
SHE'S GOT THINGS UNDER CONTROL.
THAT'S WHY MOM ISN'T MAKING A MOVE, EVEN IF SHE KNOWS THE TARGETS.
81194

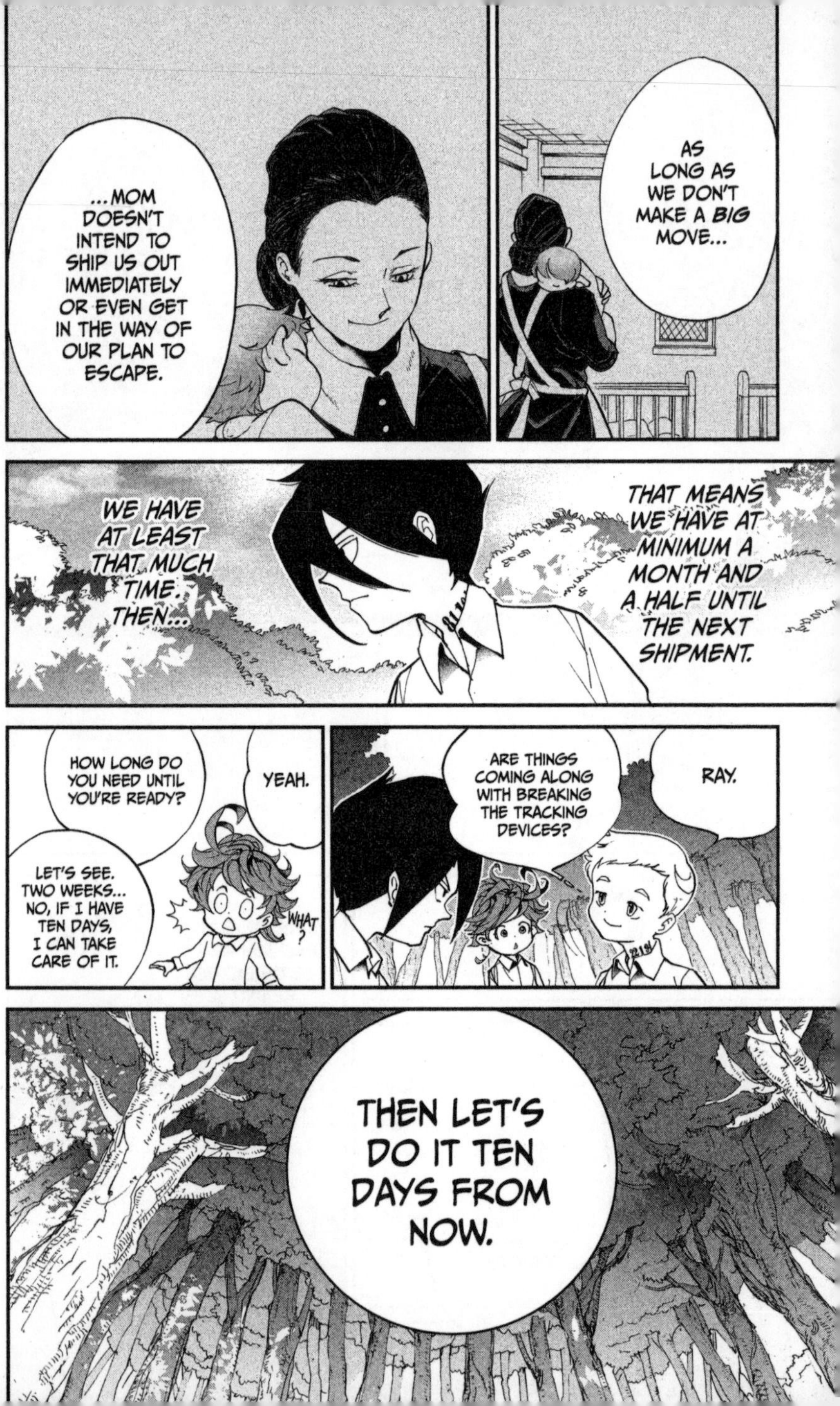
AS LONG AS WE DON'T MAKE A BIG MOVE...
...MOM DOESN'T INTEND TO SHIP US OUT IMMEDIATELY OR EVEN GET IN THE WAY OF OUR PLAN TO ESCAPE.
THAT MEANS WE HAVE AT MINIMUM A MONTH AND A HALF UNTIL THE NEXT SHIPMENT.
WE HAVE AT LEAST THAT MUCH TIME. THEN...
RAY.
ARE THINGS COMING ALONG WITH BREAKING THE TRACKING DEVICES?
YEAH.
HOW LONG DO YOU NEED UNTIL YOU'RE READY?
WHAT?
LET'S SEE. TWO WEEKS... NO, IF I HAVE TEN DAYS, I CAN TAKE CARE OF IT.
THEN LET'S DO IT TEN DAYS FROM NOW.

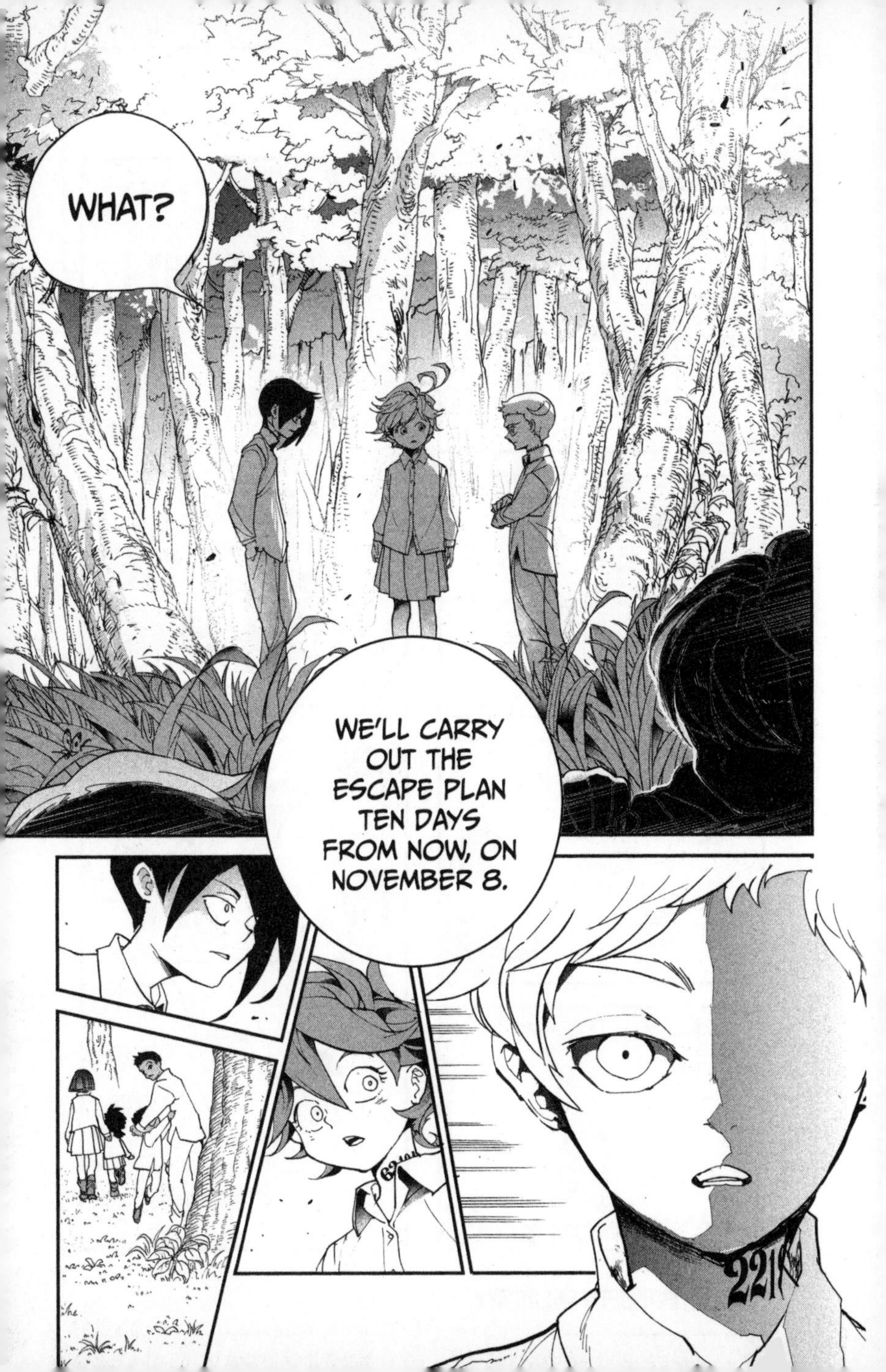
WHAT?
WE'LL CARRY OUT THE ESCAPE PLAN TEN DAYS FROM NOW, ON NOVEMBER 8.

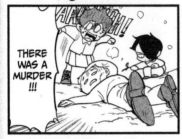

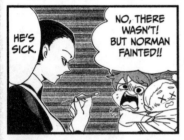

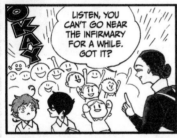

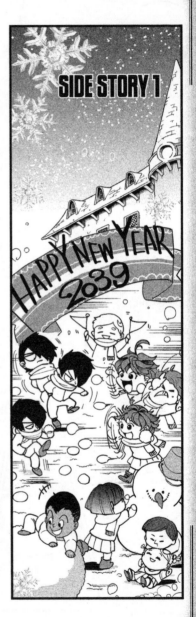

SIDE STORY 1
HAPPY NEW YEAR
2039

Starting the New Year

THERE WAS A MURDER !!!
NO, THERE WASN'T! BUT NORMAN FAINTED!!
HE'S SICK.
LISTEN, YOU CAN'T GO NEAR THE INFIRMARY FOR A WHILE. GOT IT?
OKAY
GOT IT?

TO BE CONTINUED IN SIDE STORY 2

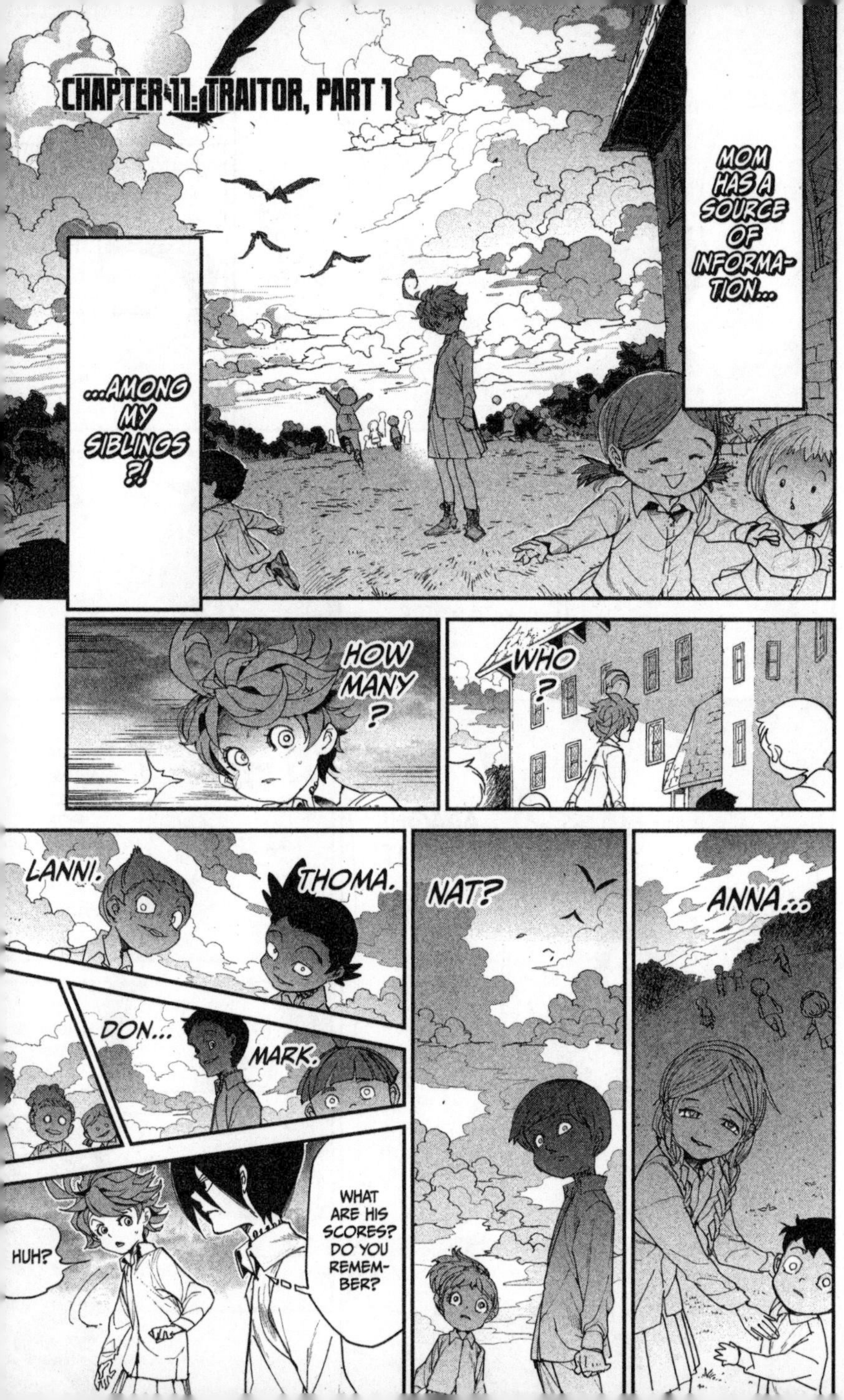
CHAPTER 11: TRAITOR, PART 1
MOM HAS A SOURCE OF INFORMA-TION...
...AMONG MY SIBLINGS?!
WHO?
HOW MANY?
ANNA...
NAT?
THOMA.
LANNI.
MARK.
DON...
WHAT ARE HIS SCORES? DO YOU REMEM-BER?
HUH?

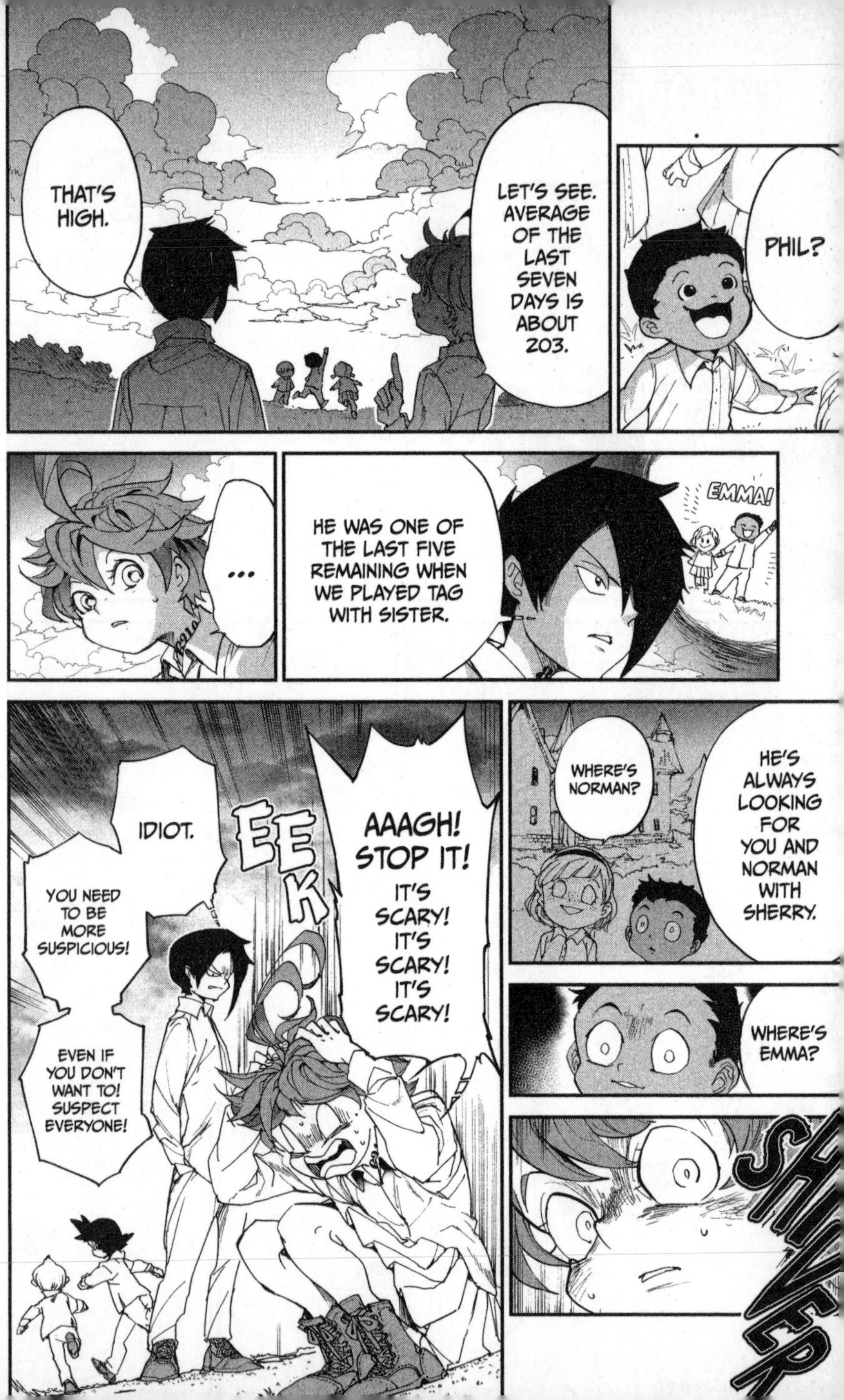
PHIL?
LET'S SEE. AVERAGE OF THE LAST SEVEN DAYS IS ABOUT 203.
THAT'S HIGH.
EMMA!
HE WAS ONE OF THE LAST FIVE REMAINING WHEN WE PLAYED TAG WITH SISTER.
...
HE'S ALWAYS LOOKING FOR YOU AND NORMAN WITH SHERRY.
WHERE'S NORMAN?
WHERE'S EMMA?
SHIVER
AAAGH! STOP IT!
IT'S SCARY! IT'S SCARY! IT'S SCARY!
EEK
IDIOT.
YOU NEED TO BE MORE SUSPICIOUS!
EVEN IF YOU DON'T WANT TO! SUSPECT EVERYONE!

CHAPTER 11: TRAITOR, PART 1

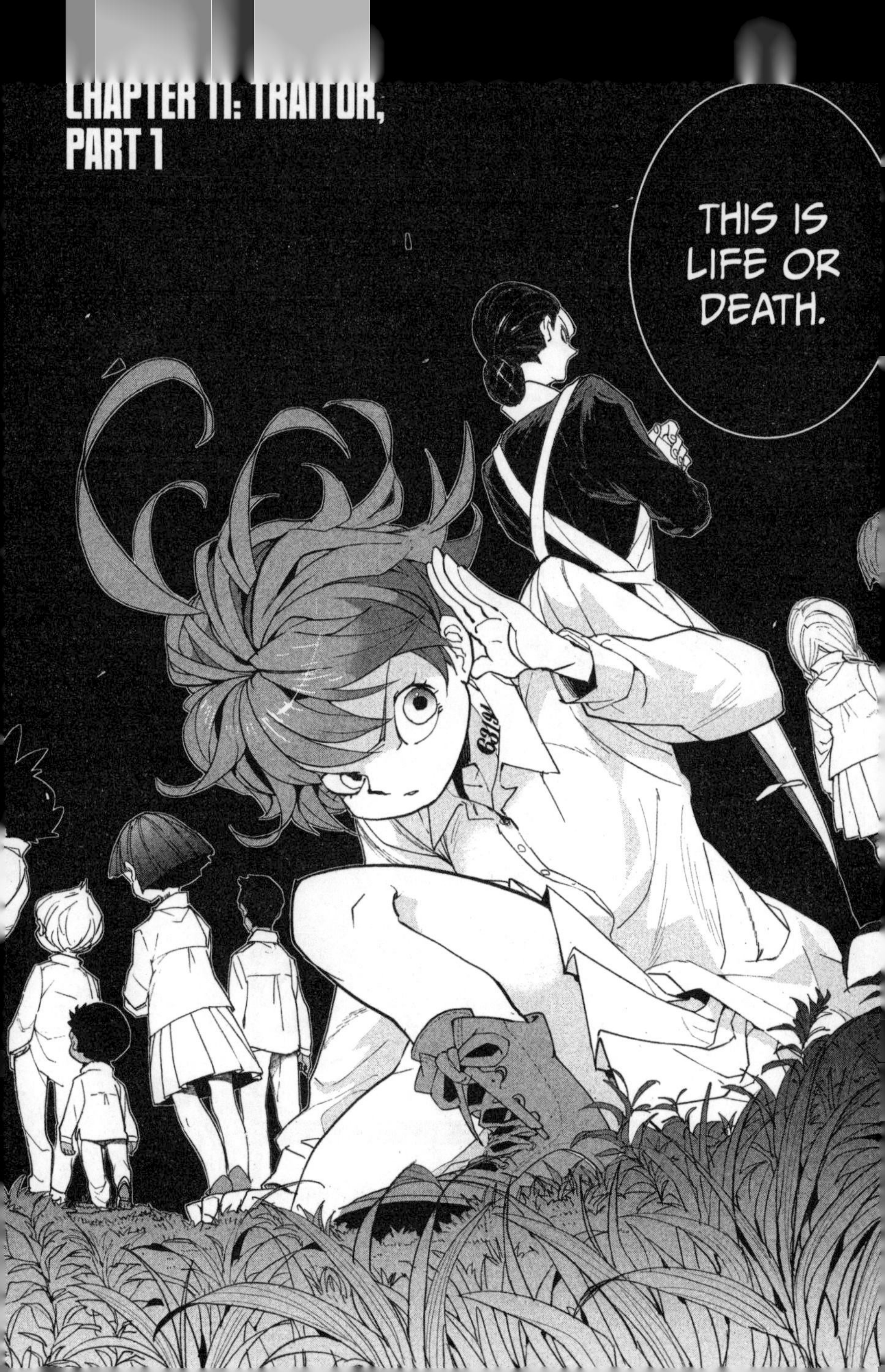
THIS IS LIFE OR DEATH.
63194

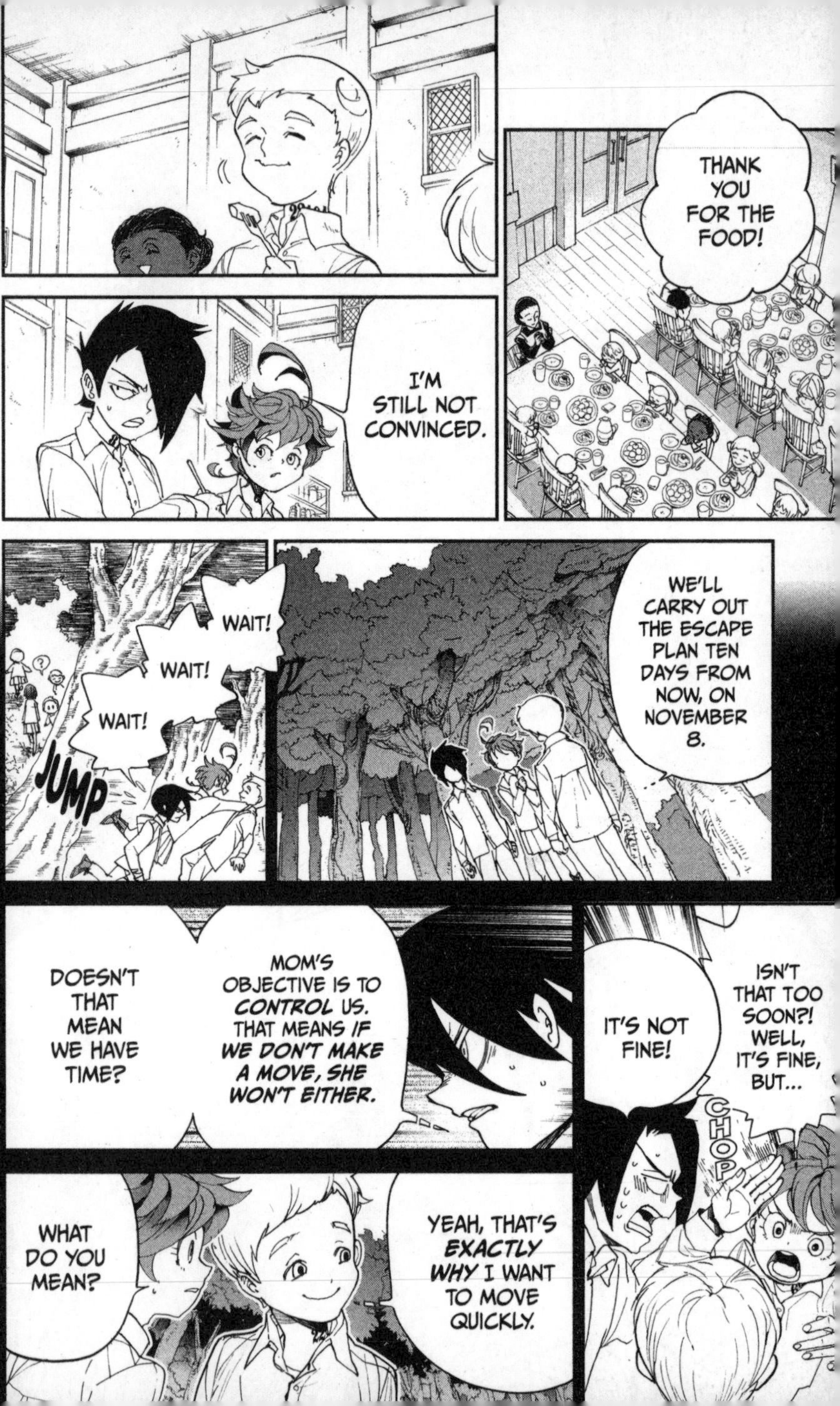
THANK YOU FOR THE FOOD!
I'M STILL NOT CONVINCED.
WE'LL CARRY OUT THE ESCAPE PLAN TEN DAYS FROM NOW, ON NOVEMBER 8.
WAIT!
WAIT!
WAIT!
JUMP
ISN'T THAT TOO SOON?! WELL, IT'S FINE, BUT...
IT'S NOT FINE!
CHOP
MOM'S OBJECTIVE IS TO CONTROL US. THAT MEANS IF WE DON'T MAKE A MOVE, SHE WON'T EITHER.
DOESN'T THAT MEAN WE HAVE TIME?
YEAH, THAT'S EXACTLY WHY I WANT TO MOVE QUICKLY.
WHAT DO YOU MEAN?

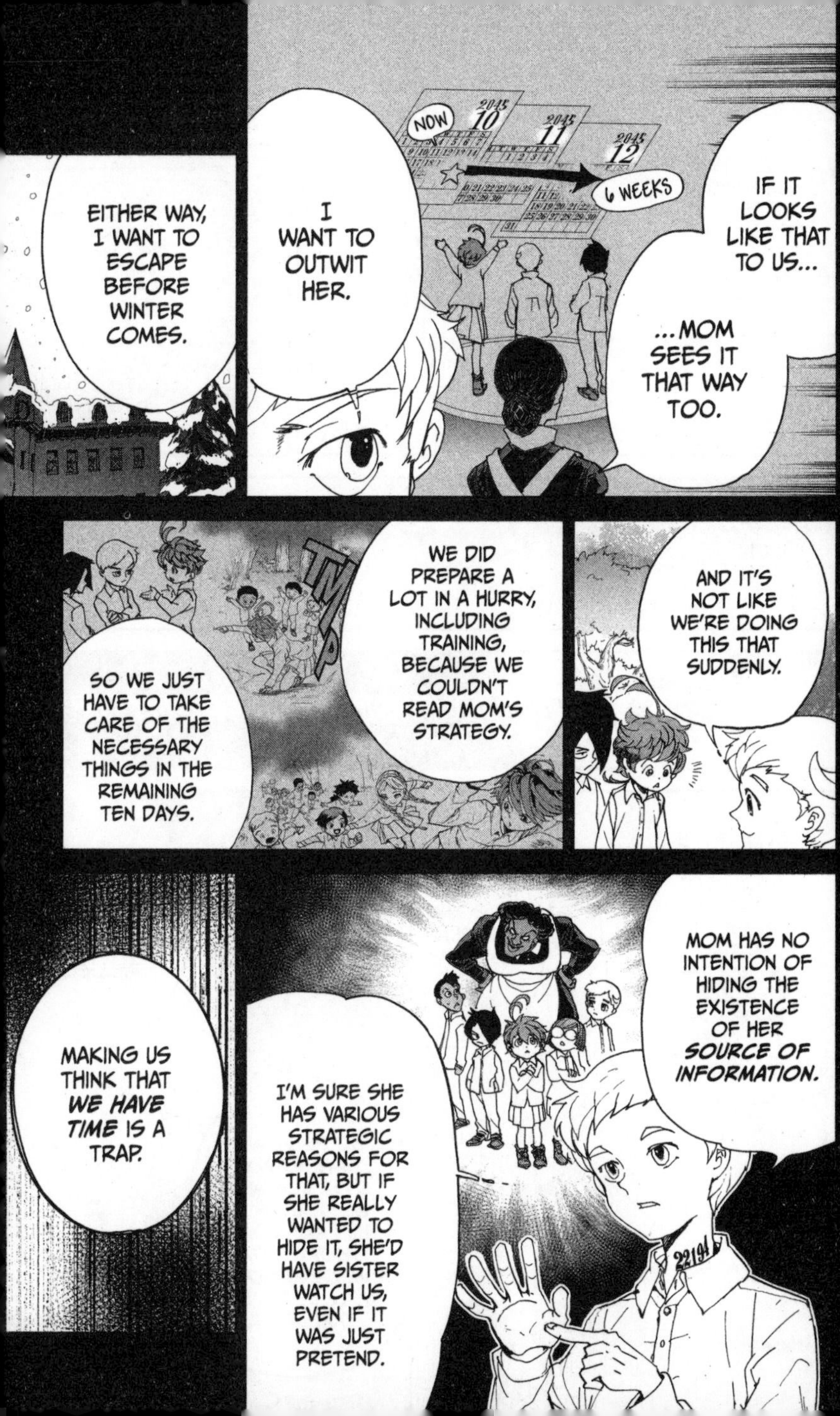
IF IT LOOKS LIKE THAT TO US...
...MOM SEES IT THAT WAY TOO.
6 WEEKS
2045 12
2045 11
2045 10
NOW
I WANT TO OUTWIT HER.
EITHER WAY, I WANT TO ESCAPE BEFORE WINTER COMES.
AND IT'S NOT LIKE WE'RE DOING THIS THAT SUDDENLY.
WE DID PREPARE A LOT IN A HURRY, INCLUDING TRAINING, BECAUSE WE COULDN'T READ MOM'S STRATEGY.
SO WE JUST HAVE TO TAKE CARE OF THE NECESSARY THINGS IN THE REMAINING TEN DAYS.
MOM HAS NO INTENTION OF HIDING THE EXISTENCE OF HER *SOURCE OF INFORMATION.*
I'M SURE SHE HAS VARIOUS STRATEGIC REASONS FOR THAT, BUT IF SHE REALLY WANTED TO HIDE IT, SHE'D HAVE SISTER WATCH US, EVEN IF IT WAS JUST PRETEND.
MAKING US THINK THAT *WE HAVE TIME* IS A TRAP.
22194

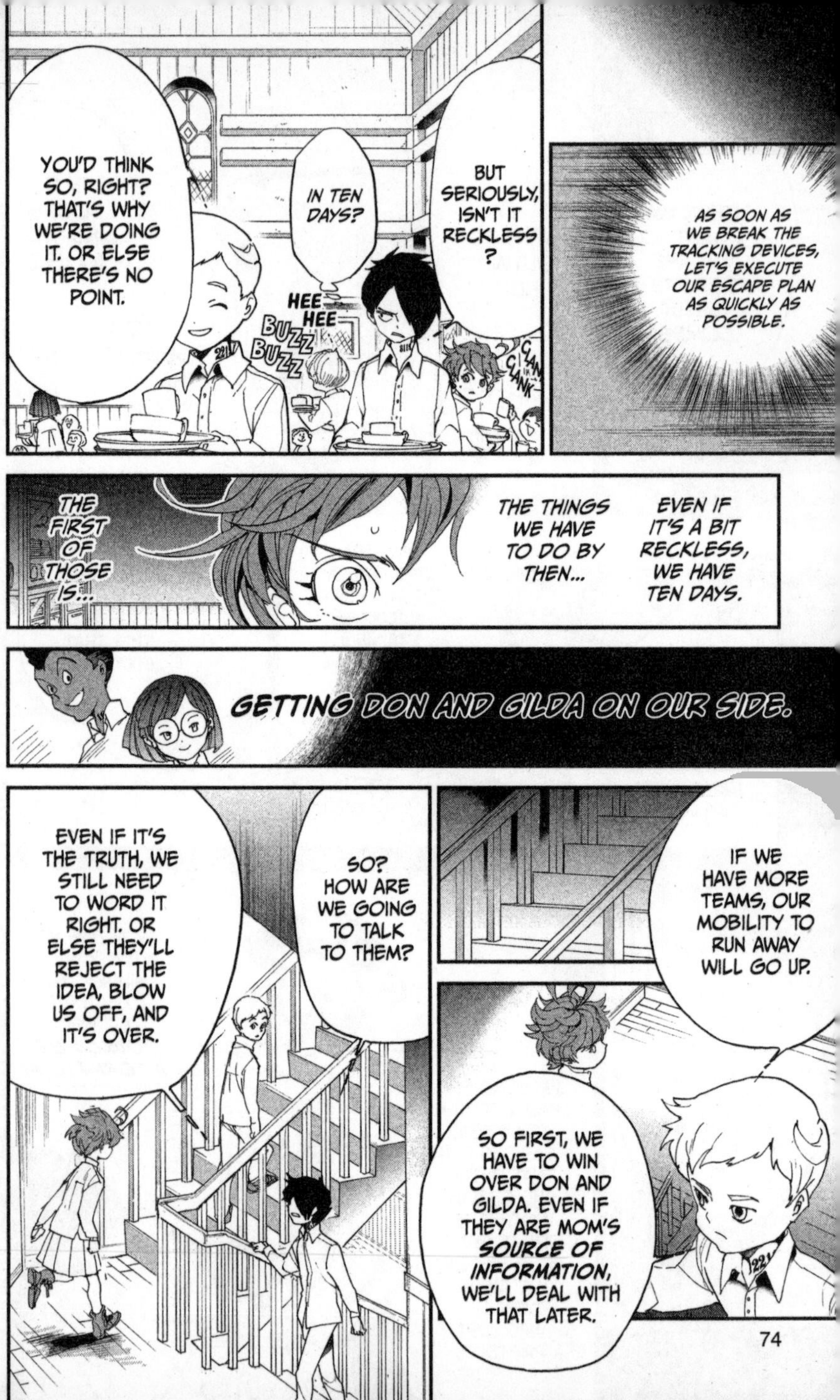
AS SOON AS WE BREAK THE TRACKING DEVICES, LET'S EXECUTE OUR ESCAPE PLAN AS QUICKLY AS POSSIBLE.
BUT SERIOUSLY, ISN'T IT RECKLESS?
IN TEN DAYS?
YOU'D THINK SO, RIGHT? THAT'S WHY WE'RE DOING IT. OR ELSE THERE'S NO POINT.
HEE HEE
BUZZ BUZZ
CLANK CLANK
EVEN IF IT'S A BIT RECKLESS, WE HAVE TEN DAYS.
THE THINGS WE HAVE TO DO BY THEN...
THE FIRST OF THOSE IS...
GETTING DON AND GILDA ON OUR SIDE.
IF WE HAVE MORE TEAMS, OUR MOBILITY TO RUN AWAY WILL GO UP.
SO FIRST, WE HAVE TO WIN OVER DON AND GILDA. EVEN IF THEY ARE MOM'S SOURCE OF INFORMATION, WE'LL DEAL WITH THAT LATER.
SO? HOW ARE WE GOING TO TALK TO THEM?
EVEN IF IT'S THE TRUTH, WE STILL NEED TO WORD IT RIGHT. OR ELSE THEY'LL REJECT THE IDEA, BLOW US OFF, AND IT'S OVER.

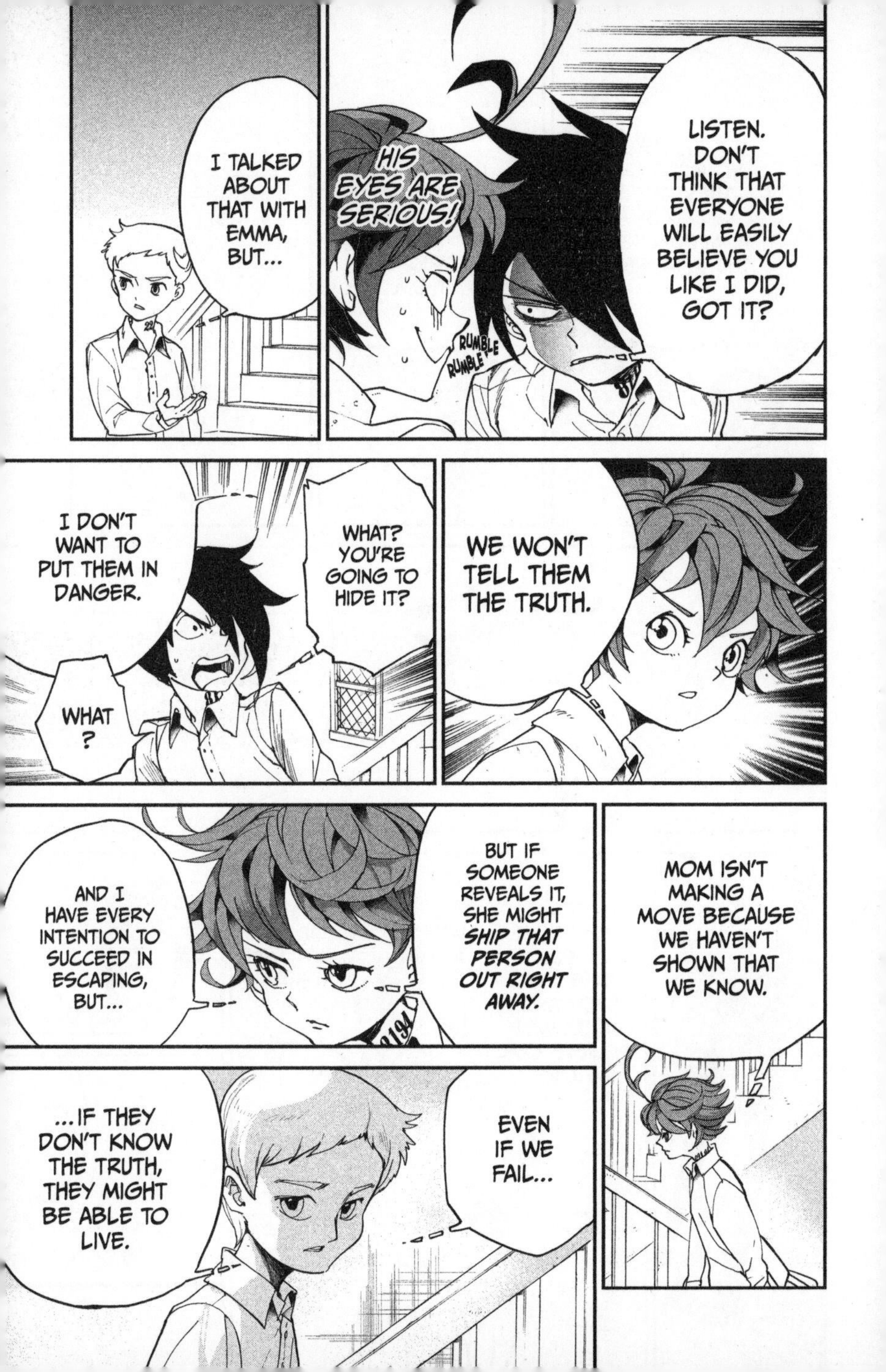
LISTEN. DON'T THINK THAT EVERYONE WILL EASILY BELIEVE YOU LIKE I DID, GOT IT?
HIS EYES ARE SERIOUS!
RUMBLE RUMBLE
I TALKED ABOUT THAT WITH EMMA, BUT...
WE WON'T TELL THEM THE TRUTH.
WHAT? YOU'RE GOING TO HIDE IT?
I DON'T WANT TO PUT THEM IN DANGER.
WHAT ?
MOM ISN'T MAKING A MOVE BECAUSE WE HAVEN'T SHOWN THAT WE KNOW.
BUT IF SOMEONE REVEALS IT, SHE MIGHT *SHIP THAT PERSON OUT RIGHT AWAY.*
AND I HAVE EVERY INTENTION TO SUCCEED IN ESCAPING, BUT...
EVEN IF WE FAIL...
...IF THEY DON'T KNOW THE TRUTH, THEY MIGHT BE ABLE TO LIVE.

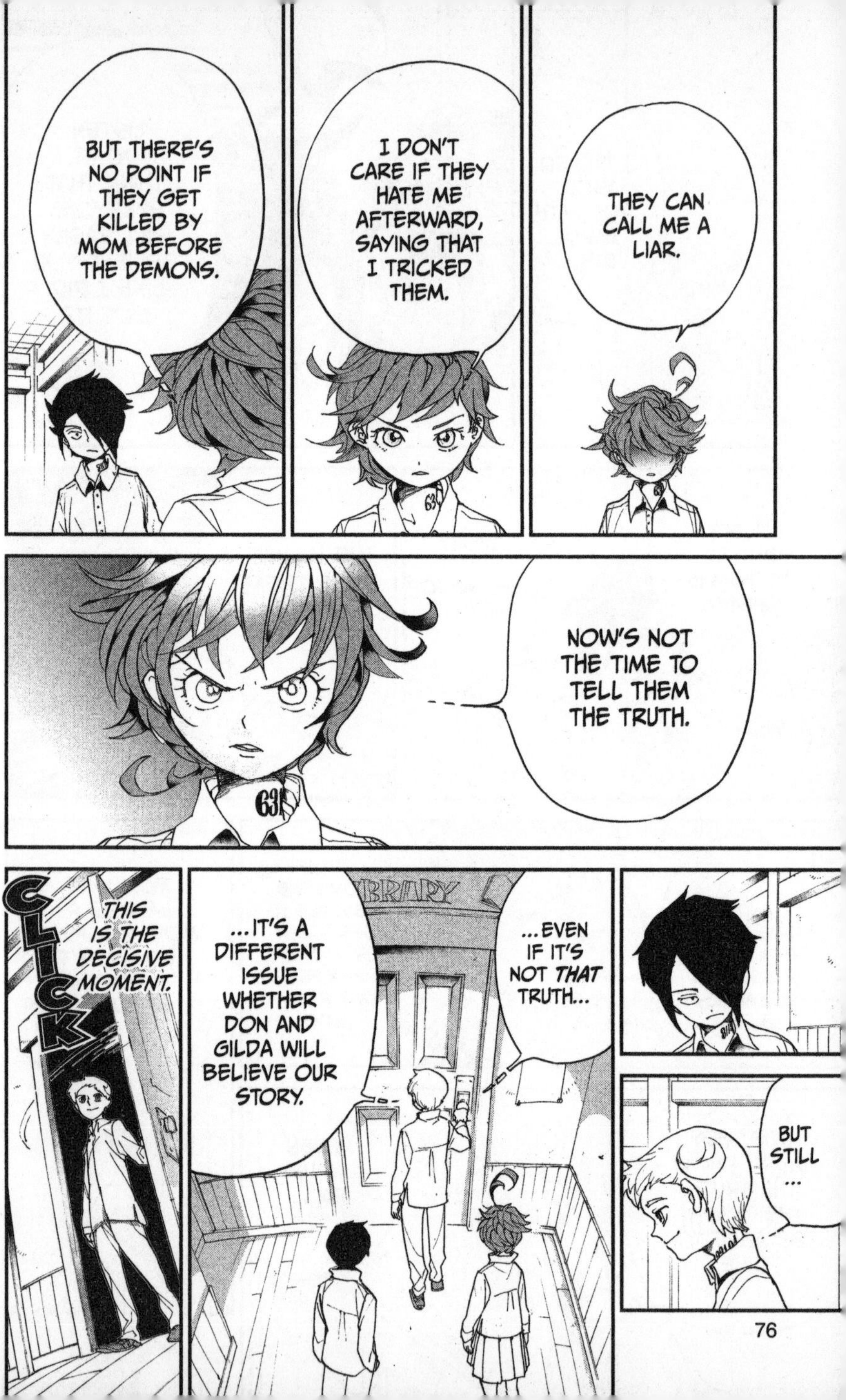
THEY CAN CALL ME A LIAR.
I DON'T CARE IF THEY HATE ME AFTERWARD, SAYING THAT I TRICKED THEM.
BUT THERE'S NO POINT IF THEY GET KILLED BY MOM BEFORE THE DEMONS.
NOW'S NOT THE TIME TO TELL THEM THE TRUTH.
BUT STILL ...
...EVEN IF IT'S NOT *THAT* TRUTH...
...IT'S A DIFFERENT ISSUE WHETHER DON AND GILDA WILL BELIEVE OUR STORY.
CLICK
THIS IS THE DECISIVE MOMENT.

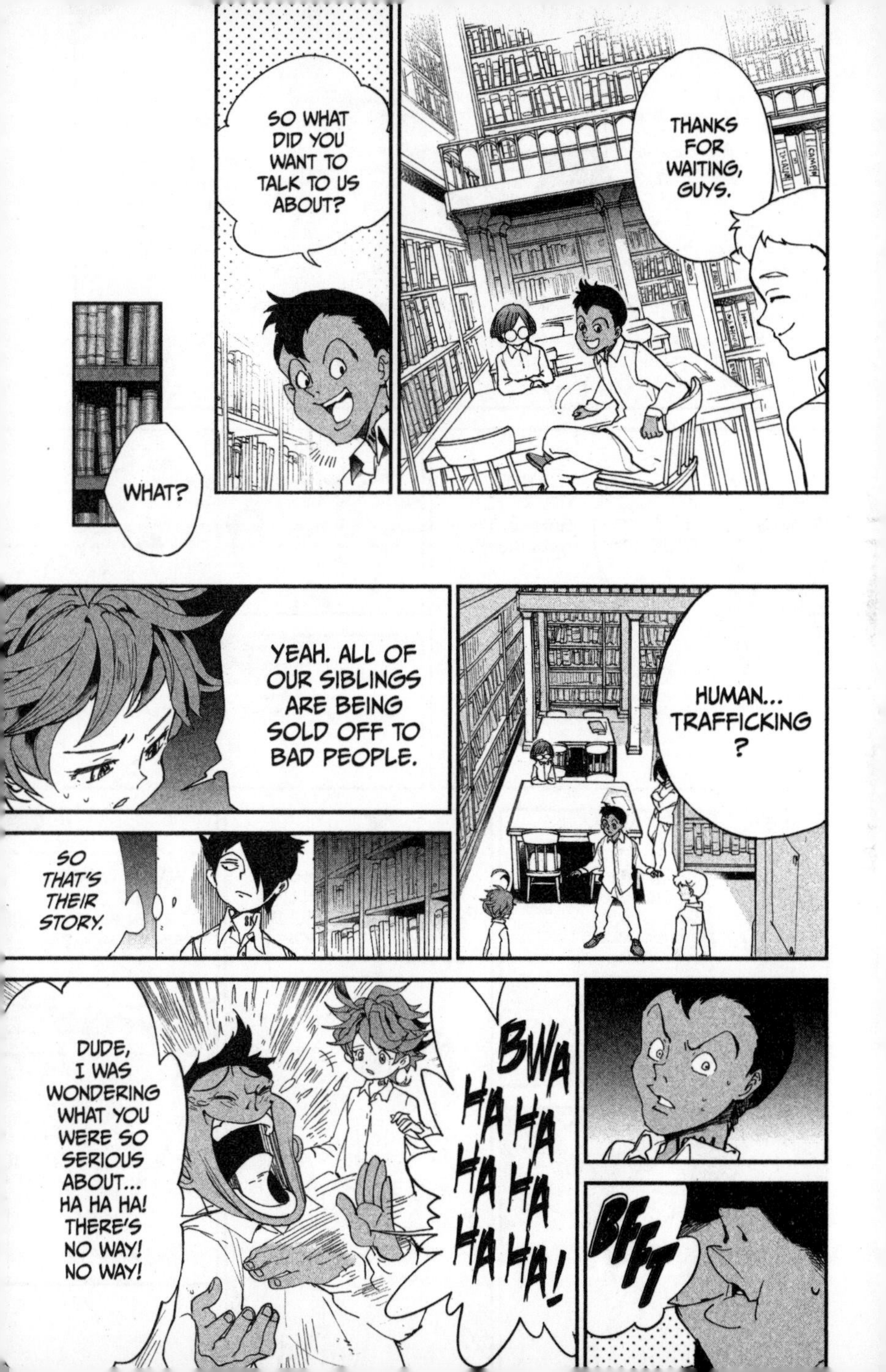
THANKS FOR WAITING, GUYS.
SO WHAT DID YOU WANT TO TALK TO US ABOUT?
WHAT?
HUMAN... TRAFFICKING?
YEAH. ALL OF OUR SIBLINGS ARE BEING SOLD OFF TO BAD PEOPLE.
SO THAT'S THEIR STORY.
BFFT
BWA HA HA HA HA HA HA HA HA!
DUDE, I WAS WONDERING WHAT YOU WERE SO SERIOUS ABOUT... HA HA HA! THERE'S NO WAY! NO WAY!

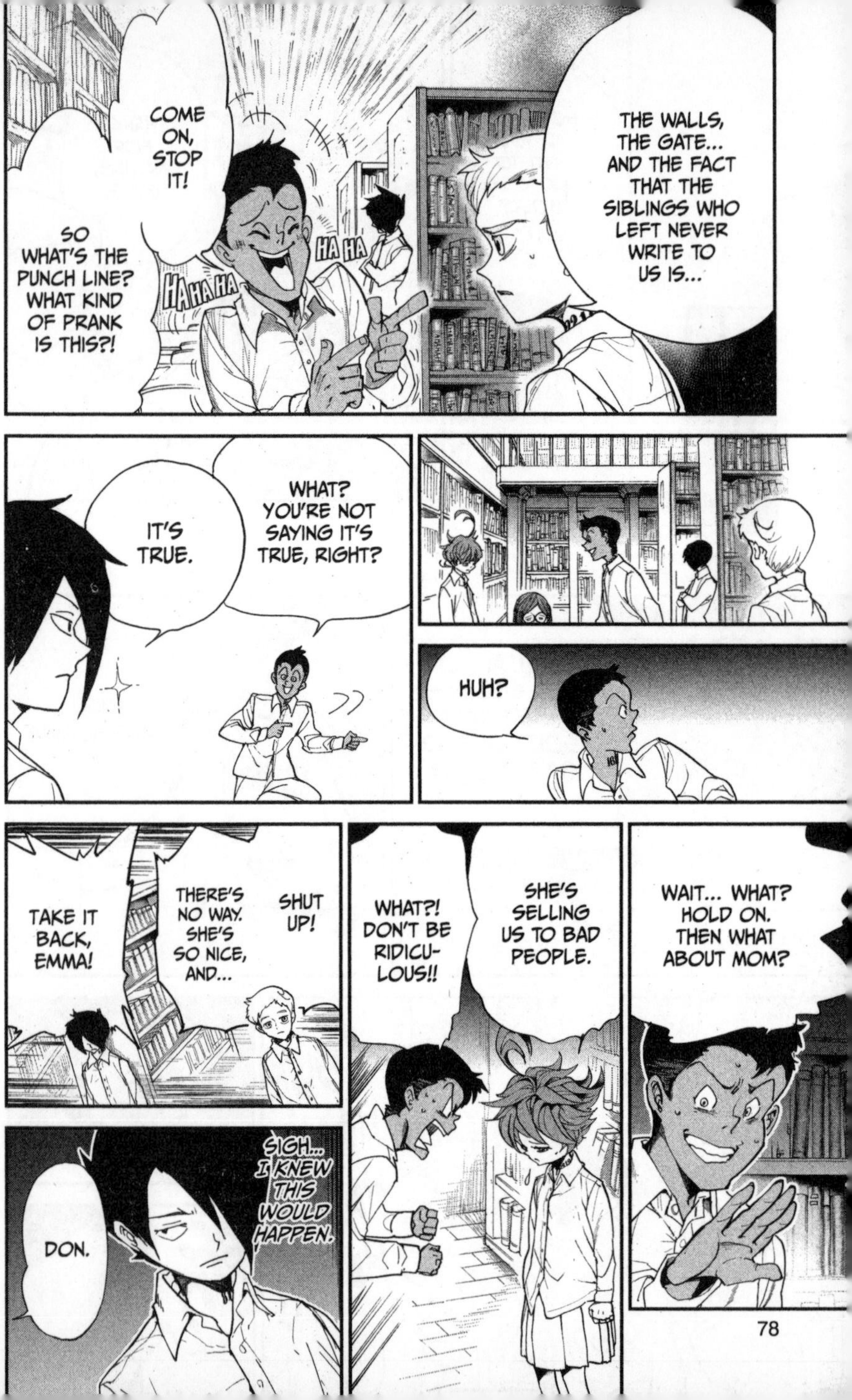
THE WALLS, THE GATE... AND THE FACT THAT THE SIBLINGS WHO LEFT NEVER WRITE TO US IS...
COME ON, STOP IT!
HA HA
SO WHAT'S THE PUNCH LINE? WHAT KIND OF PRANK IS THIS?!
HAHAHA
HUH?
WHAT? YOU'RE NOT SAYING IT'S TRUE, RIGHT?
IT'S TRUE.
WAIT... WHAT? HOLD ON. THEN WHAT ABOUT MOM?
SHE'S SELLING US TO BAD PEOPLE.
WHAT?! DON'T BE RIDICU-LOUS!!
SHUT UP!
THERE'S NO WAY. SHE'S SO NICE, AND...
TAKE IT BACK, EMMA!
SIGH... I KNEW THIS WOULD HAPPEN.
DON.

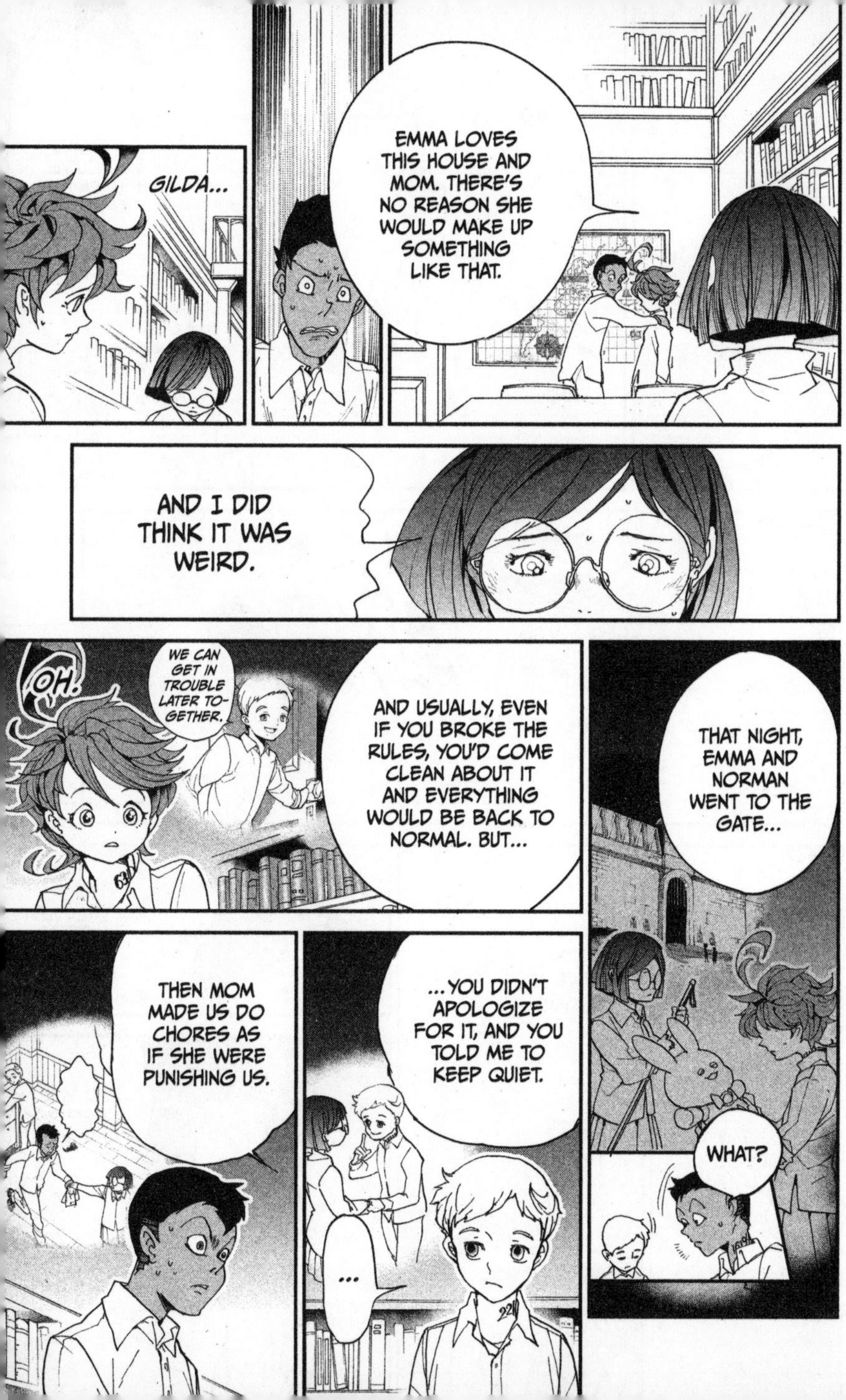
EMMA LOVES THIS HOUSE AND MOM. THERE'S NO REASON SHE WOULD MAKE UP SOMETHING LIKE THAT.
GILDA...
AND I DID THINK IT WAS WEIRD.
THAT NIGHT, EMMA AND NORMAN WENT TO THE GATE...
WHAT?
AND USUALLY, EVEN IF YOU BROKE THE RULES, YOU'D COME CLEAN ABOUT IT AND EVERYTHING WOULD BE BACK TO NORMAL. BUT...
WE CAN GET IN TROUBLE LATER TO-GETHER.
OH!
...YOU DIDN'T APOLOGIZE FOR IT, AND YOU TOLD ME TO KEEP QUIET.
...
THEN MOM MADE US DO CHORES AS IF SHE WERE PUNISHING US.

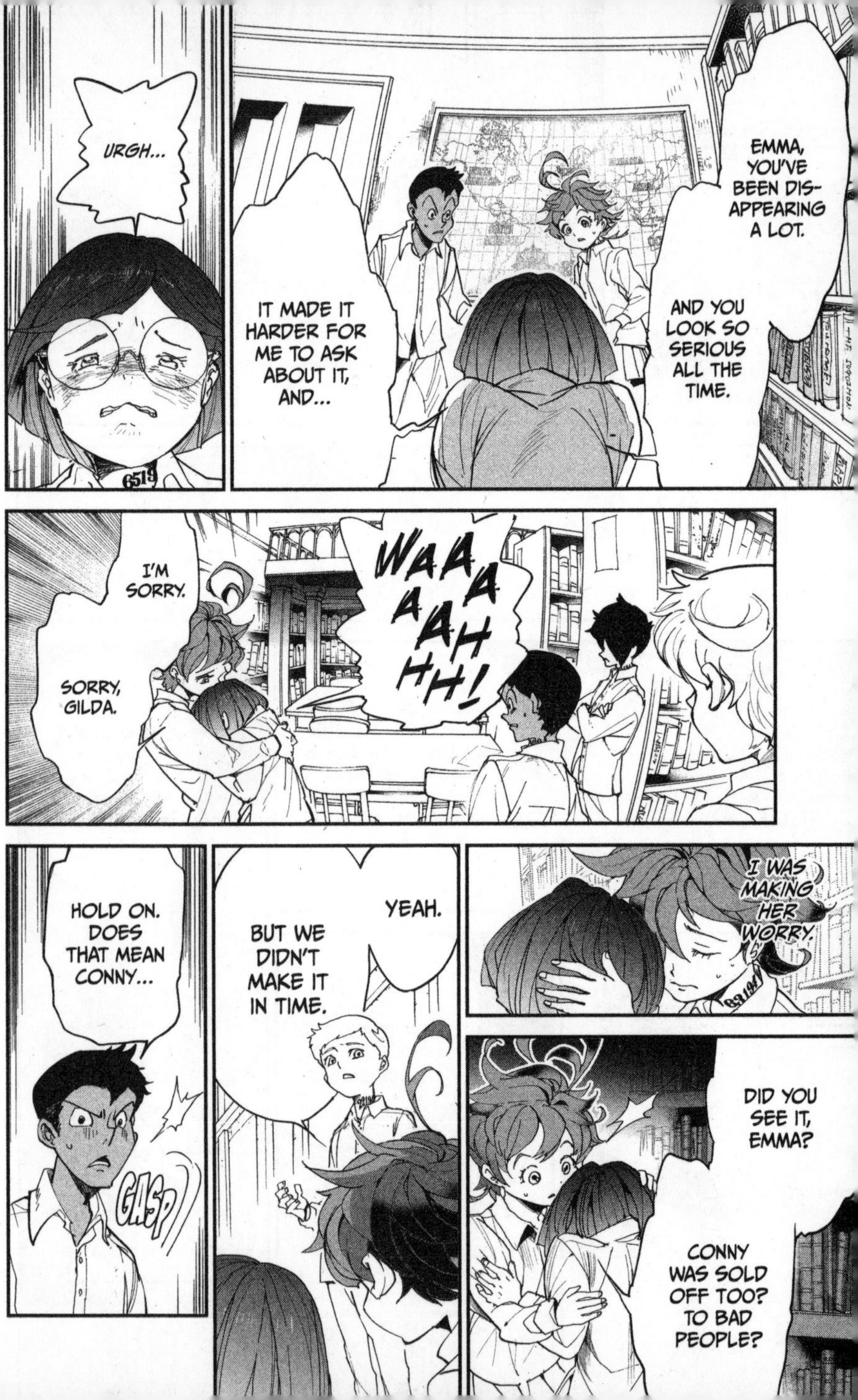

EMMA, YOU'VE BEEN DIS-APPEARING A LOT.
AND YOU LOOK SO SERIOUS ALL THE TIME.
IT MADE IT HARDER FOR ME TO ASK ABOUT IT, AND...
URGH...
WAAAAAHHH!
I'M SORRY.
SORRY, GILDA.
I WAS MAKING HER WORRY.
DID YOU SEE IT, EMMA?
CONNY WAS SOLD OFF TOO? TO BAD PEOPLE?
YEAH.
BUT WE DIDN'T MAKE IT IN TIME.
HOLD ON. DOES THAT MEAN CONNY...
GASP

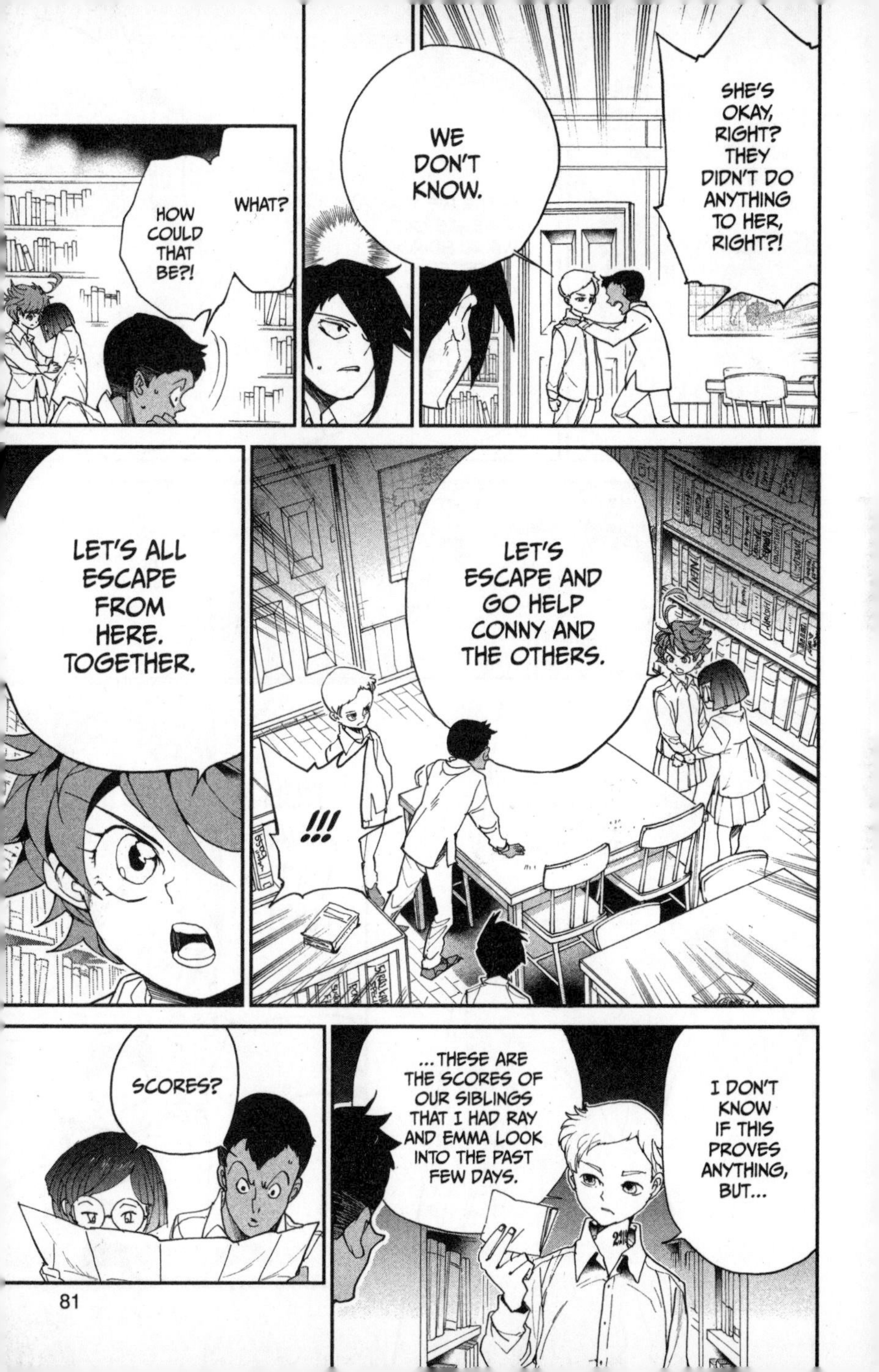
SHE'S OKAY, RIGHT? THEY DIDN'T DO ANYTHING TO HER, RIGHT?!
WE DON'T KNOW.
WHAT?
HOW COULD THAT BE?!
LET'S ESCAPE AND GO HELP CONNY AND THE OTHERS.
!!!
LET'S ALL ESCAPE FROM HERE. TOGETHER.
I DON'T KNOW IF THIS PROVES ANYTHING, BUT...
...THESE ARE THE SCORES OF OUR SIBLINGS THAT I HAD RAY AND EMMA LOOK INTO THE PAST FEW DAYS.
SCORES?

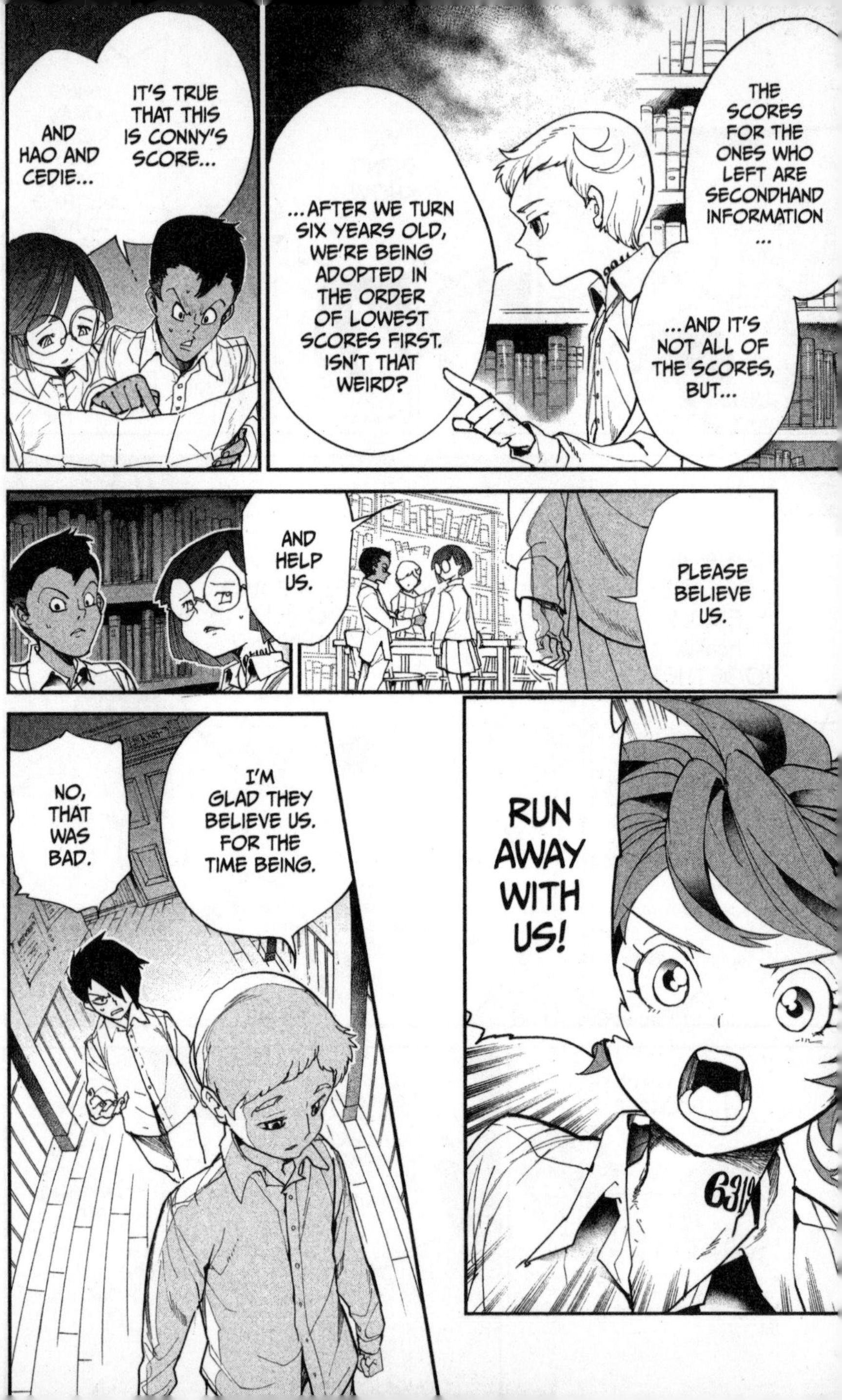
THE SCORES FOR THE ONES WHO LEFT ARE SECONDHAND INFORMATION ...
...AND IT'S NOT ALL OF THE SCORES, BUT...
...AFTER WE TURN SIX YEARS OLD, WE'RE BEING ADOPTED IN THE ORDER OF LOWEST SCORES FIRST. ISN'T THAT WEIRD?
IT'S TRUE THAT THIS IS CONNY'S SCORE...
AND HAO AND CEDIE...
PLEASE BELIEVE US.
AND HELP US.
RUN AWAY WITH US!
I'M GLAD THEY BELIEVE US. FOR THE TIME BEING.
NO, THAT WAS BAD.

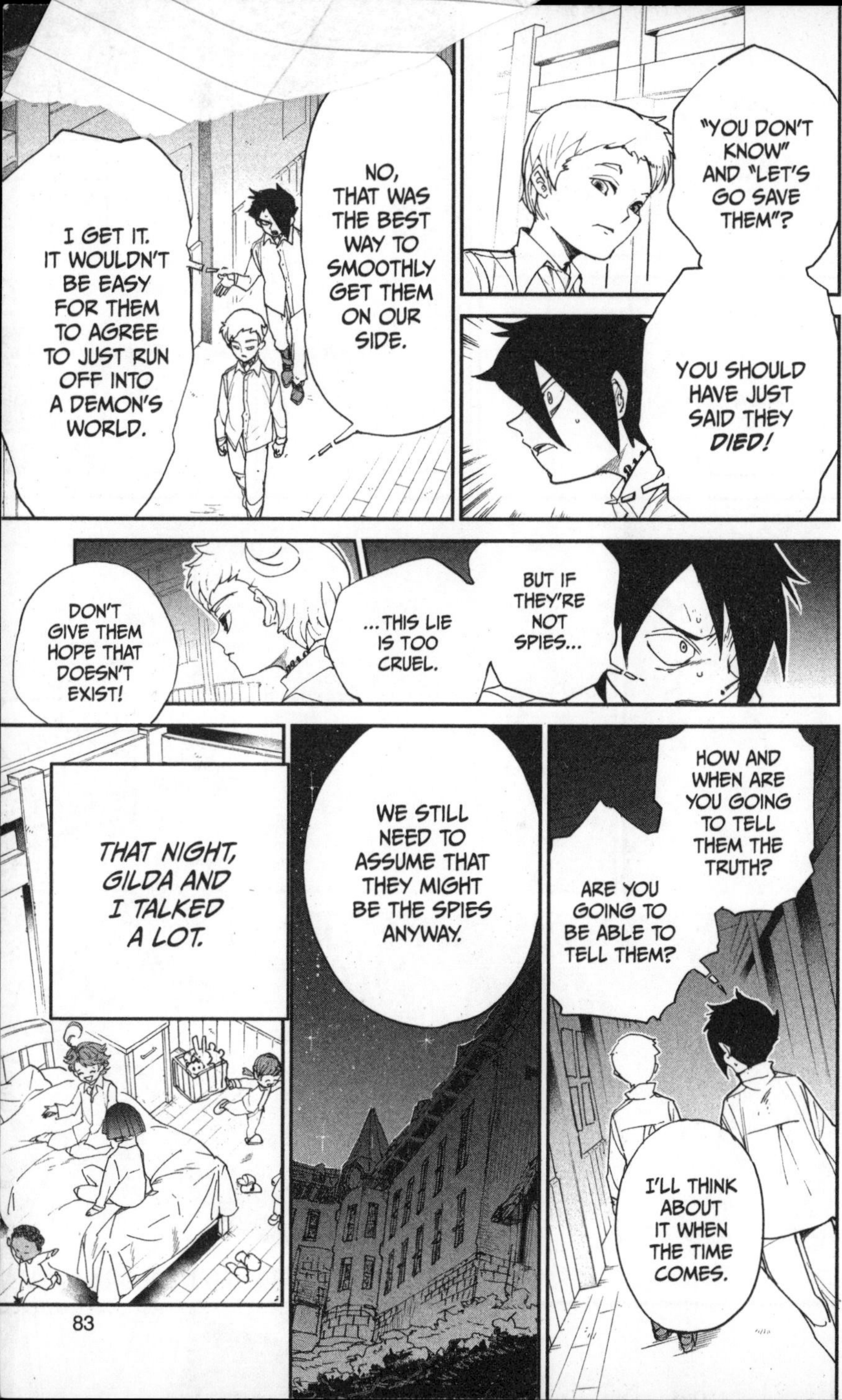
"YOU DON'T KNOW" AND "LET'S GO SAVE THEM"?
YOU SHOULD HAVE JUST SAID THEY *DIED!*
NO, THAT WAS THE BEST WAY TO SMOOTHLY GET THEM ON OUR SIDE.
I GET IT. IT WOULDN'T BE EASY FOR THEM TO AGREE TO JUST RUN OFF INTO A DEMON'S WORLD.
BUT IF THEY'RE NOT SPIES...
...THIS LIE IS TOO CRUEL.
DON'T GIVE THEM HOPE THAT DOESN'T EXIST!
HOW AND WHEN ARE YOU GOING TO TELL THEM THE TRUTH?
ARE YOU GOING TO BE ABLE TO TELL THEM?
I'LL THINK ABOUT IT WHEN THE TIME COMES.
WE STILL NEED TO ASSUME THAT THEY MIGHT BE THE SPIES ANYWAY.
THAT NIGHT, GILDA AND I TALKED A LOT.

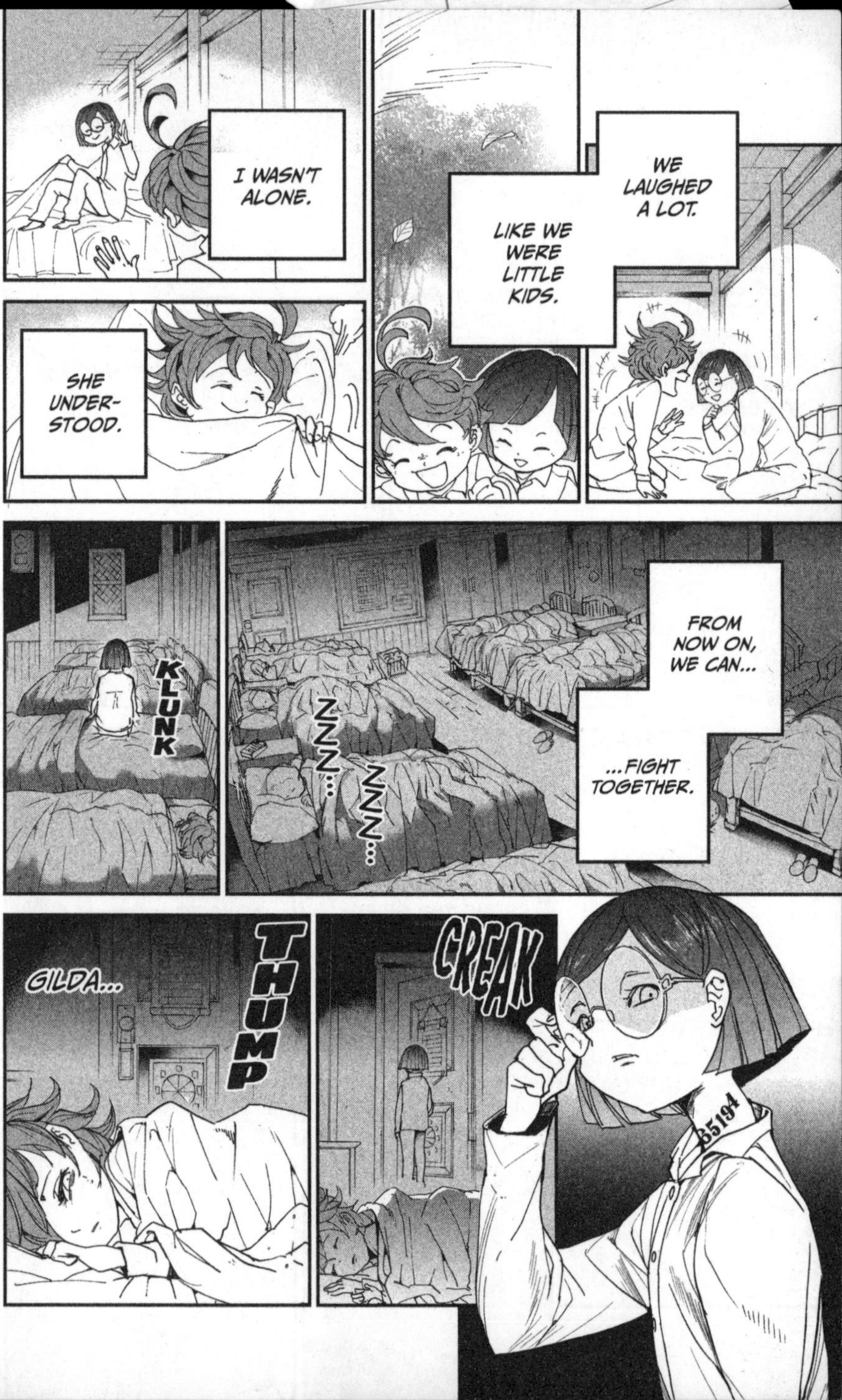
WE LAUGHED A LOT.
LIKE WE WERE LITTLE KIDS.
I WASN'T ALONE.
SHE UNDER-STOOD.
FROM NOW ON, WE CAN...
...FIGHT TOGETHER.
ZZZ...
ZZZ...
KLUNK
CREAK
THUMP
GILDA...

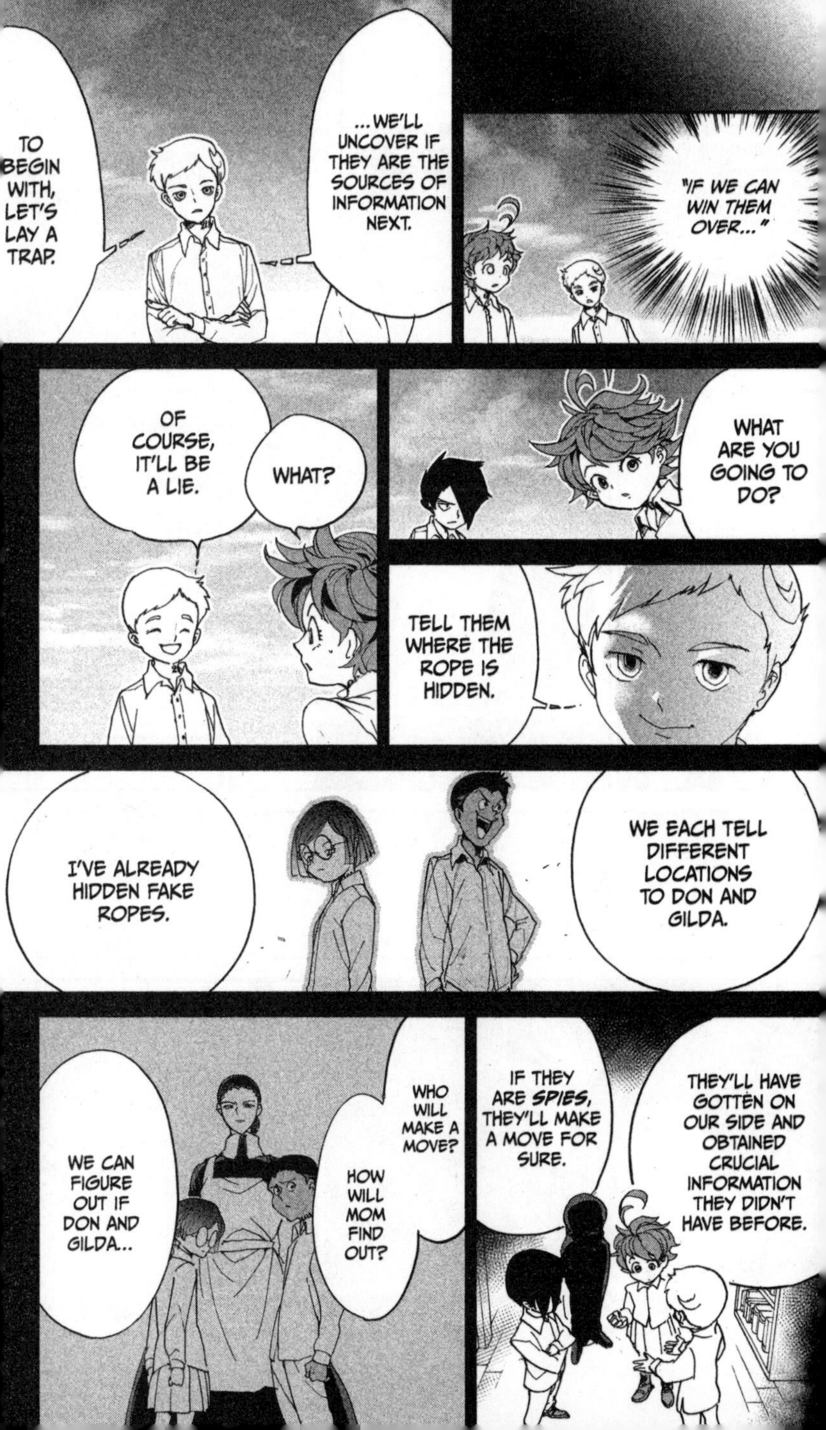
"IF WE CAN WIN THEM OVER..."
...WE'LL UNCOVER IF THEY ARE THE SOURCES OF INFORMATION NEXT.
TO BEGIN WITH, LET'S LAY A TRAP.
WHAT ARE YOU GOING TO DO?
TELL THEM WHERE THE ROPE IS HIDDEN.
WHAT?
OF COURSE, IT'LL BE A LIE.
WE EACH TELL DIFFERENT LOCATIONS TO DON AND GILDA.
I'VE ALREADY HIDDEN FAKE ROPES.
THEY'LL HAVE GOTTEN ON OUR SIDE AND OBTAINED CRUCIAL INFORMATION THEY DIDN'T HAVE BEFORE.
IF THEY ARE *SPIES*, THEY'LL MAKE A MOVE FOR SURE.
WHO WILL MAKE A MOVE?
HOW WILL MOM FIND OUT?
WE CAN FIGURE OUT IF DON AND GILDA...

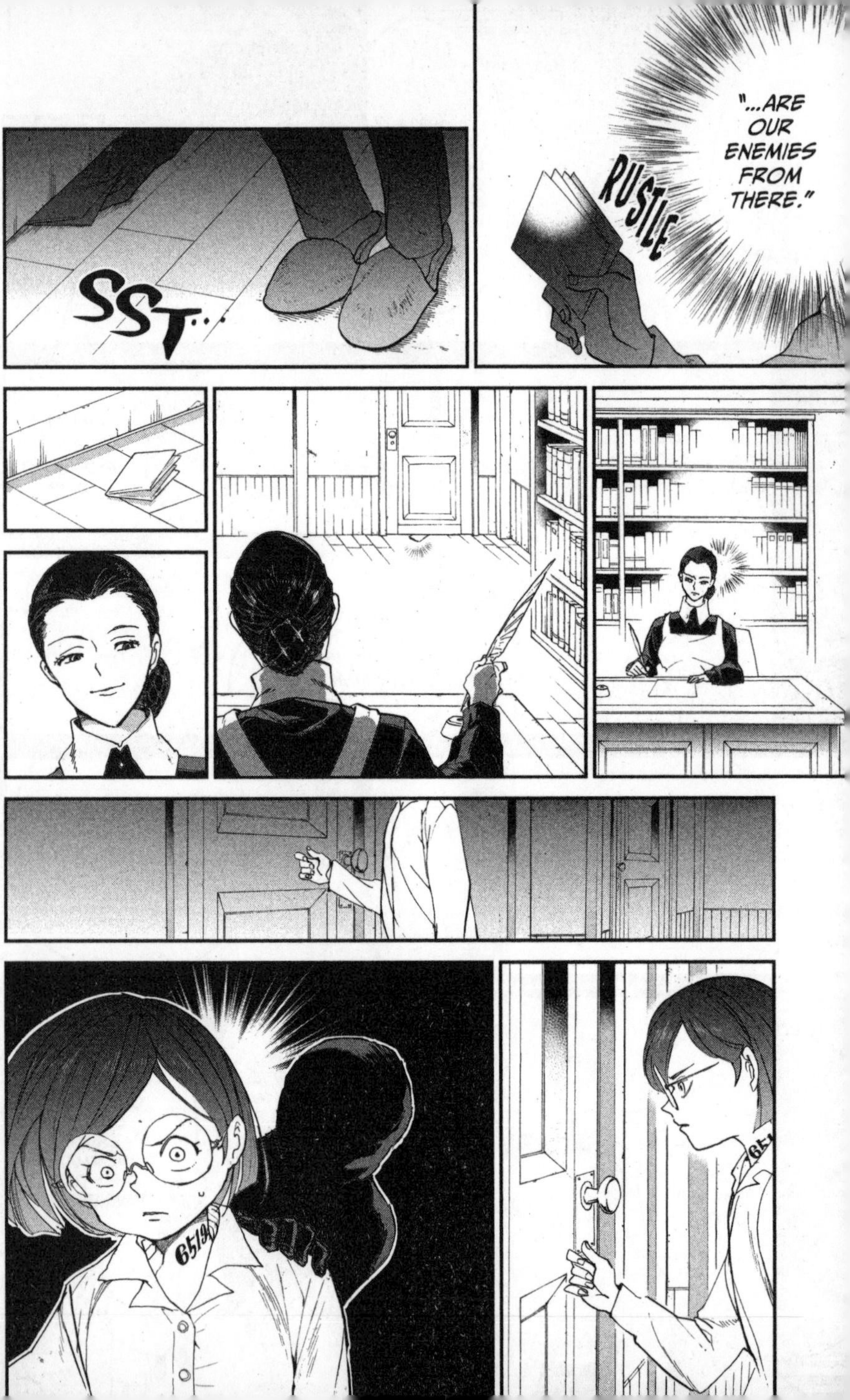
"...ARE OUR ENEMIES FROM THERE."
RUSTLE
SST...

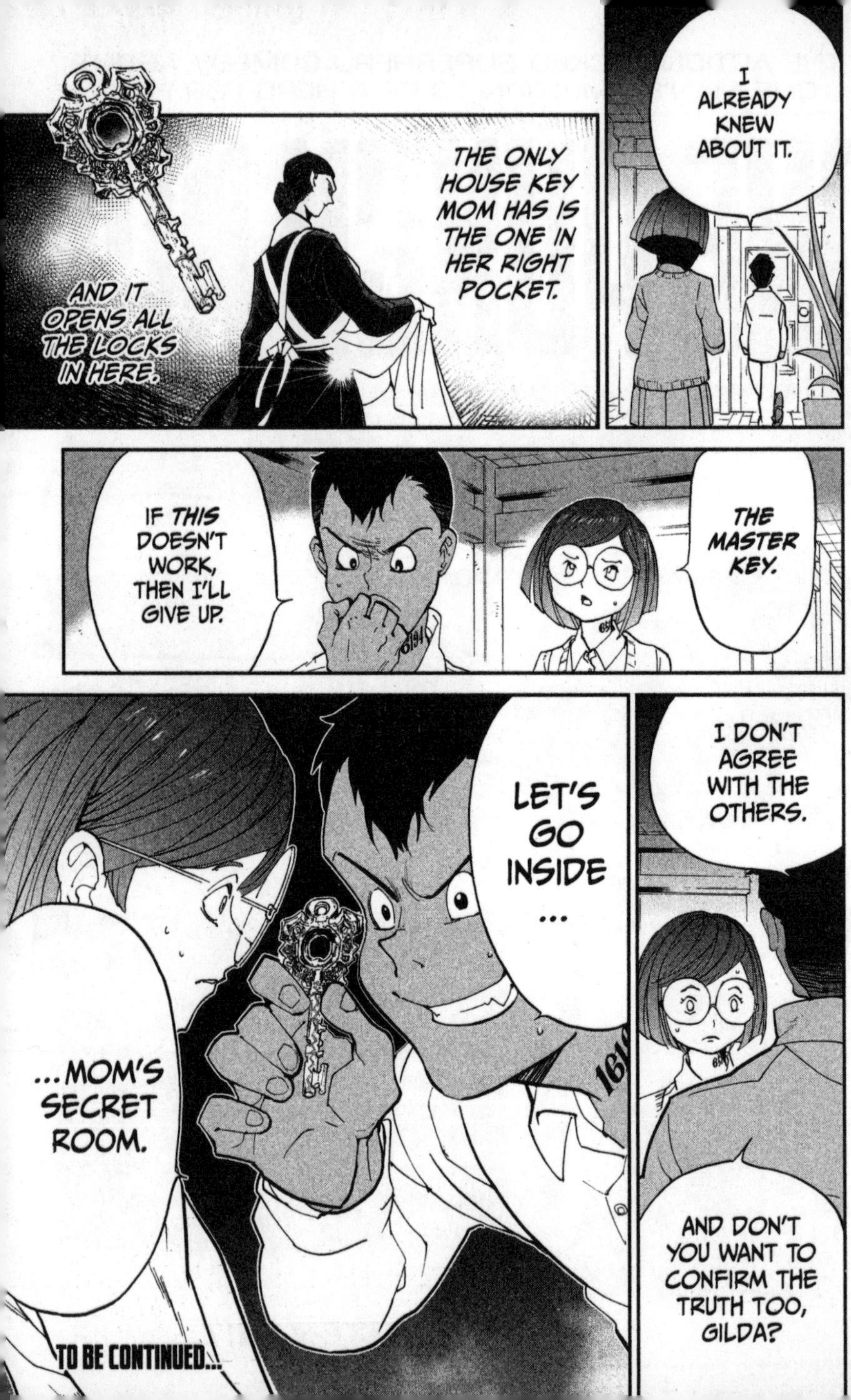
I ALREADY KNEW ABOUT IT.
THE ONLY HOUSE KEY MOM HAS IS THE ONE IN HER RIGHT POCKET.
AND IT OPENS ALL THE LOCKS IN HERE.
THE MASTER KEY.
IF THIS DOESN'T WORK, THEN I'LL GIVE UP.
I DON'T AGREE WITH THE OTHERS.
AND DON'T YOU WANT TO CONFIRM THE TRUTH TOO, GILDA?
LET'S GO INSIDE ...
...MOM'S SECRET ROOM.
TO BE CONTINUED...

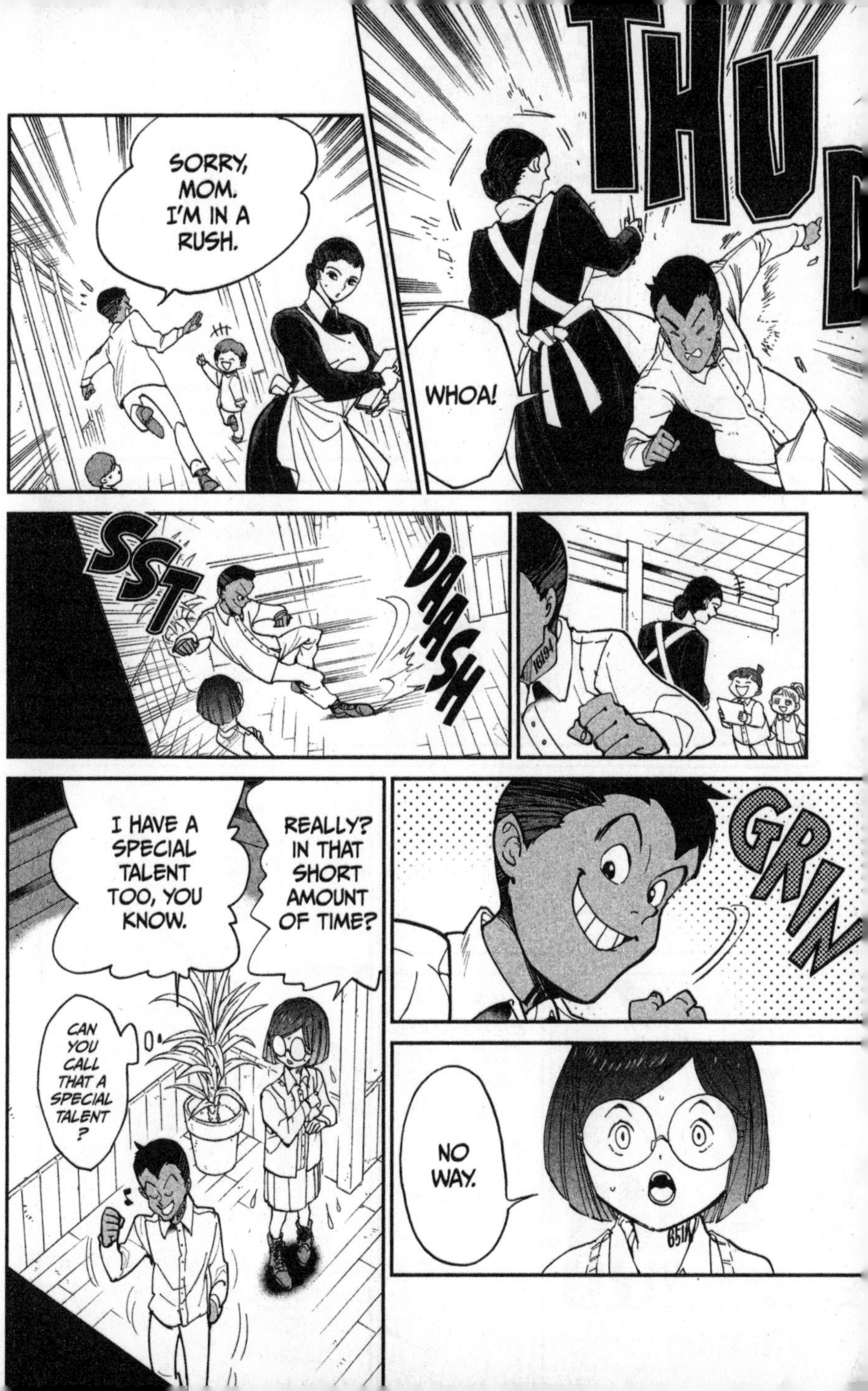
THUD
WHOA!
SORRY, MOM. I'M IN A RUSH.
16194
SST
DAASH
GRIN
NO WAY.
REALLY? IN THAT SHORT AMOUNT OF TIME?
I HAVE A SPECIAL TALENT TOO, YOU KNOW.
CAN YOU CALL THAT A SPECIAL TALENT?

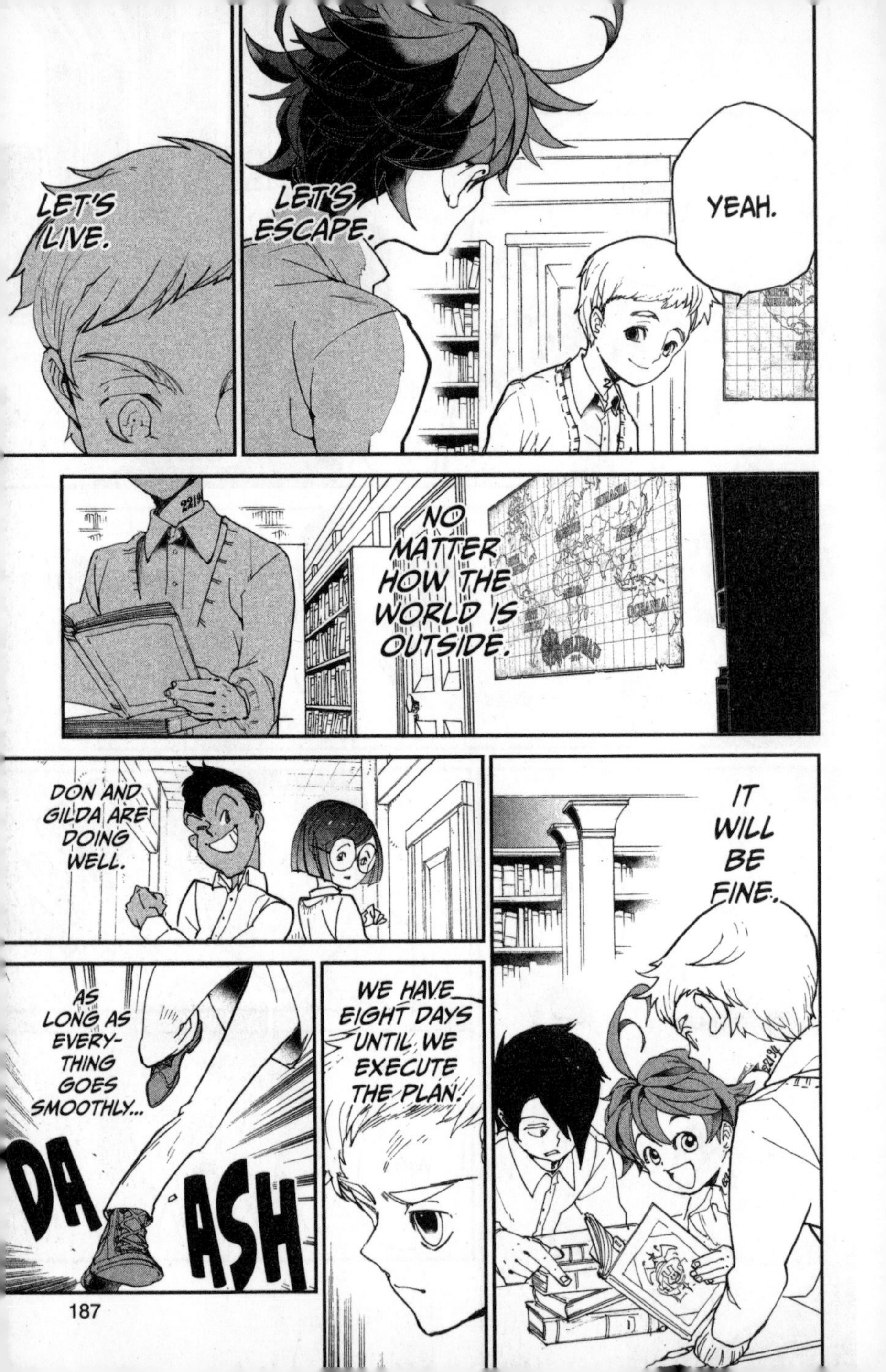
YEAH.
LET'S ESCAPE.
LET'S LIVE.
NO MATTER HOW THE WORLD IS OUTSIDE.
IT WILL BE FINE.
DON AND GILDA ARE DOING WELL.
WE HAVE EIGHT DAYS UNTIL WE EXECUTE THE PLAN.
AS LONG AS EVERYTHING GOES SMOOTHLY...
DA ASH

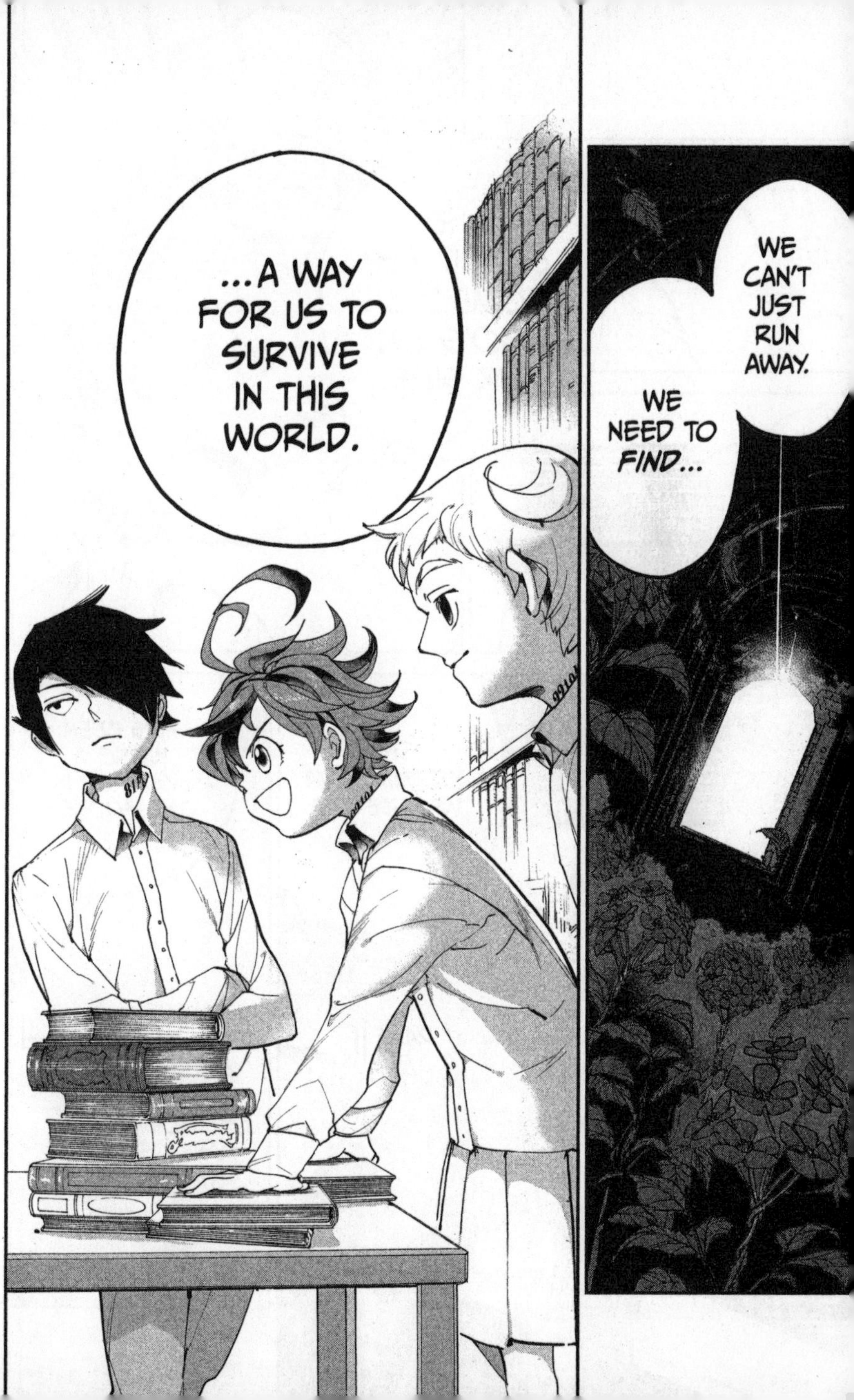
WE CAN'T JUST RUN AWAY.
WE NEED TO *FIND*...
...A WAY FOR US TO SURVIVE IN THIS WORLD.

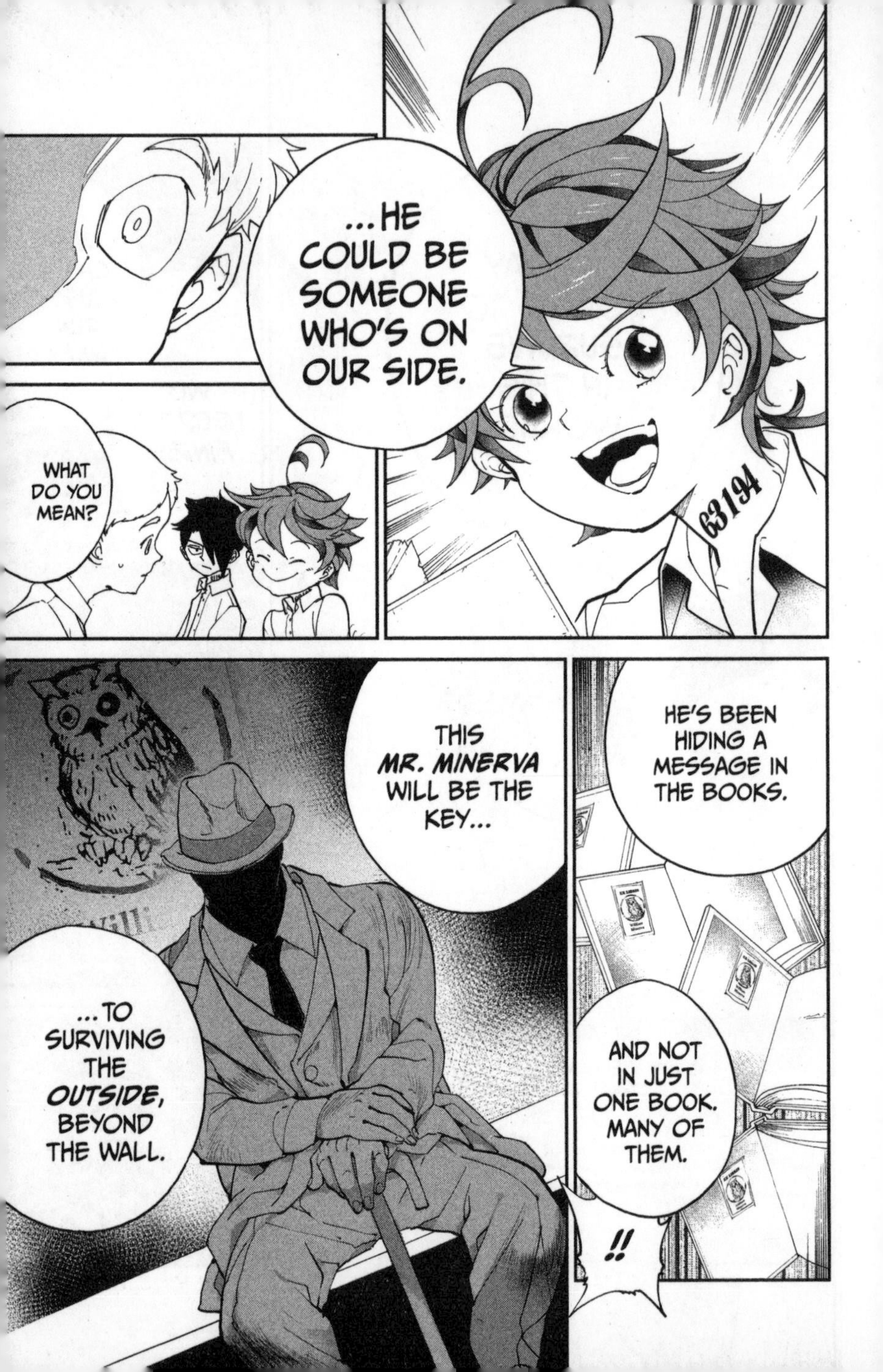

...HE COULD BE SOMEONE WHO'S ON OUR SIDE.
63194
WHAT DO YOU MEAN?
HE'S BEEN HIDING A MESSAGE IN THE BOOKS.
AND NOT IN JUST ONE BOOK. MANY OF THEM.
!!
THIS *MR. MINERVA* WILL BE THE KEY...
...TO SURVIVING THE *OUTSIDE*, BEYOND THE WALL.

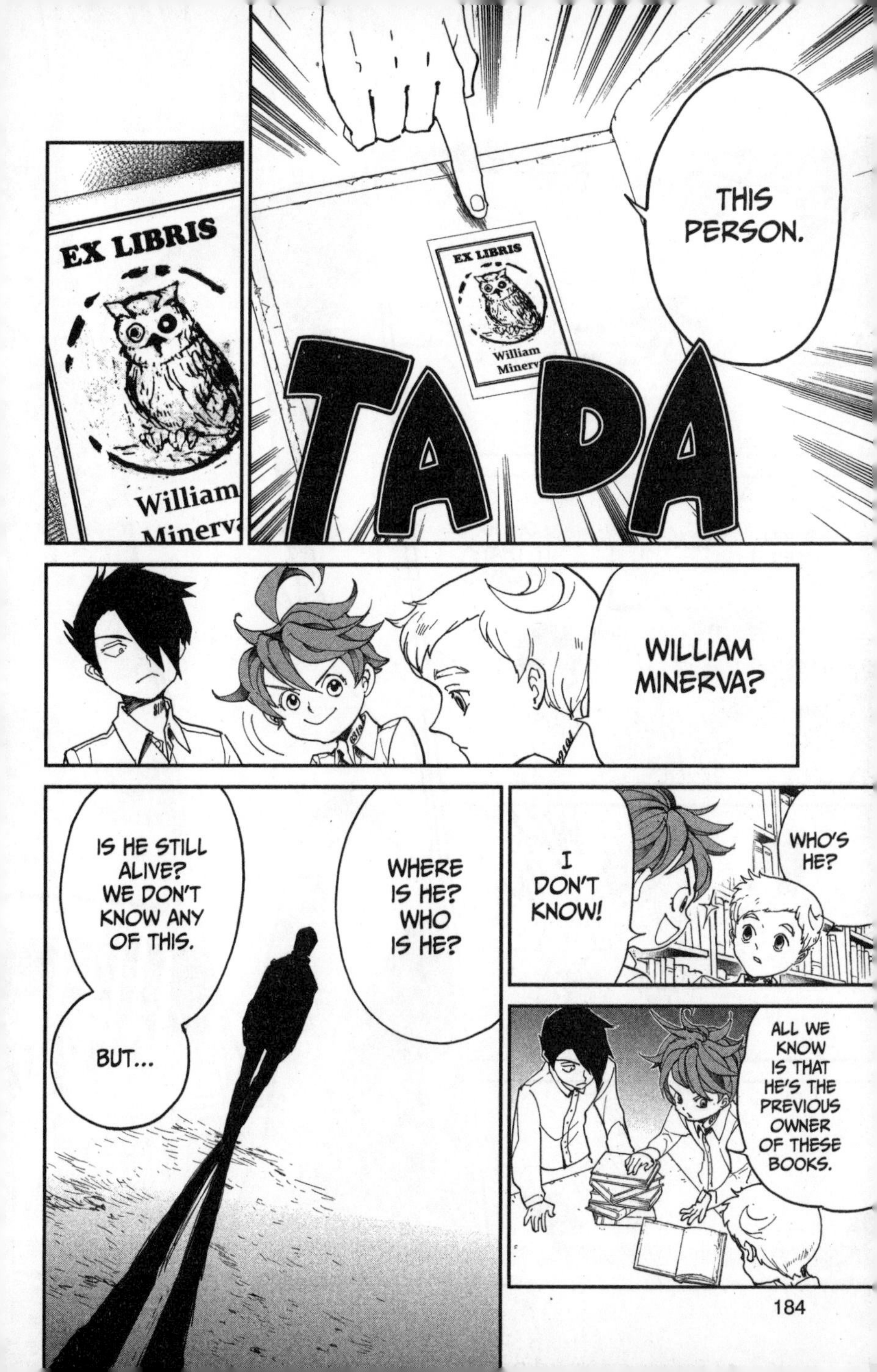
THIS PERSON.
EX LIBRIS
William Minerva
TA DA
EX LIBRIS
William Minerva
WILLIAM MINERVA?
WHO'S HE?
I DON'T KNOW!
ALL WE KNOW IS THAT HE'S THE PREVIOUS OWNER OF THESE BOOKS.
WHERE IS HE? WHO IS HE?
IS HE STILL ALIVE? WE DON'T KNOW ANY OF THIS.
BUT...

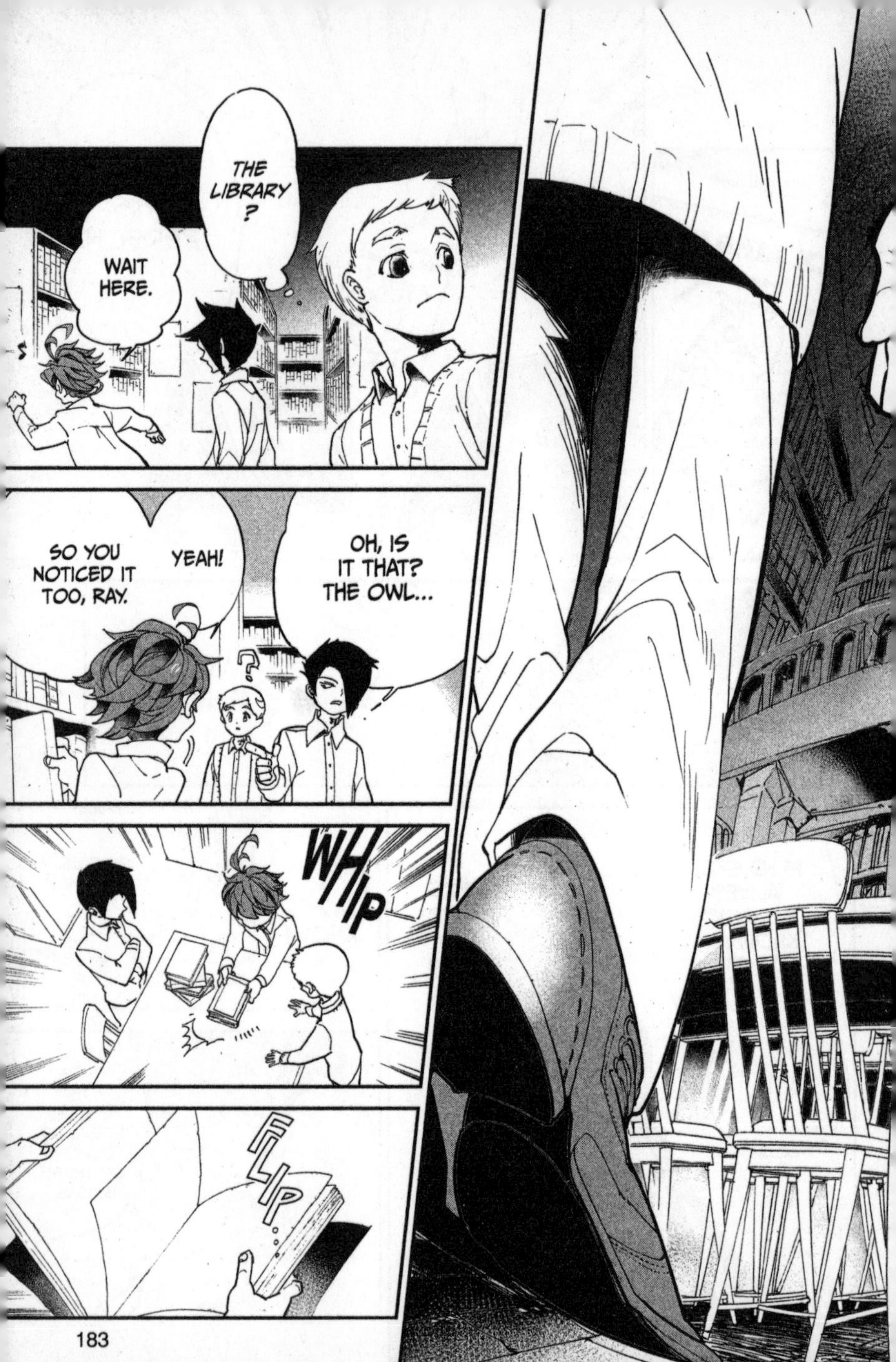
THE LIBRARY?
WAIT HERE.
OH, IS IT THAT? THE OWL...
YEAH!
SO YOU NOTICED IT TOO, RAY.
WHIP
FLIP

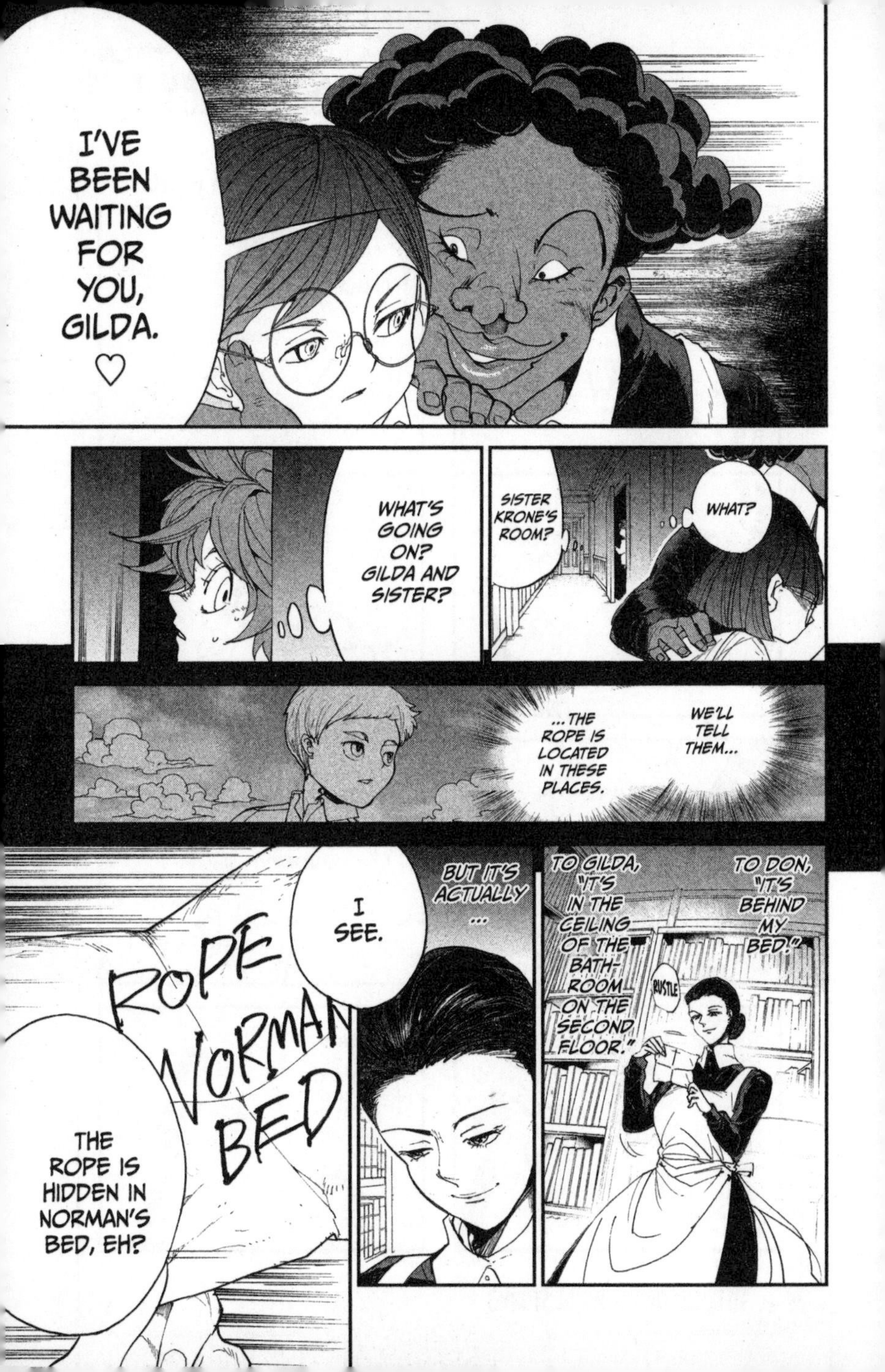
I'VE BEEN WAITING FOR YOU, GILDA. ♡
WHAT?
SISTER KRONE'S ROOM?
WHAT'S GOING ON? GILDA AND SISTER?
WE'LL TELL THEM...
...THE ROPE IS LOCATED IN THESE PLACES.
TO DON, "IT'S BEHIND MY BED."
TO GILDA, "IT'S IN THE CEILING OF THE BATHROOM ON THE SECOND FLOOR."
RUSTLE
BUT IT'S ACTUALLY ...
I SEE.
ROPE NORMAN BED
THE ROPE IS HIDDEN IN NORMAN'S BED, EH?

SIDE STORY 2

Although Mom Said...

I CAME TO VISIT!
POINK
EMMA!
NO, YOU CAN'T BE HERE. YOU'LL CATCH MY COLD.
COUGH COUGH COUGH
I WON'T CATCH IT.
I CAN'T GET SICK, SO DON'T WORRY!
BA DUM
AND WHO TOLD YOU THAT?
IT SAYS IN THIS BOOK THAT IDIOTS CANNOT CATCH COLDS.

Never Give Up

I CAME TO VISIT AGAIN!
YAY
YOU SHOULDN'T! YOU'LL CATCH COLD, AND MOM WILL FIND OUT!
TURN
COUGH COUGH
THEN JUST GIVE ME YOUR COLD.
THWUMP
HUH?
!!
THAT WAY, WE CAN STAY HERE BEING SICK TOGETHER.
BA DUM DUM
IT SAYS THAT YOU GET BETTER FASTER IF YOU GIVE IT TO SOME-ONE ELSE.
YOU AGAIN, EH?

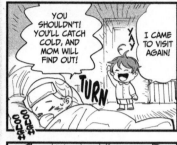

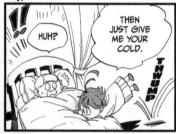

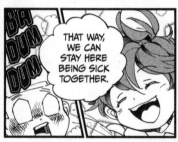

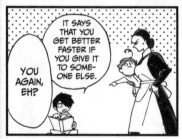

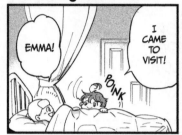

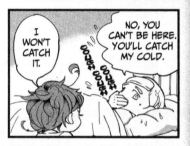

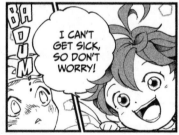

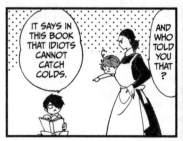

TO BE CONTINUED IN SIDE STORY 3

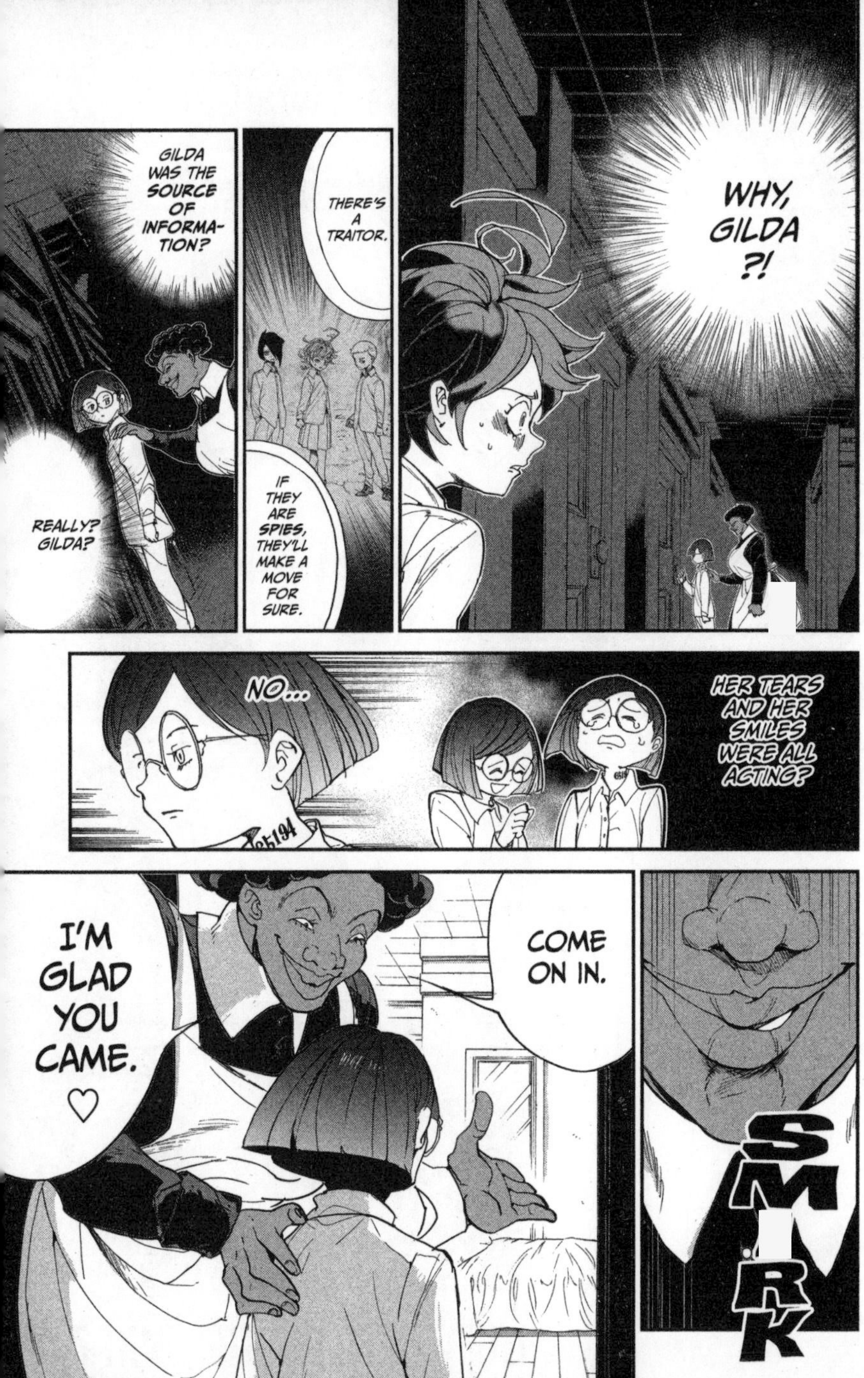
WHY, GILDA ?!
THERE'S A TRAITOR.
IF THEY ARE SPIES, THEY'LL MAKE A MOVE FOR SURE.
GILDA WAS THE SOURCE OF INFORMATION?
REALLY? GILDA?
HER TEARS AND HER SMILES WERE ALL ACTING?
NO...
SMIRK
COME ON IN.
I'M GLAD YOU CAME. ♡

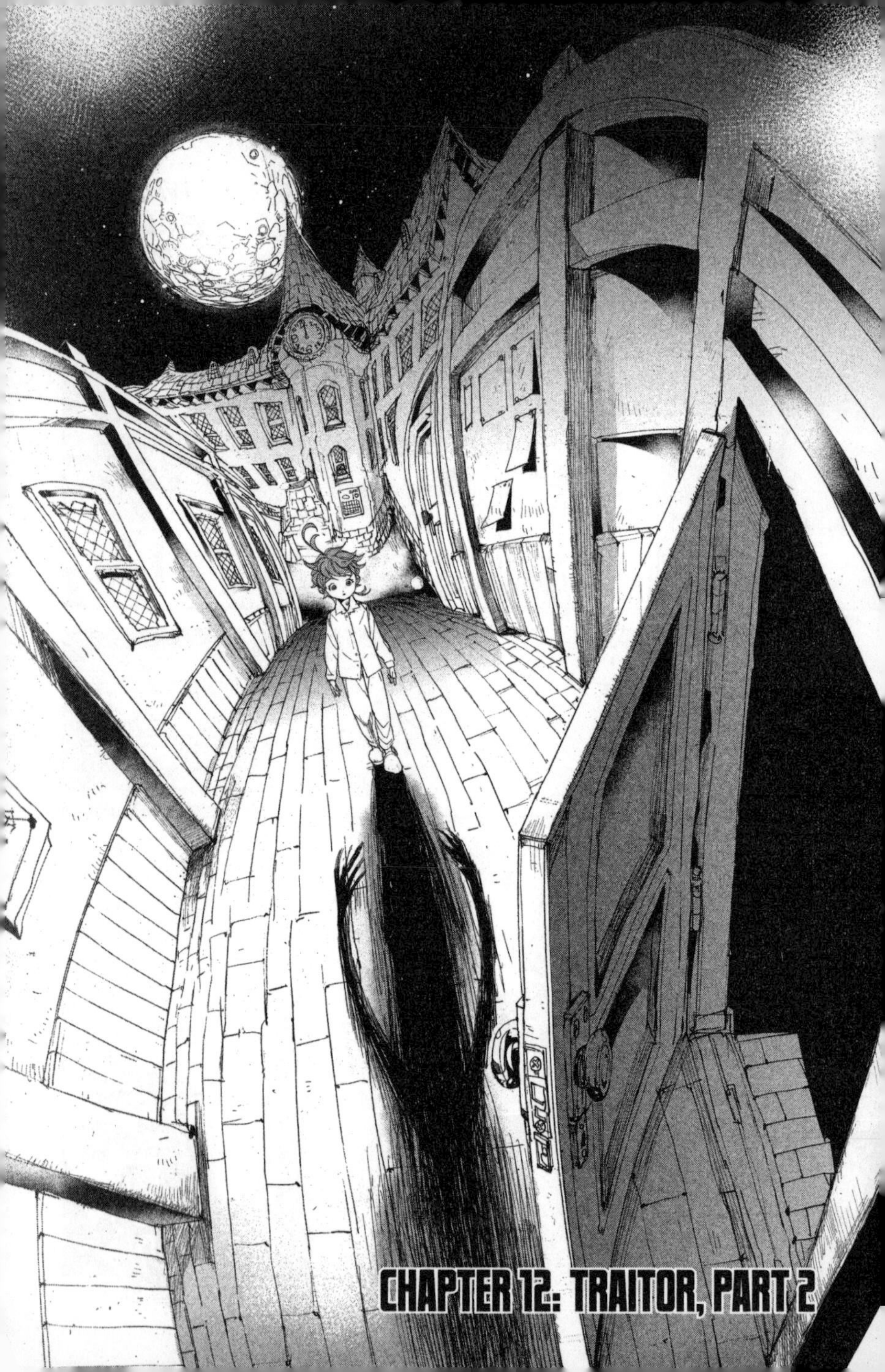
CHAPTER 12: TRAITOR, PART 2

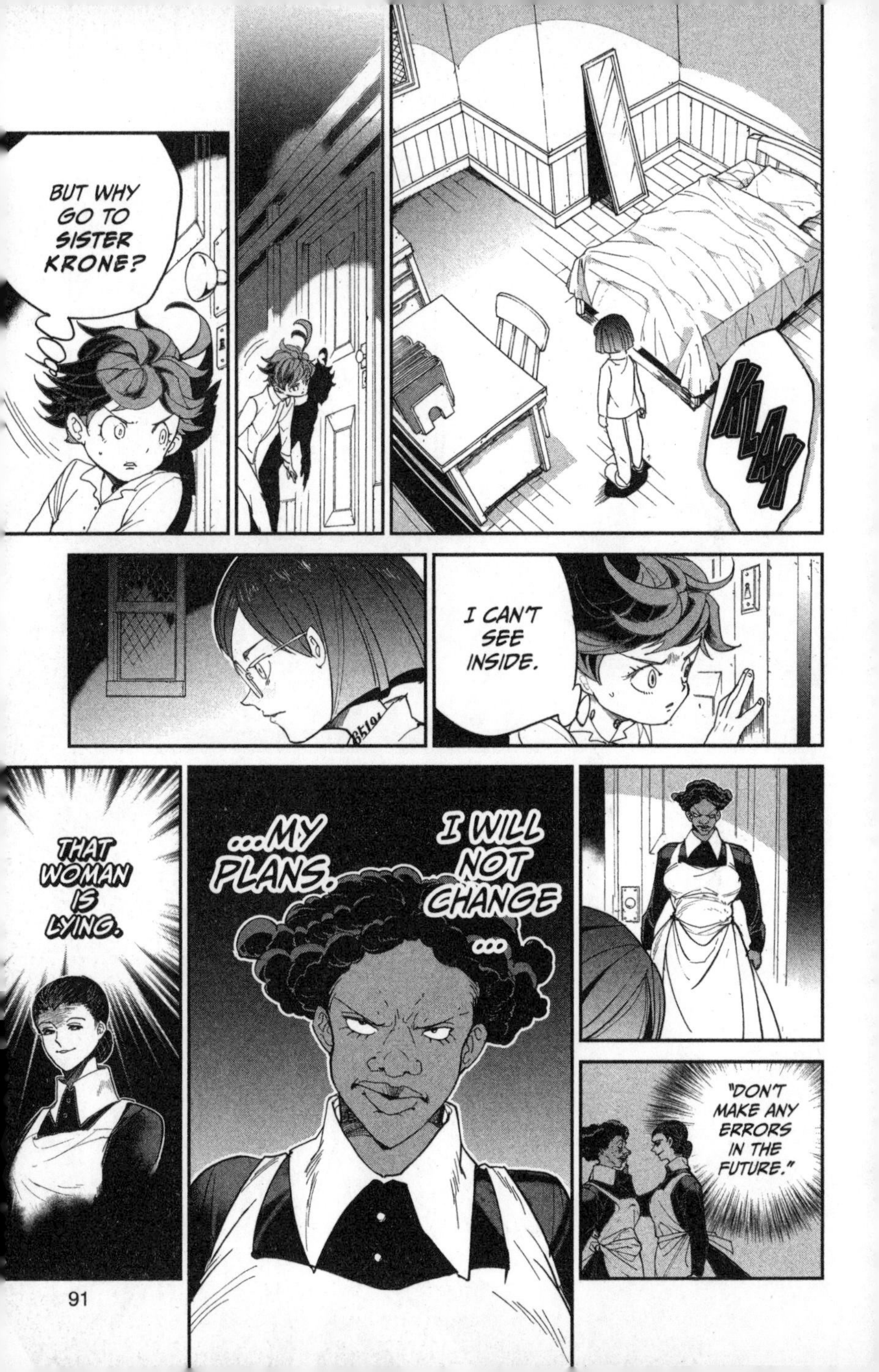
KLAK
BUT WHY GO TO SISTER KRONE?
I CAN'T SEE INSIDE.
"DON'T MAKE ANY ERRORS IN THE FUTURE."
I WILL NOT CHANGE...
...MY PLANS.
THAT WOMAN IS LYING.

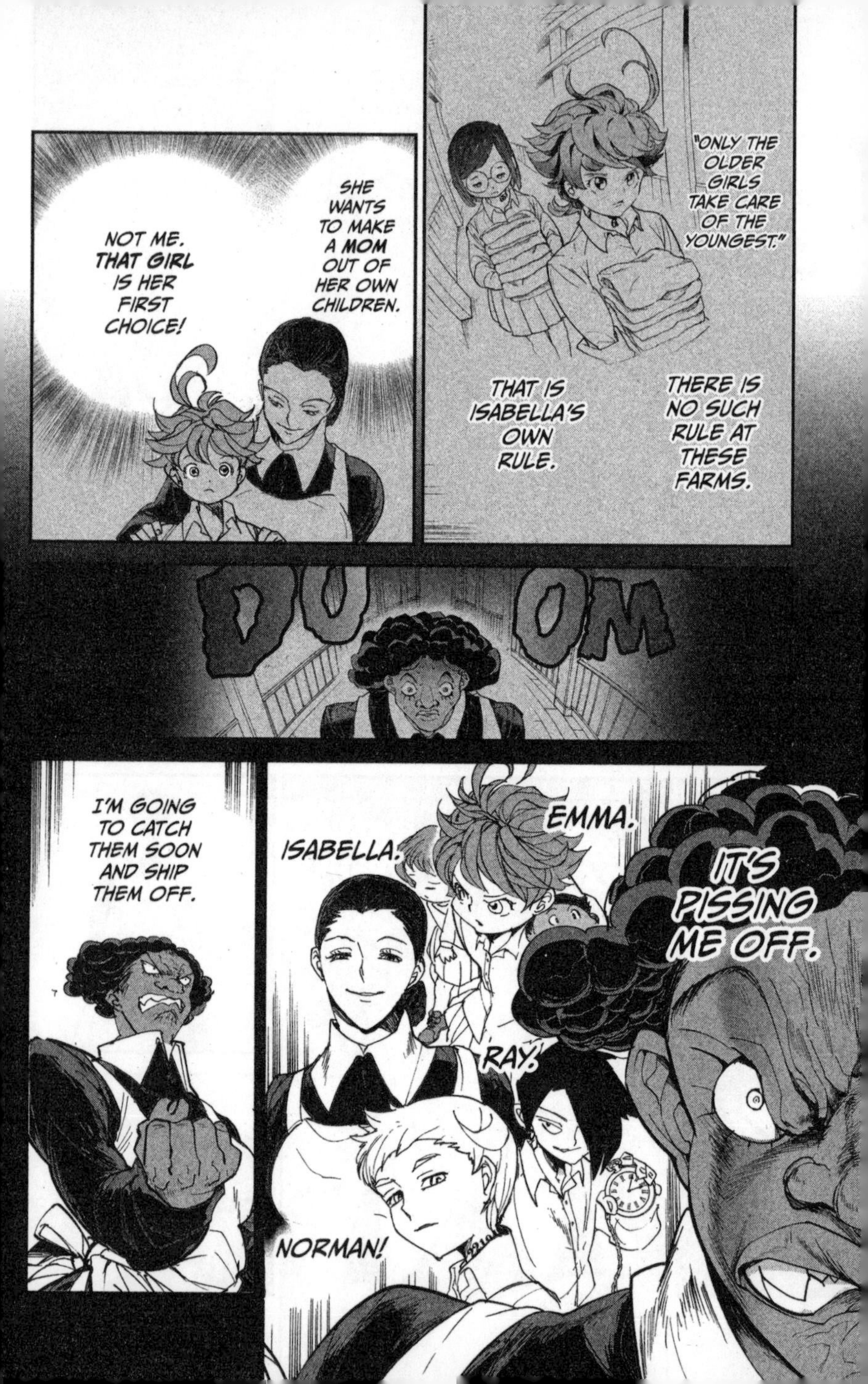
"ONLY THE OLDER GIRLS TAKE CARE OF THE YOUNGEST."
THERE IS NO SUCH RULE AT THESE FARMS.
THAT IS ISABELLA'S OWN RULE.
SHE WANTS TO MAKE A MOM OUT OF HER OWN CHILDREN.
NOT ME. THAT GIRL IS HER FIRST CHOICE!
DOOM
IT'S PISSING ME OFF.
EMMA.
ISABELLA.
RAY.
NORMAN!
I'M GOING TO CATCH THEM SOON AND SHIP THEM OFF.

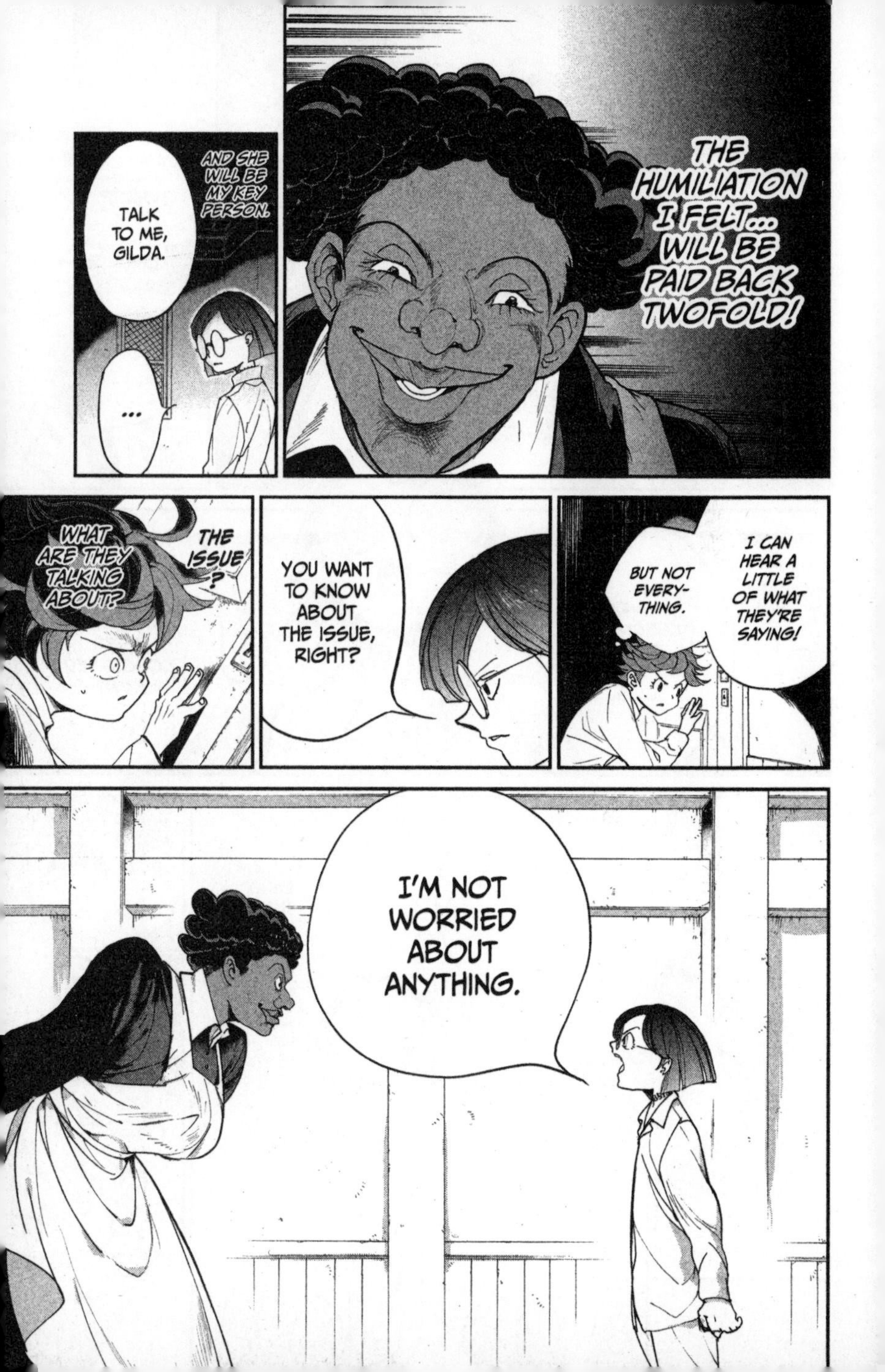
THE HUMILIATION I FELT... WILL BE PAID BACK TWOFOLD!
AND SHE WILL BE MY KEY PERSON.
TALK TO ME, GILDA.
...
I CAN HEAR A LITTLE OF WHAT THEY'RE SAYING!
BUT NOT EVERY-THING.
YOU WANT TO KNOW ABOUT THE ISSUE, RIGHT?
THE ISSUE?
WHAT ARE THEY TALKING ABOUT?
I'M NOT WORRIED ABOUT ANYTHING.

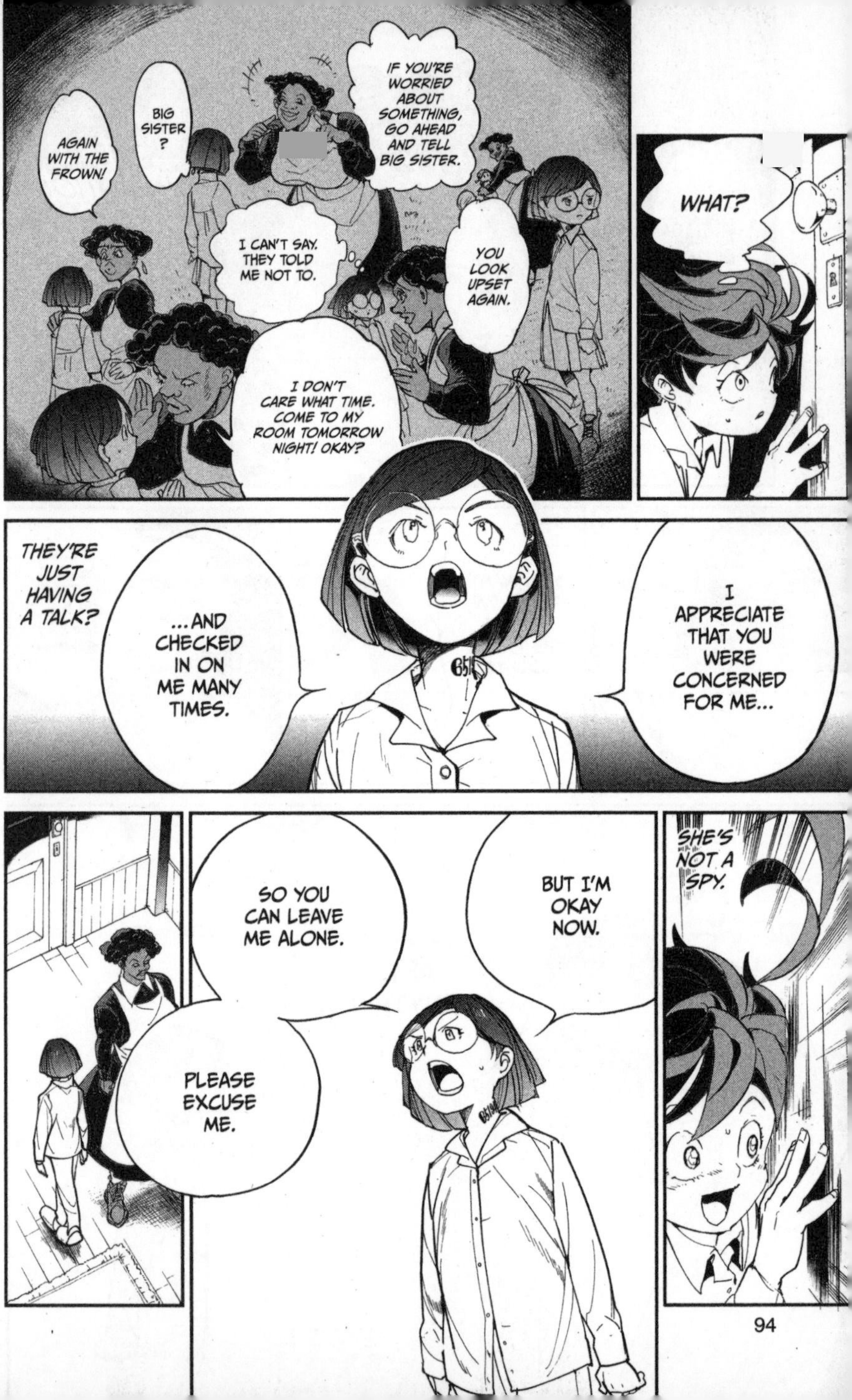
WHAT?
IF YOU'RE WORRIED ABOUT SOMETHING, GO AHEAD AND TELL BIG SISTER.
BIG SISTER?
AGAIN WITH THE FROWN!
YOU LOOK UPSET AGAIN.
I CAN'T SAY. THEY TOLD ME NOT TO.
I DON'T CARE WHAT TIME. COME TO MY ROOM TOMORROW NIGHT! OKAY?
I APPRECIATE THAT YOU WERE CONCERNED FOR ME...
...AND CHECKED IN ON ME MANY TIMES.
THEY'RE JUST HAVING A TALK?
SHE'S NOT A SPY.
BUT I'M OKAY NOW.
SO YOU CAN LEAVE ME ALONE.
PLEASE EXCUSE ME.

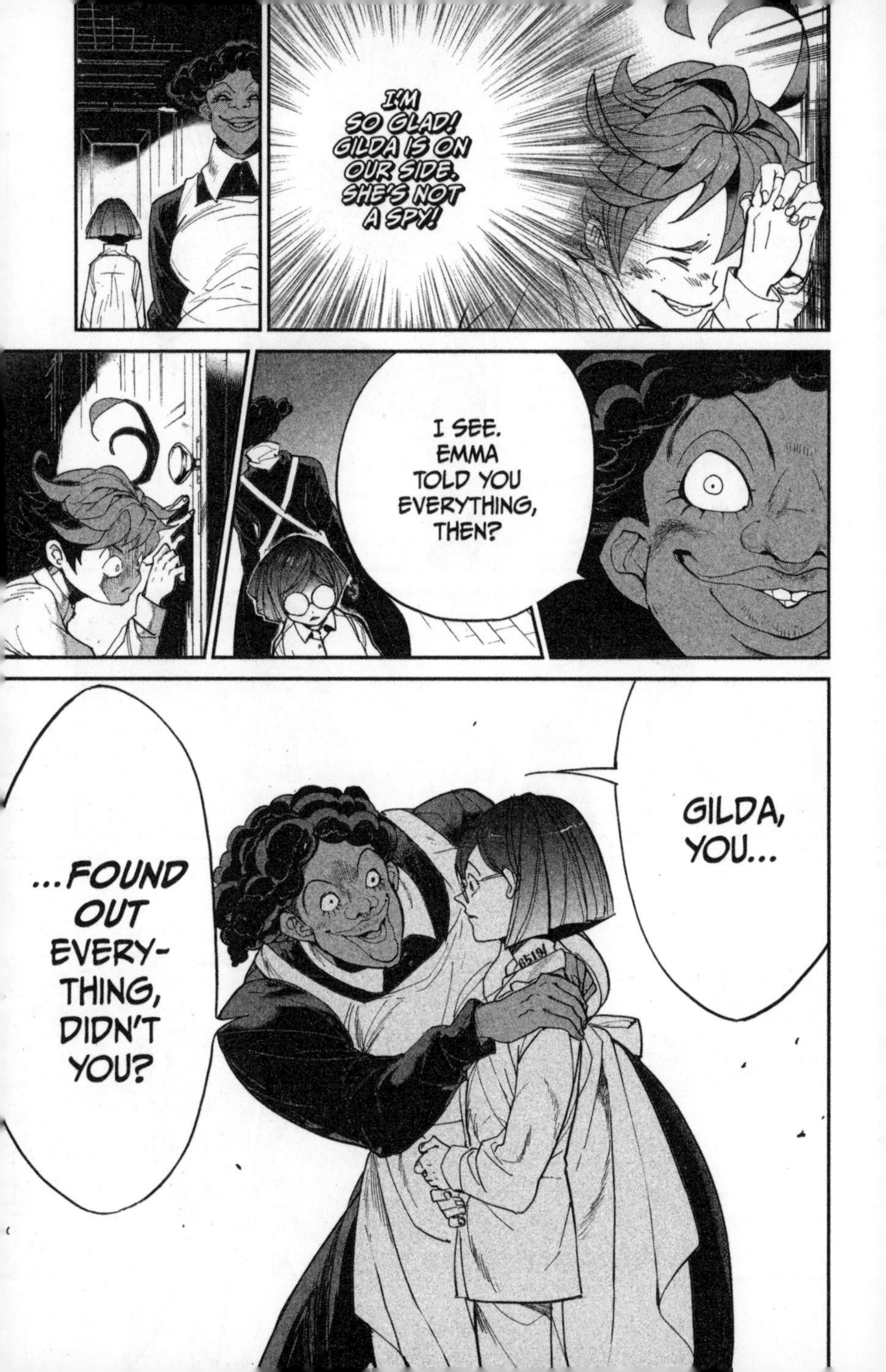
I'M SO GLAD! GILDA IS ON OUR SIDE. SHE'S NOT A SPY!
I SEE. EMMA TOLD YOU EVERYTHING, THEN?
GILDA, YOU...
...FOUND OUT EVERY-THING, DIDN'T YOU?

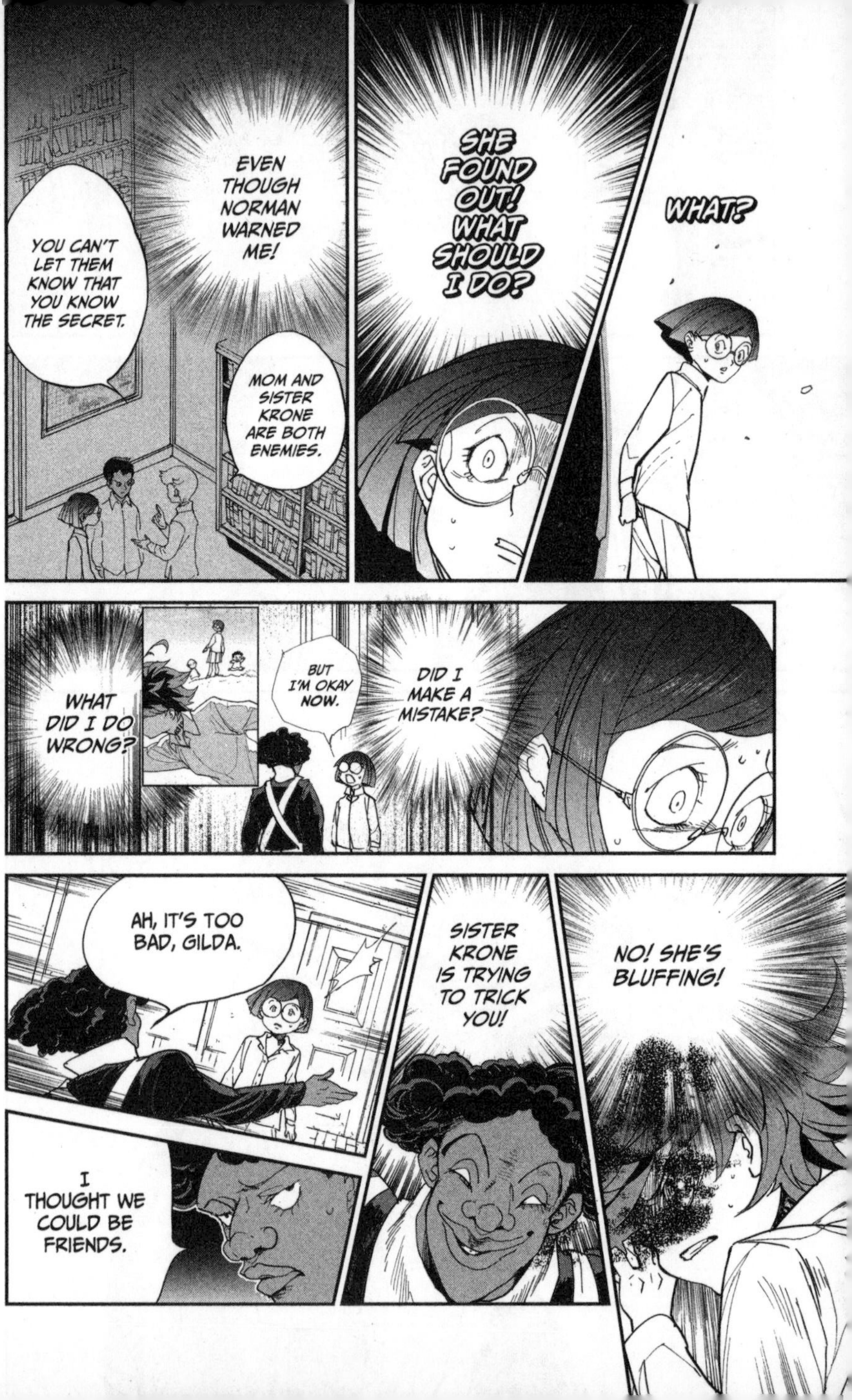
WHAT?
SHE FOUND OUT! WHAT SHOULD I DO?
EVEN THOUGH NORMAN WARNED ME!
YOU CAN'T LET THEM KNOW THAT YOU KNOW THE SECRET.
MOM AND SISTER KRONE ARE BOTH ENEMIES.
DID I MAKE A MISTAKE?
BUT I'M OKAY NOW.
WHAT DID I DO WRONG?
NO! SHE'S BLUFFING!
SISTER KRONE IS TRYING TO TRICK YOU!
AH, IT'S TOO BAD, GILDA.
I THOUGHT WE COULD BE FRIENDS.

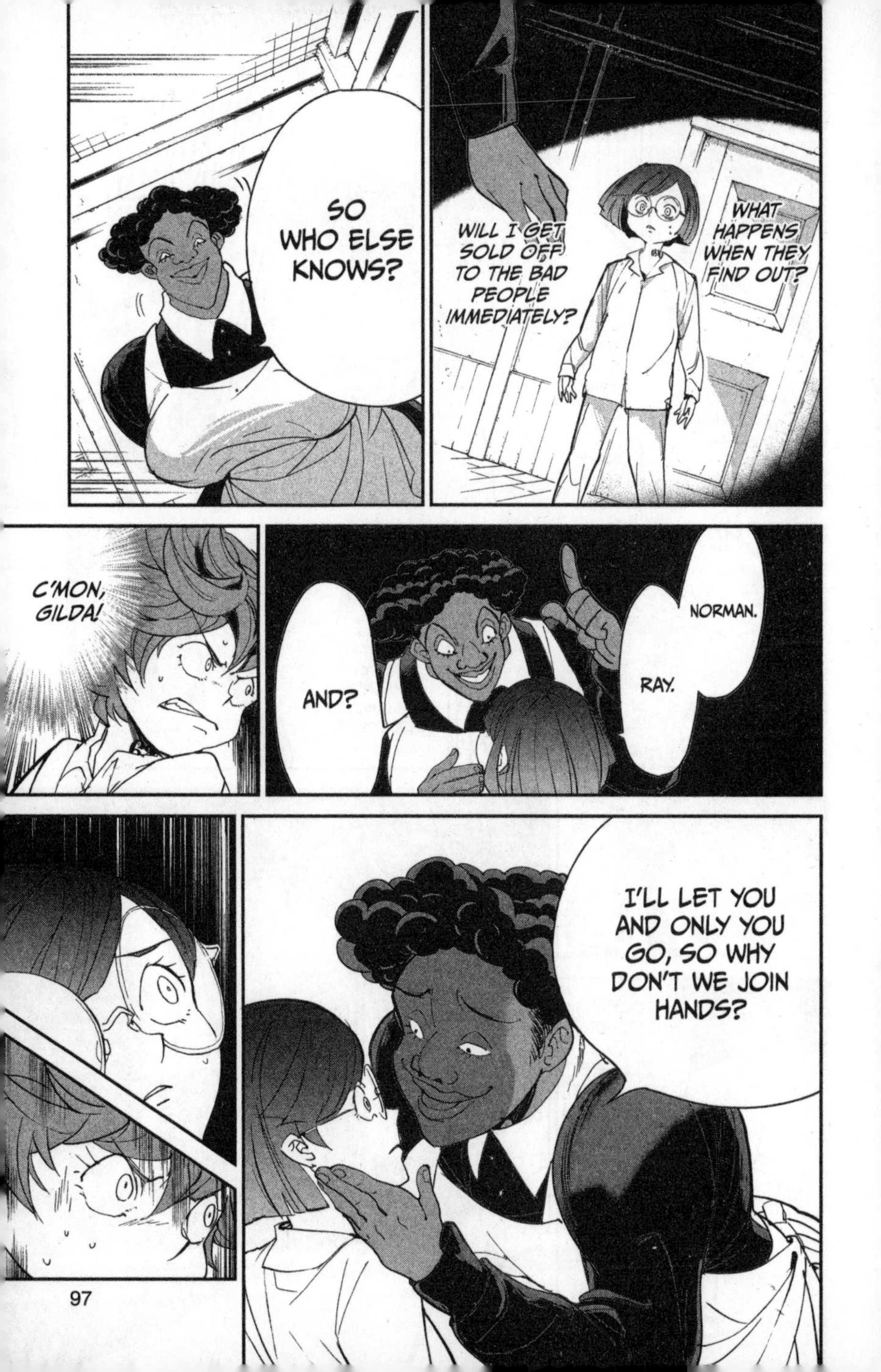
WHAT HAPPENS WHEN THEY FIND OUT?
WILL I GET SOLD OFF TO THE BAD PEOPLE IMMEDIATELY?
SO WHO ELSE KNOWS?
NORMAN.
RAY.
AND?
C'MON, GILDA!
I'LL LET YOU AND ONLY YOU GO, SO WHY DON'T WE JOIN HANDS?

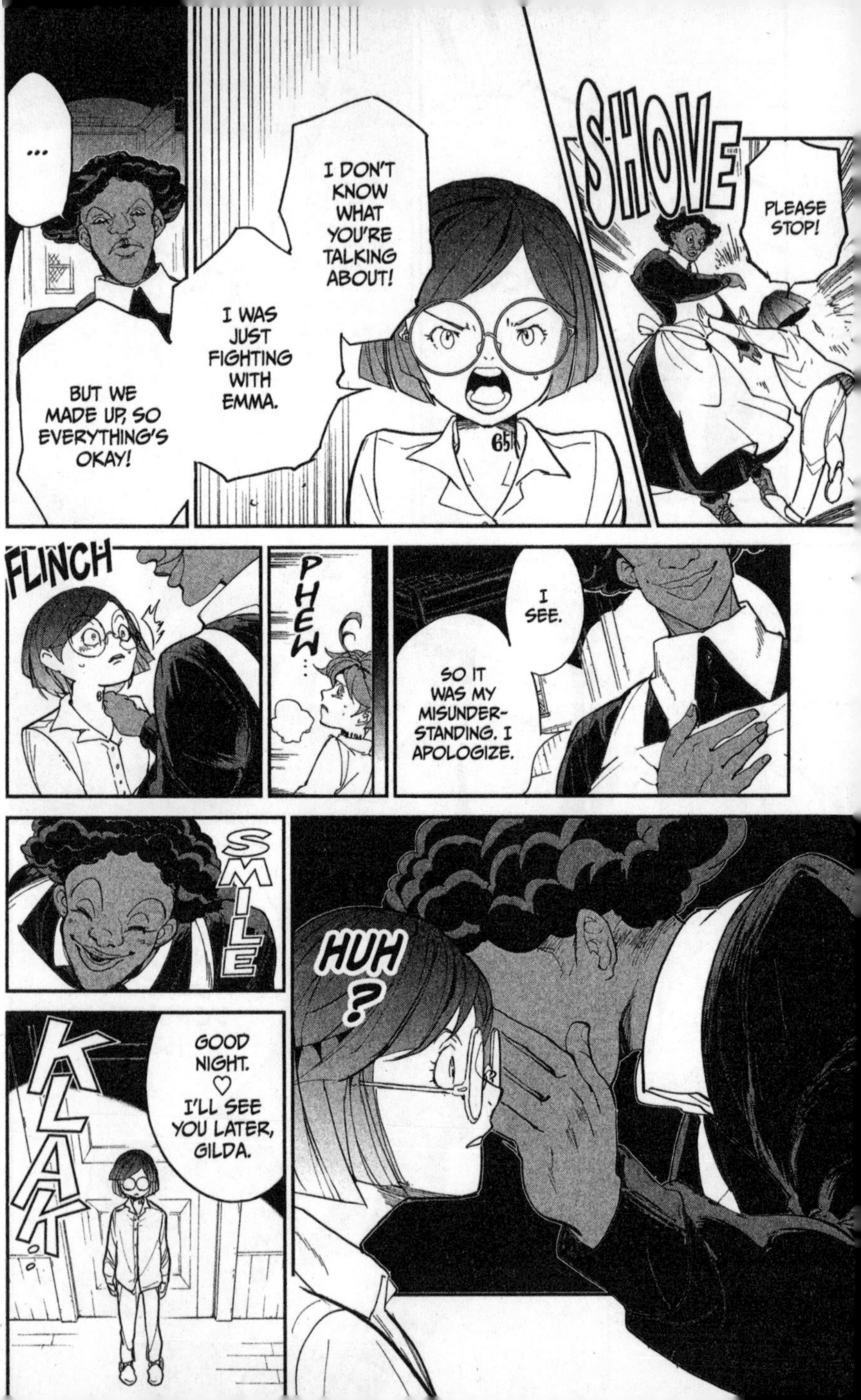
SHOVE
PLEASE STOP!
I DON'T KNOW WHAT YOU'RE TALKING ABOUT!
I WAS JUST FIGHTING WITH EMMA.
BUT WE MADE UP, SO EVERYTHING'S OKAY!
...
I SEE.
SO IT WAS MY MISUNDER-STANDING. I APOLOGIZE.
PHEW...
FLINCH
HUH?
SMILE
GOOD NIGHT. ♡ I'LL SEE YOU LATER, GILDA.
KLAK

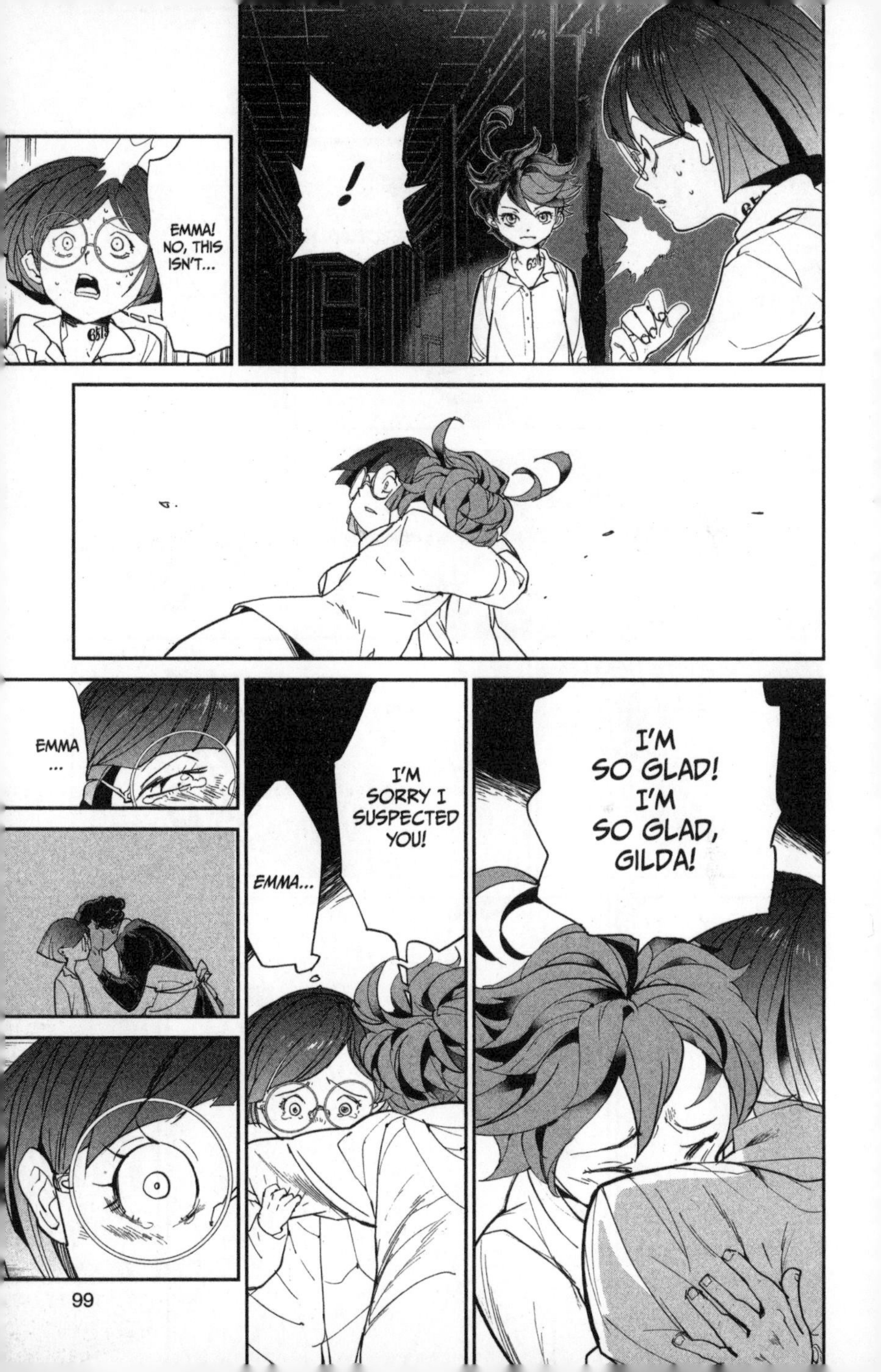
!
EMMA! NO, THIS ISN'T...
I'M SO GLAD! I'M SO GLAD, GILDA!
I'M SORRY I SUSPECTED YOU!
EMMA...
EMMA ...

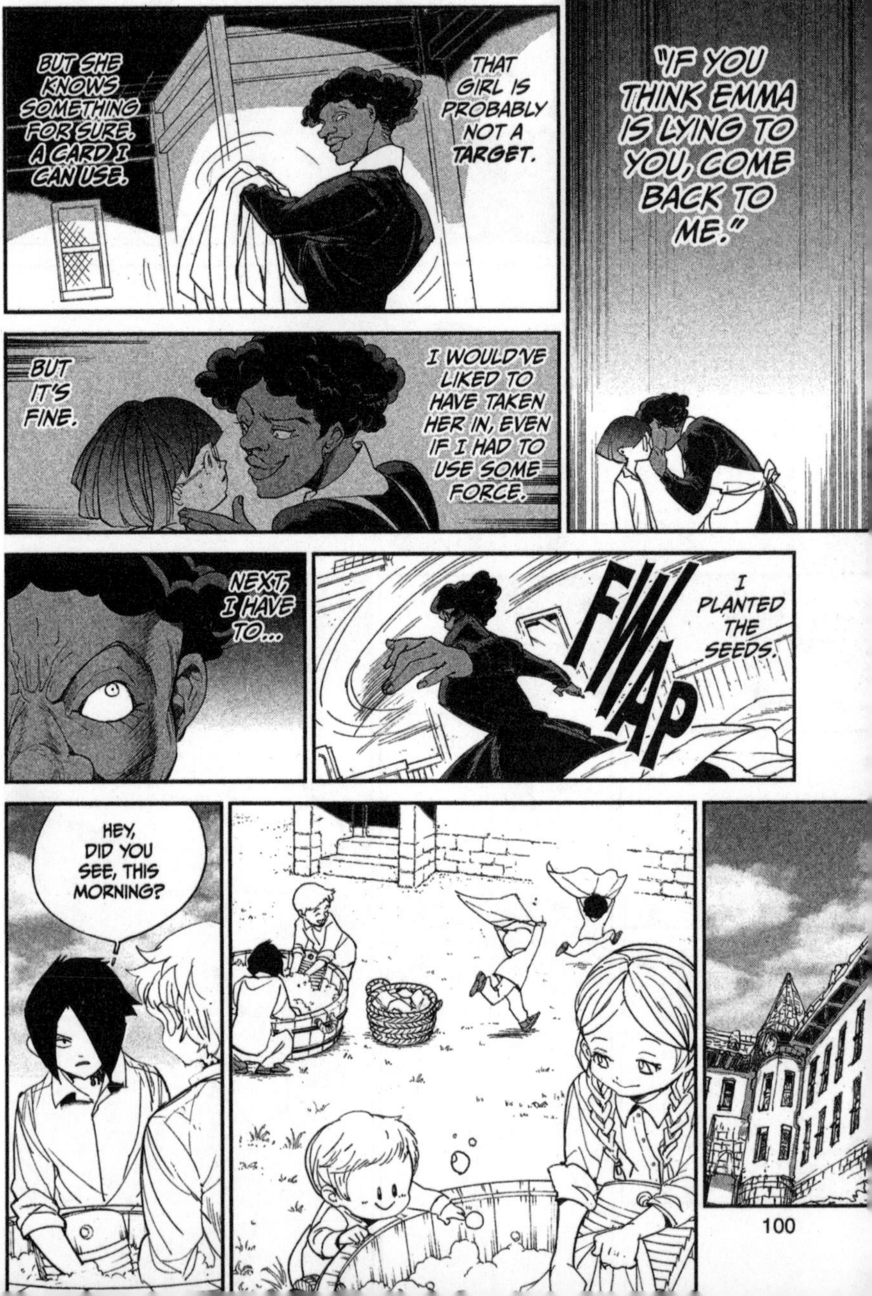
"IF YOU THINK EMMA IS LYING TO YOU, COME BACK TO ME."
THAT GIRL IS PROBABLY NOT A TARGET.
BUT SHE KNOWS SOMETHING FOR SURE. A CARD I CAN USE.
I WOULD'VE LIKED TO HAVE TAKEN HER IN, EVEN IF I HAD TO USE SOME FORCE.
BUT IT'S FINE.
I PLANTED THE SEEDS.
FWAP
NEXT, I HAVE TO...
HEY, DID YOU SEE, THIS MORNING?

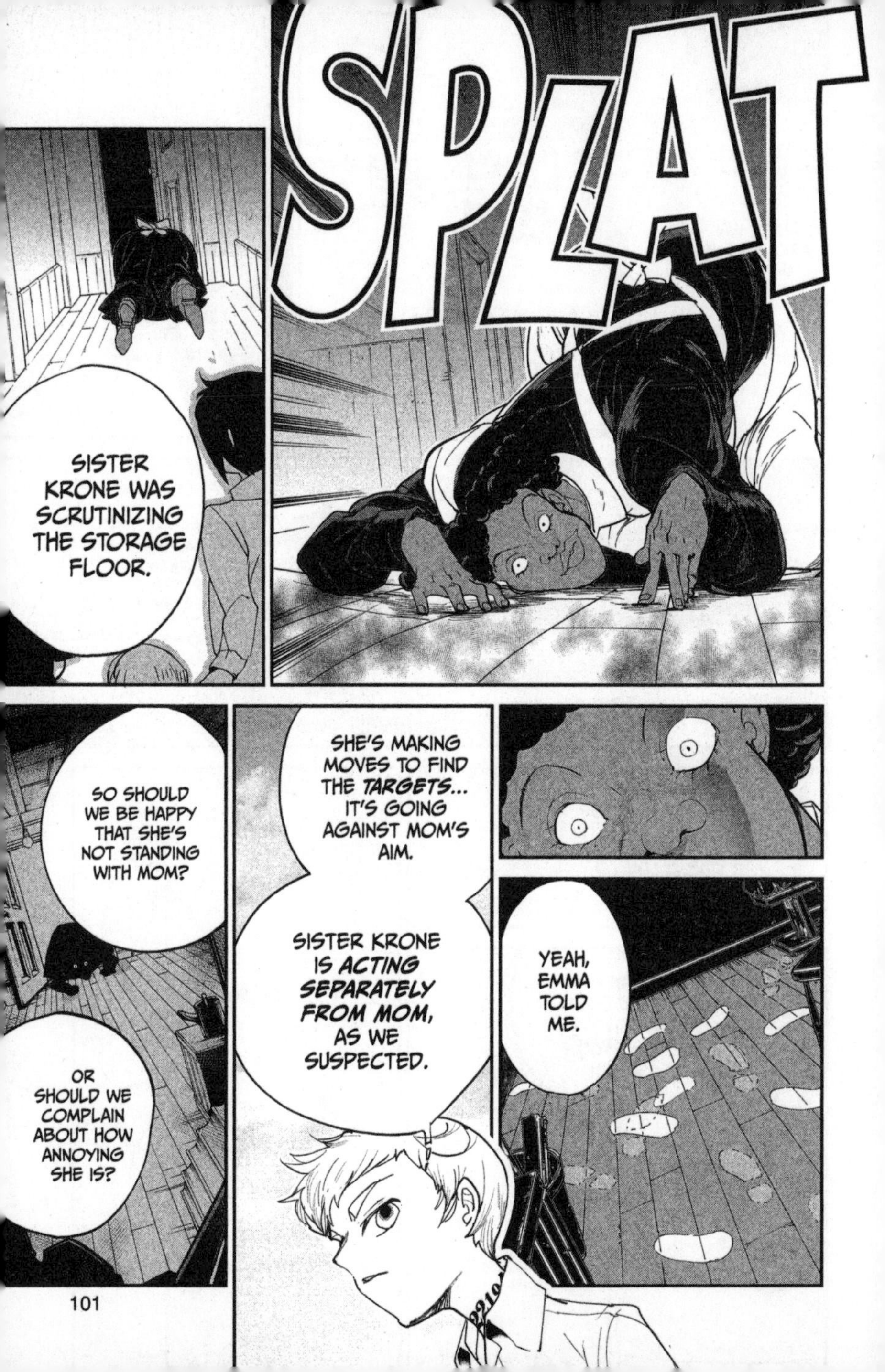
SPLAT
SISTER KRONE WAS SCRUTINIZING THE STORAGE FLOOR.
YEAH, EMMA TOLD ME.
SHE'S MAKING MOVES TO FIND THE *TARGETS*... IT'S GOING AGAINST MOM'S AIM.
SISTER KRONE IS *ACTING SEPARATELY FROM MOM*, AS WE SUSPECTED.
SO SHOULD WE BE HAPPY THAT SHE'S NOT STANDING WITH MOM?
OR SHOULD WE COMPLAIN ABOUT HOW ANNOYING SHE IS?

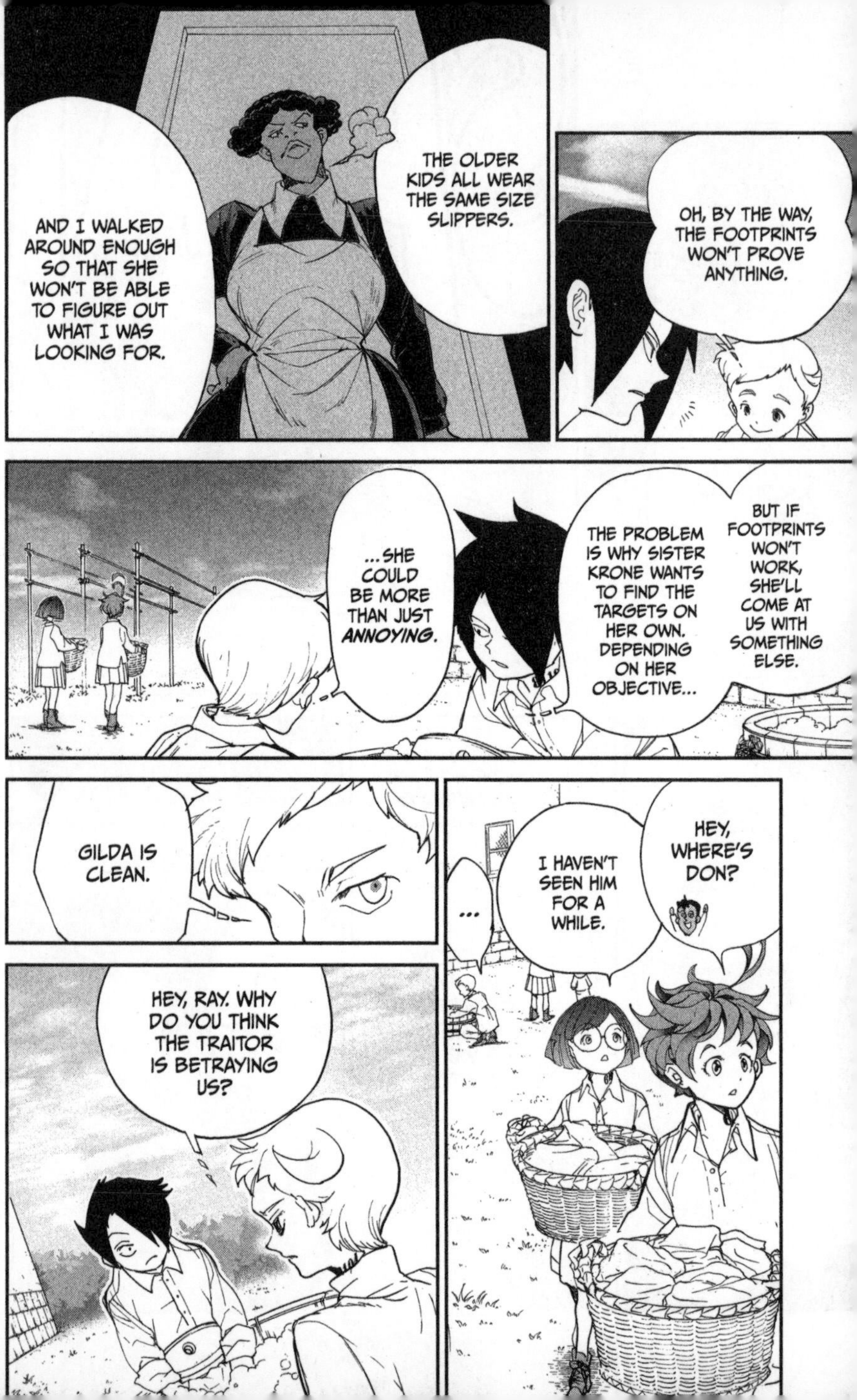
OH, BY THE WAY, THE FOOTPRINTS WON'T PROVE ANYTHING.
THE OLDER KIDS ALL WEAR THE SAME SIZE SLIPPERS.
AND I WALKED AROUND ENOUGH SO THAT SHE WON'T BE ABLE TO FIGURE OUT WHAT I WAS LOOKING FOR.
BUT IF FOOTPRINTS WON'T WORK, SHE'LL COME AT US WITH SOMETHING ELSE.
THE PROBLEM IS WHY SISTER KRONE WANTS TO FIND THE TARGETS ON HER OWN. DEPENDING ON HER OBJECTIVE...
...SHE COULD BE MORE THAN JUST *ANNOYING*.
HEY, WHERE'S DON?
I HAVEN'T SEEN HIM FOR A WHILE.
...
GILDA IS CLEAN.
HEY, RAY. WHY DO YOU THINK THE TRAITOR IS BETRAYING US?

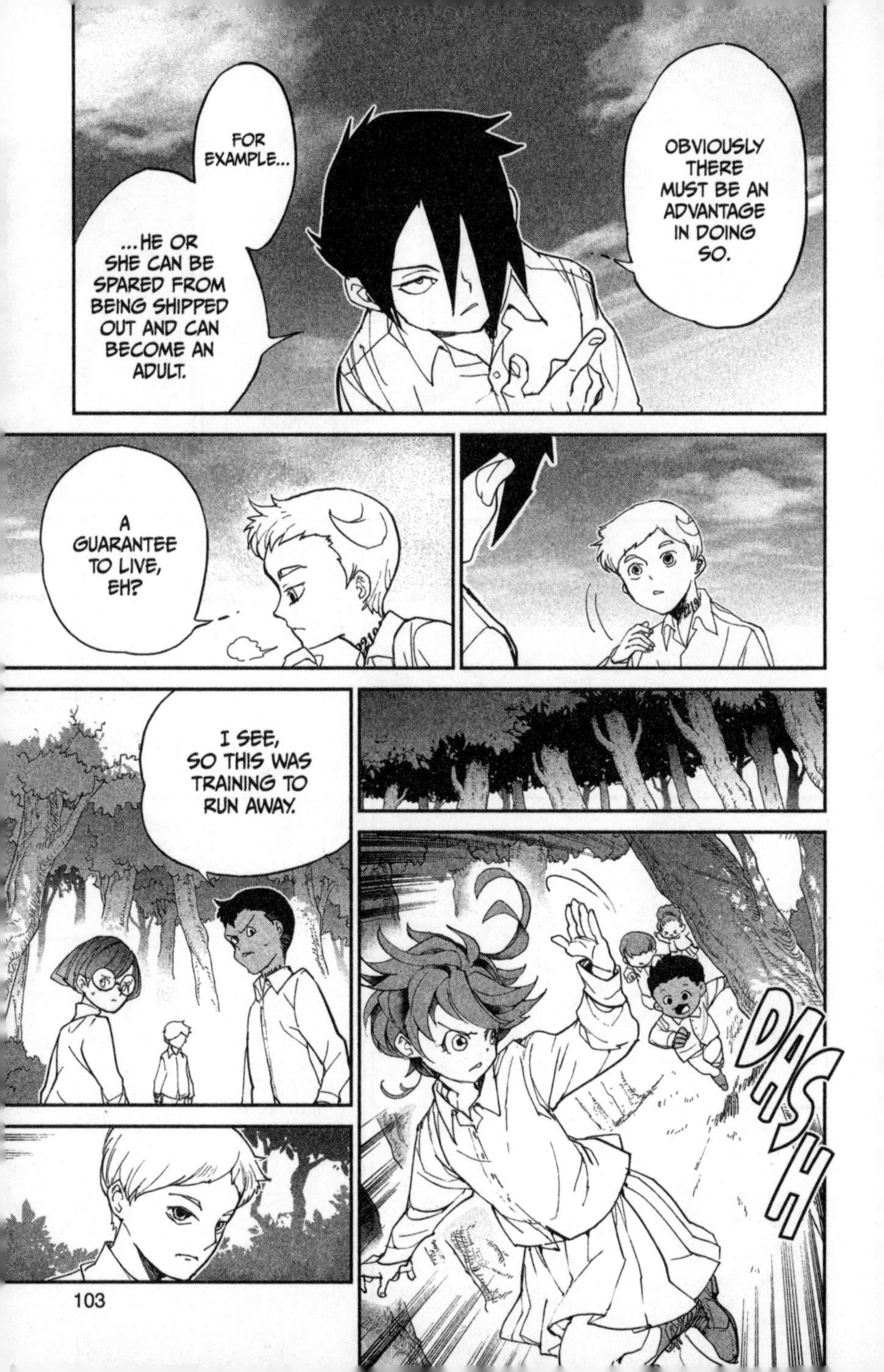
OBVIOUSLY THERE MUST BE AN ADVANTAGE IN DOING SO.
FOR EXAMPLE...
...HE OR SHE CAN BE SPARED FROM BEING SHIPPED OUT AND CAN BECOME AN ADULT.
A GUARANTEE TO LIVE, EH?
DASHH
I SEE, SO THIS WAS TRAINING TO RUN AWAY.

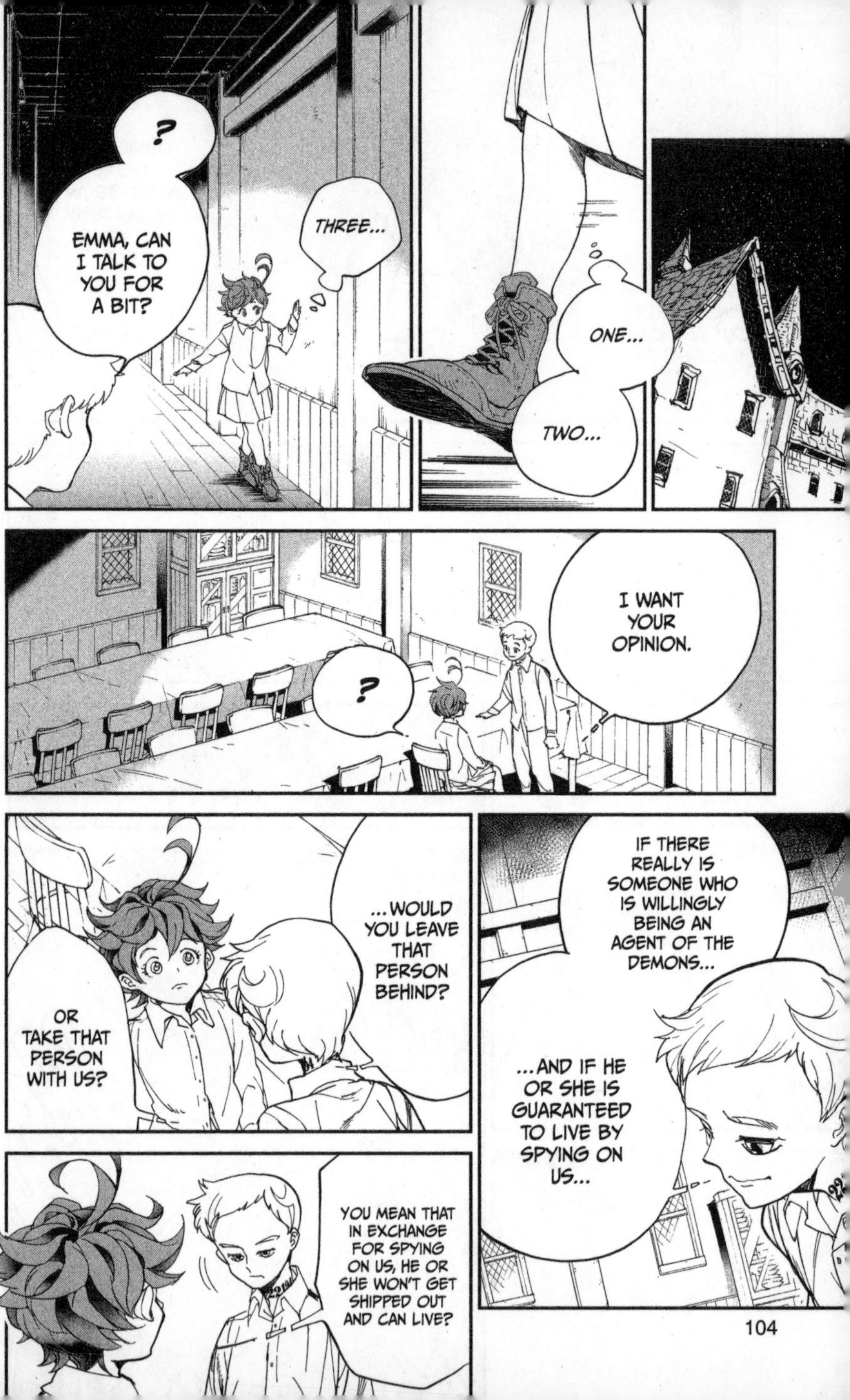
ONE...
TWO...
THREE...
?
EMMA, CAN I TALK TO YOU FOR A BIT?
I WANT YOUR OPINION.
?
IF THERE REALLY IS SOMEONE WHO IS WILLINGLY BEING AN AGENT OF THE DEMONS...
...AND IF HE OR SHE IS GUARANTEED TO LIVE BY SPYING ON US...
...WOULD YOU LEAVE THAT PERSON BEHIND?
OR TAKE THAT PERSON WITH US?
YOU MEAN THAT IN EXCHANGE FOR SPYING ON US, HE OR SHE WON'T GET SHIPPED OUT AND CAN LIVE?

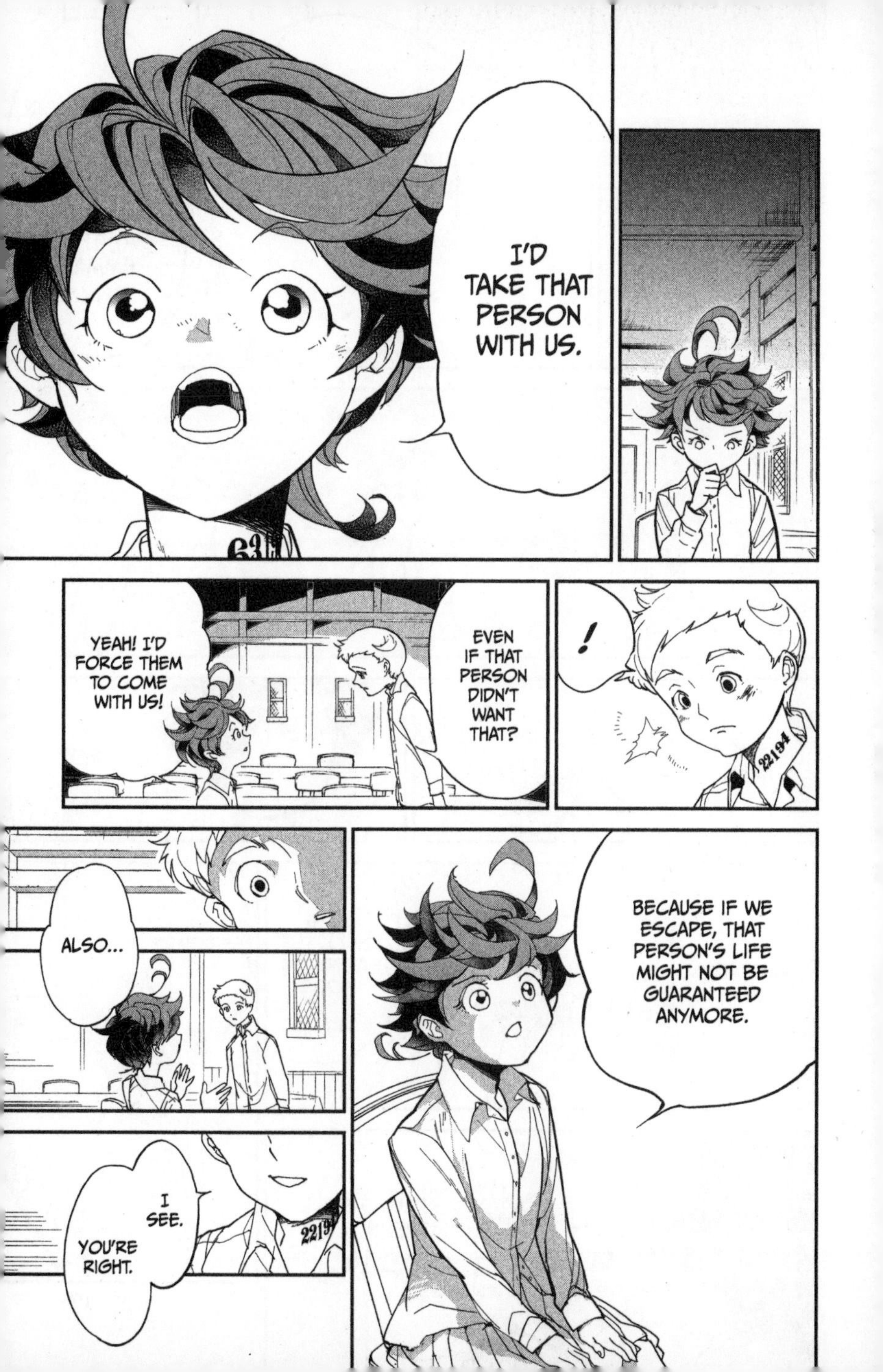
I'D TAKE THAT PERSON WITH US.
!
EVEN IF THAT PERSON DIDN'T WANT THAT?
YEAH! I'D FORCE THEM TO COME WITH US!
BECAUSE IF WE ESCAPE, THAT PERSON'S LIFE MIGHT NOT BE GUARANTEED ANYMORE.
ALSO...
I SEE.
YOU'RE RIGHT.

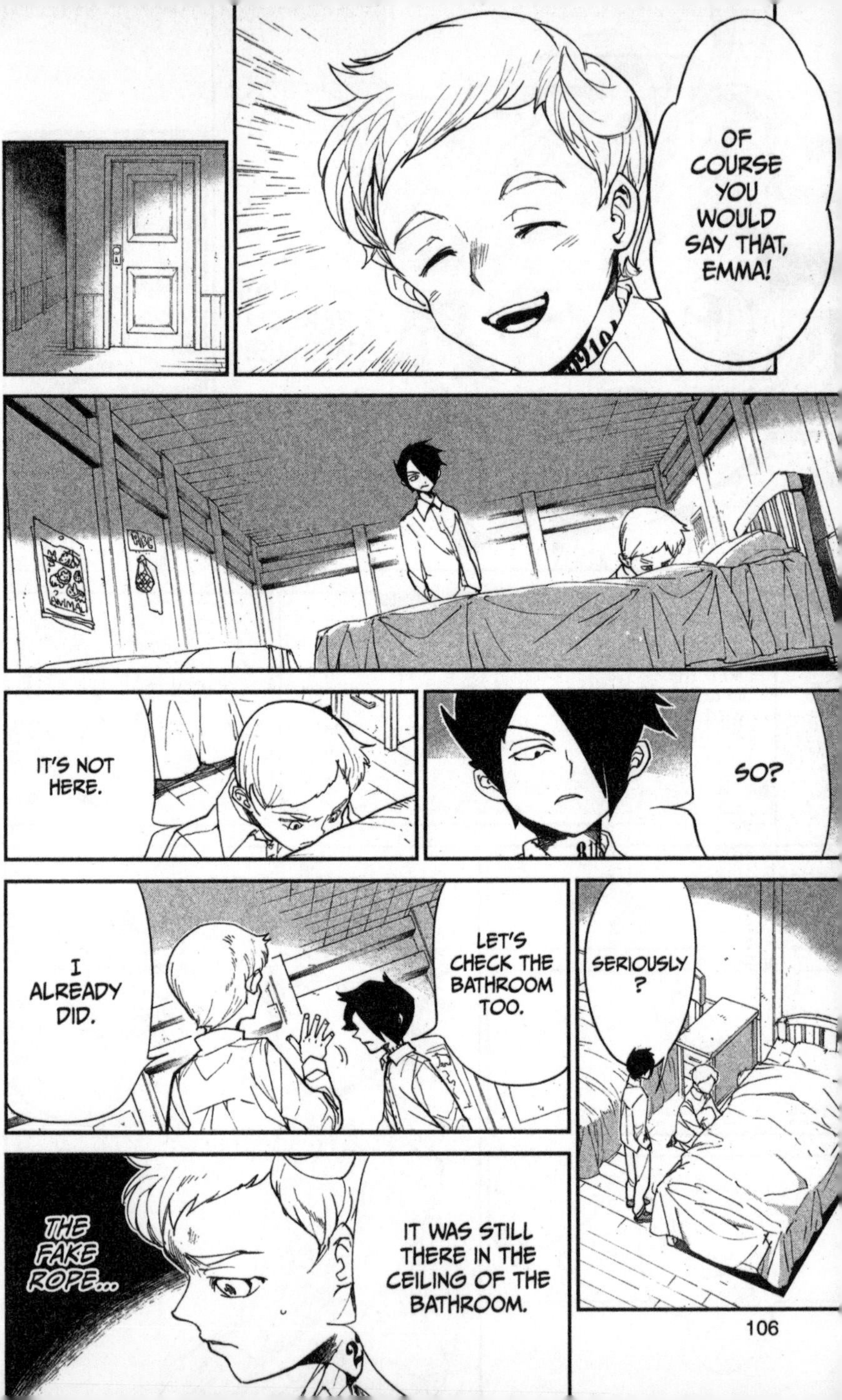
OF COURSE YOU WOULD SAY THAT, EMMA!
SO?
IT'S NOT HERE.
SERIOUSLY?
LET'S CHECK THE BATHROOM TOO.
I ALREADY DID.
IT WAS STILL THERE IN THE CEILING OF THE BATHROOM.
THE FAKE ROPE...

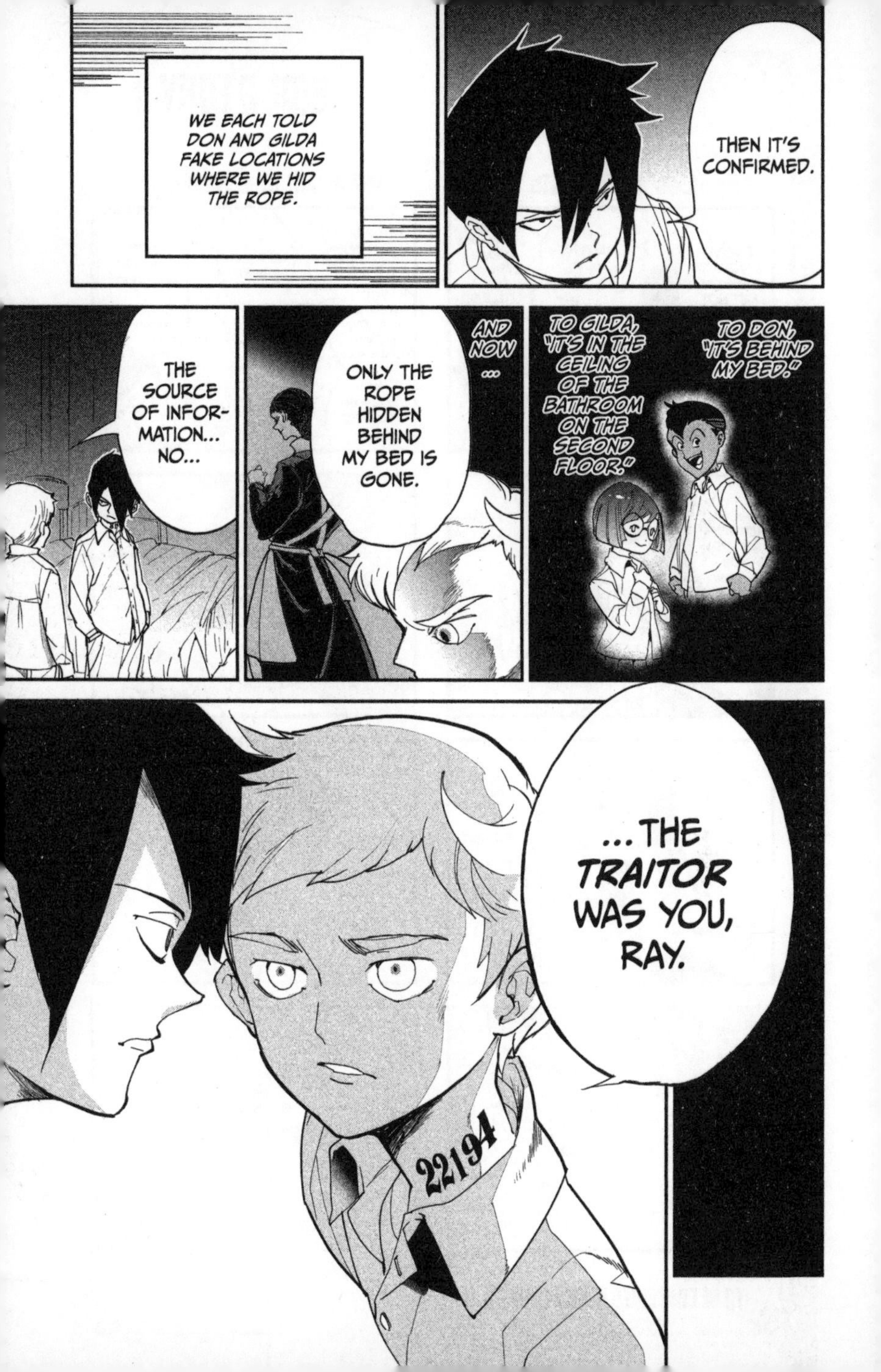
THEN IT'S CONFIRMED.
WE EACH TOLD DON AND GILDA FAKE LOCATIONS WHERE WE HID THE ROPE.
TO DON, "IT'S BEHIND MY BED."
TO GILDA, "IT'S IN THE CEILING OF THE BATHROOM ON THE SECOND FLOOR."
AND NOW...
ONLY THE ROPE HIDDEN BEHIND MY BED IS GONE.
THE SOURCE OF INFORMATION... NO...
...THE TRAITOR WAS YOU, RAY.
22194

SIDE STORY 3

Let's Go Visit With All the Siblings

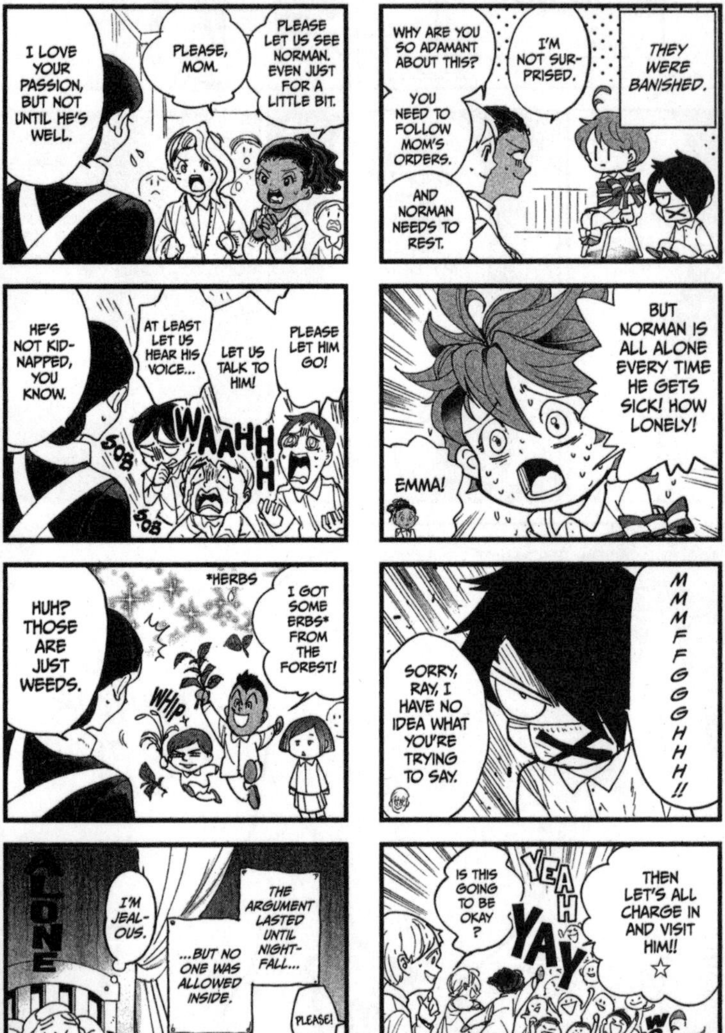
THEY WERE BANISHED.
I'M NOT SURPRISED.
WHY ARE YOU SO ADAMANT ABOUT THIS?
YOU NEED TO FOLLOW MOM'S ORDERS.
AND NORMAN NEEDS TO REST.
BUT NORMAN IS ALL ALONE EVERY TIME HE GETS SICK! HOW LONELY!
EMMA!
MMMFFGGGHHH!!
SORRY, RAY, I HAVE NO IDEA WHAT YOU'RE TRYING TO SAY.
THEN LET'S ALL CHARGE IN AND VISIT HIM!! ☆
YEAH
YAY
IS THIS GOING TO BE OKAY?
WOO
PLEASE LET US SEE NORMAN. EVEN JUST FOR A LITTLE BIT.
PLEASE, MOM.
I LOVE YOUR PASSION, BUT NOT UNTIL HE'S WELL.
PLEASE LET HIM GO!
LET US TALK TO HIM!
AT LEAST LET US HEAR HIS VOICE...
WAAHHHH
HE'S NOT KIDNAPPED, YOU KNOW.
SOB
SOB
*HERBS
I GOT SOME ERBS* FROM THE FOREST!
WHIP
HUH? THOSE ARE JUST WEEDS.
THE ARGUMENT LASTED UNTIL NIGHTFALL...
...BUT NO ONE WAS ALLOWED INSIDE.
I'M JEALOUS.
PLEASE!
NO.
ALONE

TO BE CONTINUED IN SIDE STORY 4

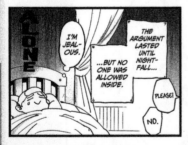

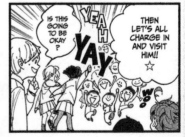

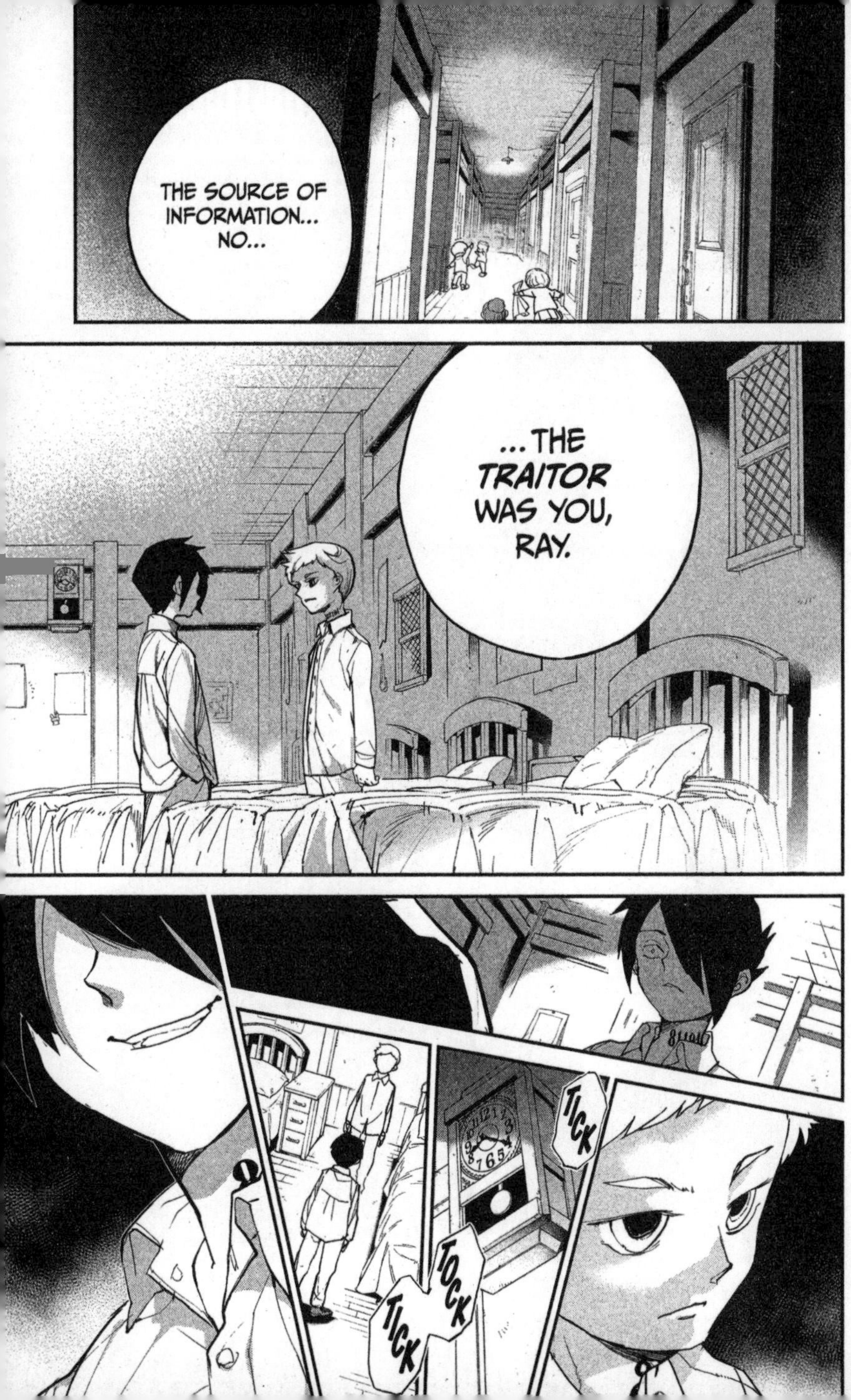
THE SOURCE OF INFORMATION... NO...
...THE TRAITOR WAS YOU, RAY.
TICK
TOCK
TICK

CHAPTER 13: TRAITOR, PART 3

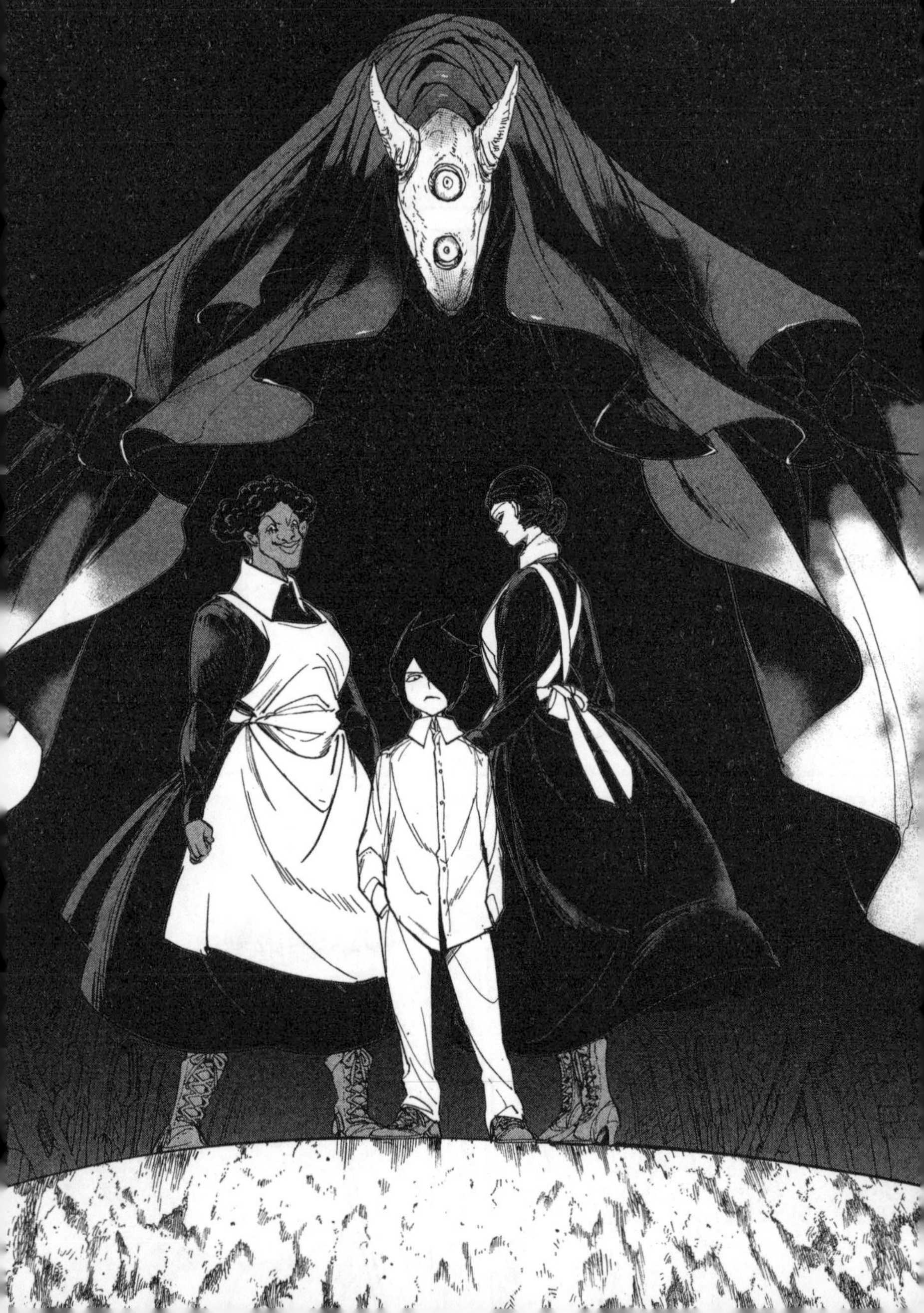

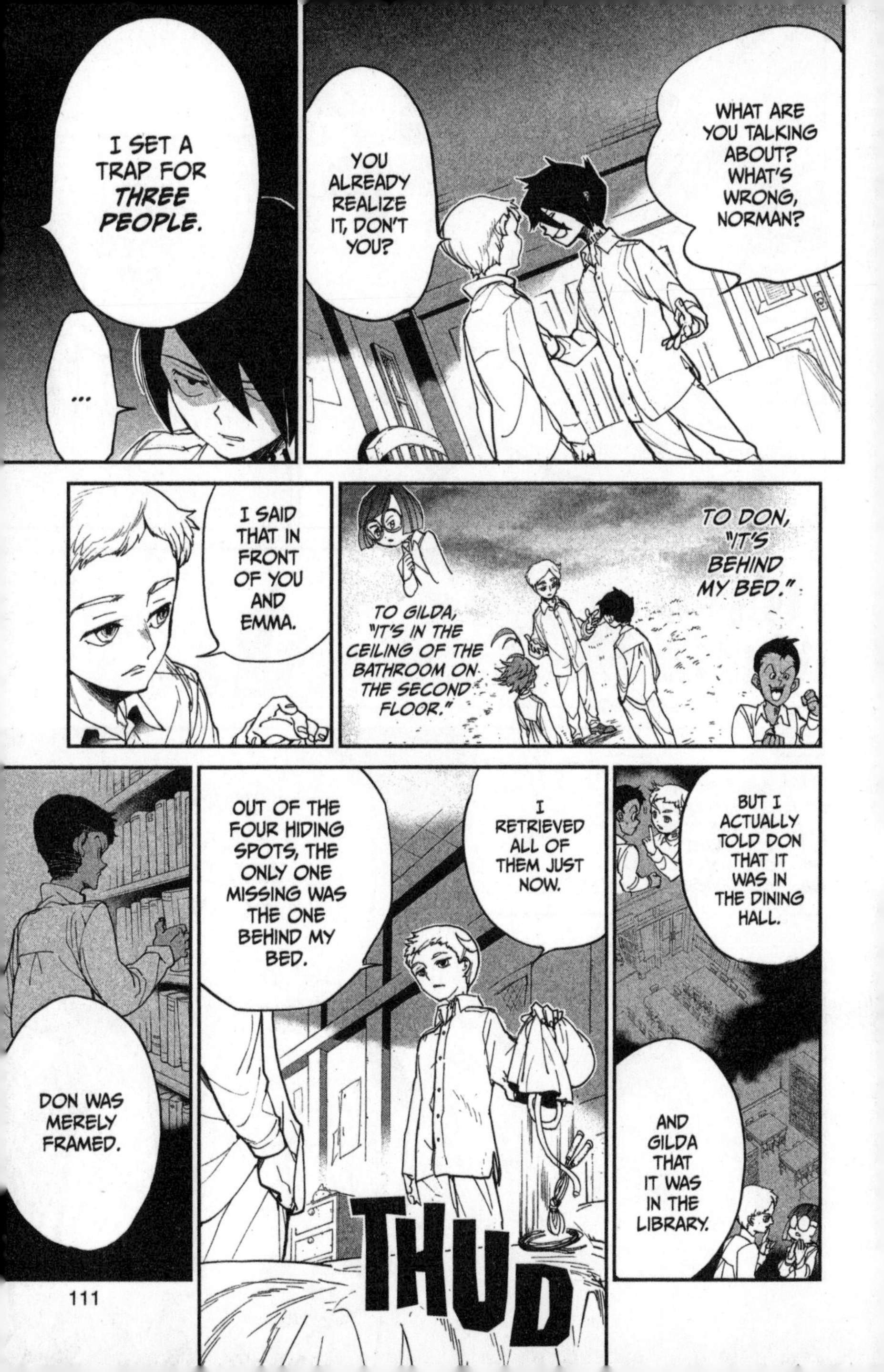
WHAT ARE YOU TALKING ABOUT? WHAT'S WRONG, NORMAN?
YOU ALREADY REALIZE IT, DON'T YOU?
I SET A TRAP FOR *THREE PEOPLE*.
...
TO DON, "IT'S BEHIND MY BED."
TO GILDA, "IT'S IN THE CEILING OF THE BATHROOM ON THE SECOND FLOOR."
I SAID THAT IN FRONT OF YOU AND EMMA.
BUT I ACTUALLY TOLD DON THAT IT WAS IN THE DINING HALL.
AND GILDA THAT IT WAS IN THE LIBRARY.
I RETRIEVED ALL OF THEM JUST NOW.
OUT OF THE FOUR HIDING SPOTS, THE ONLY ONE MISSING WAS THE ONE BEHIND MY BED.
THUD
DON WAS MERELY FRAMED.

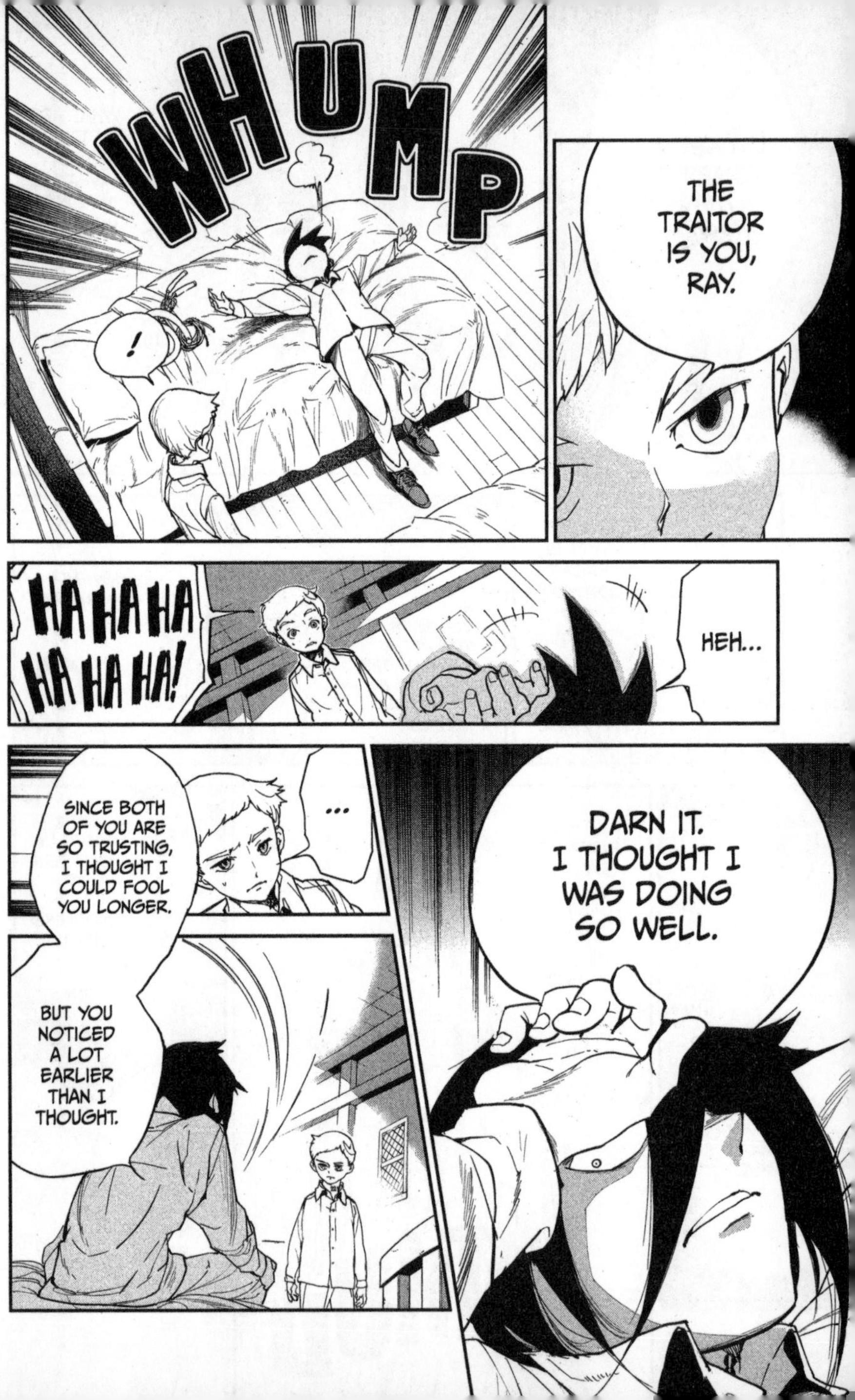
THE TRAITOR IS YOU, RAY.
WHUMP
!
HEH...
HA HA HA HA HA HA!
DARN IT. I THOUGHT I WAS DOING SO WELL.
...
SINCE BOTH OF YOU ARE SO TRUSTING, I THOUGHT I COULD FOOL YOU LONGER.
BUT YOU NOTICED A LOT EARLIER THAN I THOUGHT.

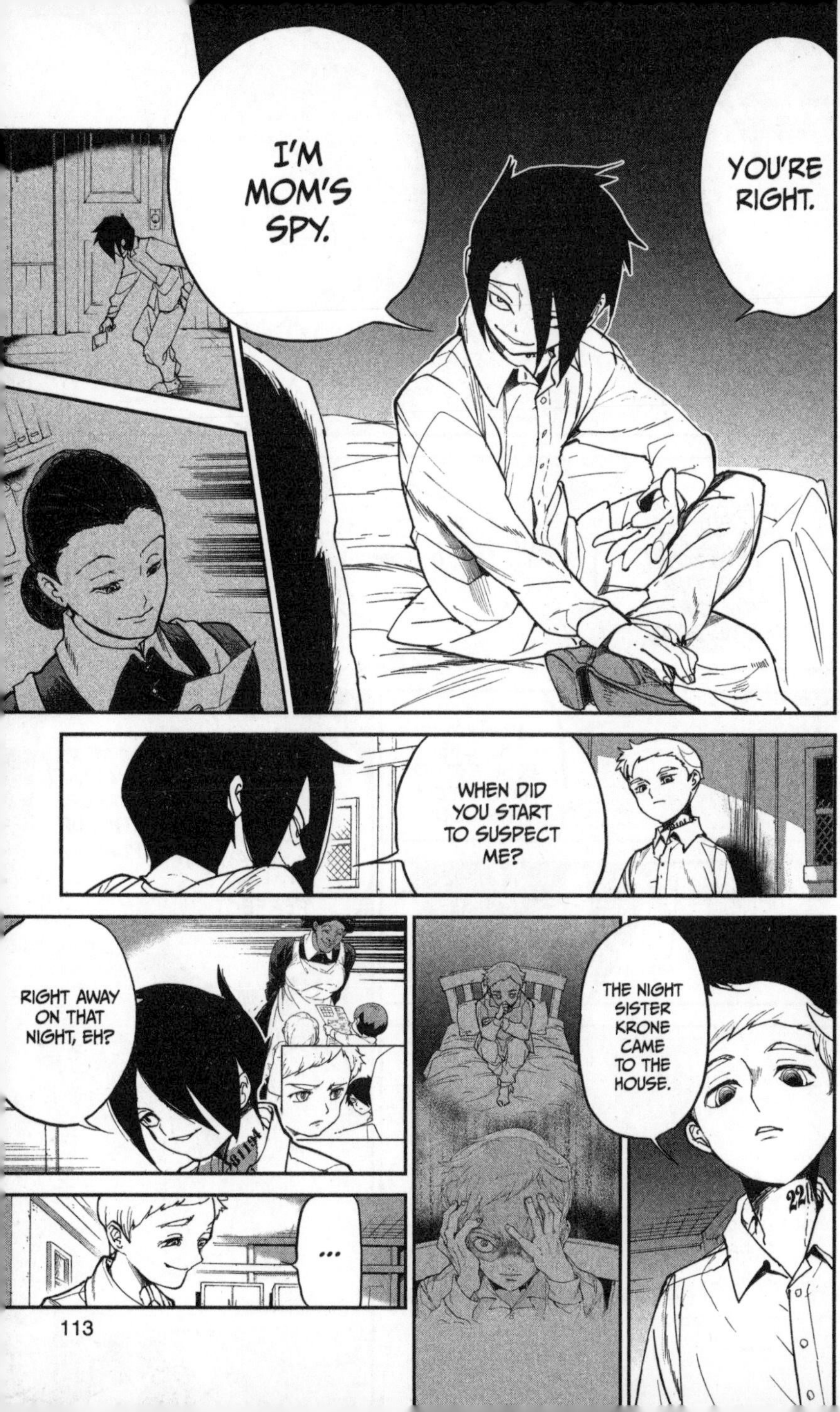
YOU'RE RIGHT.
I'M MOM'S SPY.
WHEN DID YOU START TO SUSPECT ME?
THE NIGHT SISTER KRONE CAME TO THE HOUSE.
RIGHT AWAY ON THAT NIGHT, EH?
...

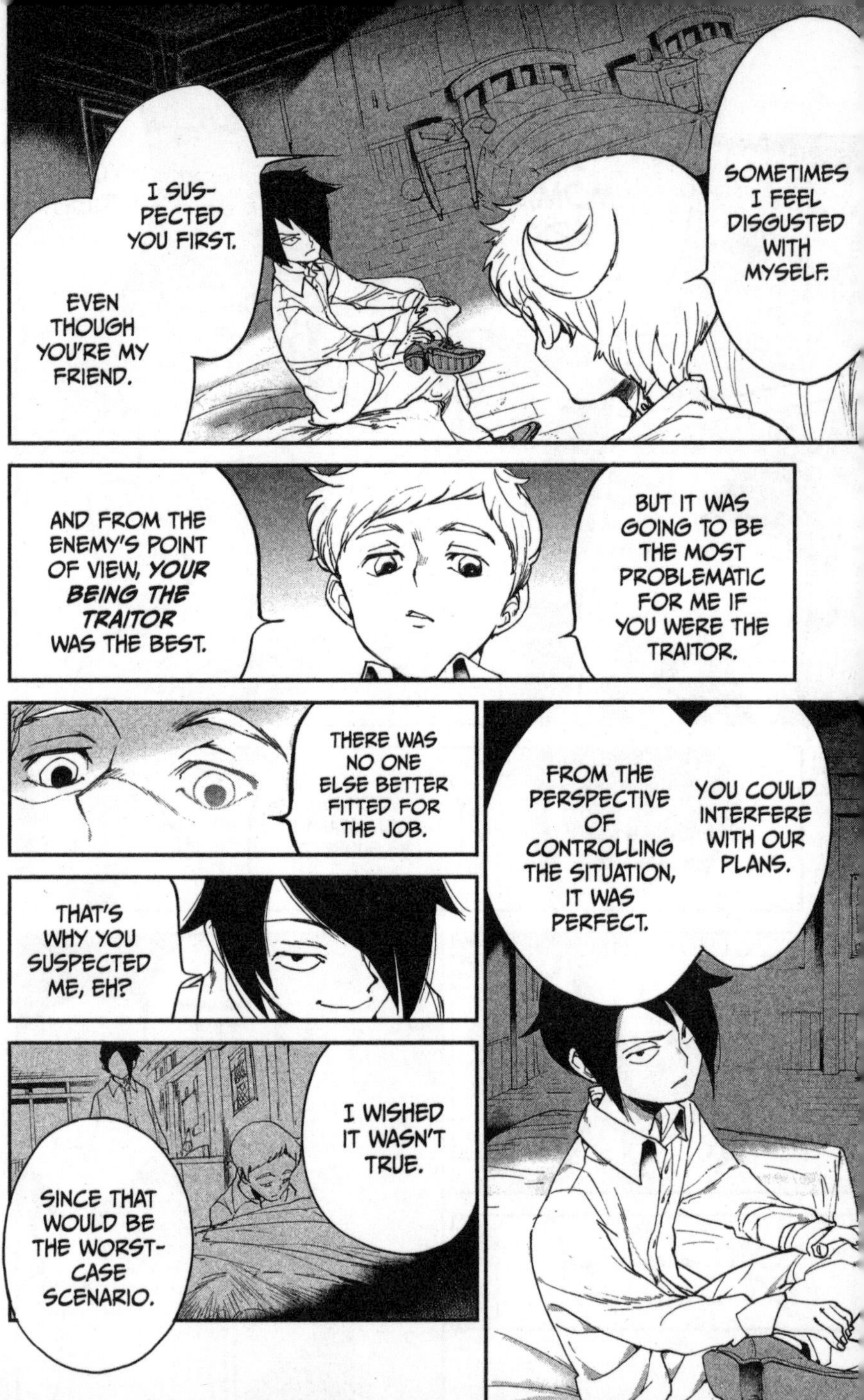
SOMETIMES I FEEL DISGUSTED WITH MYSELF.
I SUS-PECTED YOU FIRST.
EVEN THOUGH YOU'RE MY FRIEND.
BUT IT WAS GOING TO BE THE MOST PROBLEMATIC FOR ME IF YOU WERE THE TRAITOR.
AND FROM THE ENEMY'S POINT OF VIEW, *YOUR BEING THE TRAITOR* WAS THE BEST.
YOU COULD INTERFERE WITH OUR PLANS.
FROM THE PERSPECTIVE OF CONTROLLING THE SITUATION, IT WAS PERFECT.
THERE WAS NO ONE ELSE BETTER FITTED FOR THE JOB.
THAT'S WHY YOU SUSPECTED ME, EH?
I WISHED IT WASN'T TRUE.
SINCE THAT WOULD BE THE WORST-CASE SCENARIO.

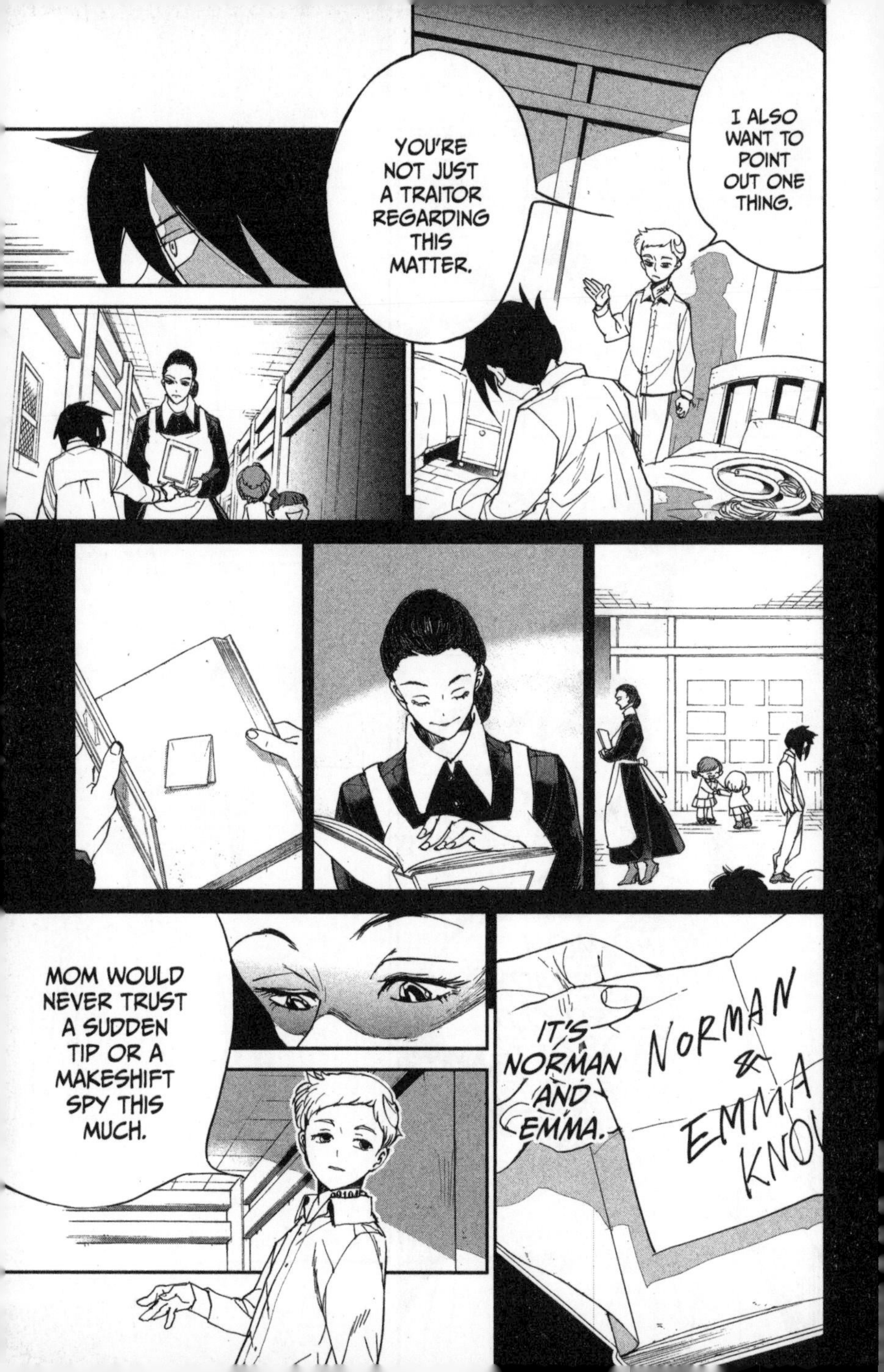
I ALSO WANT TO POINT OUT ONE THING.
YOU'RE NOT JUST A TRAITOR REGARDING THIS MATTER.
IT'S NORMAN AND EMMA.
NORMAN & EMMA
MOM WOULD NEVER TRUST A SUDDEN TIP OR A MAKESHIFT SPY THIS MUCH.

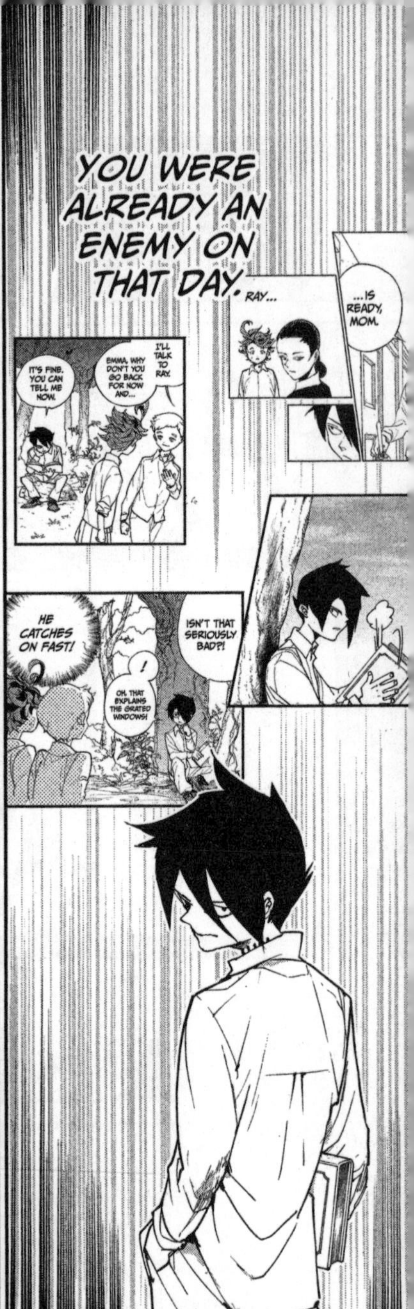
YOU WERE ALREADY AN ENEMY ON THAT DAY.
...IS READY, MOM.
RAY...
I'LL TALK TO RAY.
EMMA, WHY DON'T YOU GO BACK FOR NOW AND...
IT'S FINE. YOU CAN TELL ME NOW.
ISN'T THAT SERIOUSLY BAD?!
OH, THAT EXPLAINS THE GRATED WINDOWS!
HE CATCHES ON FAST!
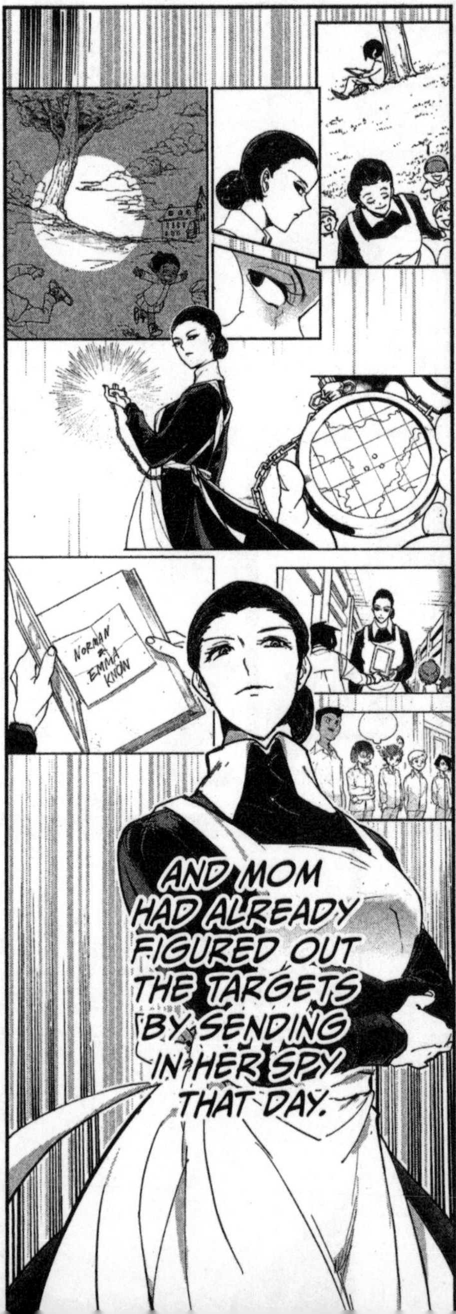
NORMAN & EMMA KNOW
AND MOM HAD ALREADY FIGURED OUT THE TARGETS BY SENDING IN HER SPY THAT DAY.

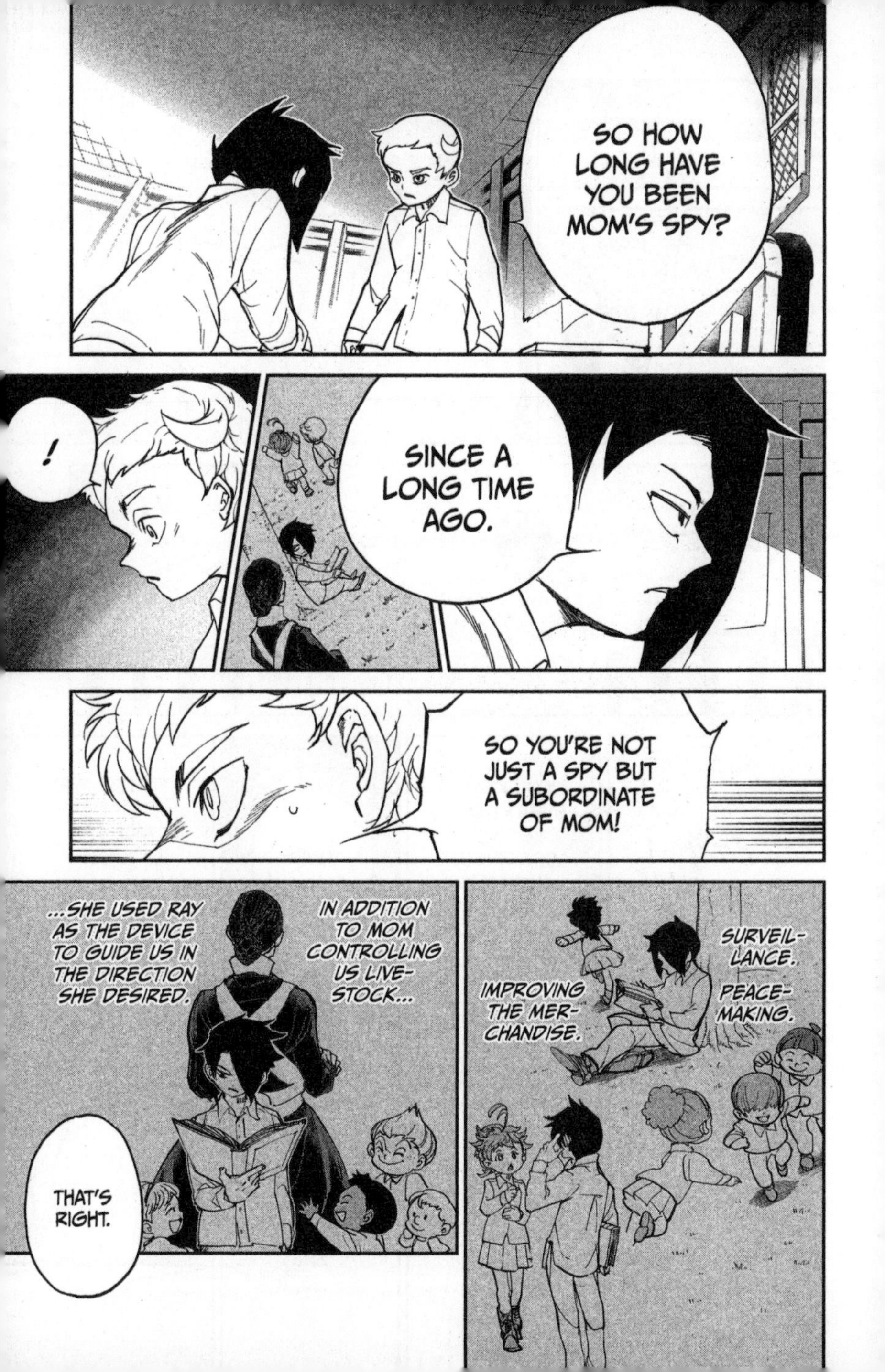
SO HOW LONG HAVE YOU BEEN MOM'S SPY?
SINCE A LONG TIME AGO.
!
SO YOU'RE NOT JUST A SPY BUT A SUBORDINATE OF MOM!
SURVEIL-LANCE.
PEACE-MAKING.
IMPROVING THE MER-CHANDISE.
IN ADDITION TO MOM CONTROLLING US LIVE-STOCK...
...SHE USED RAY AS THE DEVICE TO GUIDE US IN THE DIRECTION SHE DESIRED.
THAT'S RIGHT.

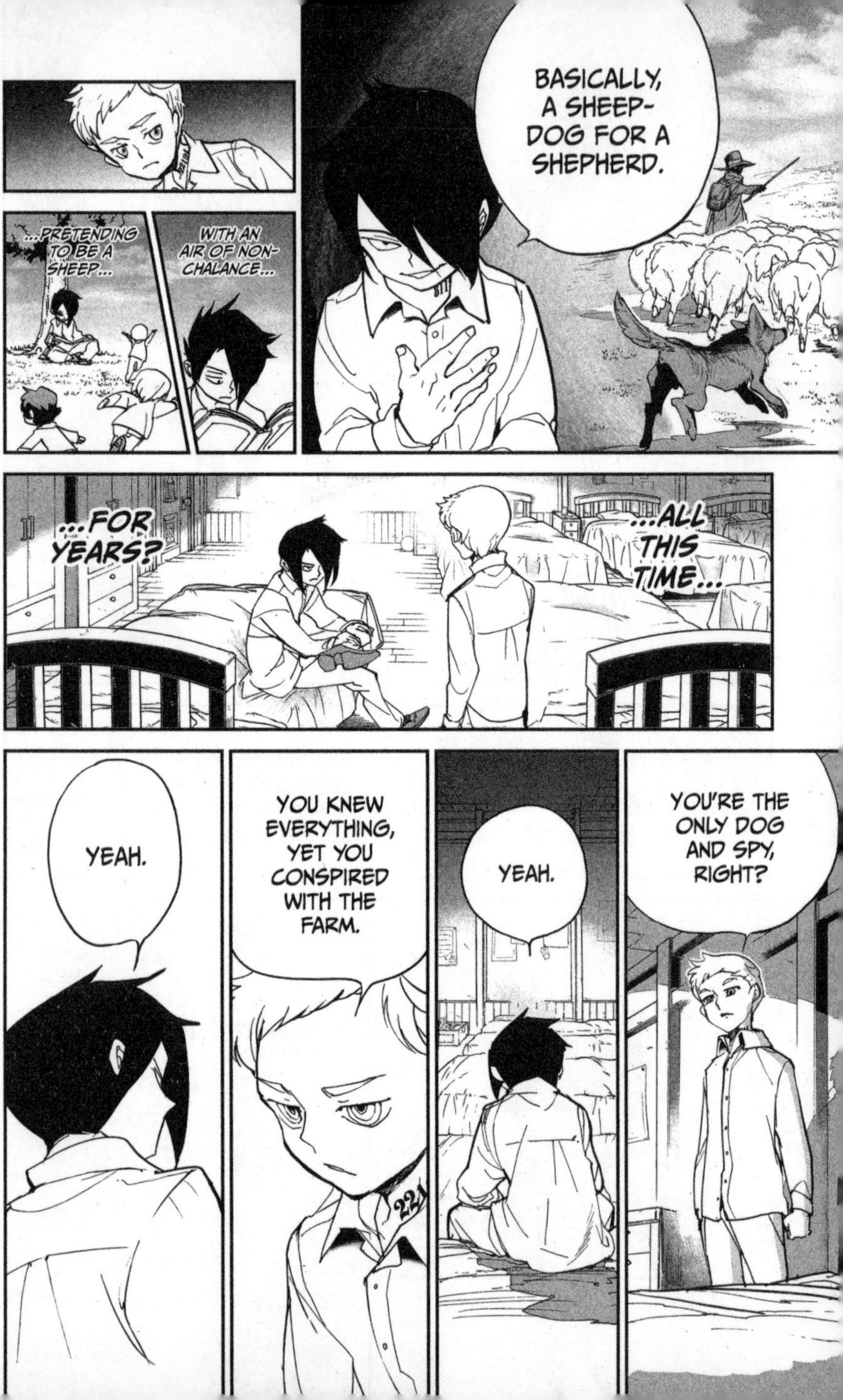
BASICALLY, A SHEEP-DOG FOR A SHEPHERD.
WITH AN AIR OF NON-CHALANCE...
...PRETENDING TO BE A SHEEP...
...ALL THIS TIME...
...FOR YEARS?
YOU'RE THE ONLY DOG AND SPY, RIGHT?
YEAH.
YOU KNEW EVERYTHING, YET YOU CONSPIRED WITH THE FARM.
YEAH.

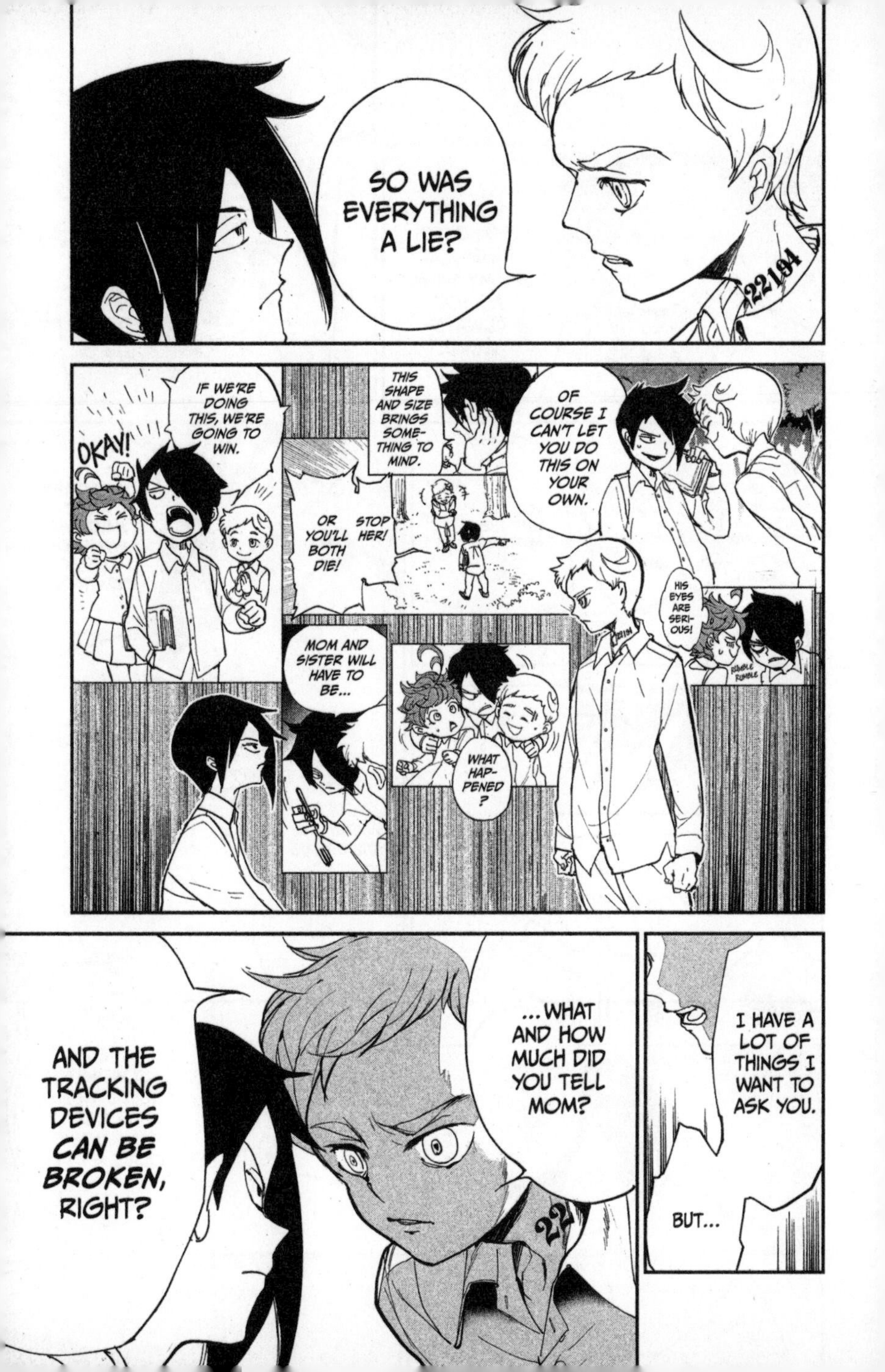
SO WAS EVERYTHING A LIE?
22194
OF COURSE I CAN'T LET YOU DO THIS ON YOUR OWN.
THIS SHAPE AND SIZE BRINGS SOMETHING TO MIND.
STOP HER!
OR YOU'LL BOTH DIE!
IF WE'RE DOING THIS, WE'RE GOING TO WIN.
OKAY!
HIS EYES ARE SERIOUS!
RUMBLE RUMBLE
WHAT HAPPENED?
MOM AND SISTER WILL HAVE TO BE...
I HAVE A LOT OF THINGS I WANT TO ASK YOU.
BUT...
...WHAT AND HOW MUCH DID YOU TELL MOM?
AND THE TRACKING DEVICES CAN BE BROKEN, RIGHT?

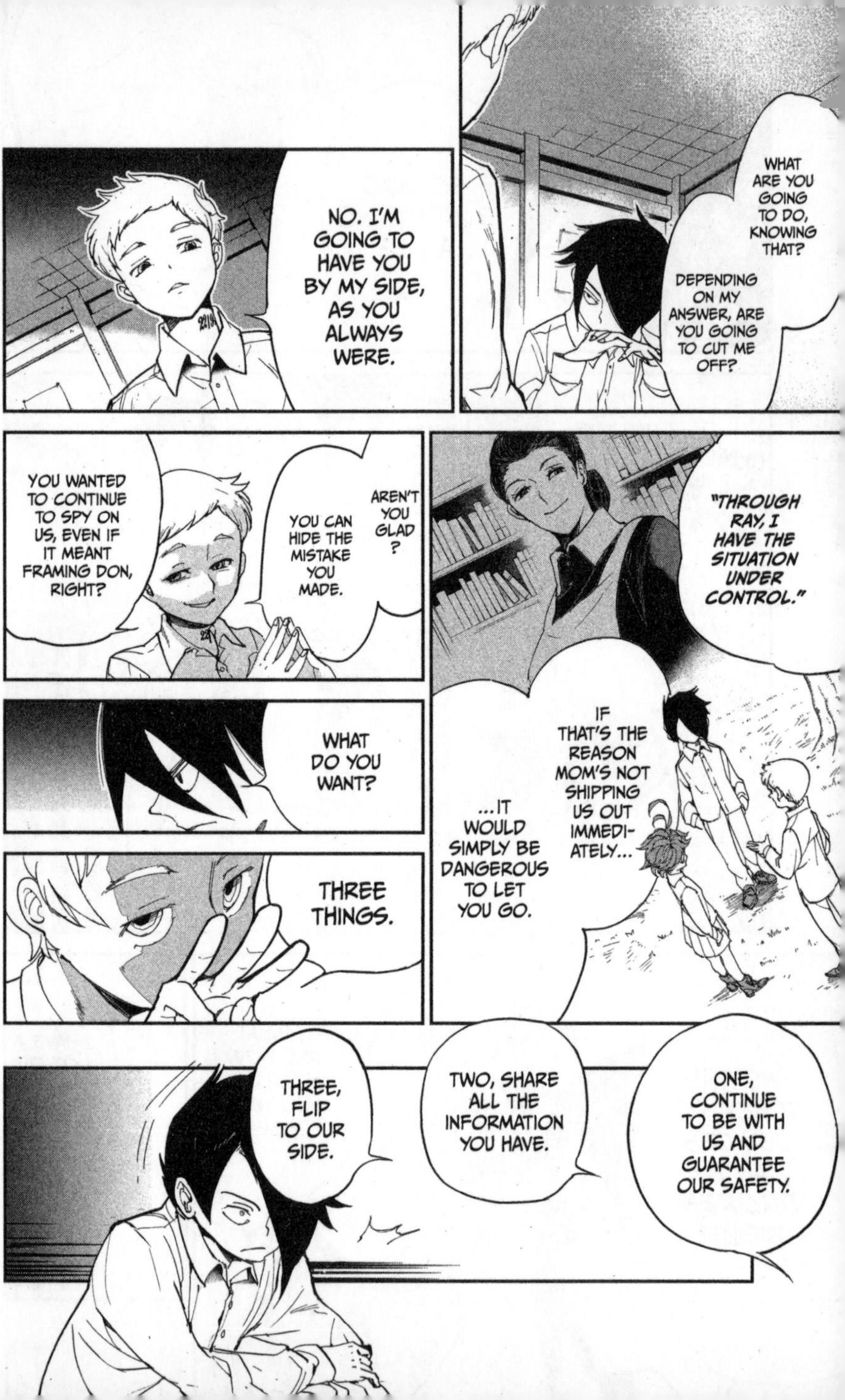
WHAT ARE YOU GOING TO DO, KNOWING THAT?
DEPENDING ON MY ANSWER, ARE YOU GOING TO CUT ME OFF?
NO. I'M GOING TO HAVE YOU BY MY SIDE, AS YOU ALWAYS WERE.
"THROUGH RAY, I HAVE THE SITUATION UNDER CONTROL."
IF THAT'S THE REASON MOM'S NOT SHIPPING US OUT IMMEDIATELY...
...IT WOULD SIMPLY BE DANGEROUS TO LET YOU GO.
AREN'T YOU GLAD?
YOU CAN HIDE THE MISTAKE YOU MADE.
YOU WANTED TO CONTINUE TO SPY ON US, EVEN IF IT MEANT FRAMING DON, RIGHT?
WHAT DO YOU WANT?
THREE THINGS.
ONE, CONTINUE TO BE WITH US AND GUARANTEE OUR SAFETY.
TWO, SHARE ALL THE INFORMATION YOU HAVE.
THREE, FLIP TO OUR SIDE.

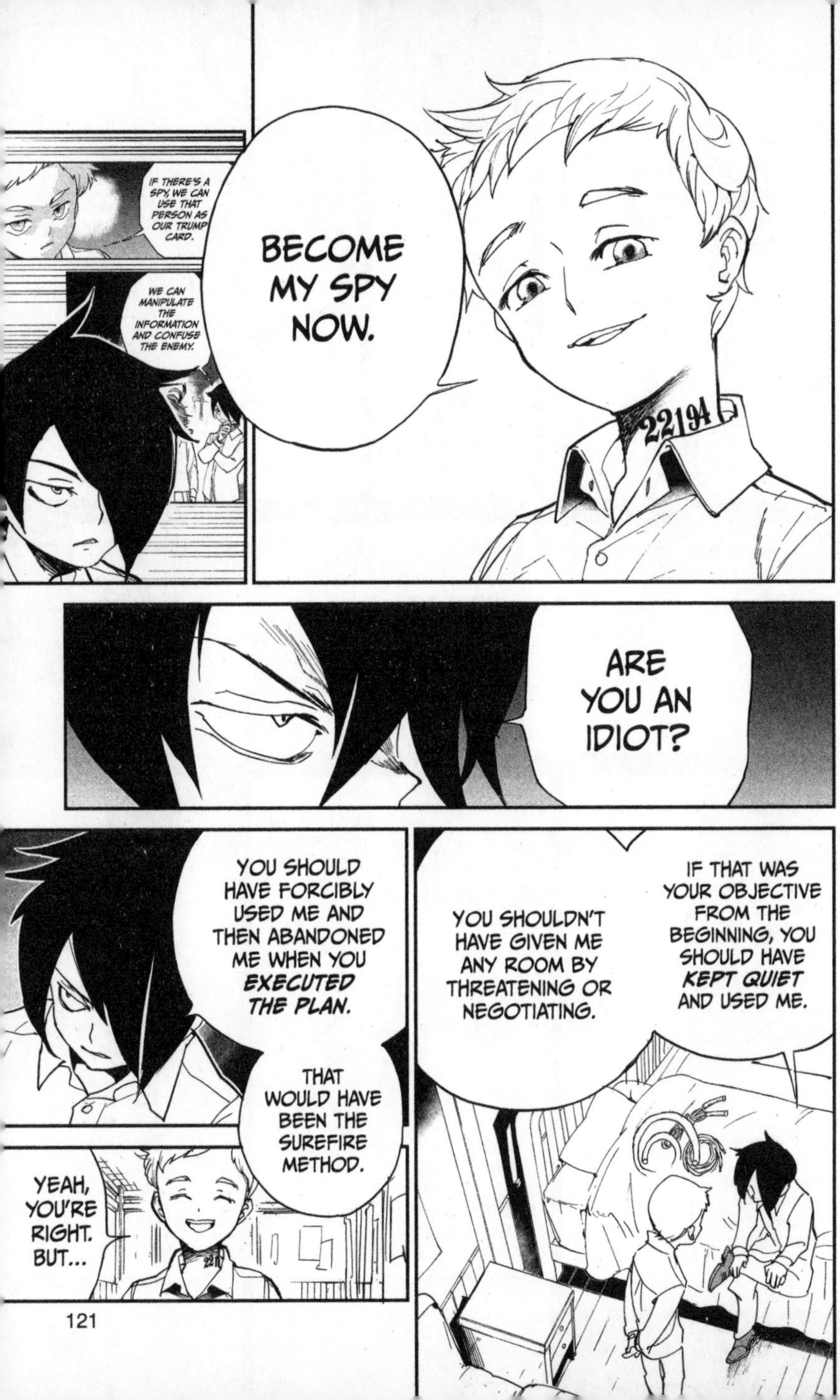
BECOME MY SPY NOW.
IF THERE'S A SPY, WE CAN USE THAT PERSON AS OUR TRUMP CARD.
WE CAN MANIPULATE THE INFORMATION AND CONFUSE THE ENEMY.
ARE YOU AN IDIOT?
IF THAT WAS YOUR OBJECTIVE FROM THE BEGINNING, YOU SHOULD HAVE *KEPT QUIET* AND USED ME.
YOU SHOULDN'T HAVE GIVEN ME ANY ROOM BY THREATENING OR NEGOTIATING.
YOU SHOULD HAVE FORCIBLY USED ME AND THEN ABANDONED ME WHEN YOU *EXECUTED THE PLAN.*
THAT WOULD HAVE BEEN THE SUREFIRE METHOD.
YEAH, YOU'RE RIGHT. BUT...

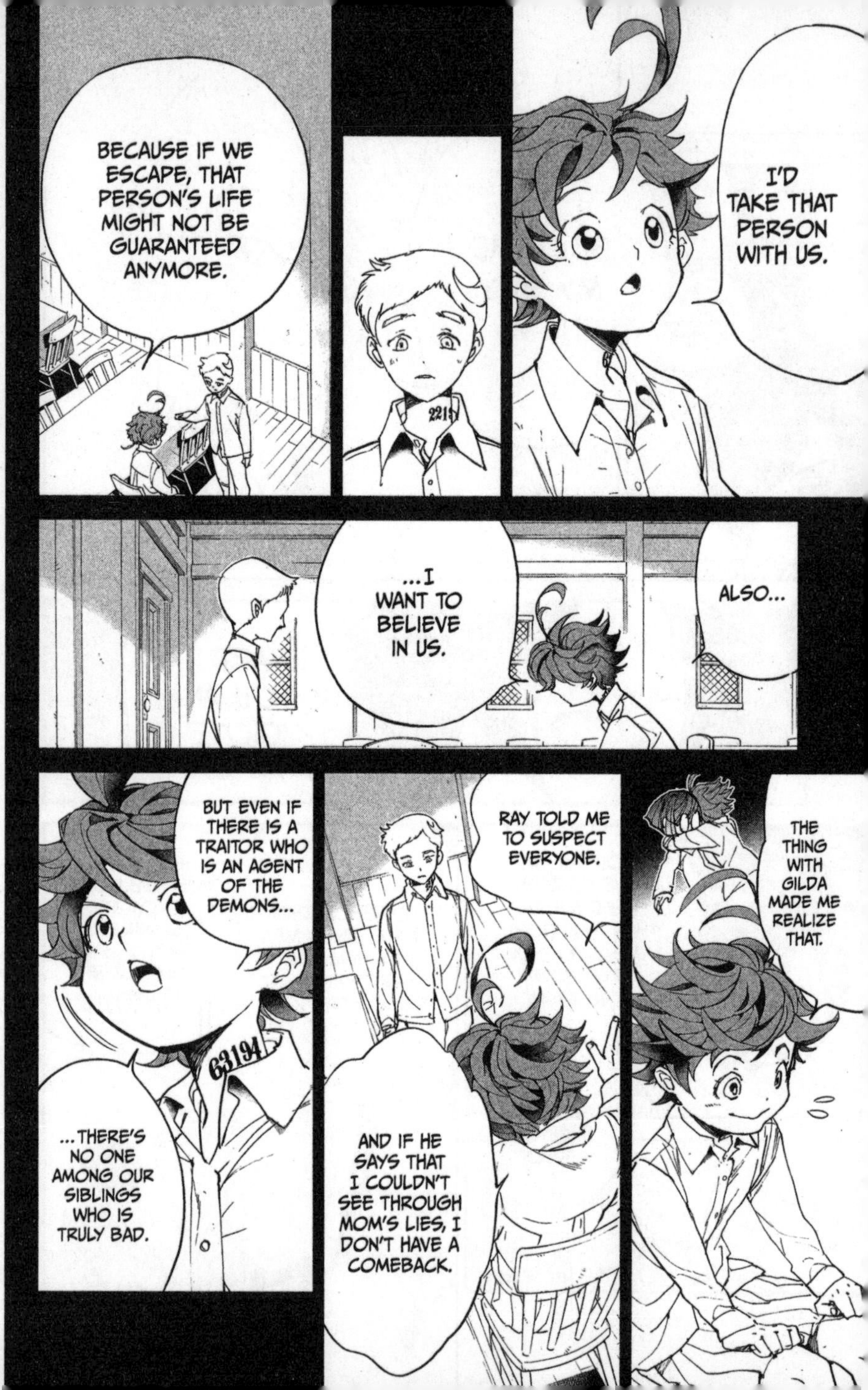
I'D TAKE THAT PERSON WITH US.
BECAUSE IF WE ESCAPE, THAT PERSON'S LIFE MIGHT NOT BE GUARANTEED ANYMORE.
ALSO...
...I WANT TO BELIEVE IN US.
THE THING WITH GILDA MADE ME REALIZE THAT.
RAY TOLD ME TO SUSPECT EVERYONE.
AND IF HE SAYS THAT I COULDN'T SEE THROUGH MOM'S LIES, I DON'T HAVE A COMEBACK.
BUT EVEN IF THERE IS A TRAITOR WHO IS AN AGENT OF THE DEMONS...
63194
...THERE'S NO ONE AMONG OUR SIBLINGS WHO IS TRULY BAD.

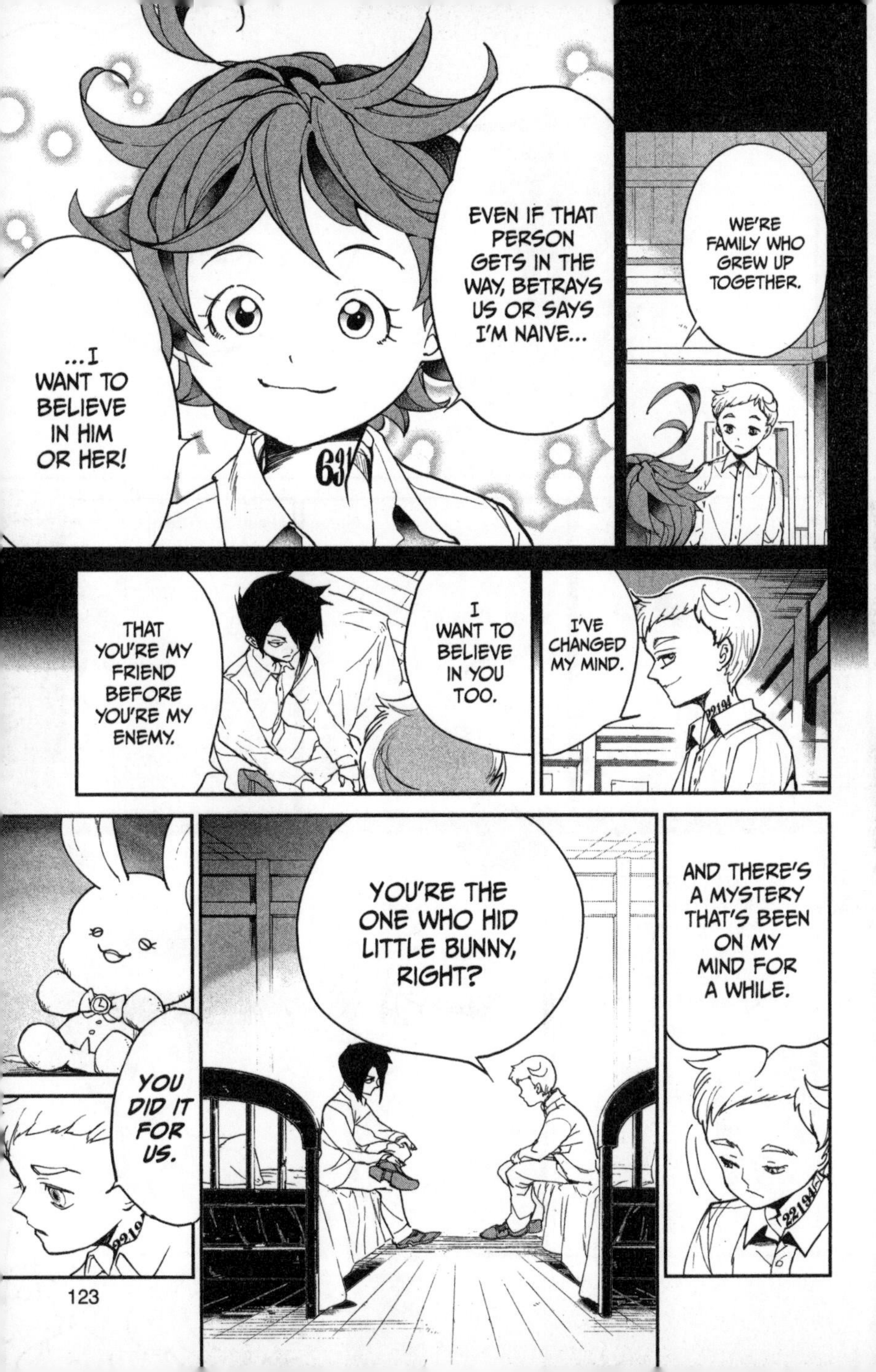
WE'RE FAMILY WHO GREW UP TOGETHER.
EVEN IF THAT PERSON GETS IN THE WAY, BETRAYS US OR SAYS I'M NAIVE...
...I WANT TO BELIEVE IN HIM OR HER!
I'VE CHANGED MY MIND.
I WANT TO BELIEVE IN YOU TOO.
THAT YOU'RE MY FRIEND BEFORE YOU'RE MY ENEMY.
AND THERE'S A MYSTERY THAT'S BEEN ON MY MIND FOR A WHILE.
YOU'RE THE ONE WHO HID LITTLE BUNNY, RIGHT?
YOU DID IT FOR US.

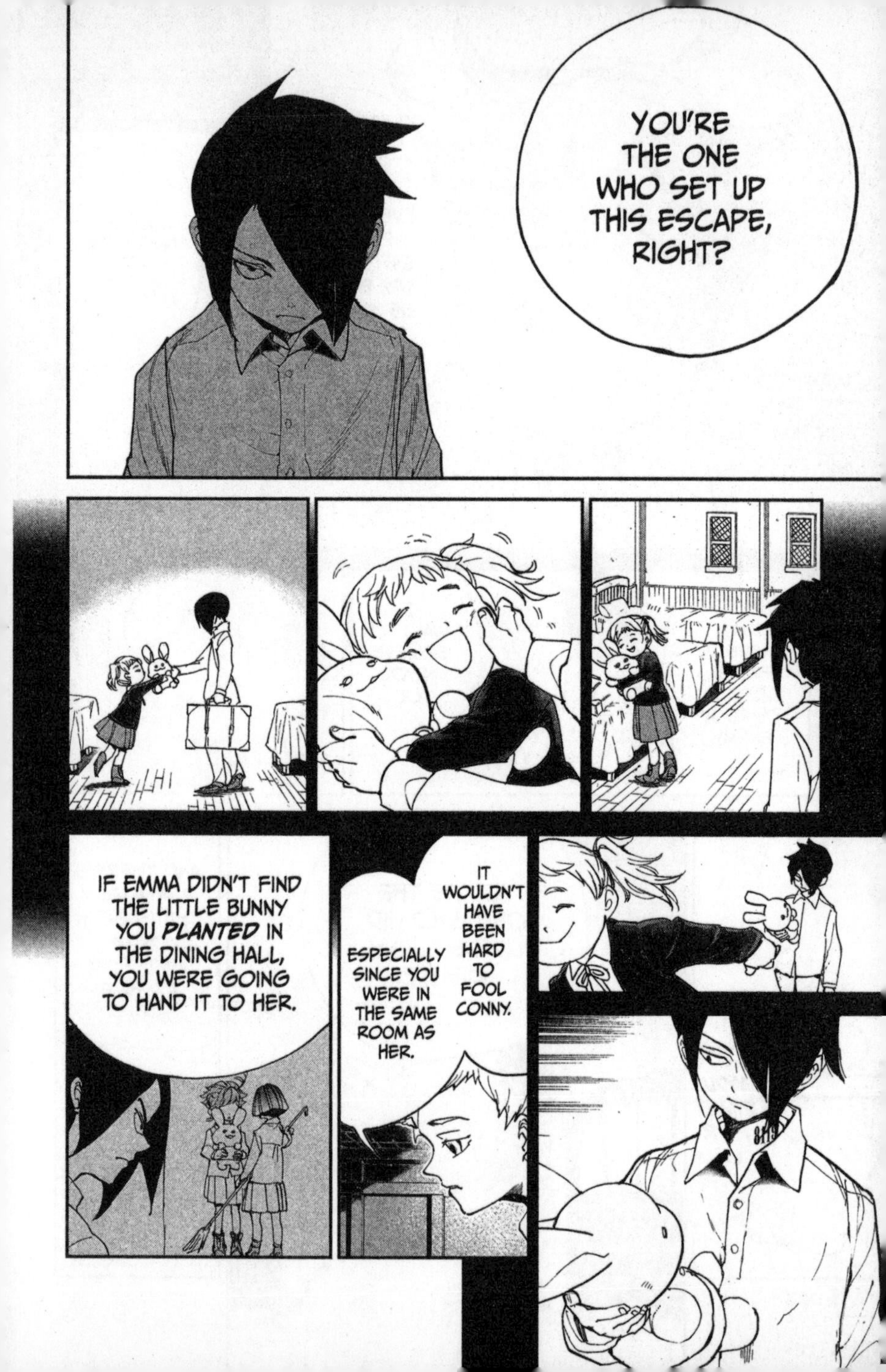
YOU'RE THE ONE WHO SET UP THIS ESCAPE, RIGHT?
IT WOULDN'T HAVE BEEN HARD TO FOOL CONNY.
ESPECIALLY SINCE YOU WERE IN THE SAME ROOM AS HER.
IF EMMA DIDN'T FIND THE LITTLE BUNNY YOU *PLANTED* IN THE DINING HALL, YOU WERE GOING TO HAND IT TO HER.

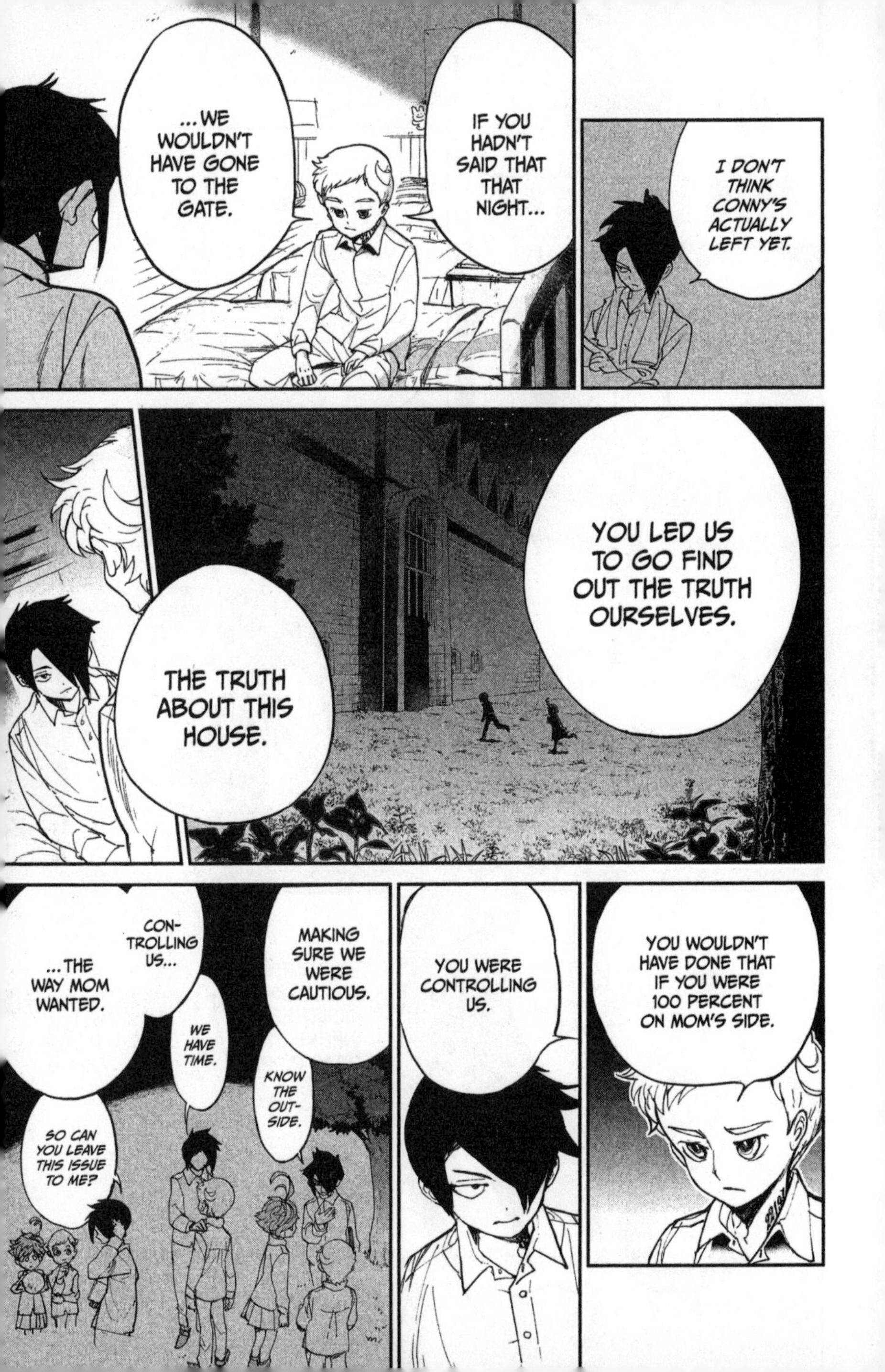
I DON'T THINK CONNY'S ACTUALLY LEFT YET.
IF YOU HADN'T SAID THAT THAT NIGHT...
...WE WOULDN'T HAVE GONE TO THE GATE.
YOU LED US TO GO FIND OUT THE TRUTH OURSELVES.
THE TRUTH ABOUT THIS HOUSE.
YOU WOULDN'T HAVE DONE THAT IF YOU WERE 100 PERCENT ON MOM'S SIDE.
YOU WERE CONTROLLING US.
MAKING SURE WE WERE CAUTIOUS.
CON-TROLLING US...
...THE WAY MOM WANTED.
KNOW THE OUT-SIDE.
WE HAVE TIME.
SO CAN YOU LEAVE THIS ISSUE TO ME?

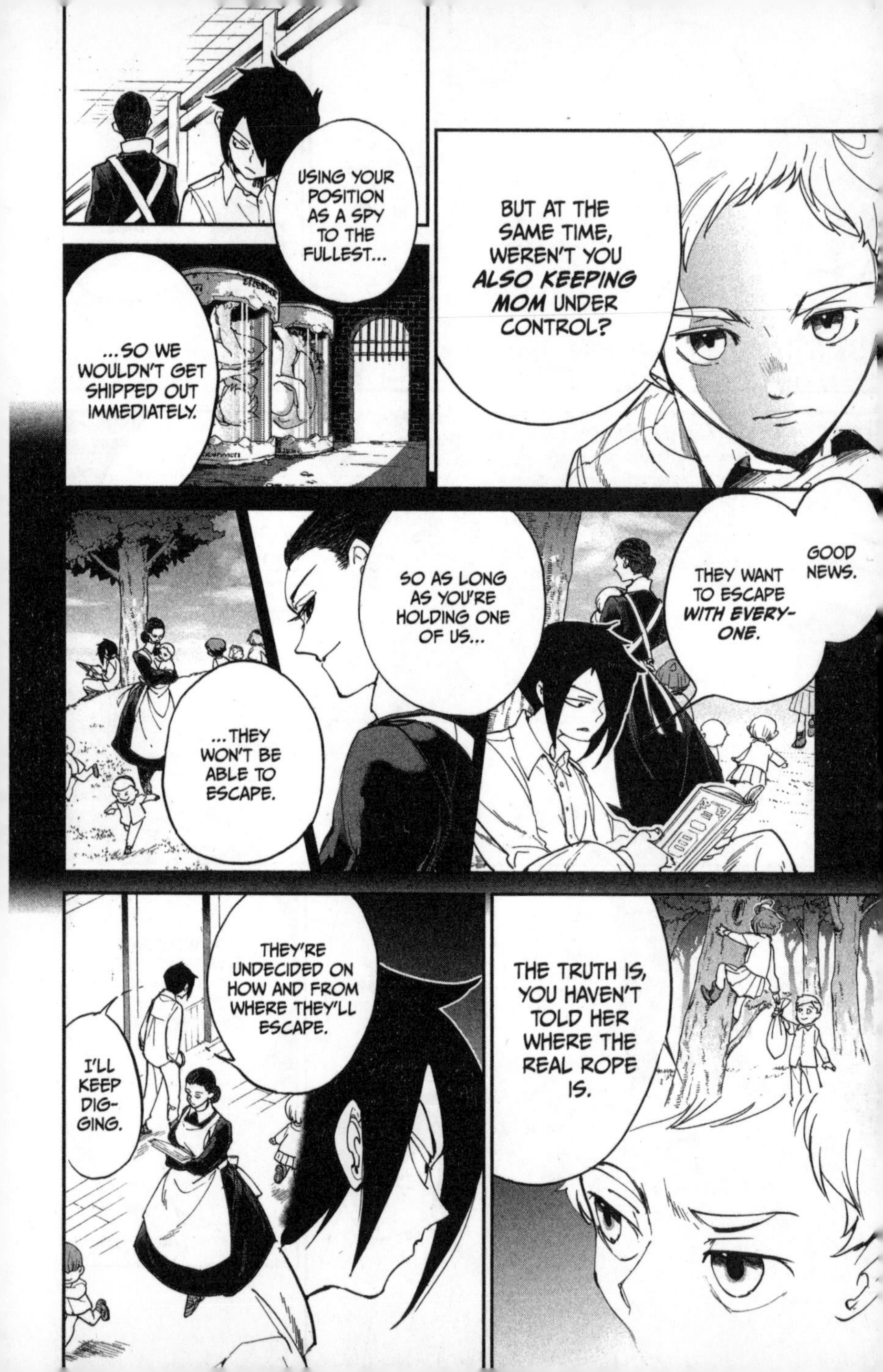
USING YOUR POSITION AS A SPY TO THE FULLEST...
...SO WE WOULDN'T GET SHIPPED OUT IMMEDIATELY.
BUT AT THE SAME TIME, WEREN'T YOU *ALSO KEEPING MOM* UNDER CONTROL?
GOOD NEWS.
THEY WANT TO ESCAPE *WITH EVERY-ONE.*
SO AS LONG AS YOU'RE HOLDING ONE OF US...
...THEY WON'T BE ABLE TO ESCAPE.
THE TRUTH IS, YOU HAVEN'T TOLD HER WHERE THE REAL ROPE IS.
THEY'RE UNDECIDED ON HOW AND FROM WHERE THEY'LL ESCAPE.
I'LL KEEP DIG-GING.

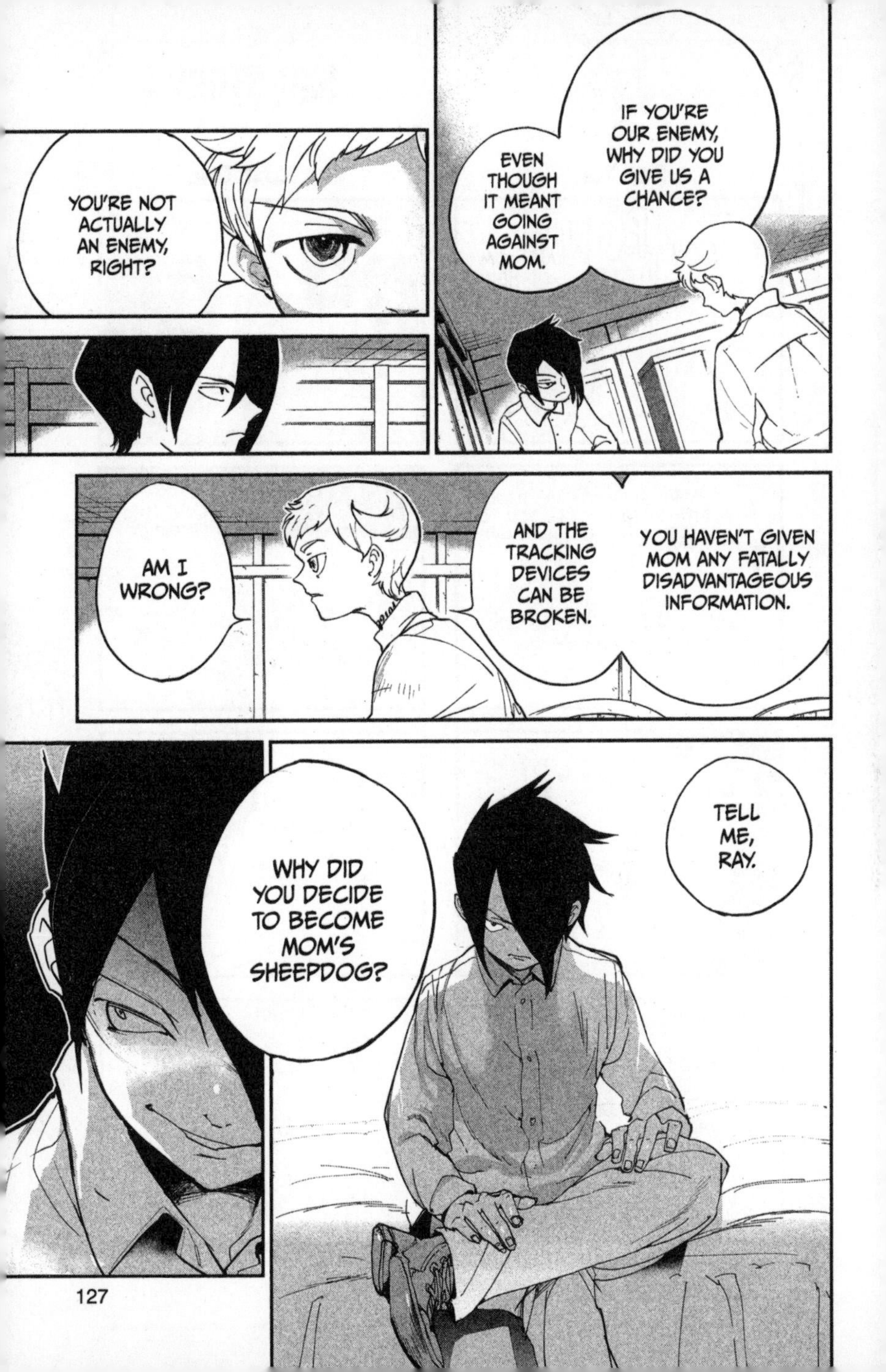
IF YOU'RE OUR ENEMY, WHY DID YOU GIVE US A CHANCE?
EVEN THOUGH IT MEANT GOING AGAINST MOM.
YOU'RE NOT ACTUALLY AN ENEMY, RIGHT?
YOU HAVEN'T GIVEN MOM ANY FATALLY DISADVANTAGEOUS INFORMATION.
AND THE TRACKING DEVICES CAN BE BROKEN.
AM I WRONG?
TELL ME, RAY.
WHY DID YOU DECIDE TO BECOME MOM'S SHEEPDOG?

SIDE STORY 4

For You

POINK
I'M HERE!
!
I TOLD YOU, YOU CAN'T.
HERE. THIS IS FOR YOU.
COUGH COUGH
A CUP?
?
HEY! EMMA!!
I REALLY CAN'T LET YOU OUT OF MY SIGHT.
NORMAN, TALK TO YOU LATER!
TALK? LATER?

The Next Day

DOOM
KEEP OUT
THE DOOR WAS TAPED UP.
ALONE
SHOCK
...
COUGH
COUGH
KEEP OUT

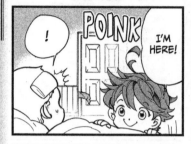

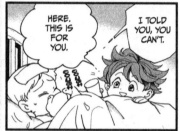

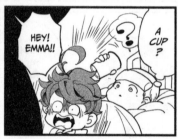

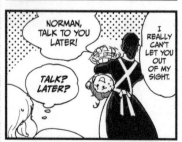

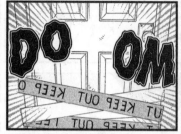

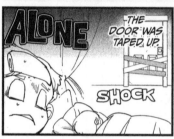

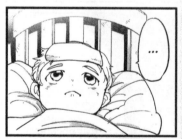

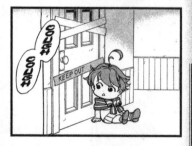

TO BE CONTINUED IN SIDE STORY 5

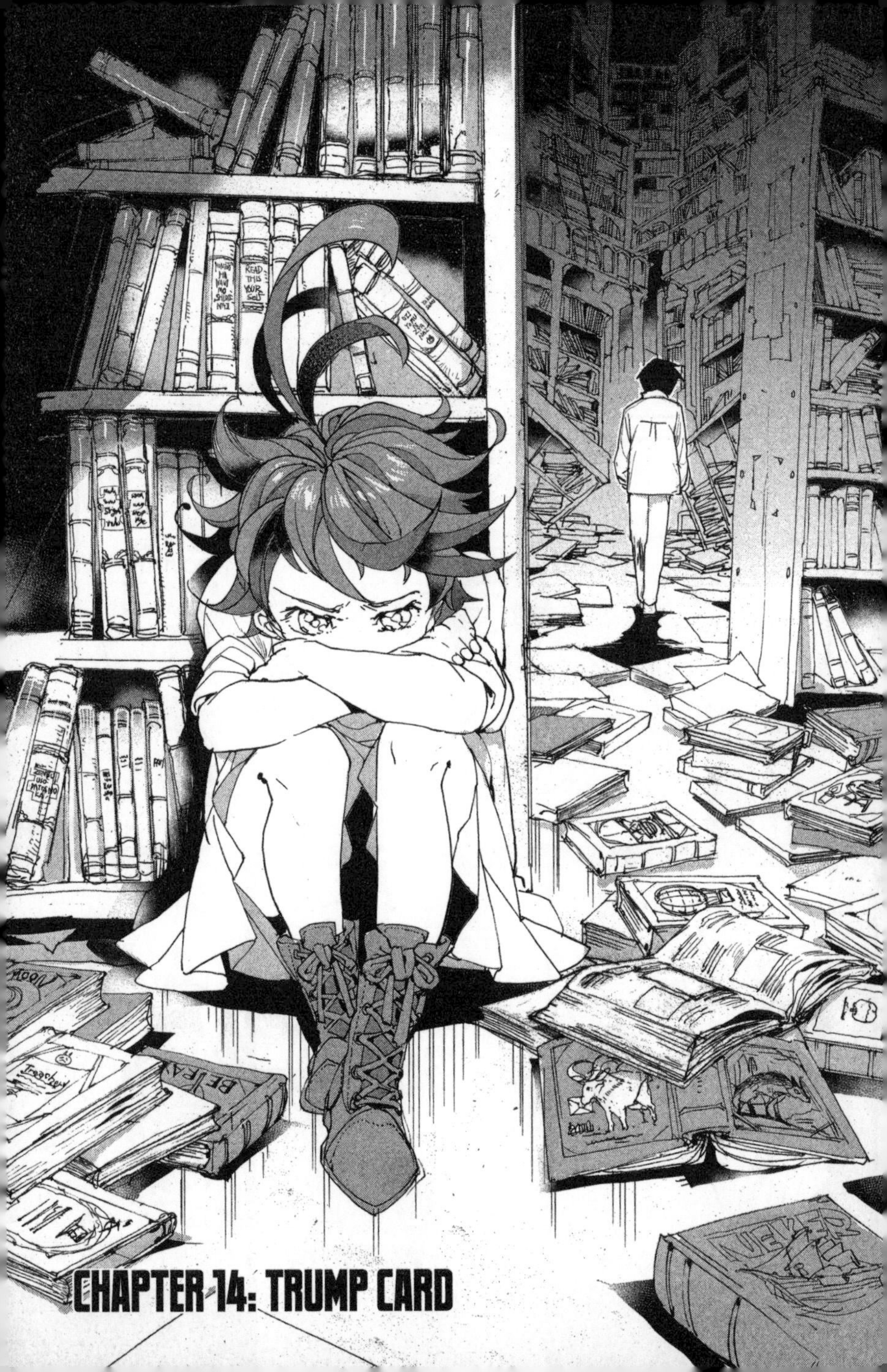

CHAPTER 14: TRUMP CARD

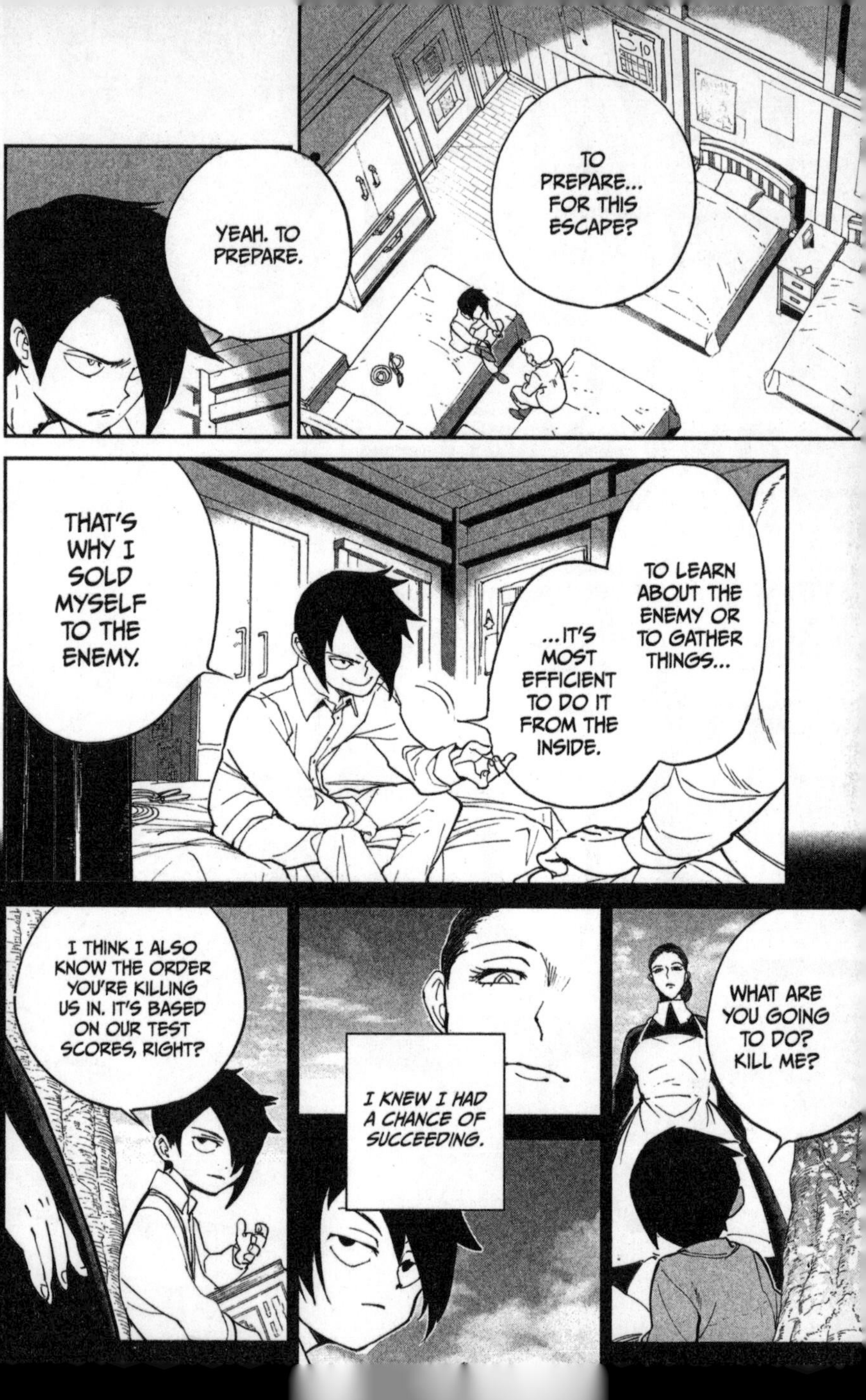
TO PREPARE... FOR THIS ESCAPE?
YEAH. TO PREPARE.
TO LEARN ABOUT THE ENEMY OR TO GATHER THINGS...
...IT'S MOST EFFICIENT TO DO IT FROM THE INSIDE.
THAT'S WHY I SOLD MYSELF TO THE ENEMY.
WHAT ARE YOU GOING TO DO? KILL ME?
I KNEW I HAD A CHANCE OF SUCCEEDING.
I THINK I ALSO KNOW THE ORDER YOU'RE KILLING US IN. IT'S BASED ON OUR TEST SCORES, RIGHT?

CHAPTER 14: TRUMP CARD

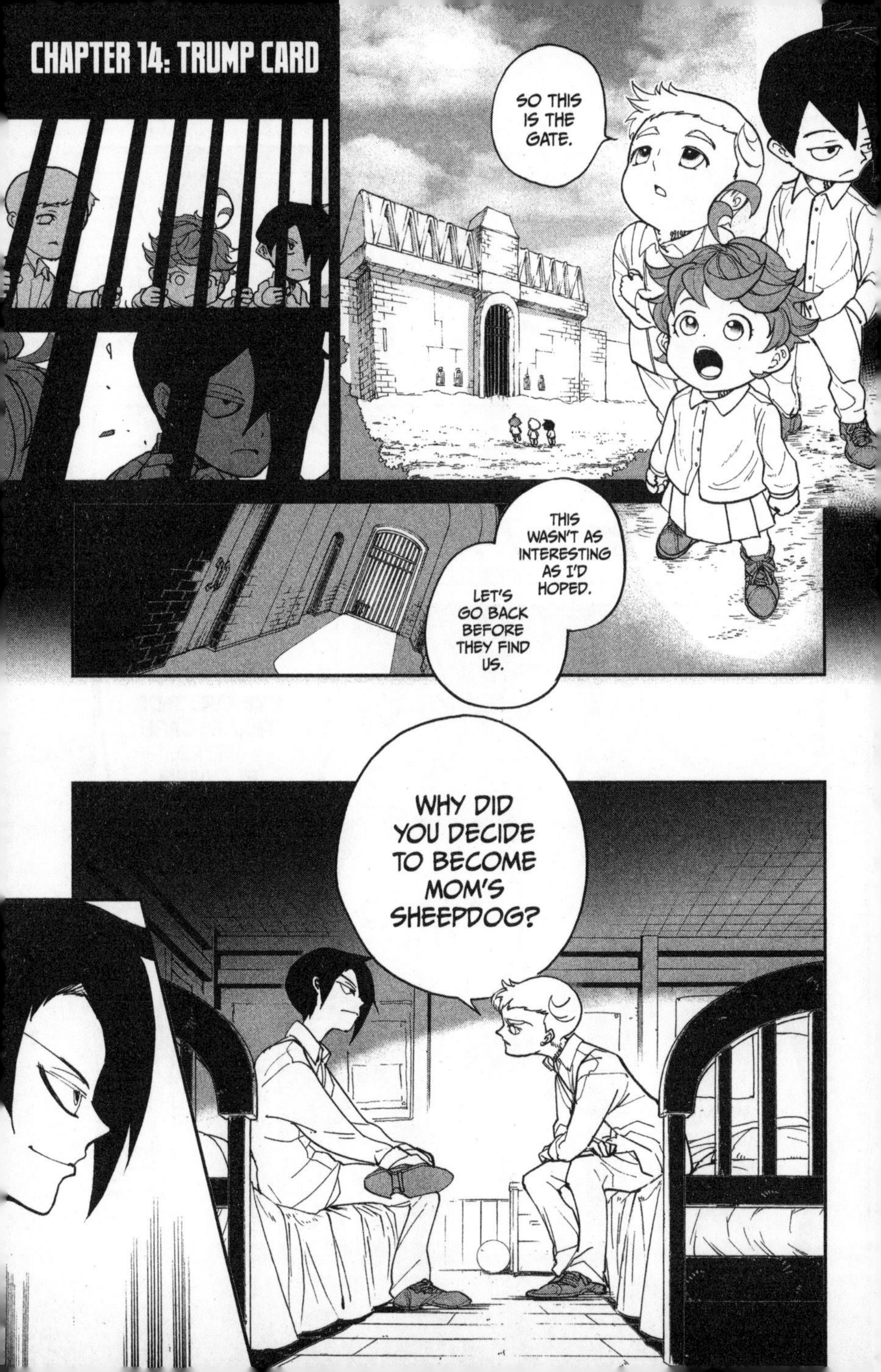

SO THIS IS THE GATE.
THIS WASN'T AS INTERESTING AS I'D HOPED.
LET'S GO BACK BEFORE THEY FIND US.
WHY DID YOU DECIDE TO BECOME MOM'S SHEEPDOG?

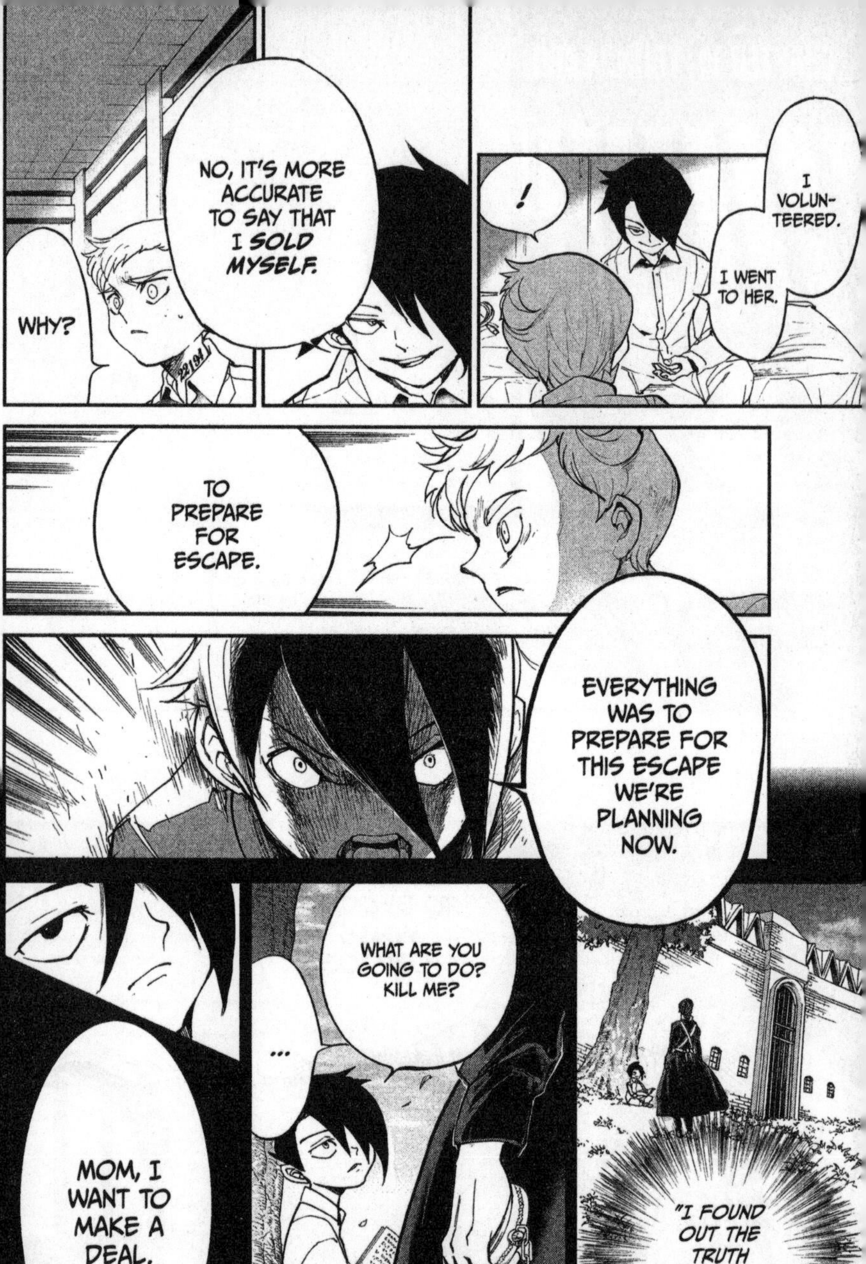
I VOLUNTEERED.
!
I WENT TO HER.
NO, IT'S MORE ACCURATE TO SAY THAT I *SOLD MYSELF.*
WHY?
TO PREPARE FOR ESCAPE.
EVERYTHING WAS TO PREPARE FOR THIS ESCAPE WE'RE PLANNING NOW.
"I FOUND OUT THE TRUTH ABOUT THIS HOUSE."
WHAT ARE YOU GOING TO DO? KILL ME?
...
MOM, I WANT TO MAKE A DEAL.

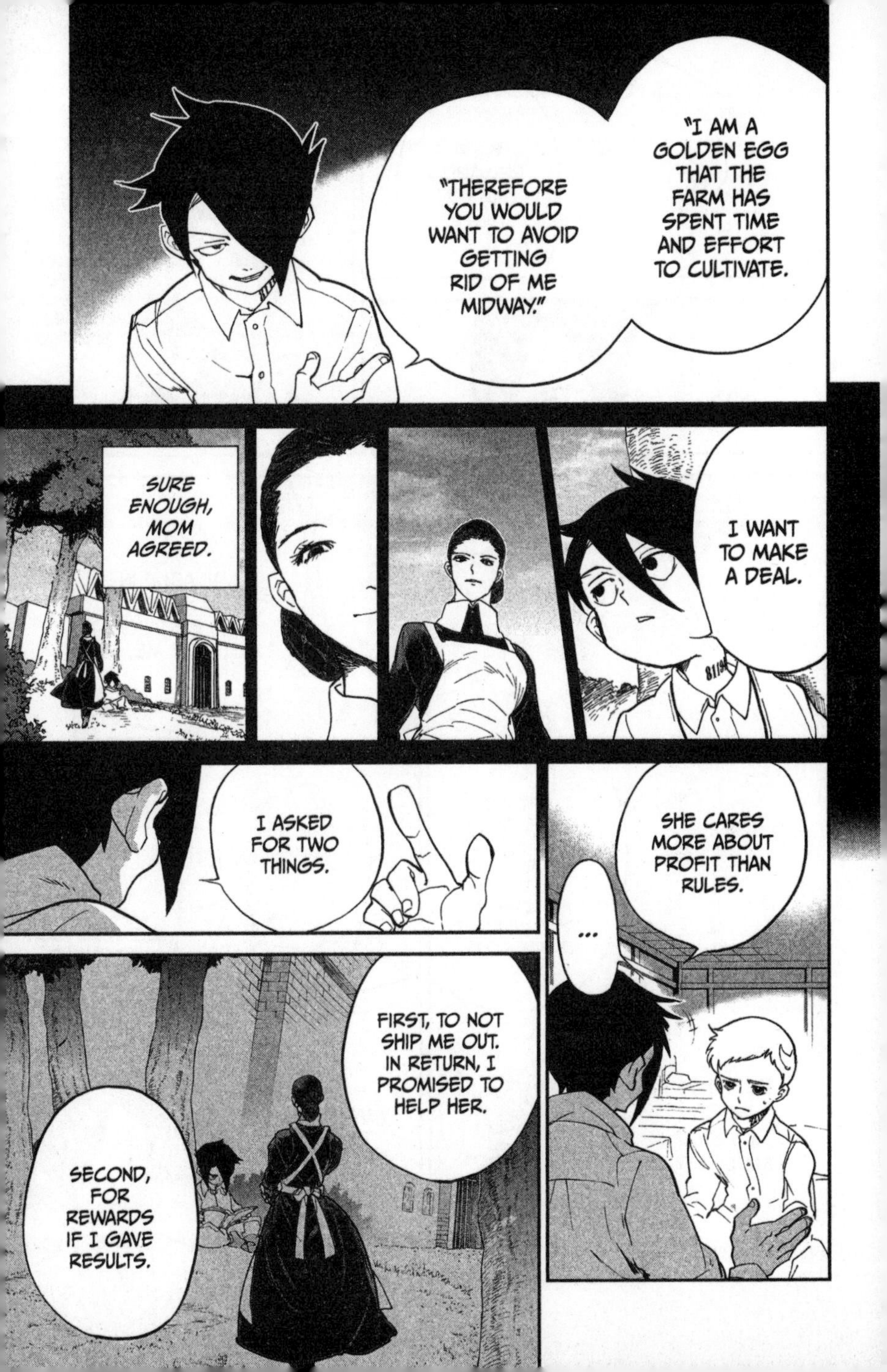
"I AM A GOLDEN EGG THAT THE FARM HAS SPENT TIME AND EFFORT TO CULTIVATE.
"THEREFORE YOU WOULD WANT TO AVOID GETTING RID OF ME MIDWAY."
I WANT TO MAKE A DEAL.
SURE ENOUGH, MOM AGREED.
SHE CARES MORE ABOUT PROFIT THAN RULES.
...
I ASKED FOR TWO THINGS.
FIRST, TO NOT SHIP ME OUT. IN RETURN, I PROMISED TO HELP HER.
SECOND, FOR REWARDS IF I GAVE RESULTS.

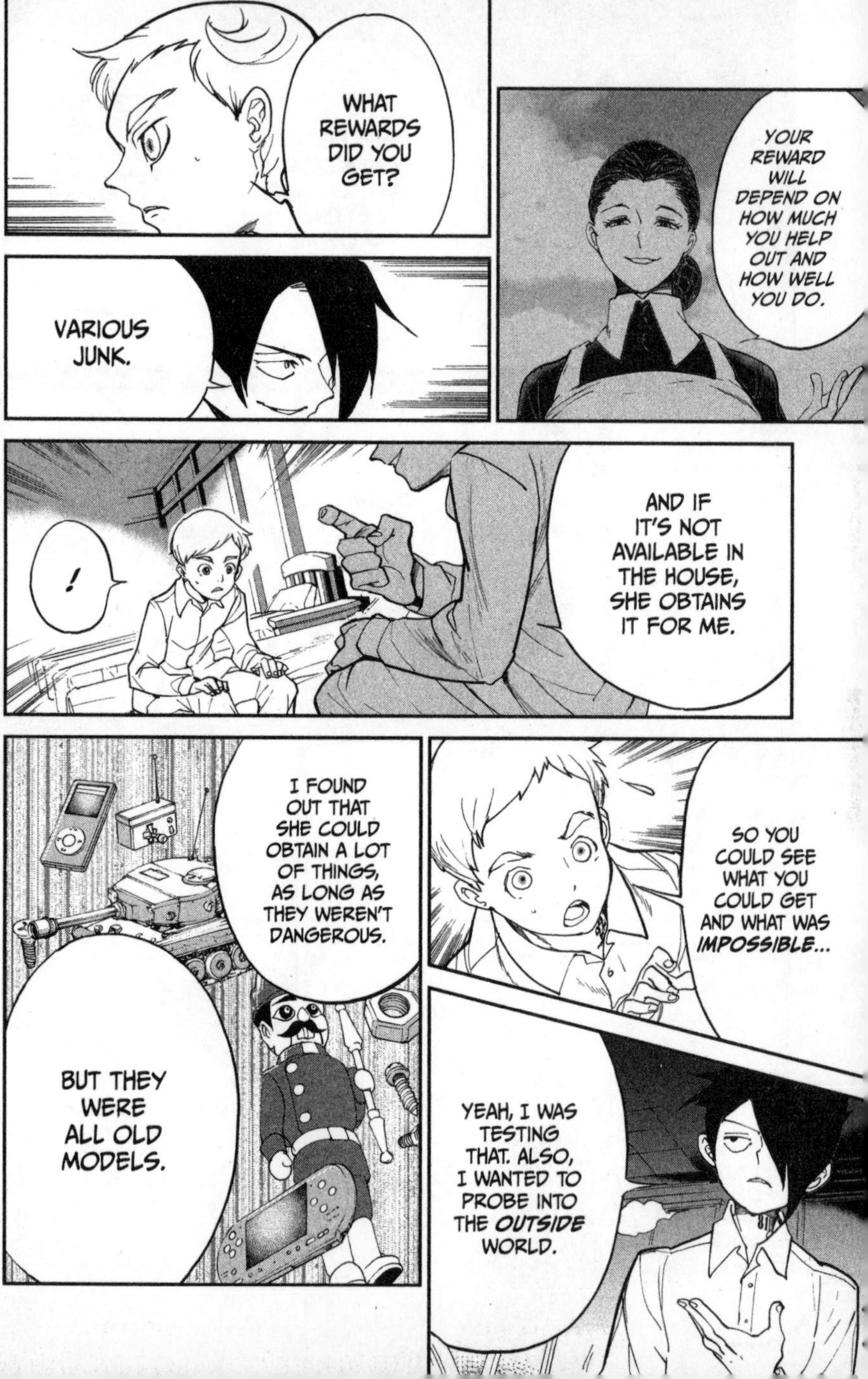
YOUR REWARD WILL DEPEND ON HOW MUCH YOU HELP OUT AND HOW WELL YOU DO.
WHAT REWARDS DID YOU GET?
VARIOUS JUNK.
AND IF IT'S NOT AVAILABLE IN THE HOUSE, SHE OBTAINS IT FOR ME.
!
SO YOU COULD SEE WHAT YOU COULD GET AND WHAT WAS *IMPOSSIBLE*...
YEAH, I WAS TESTING THAT. ALSO, I WANTED TO PROBE INTO THE *OUTSIDE* WORLD.
I FOUND OUT THAT SHE COULD OBTAIN A LOT OF THINGS, AS LONG AS THEY WEREN'T DANGEROUS.
BUT THEY WERE ALL OLD MODELS.

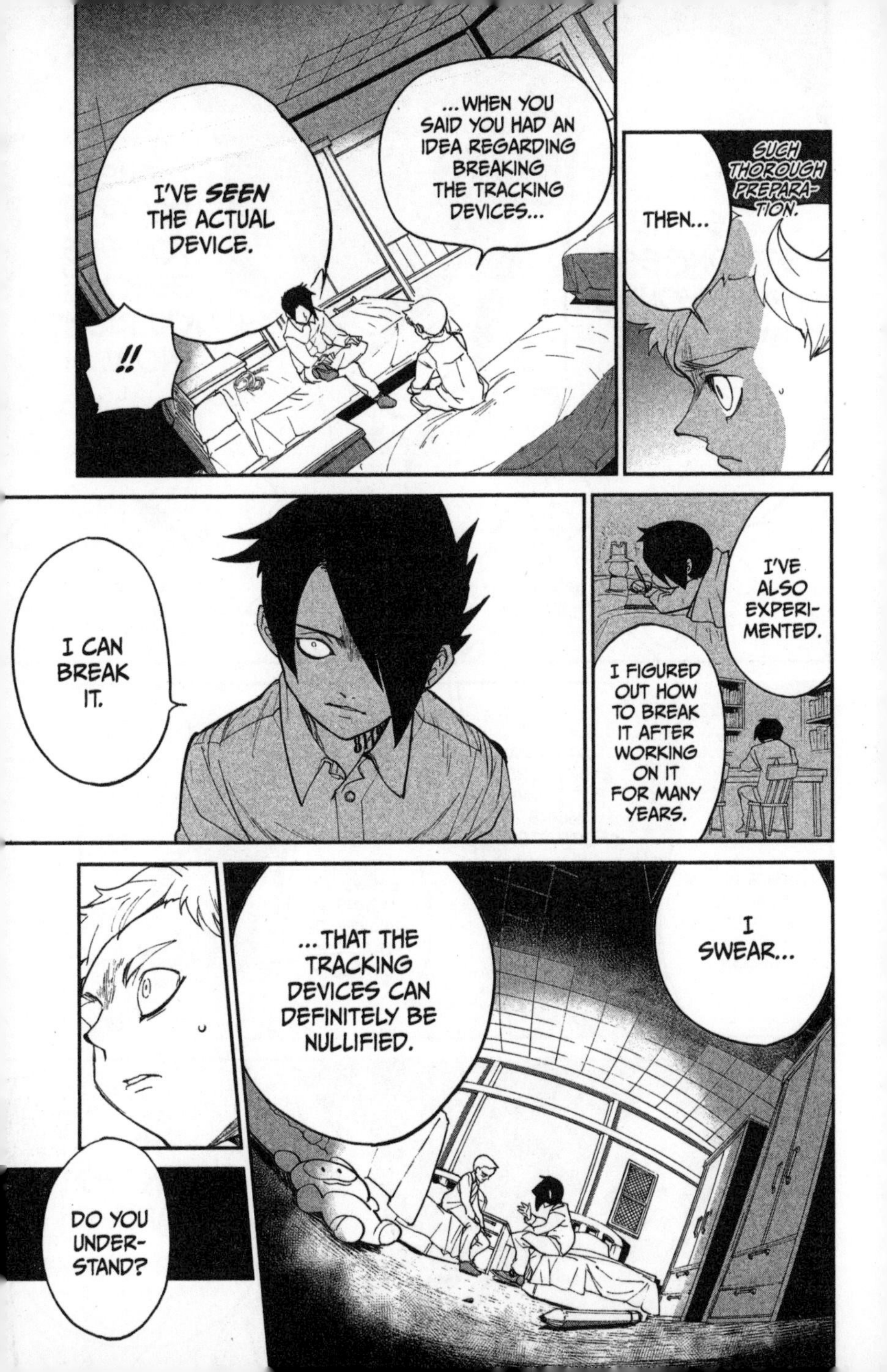
SUCH THOROUGH PREPARATION.
THEN...
...WHEN YOU SAID YOU HAD AN IDEA REGARDING BREAKING THE TRACKING DEVICES...
I'VE **SEEN** THE ACTUAL DEVICE.
!!
I'VE ALSO EXPERIMENTED.
I FIGURED OUT HOW TO BREAK IT AFTER WORKING ON IT FOR MANY YEARS.
I CAN BREAK IT.
I SWEAR...
...THAT THE TRACKING DEVICES CAN DEFINITELY BE NULLIFIED.
DO YOU UNDERSTAND?

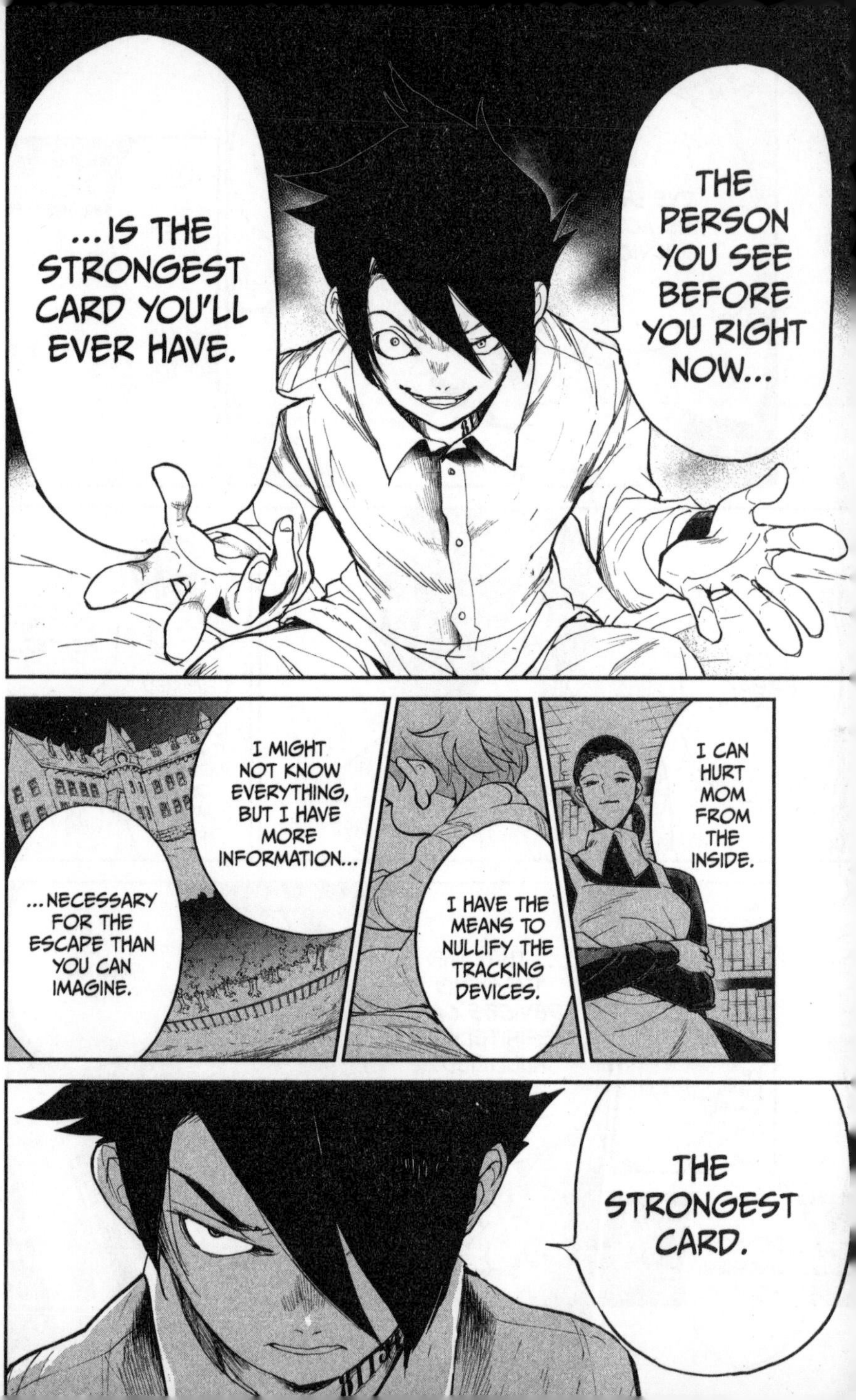
THE PERSON YOU SEE BEFORE YOU RIGHT NOW...
...IS THE STRONGEST CARD YOU'LL EVER HAVE.
I CAN HURT MOM FROM THE INSIDE.
I HAVE THE MEANS TO NULLIFY THE TRACKING DEVICES.
I MIGHT NOT KNOW EVERYTHING, BUT I HAVE MORE INFORMATION...
...NECESSARY FOR THE ESCAPE THAN YOU CAN IMAGINE.
THE STRONGEST CARD.

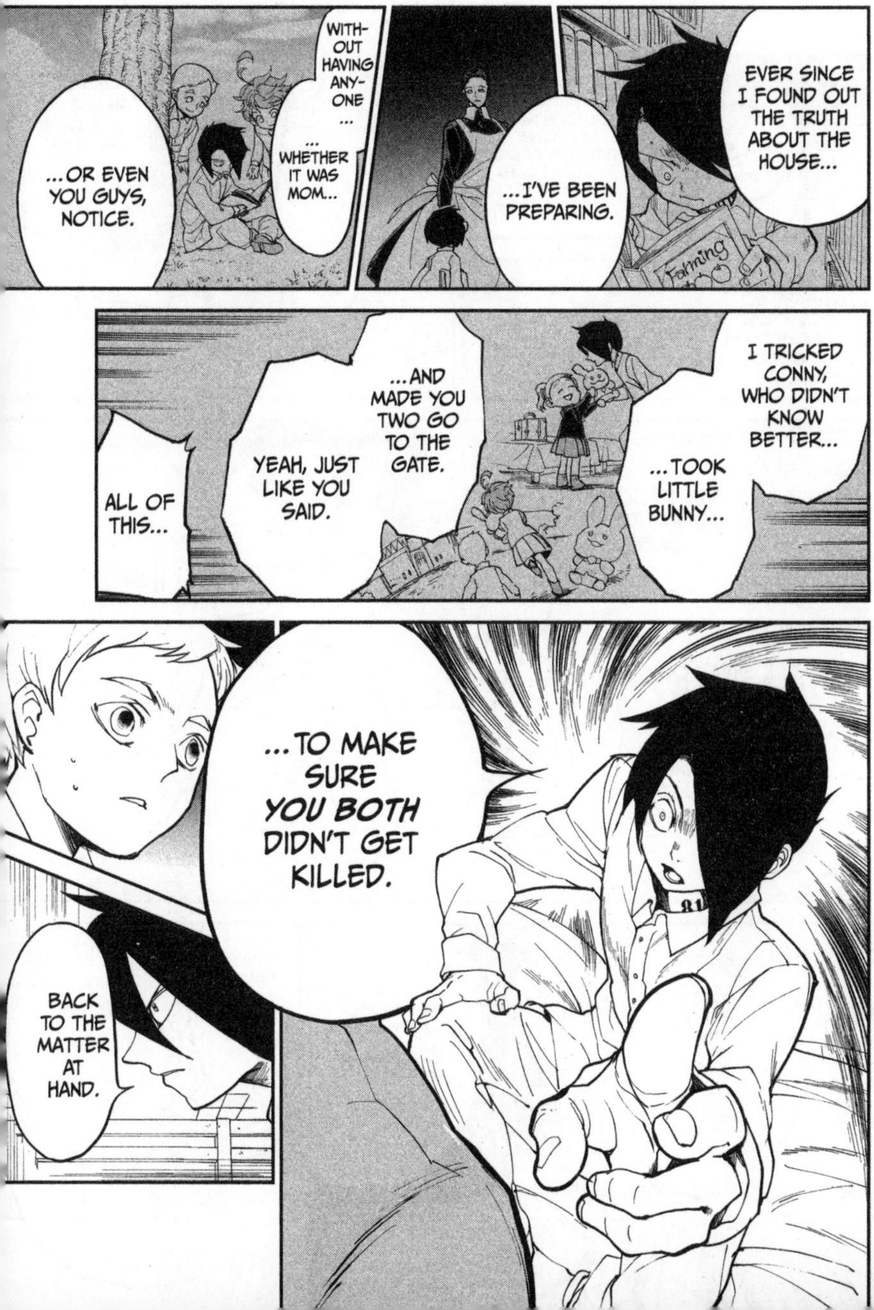
EVER SINCE I FOUND OUT THE TRUTH ABOUT THE HOUSE...
Farming
...I'VE BEEN PREPARING.
WITHOUT HAVING ANYONE ...
... WHETHER IT WAS MOM...
...OR EVEN YOU GUYS, NOTICE.
I TRICKED CONNY, WHO DIDN'T KNOW BETTER...
...TOOK LITTLE BUNNY...
...AND MADE YOU TWO GO TO THE GATE.
YEAH, JUST LIKE YOU SAID.
ALL OF THIS...
...TO MAKE SURE *YOU BOTH* DIDN'T GET KILLED.
BACK TO THE MATTER AT HAND.

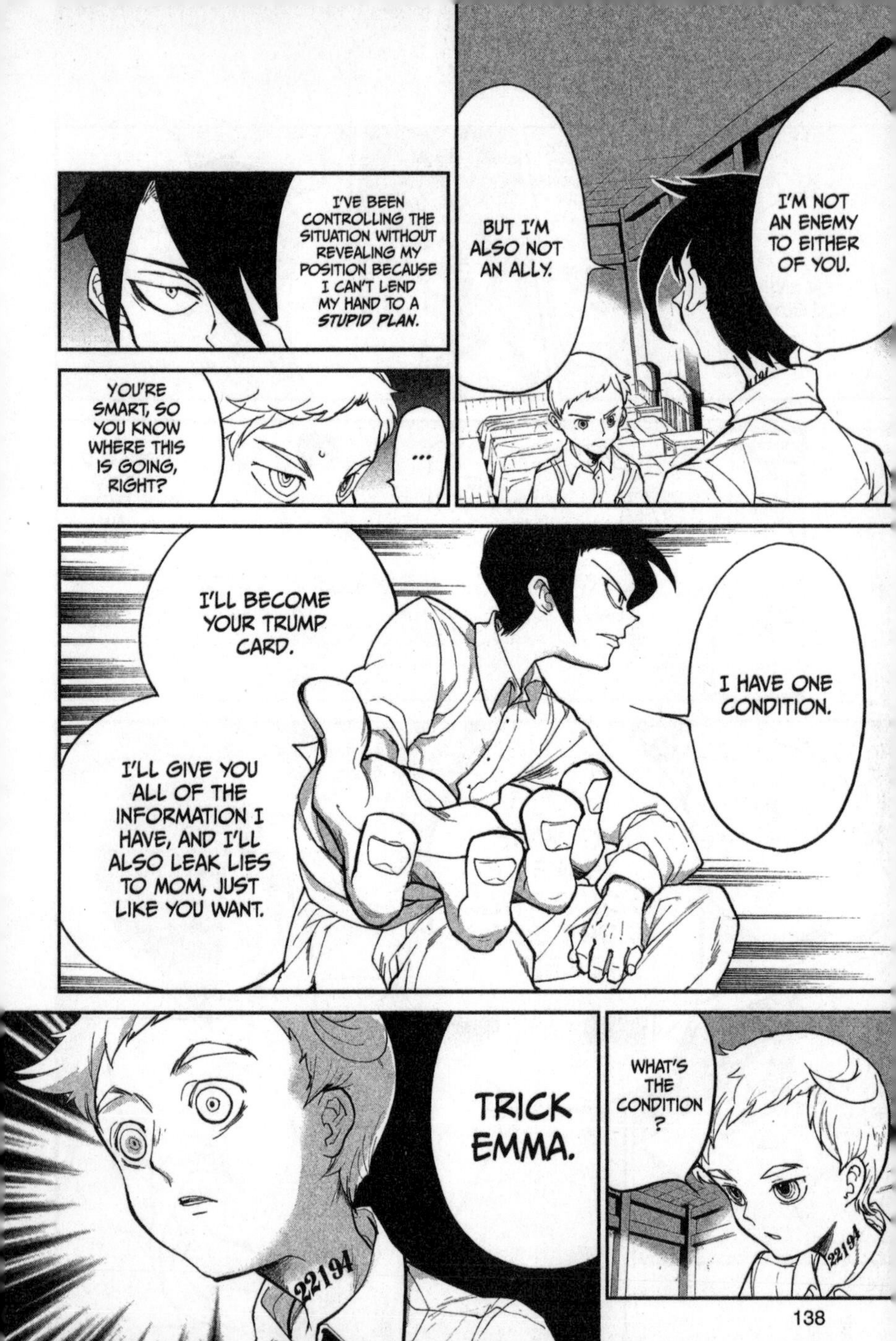
I'M NOT AN ENEMY TO EITHER OF YOU.
BUT I'M ALSO NOT AN ALLY.
I'VE BEEN CONTROLLING THE SITUATION WITHOUT REVEALING MY POSITION BECAUSE I CAN'T LEND MY HAND TO A *STUPID PLAN.*
YOU'RE SMART, SO YOU KNOW WHERE THIS IS GOING, RIGHT?
...
I'LL BECOME YOUR TRUMP CARD.
I'LL GIVE YOU ALL OF THE INFORMATION I HAVE, AND I'LL ALSO LEAK LIES TO MOM, JUST LIKE YOU WANT.
I HAVE ONE CONDITION.
WHAT'S THE CONDITION ?
TRICK EMMA.
22194
22194

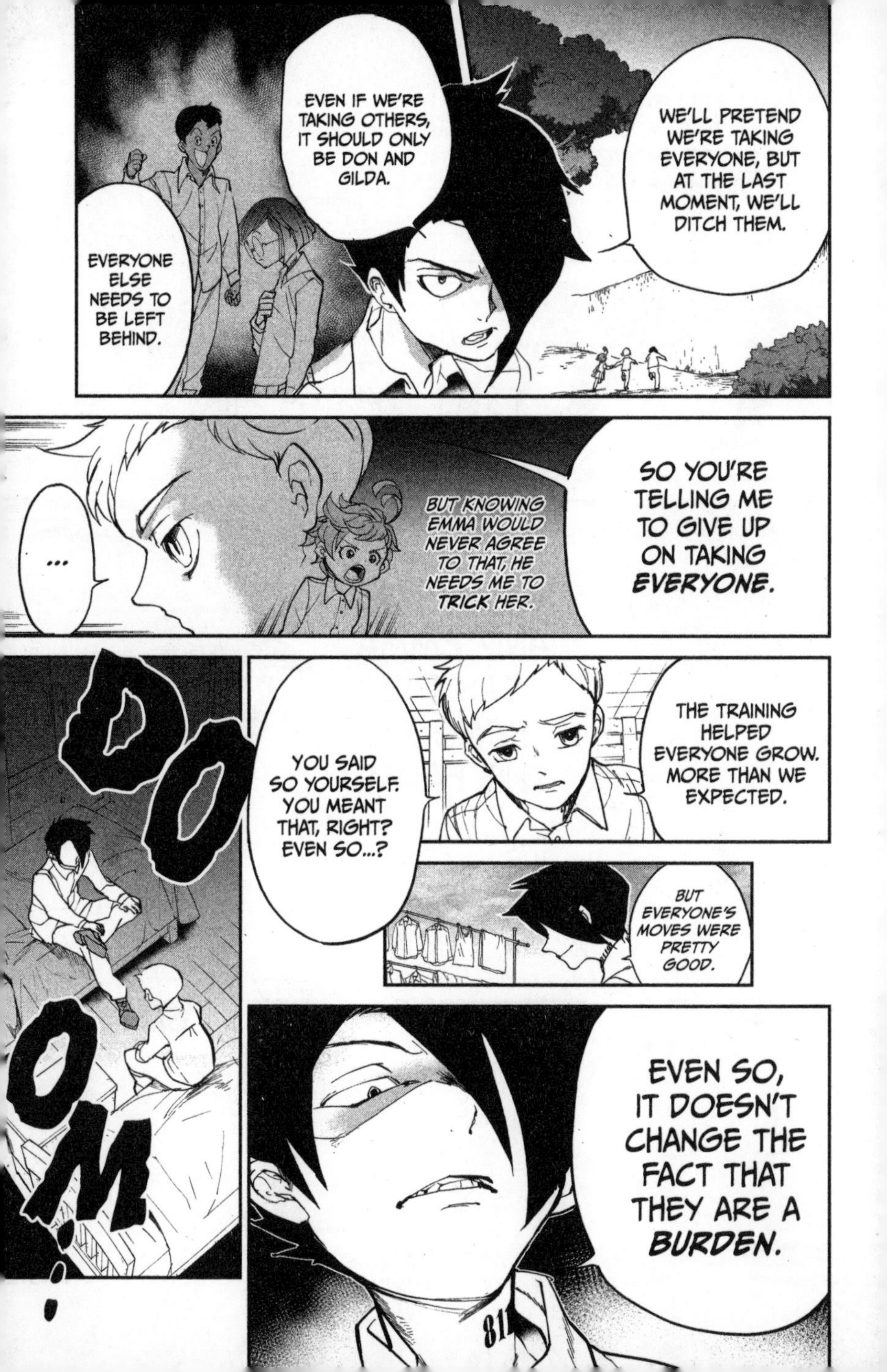
WE'LL PRETEND WE'RE TAKING EVERYONE, BUT AT THE LAST MOMENT, WE'LL DITCH THEM.
EVEN IF WE'RE TAKING OTHERS, IT SHOULD ONLY BE DON AND GILDA.
EVERYONE ELSE NEEDS TO BE LEFT BEHIND.
SO YOU'RE TELLING ME TO GIVE UP ON TAKING *EVERYONE*.
BUT KNOWING EMMA WOULD NEVER AGREE TO THAT, HE NEEDS ME TO TRICK HER.
...
THE TRAINING HELPED EVERYONE GROW. MORE THAN WE EXPECTED.
YOU SAID SO YOURSELF. YOU MEANT THAT, RIGHT? EVEN SO...?
BUT EVERYONE'S MOVES WERE PRETTY GOOD.
EVEN SO, IT DOESN'T CHANGE THE FACT THAT THEY ARE A *BURDEN*.
DOOM
811

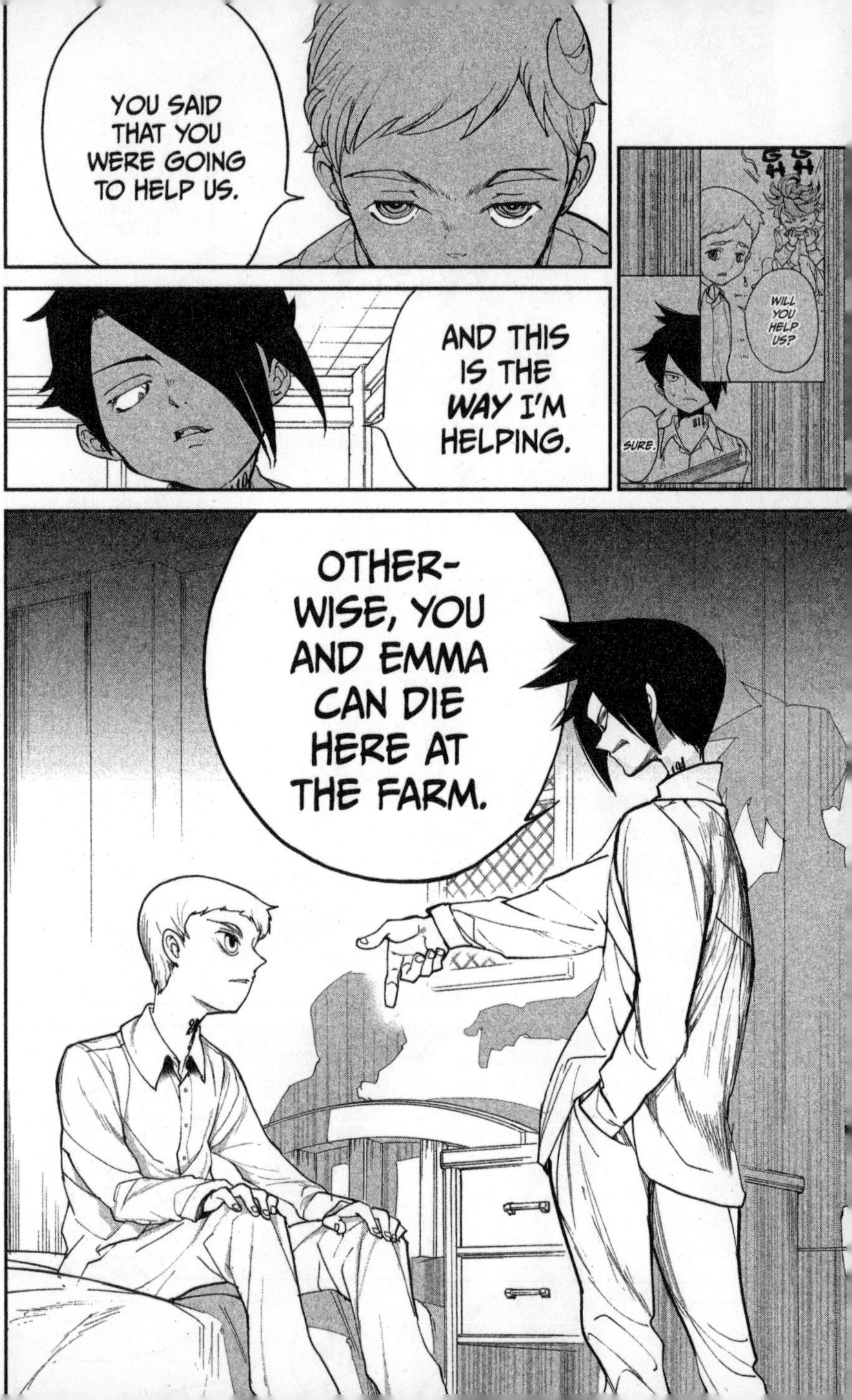
YOU SAID THAT YOU WERE GOING TO HELP US.
WILL YOU HELP US?
SURE.
AND THIS IS THE WAY I'M HELPING.
OTHER-WISE, YOU AND EMMA CAN DIE HERE AT THE FARM.

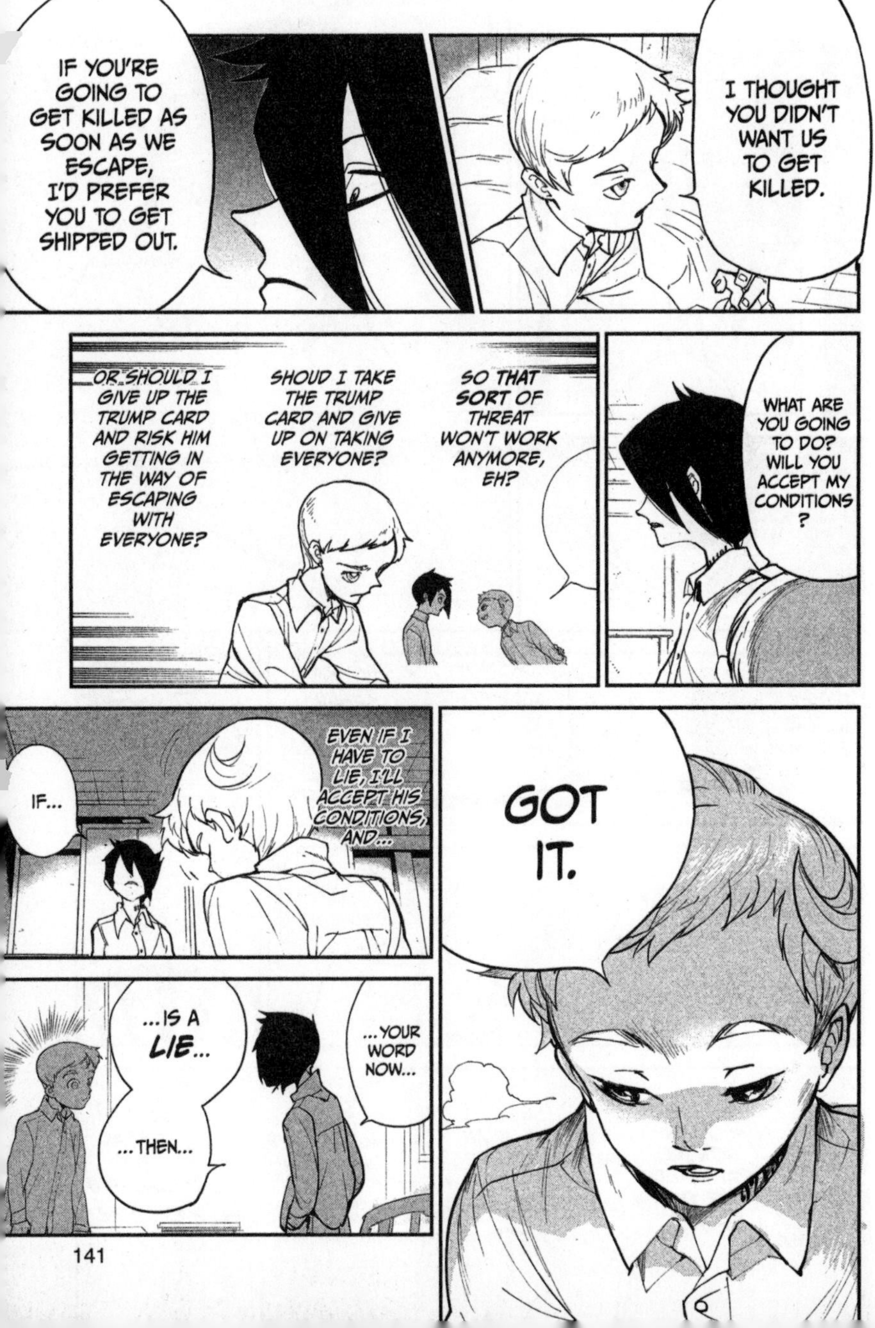
I THOUGHT YOU DIDN'T WANT US TO GET KILLED.
IF YOU'RE GOING TO GET KILLED AS SOON AS WE ESCAPE, I'D PREFER YOU TO GET SHIPPED OUT.
WHAT ARE YOU GOING TO DO? WILL YOU ACCEPT MY CONDITIONS?
SO THAT SORT OF THREAT WON'T WORK ANYMORE, EH?
SHOUD I TAKE THE TRUMP CARD AND GIVE UP ON TAKING EVERYONE?
OR SHOULD I GIVE UP THE TRUMP CARD AND RISK HIM GETTING IN THE WAY OF ESCAPING WITH EVERYONE?
GOT IT.
EVEN IF I HAVE TO LIE, I'LL ACCEPT HIS CONDITIONS, AND...
IF...
...YOUR WORD NOW...
...IS A LIE...
...THEN...

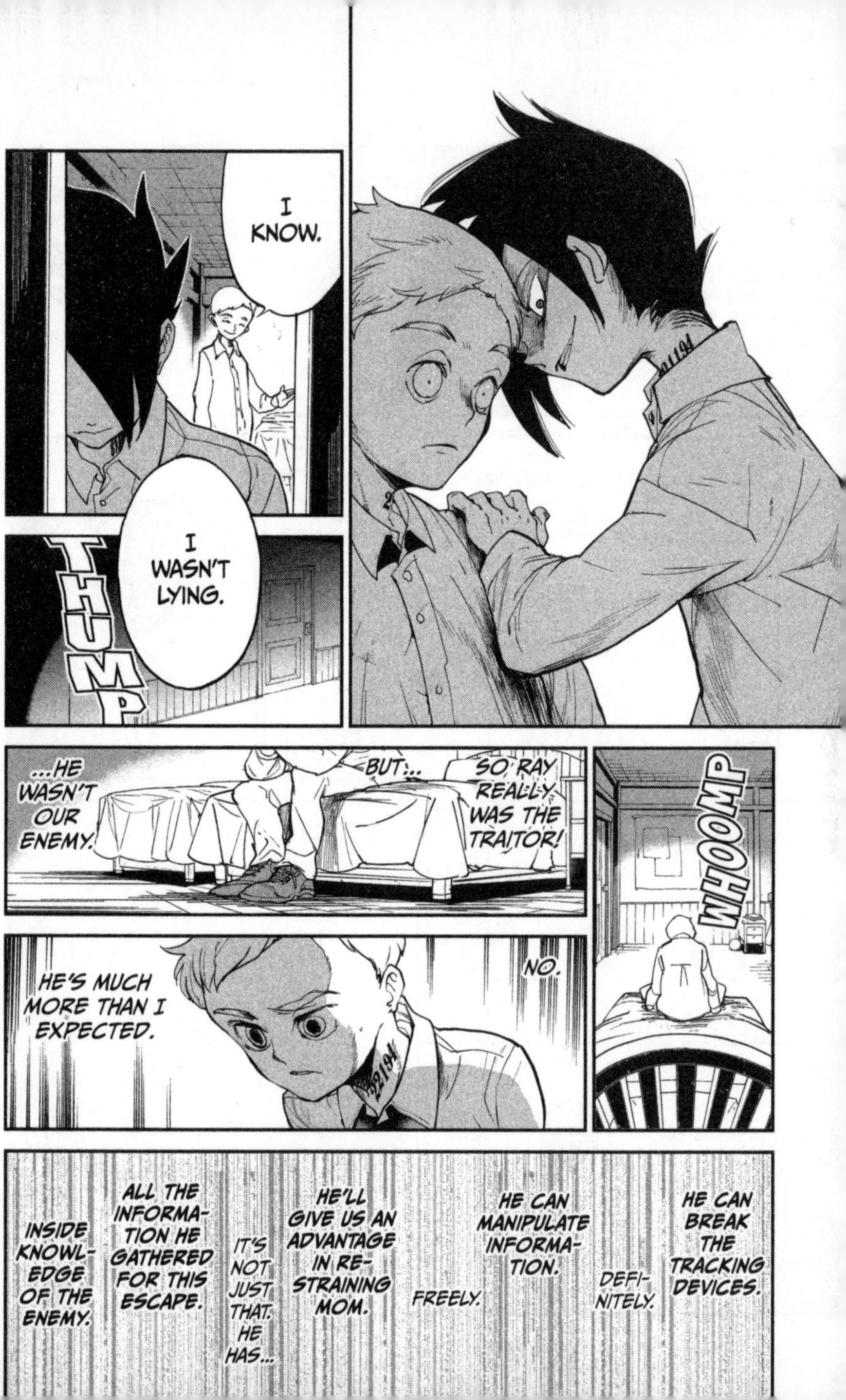
I KNOW.
I WASN'T LYING.
THUMP
WHOOMP
SO RAY REALLY WAS THE TRAITOR!
BUT...
...HE WASN'T OUR ENEMY.
NO.
HE'S MUCH MORE THAN I EXPECTED.
HE CAN BREAK THE TRACKING DEVICES.
DEFINITELY.
HE CAN MANIPULATE INFORMATION.
FREELY.
HE'LL GIVE US AN ADVANTAGE IN RESTRAINING MOM.
IT'S NOT JUST THAT. HE HAS...
ALL THE INFORMATION HE GATHERED FOR THIS ESCAPE.
INSIDE KNOWLEDGE OF THE ENEMY.

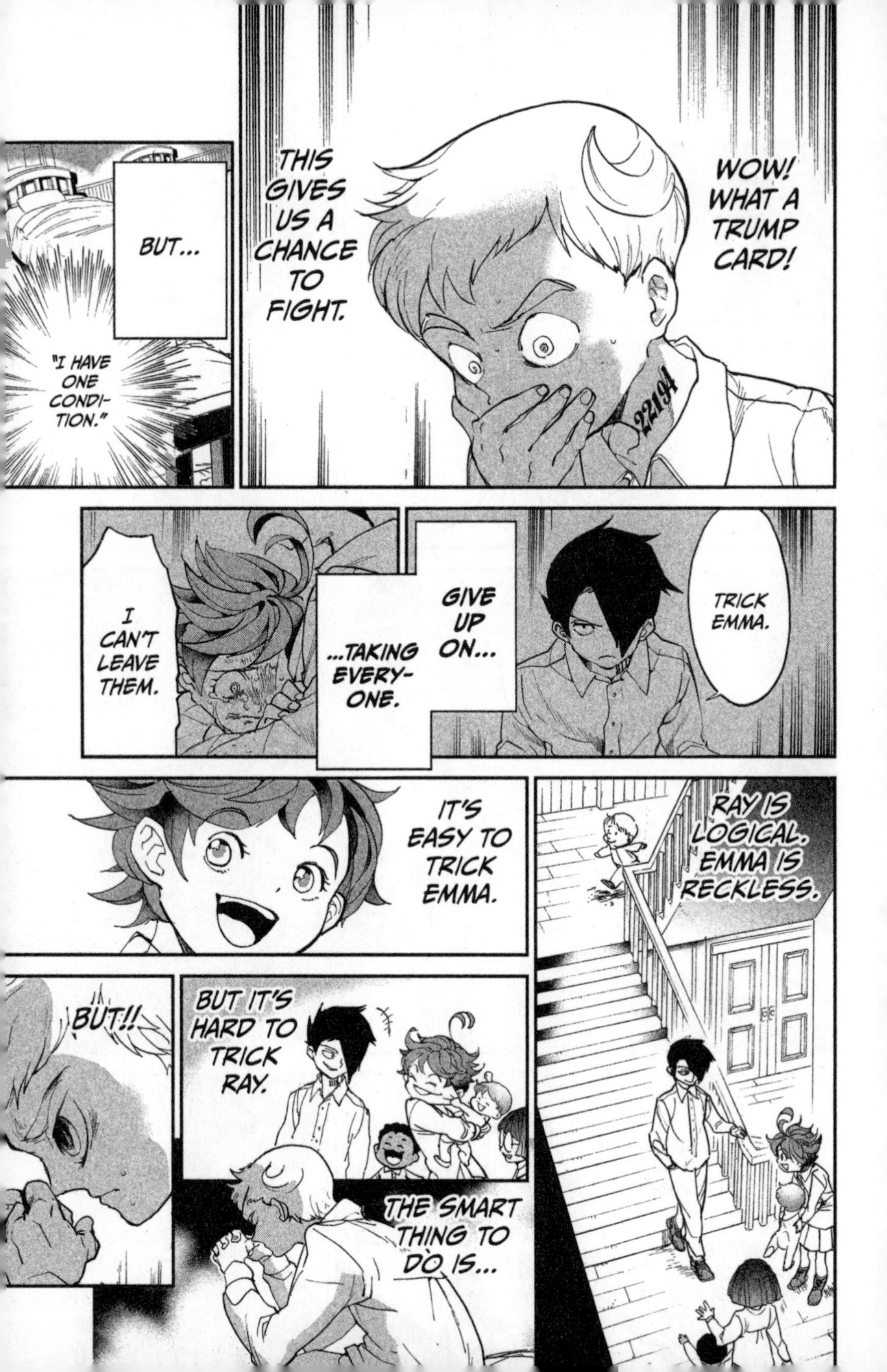
WOW! WHAT A TRUMP CARD!
22194
THIS GIVES US A CHANCE TO FIGHT.
BUT...
"I HAVE ONE CONDITION."
TRICK EMMA.
GIVE UP ON...
...TAKING EVERY-ONE.
I CAN'T LEAVE THEM.
RAY IS LOGICAL. EMMA IS RECKLESS.
IT'S EASY TO TRICK EMMA.
BUT IT'S HARD TO TRICK RAY.
THE SMART THING TO DO IS...
BUT!!

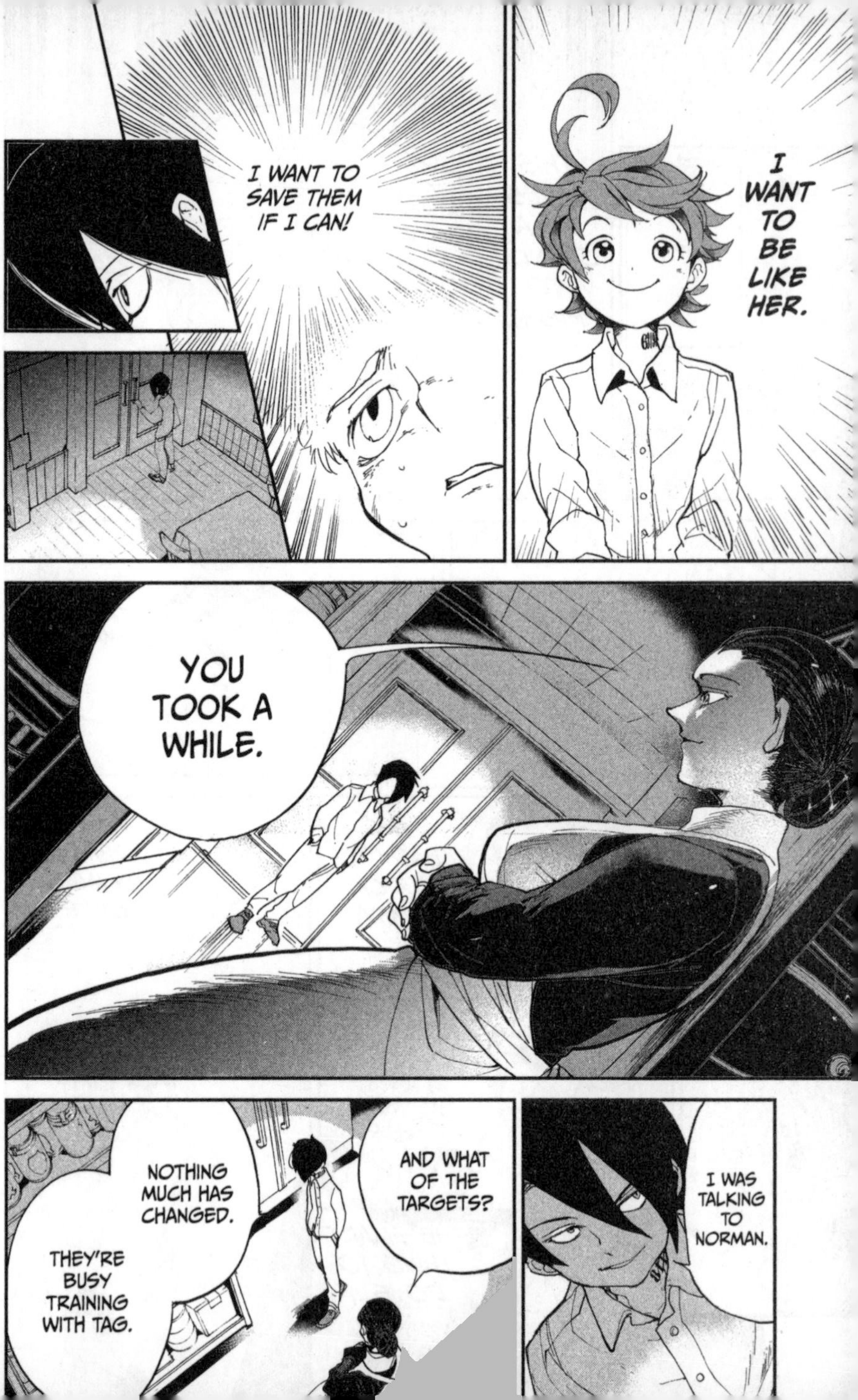
I WANT TO BE LIKE HER.
I WANT TO SAVE THEM IF I CAN!
YOU TOOK A WHILE.
I WAS TALKING TO NORMAN.
AND WHAT OF THE TARGETS?
NOTHING MUCH HAS CHANGED.
THEY'RE BUSY TRAINING WITH TAG.

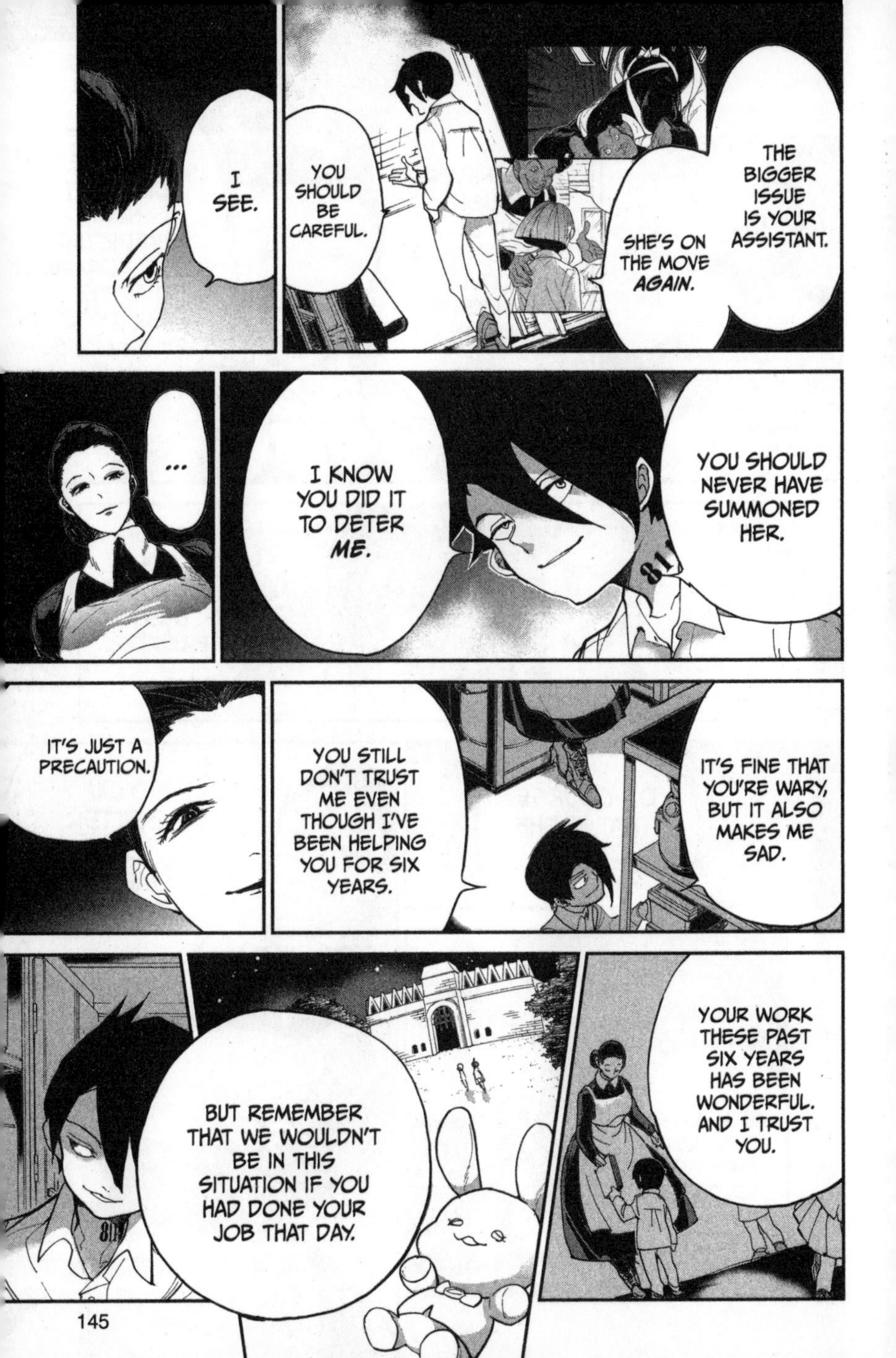
THE BIGGER ISSUE IS YOUR ASSISTANT.
SHE'S ON THE MOVE AGAIN.
YOU SHOULD BE CAREFUL.
I SEE.
YOU SHOULD NEVER HAVE SUMMONED HER.
I KNOW YOU DID IT TO DETER ME.
...
IT'S FINE THAT YOU'RE WARY, BUT IT ALSO MAKES ME SAD.
YOU STILL DON'T TRUST ME EVEN THOUGH I'VE BEEN HELPING YOU FOR SIX YEARS.
IT'S JUST A PRECAUTION.
YOUR WORK THESE PAST SIX YEARS HAS BEEN WONDERFUL. AND I TRUST YOU.
BUT REMEMBER THAT WE WOULDN'T BE IN THIS SITUATION IF YOU HAD DONE YOUR JOB THAT DAY.

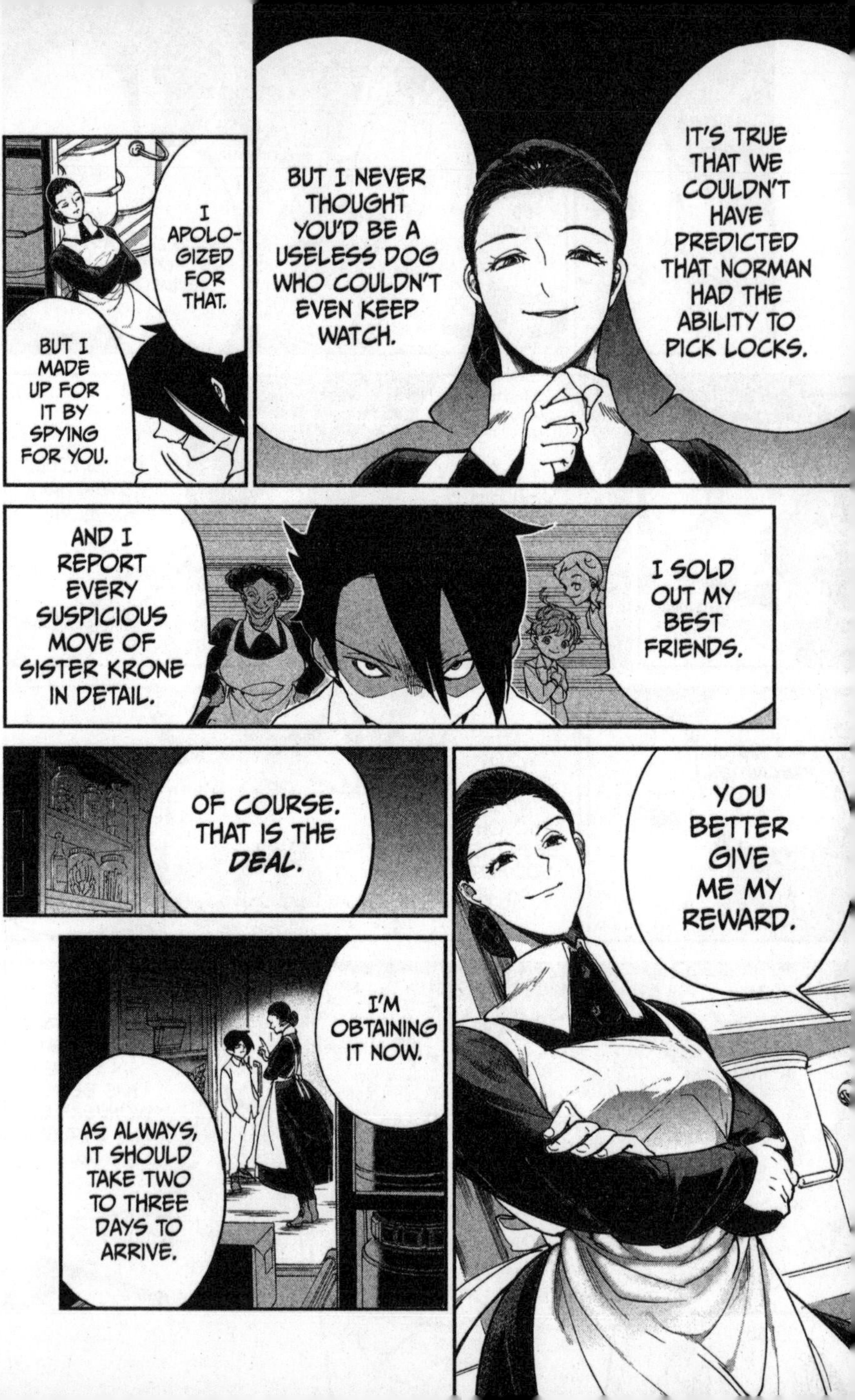
IT'S TRUE THAT WE COULDN'T HAVE PREDICTED THAT NORMAN HAD THE ABILITY TO PICK LOCKS.
BUT I NEVER THOUGHT YOU'D BE A USELESS DOG WHO COULDN'T EVEN KEEP WATCH.
I APOLOGIZED FOR THAT.
BUT I MADE UP FOR IT BY SPYING FOR YOU.
I SOLD OUT MY BEST FRIENDS.
AND I REPORT EVERY SUSPICIOUS MOVE OF SISTER KRONE IN DETAIL.
YOU BETTER GIVE ME MY REWARD.
OF COURSE. THAT IS THE *DEAL*.
I'M OBTAINING IT NOW.
AS ALWAYS, IT SHOULD TAKE TWO TO THREE DAYS TO ARRIVE.

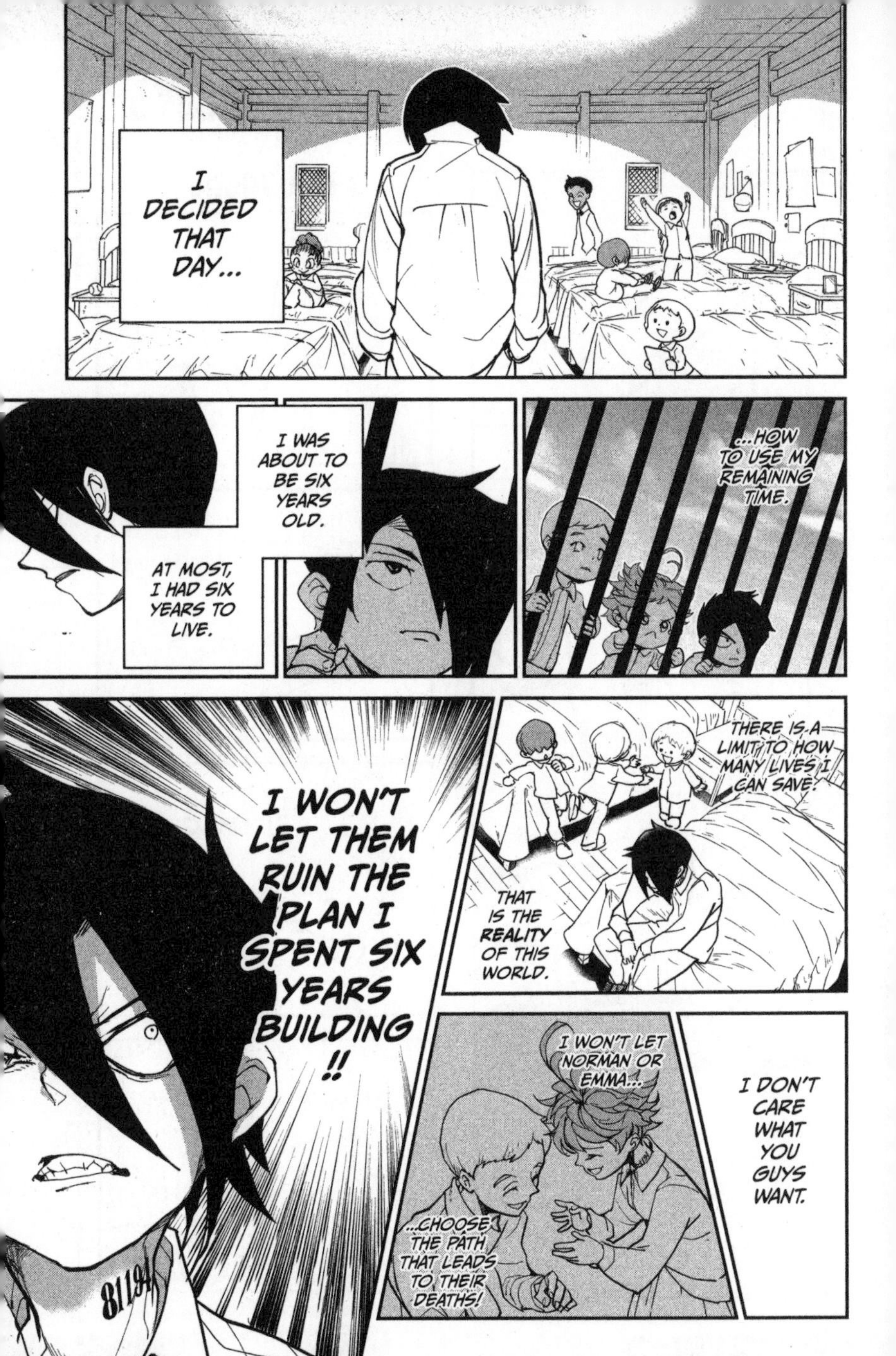
I DECIDED THAT DAY...
...HOW TO USE MY REMAINING TIME.
I WAS ABOUT TO BE SIX YEARS OLD.
AT MOST, I HAD SIX YEARS TO LIVE.
THERE IS A LIMIT TO HOW MANY LIVES I CAN SAVE.
THAT IS THE REALITY OF THIS WORLD.
I DON'T CARE WHAT YOU GUYS WANT.
I WON'T LET NORMAN OR EMMA...
...CHOOSE THE PATH THAT LEADS TO THEIR DEATHS!
I WON'T LET THEM RUIN THE PLAN I SPENT SIX YEARS BUILDING!!
81194

SIDE STORY 5

Not Alone

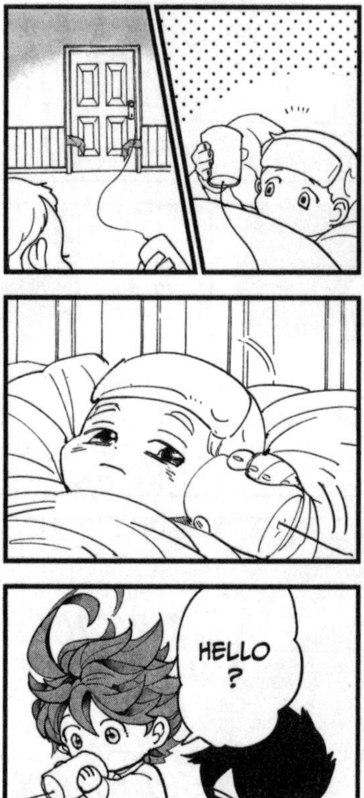

HELLO ?
NOW WE CAN TALK EVEN IF I'M OUTSIDE!

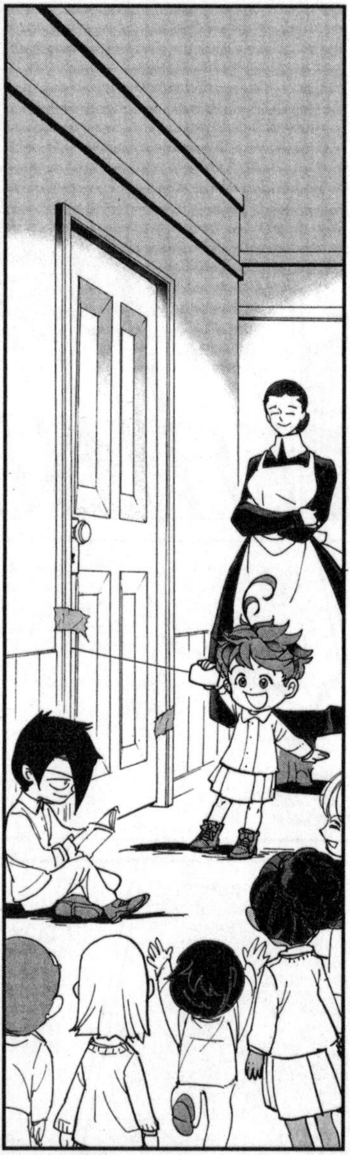

SIDE STORY – FIN

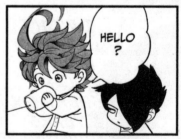

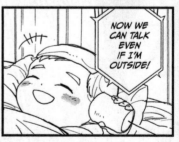

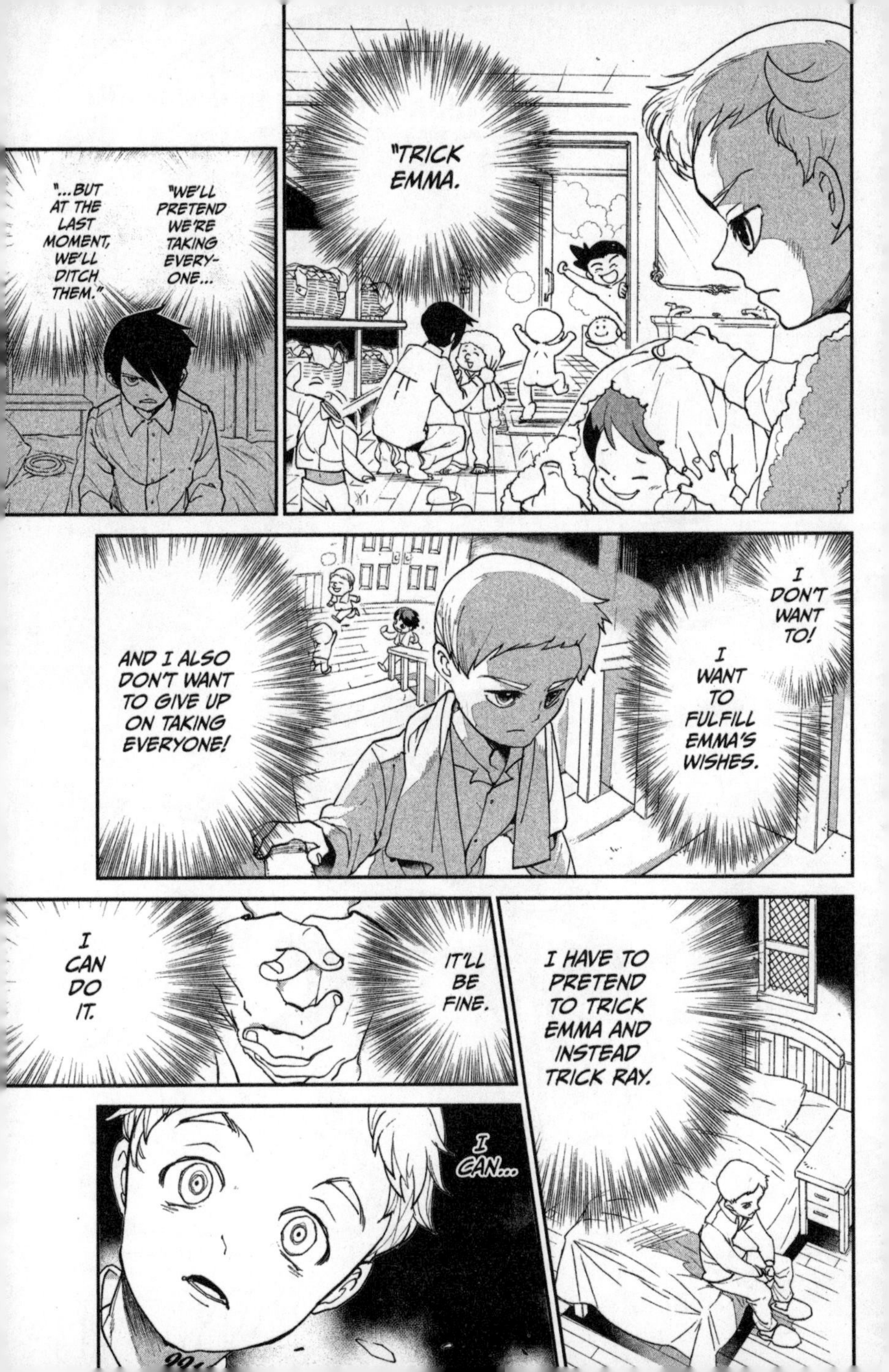
"TRICK EMMA.
"WE'LL PRETEND WE'RE TAKING EVERYONE...
"...BUT AT THE LAST MOMENT, WE'LL DITCH THEM."
I DON'T WANT TO!
I WANT TO FULFILL EMMA'S WISHES.
AND I ALSO DON'T WANT TO GIVE UP ON TAKING EVERYONE!
I HAVE TO PRETEND TO TRICK EMMA AND INSTEAD TRICK RAY.
IT'LL BE FINE.
I CAN DO IT.
I CAN...

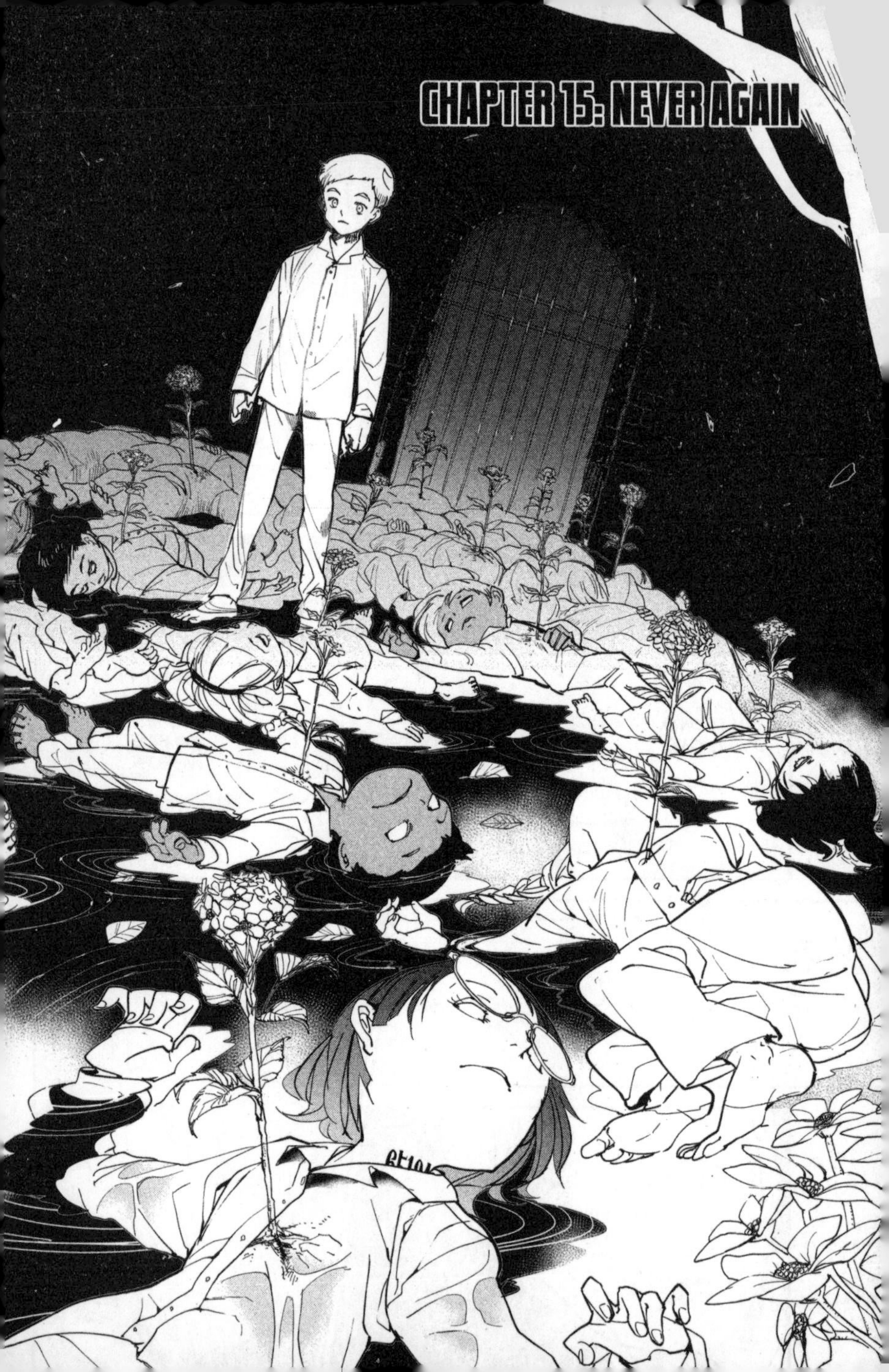
CHAPTER 15: NEVER AGAIN

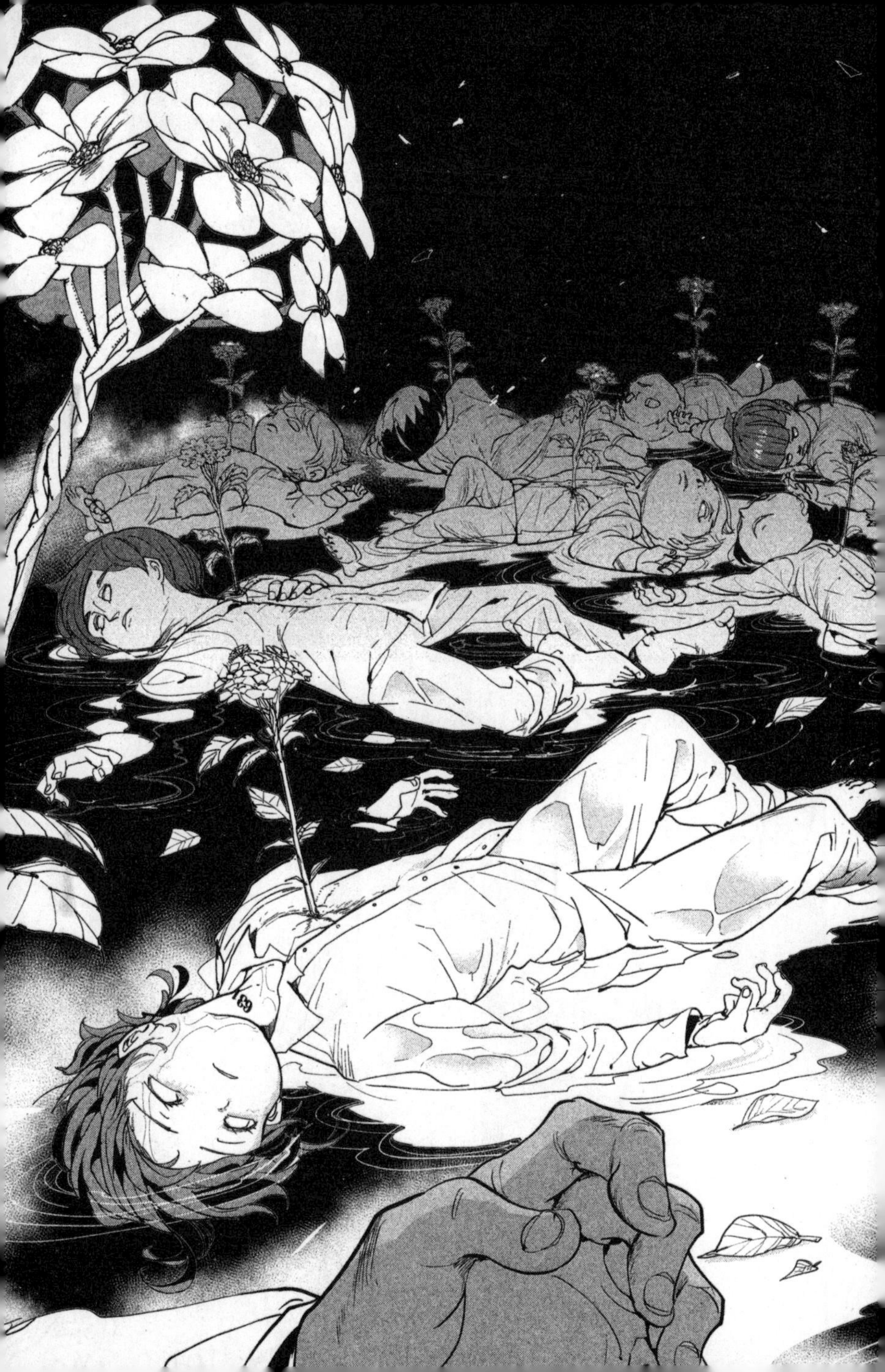

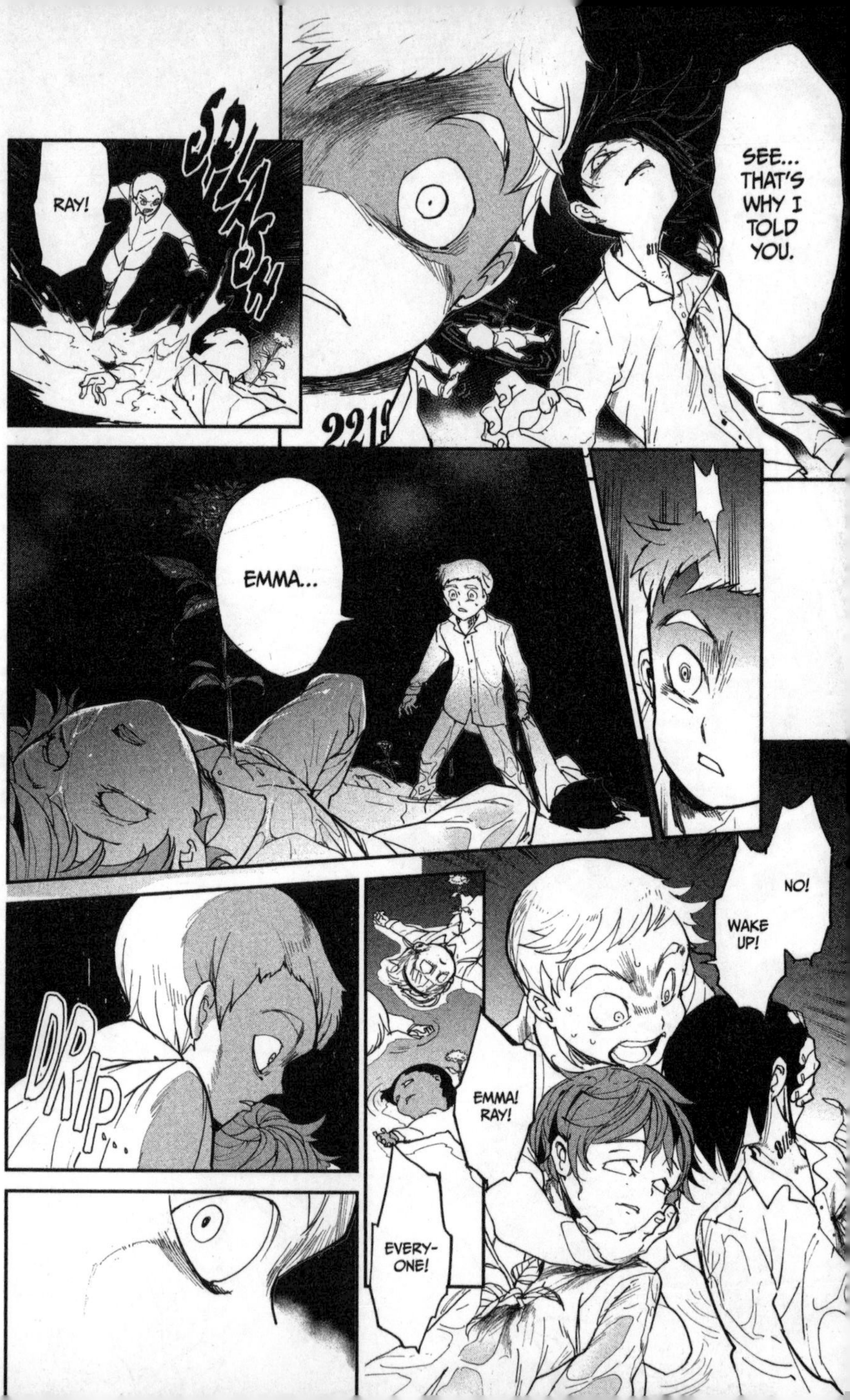
SEE... THAT'S WHY I TOLD YOU.
RAY!
SPLASH
EMMA...
NO!
WAKE UP!
EMMA! RAY!
EVERY-ONE!
DRIP...

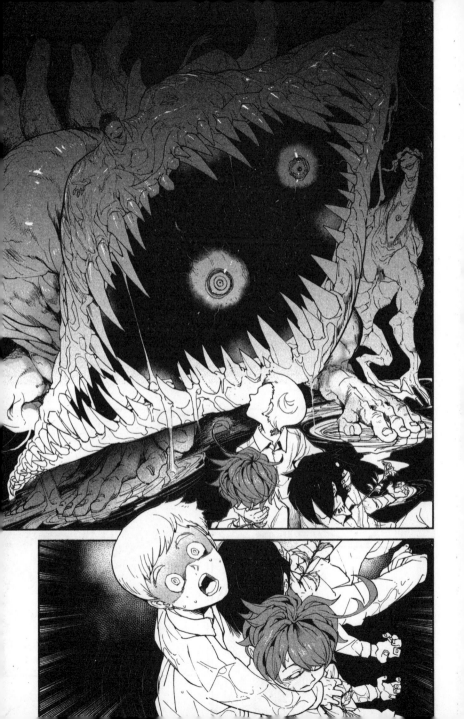

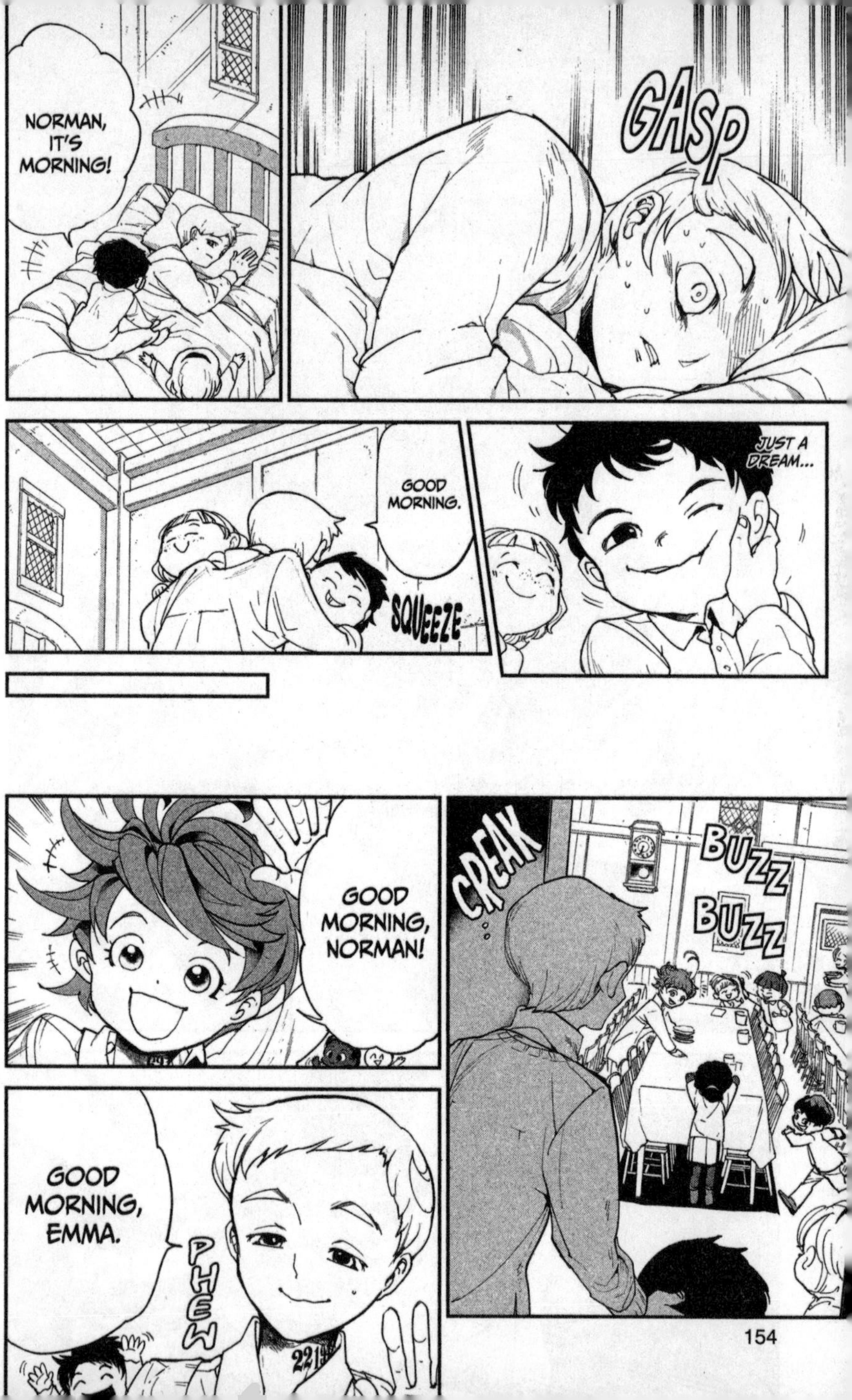
GASP
NORMAN, IT'S MORNING!
JUST A DREAM...
GOOD MORNING.
SQUEEZE
CREAK
BUZZ
BUZZ
GOOD MORNING, NORMAN!
GOOD MORNING, EMMA.
PHEW

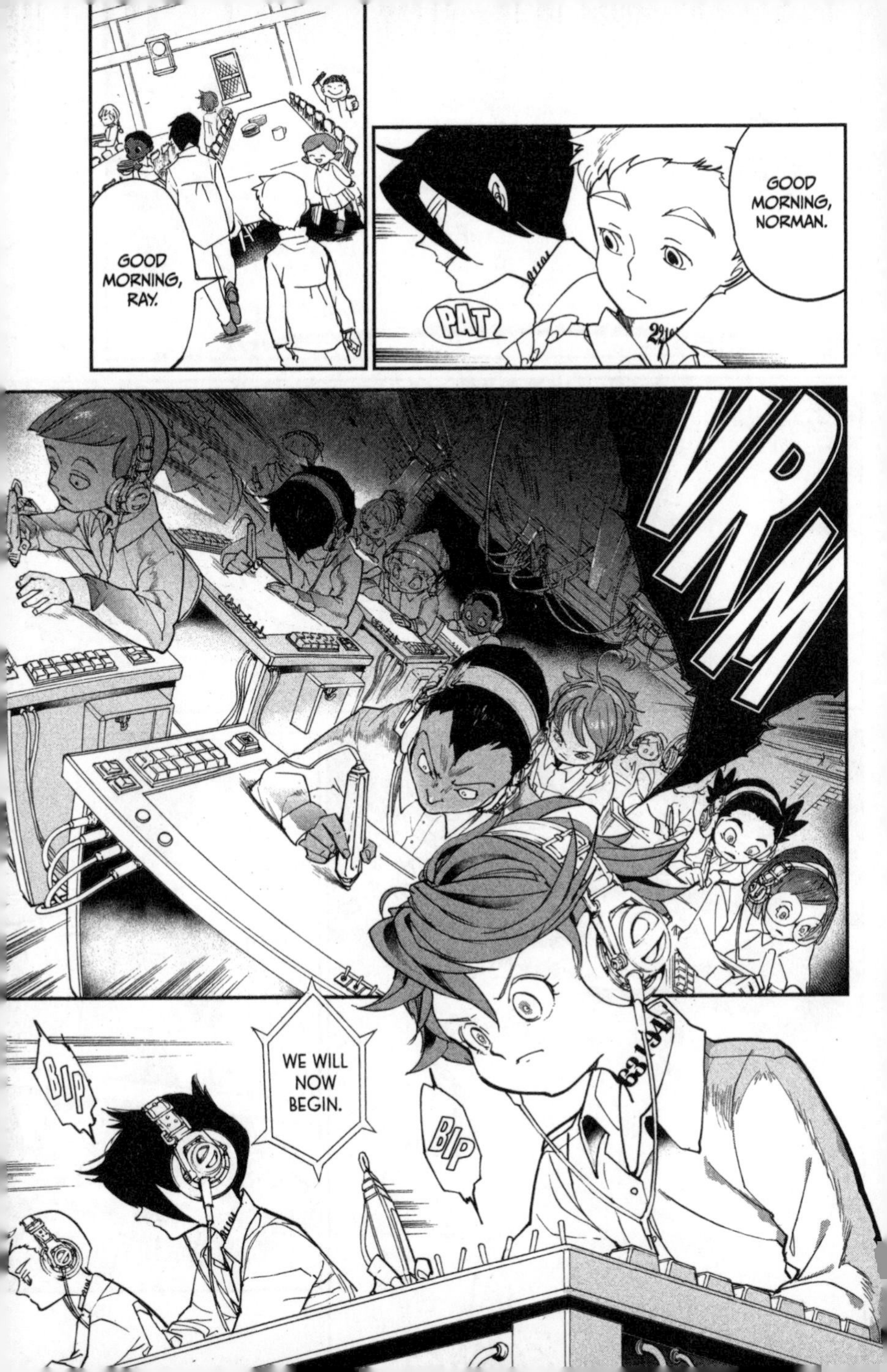
GOOD MORNING, NORMAN.
PAT
GOOD MORNING, RAY.
VRM
WE WILL NOW BEGIN.
BIP
BIP

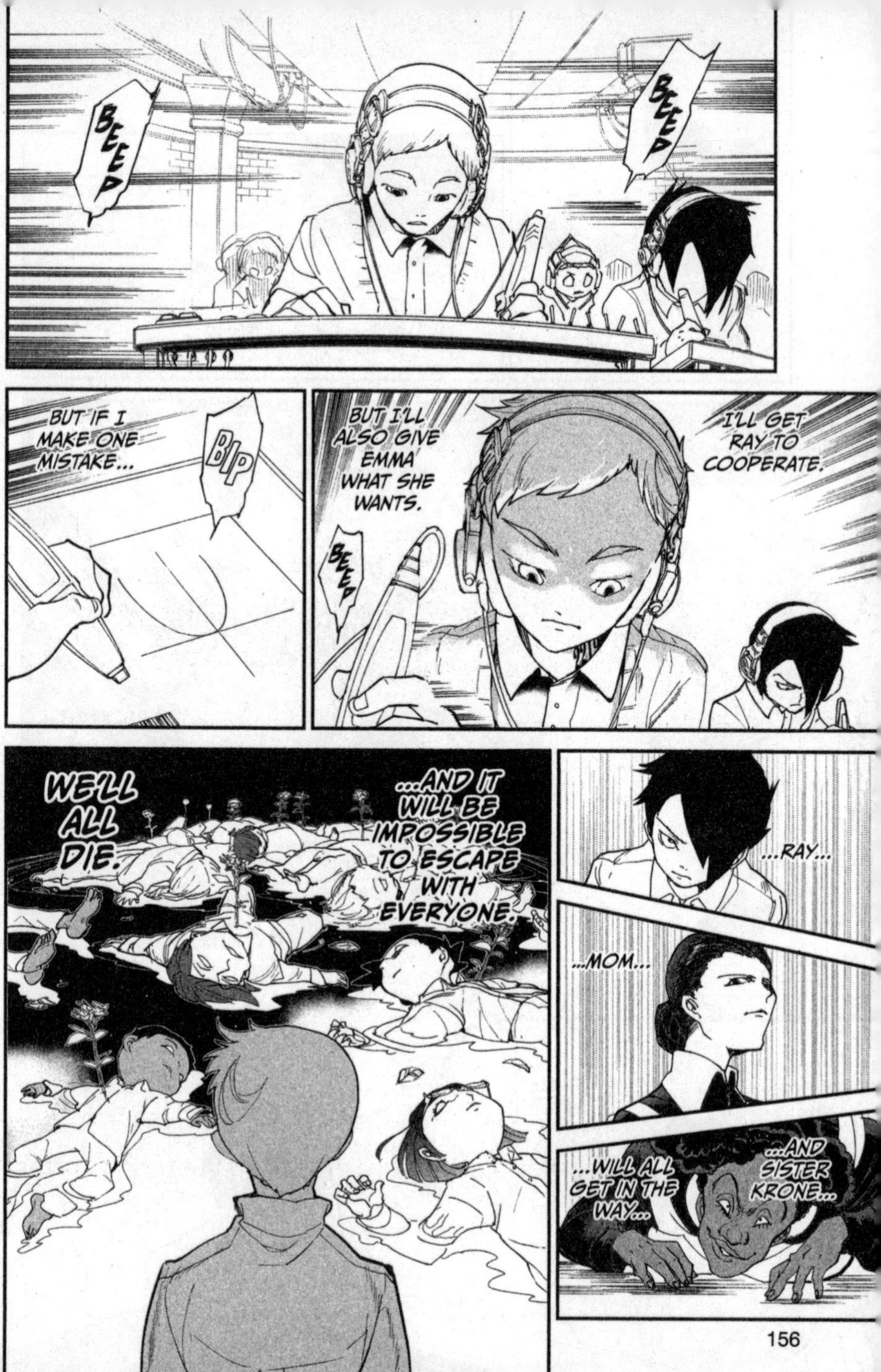
BEEEP
BEEEP
I'LL GET RAY TO COOPERATE.
BUT I'LL ALSO GIVE EMMA WHAT SHE WANTS.
BEEP
BIP
BUT IF I MAKE ONE MISTAKE...
...RAY...
...MOM...
...AND SISTER KRONE...
...WILL ALL GET IN THE WAY...
...AND IT WILL BE IMPOSSIBLE TO ESCAPE WITH EVERYONE.
WE'LL ALL DIE.

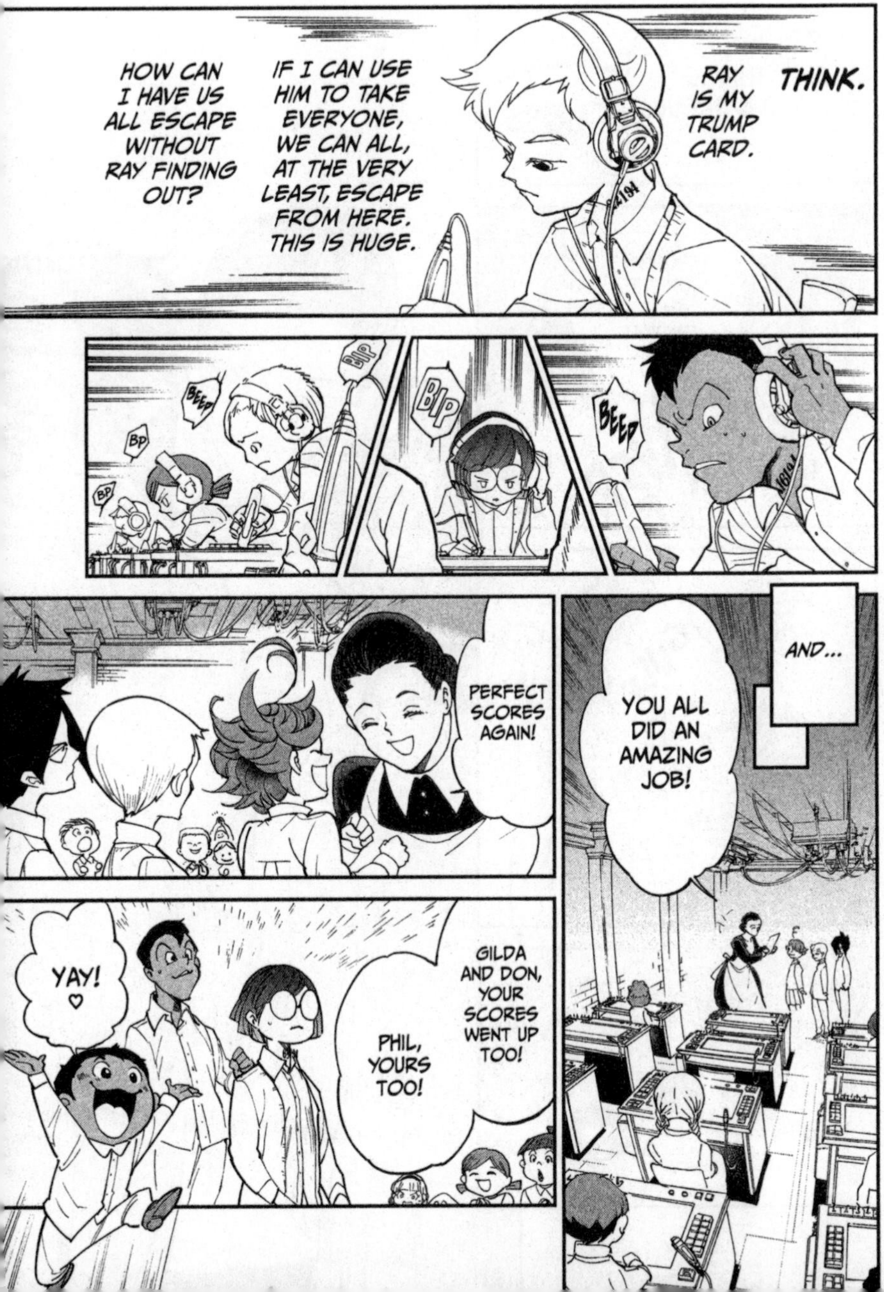
THINK.
RAY IS MY TRUMP CARD.
IF I CAN USE HIM TO TAKE EVERYONE, WE CAN ALL, AT THE VERY LEAST, ESCAPE FROM HERE. THIS IS HUGE.
HOW CAN I HAVE US ALL ESCAPE WITHOUT RAY FINDING OUT?
BEEP
BIP
BIP
BEEP
BP
BP
AND...
YOU ALL DID AN AMAZING JOB!
PERFECT SCORES AGAIN!
GILDA AND DON, YOUR SCORES WENT UP TOO!
PHIL, YOURS TOO!
YAY! ♡

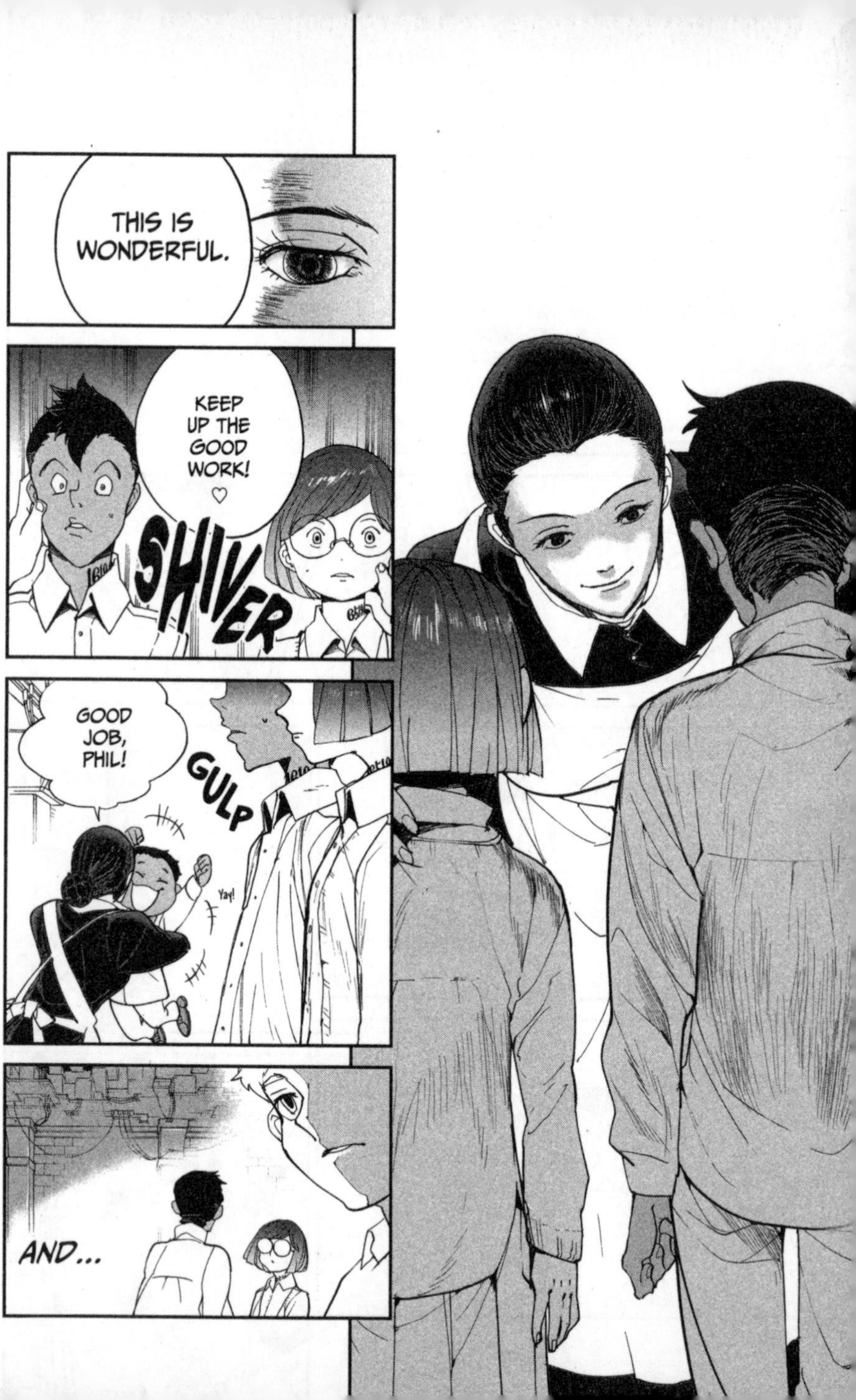
THIS IS WONDERFUL.
KEEP UP THE GOOD WORK! ♡
SHIVER
GOOD JOB, PHIL!
GULP
Yay!
AND...

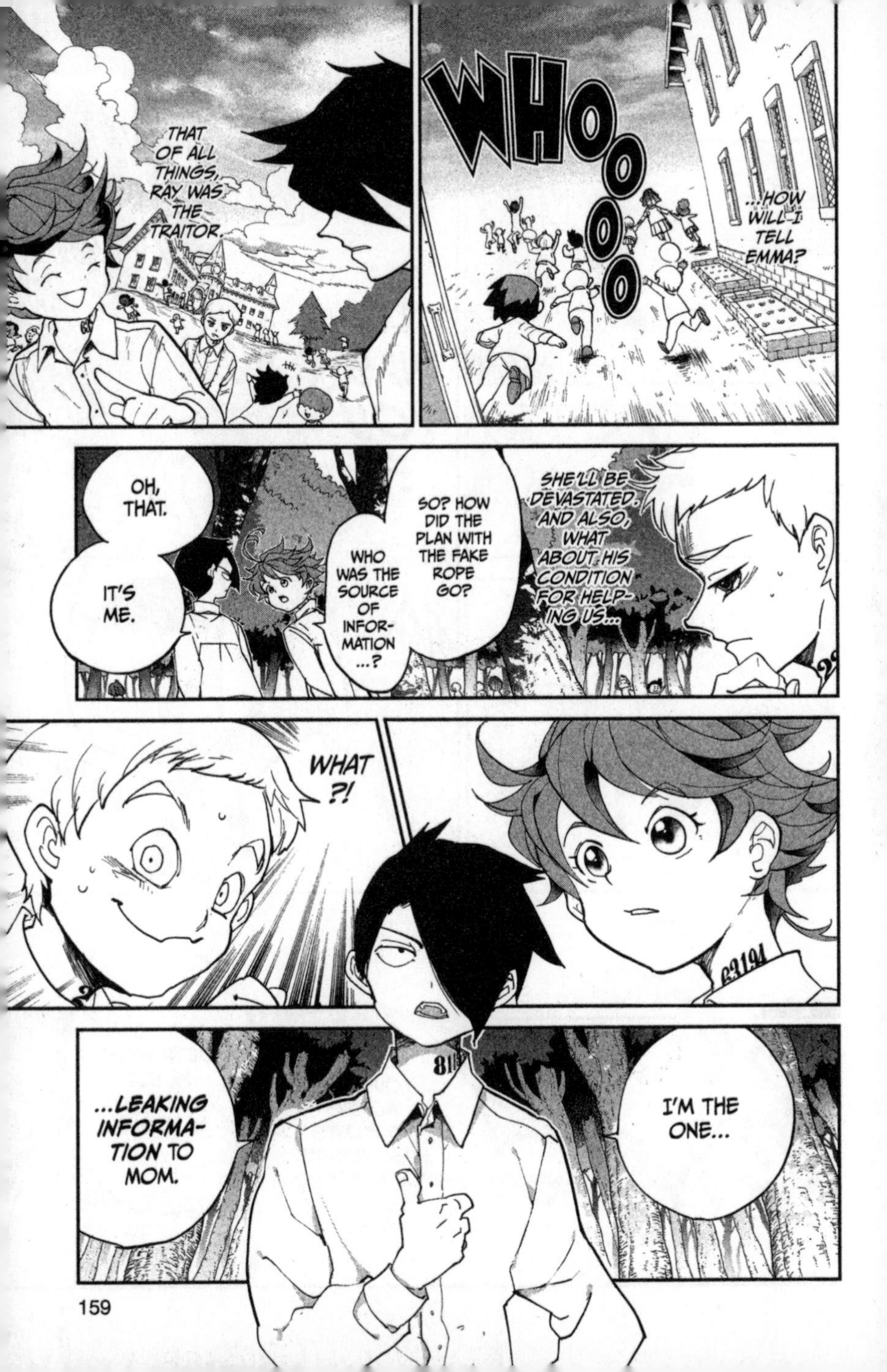
WHOOOOO
...HOW WILL I TELL EMMA?
THAT OF ALL THINGS, RAY WAS THE TRAITOR.
SHE'LL BE DEVASTATED. AND ALSO, WHAT ABOUT HIS CONDITION FOR HELPING US...
SO? HOW DID THE PLAN WITH THE FAKE ROPE GO?
WHO WAS THE SOURCE OF INFORMATION ...?
OH, THAT.
IT'S ME.
WHAT ?!
I'M THE ONE...
...LEAKING INFORMATION TO MOM.

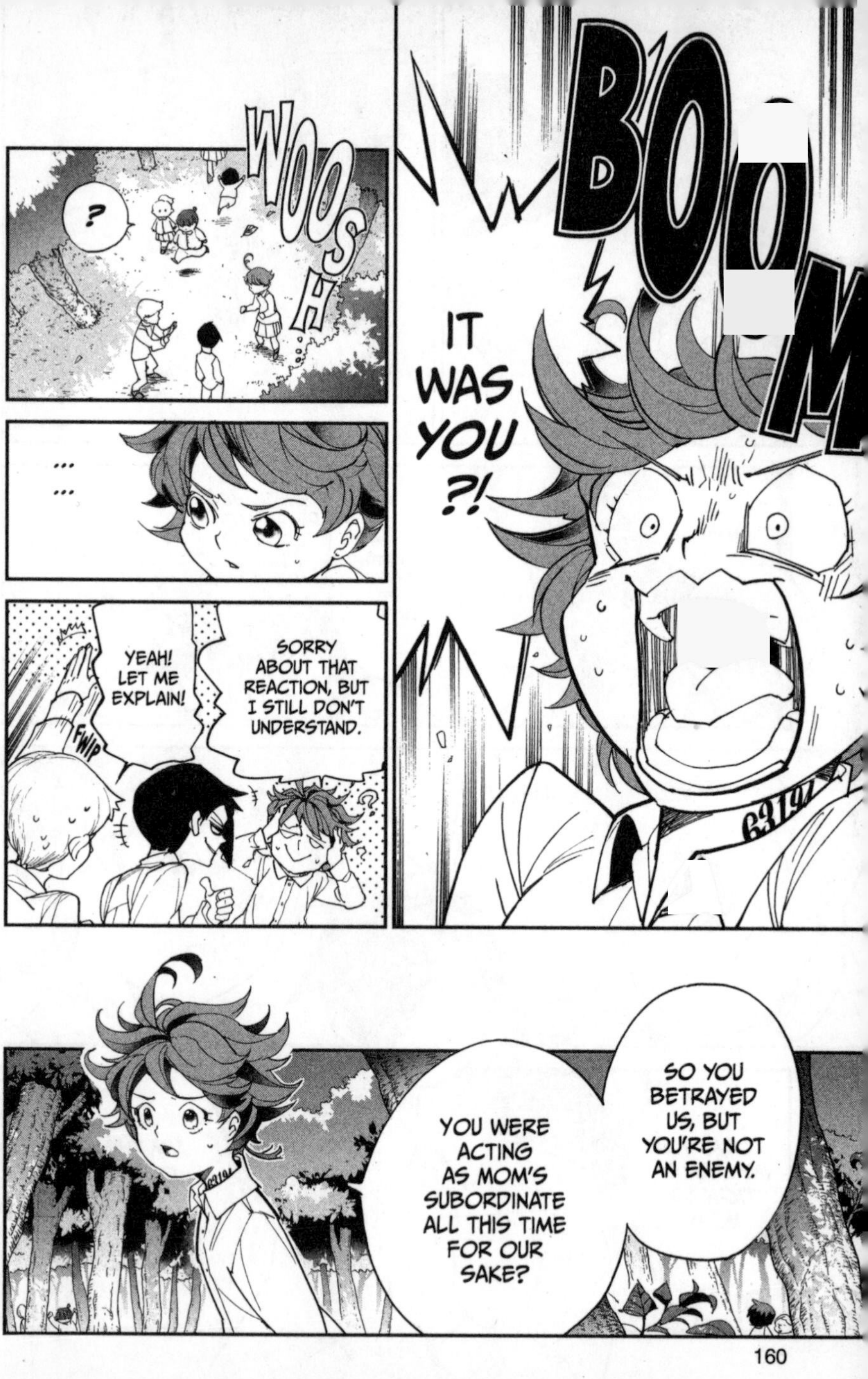
BOOM
IT WAS YOU?!
WOOSH
?
...
...
SORRY ABOUT THAT REACTION, BUT I STILL DON'T UNDERSTAND.
YEAH! LET ME EXPLAIN!
FWIP
SO YOU BETRAYED US, BUT YOU'RE NOT AN ENEMY.
YOU WERE ACTING AS MOM'S SUBORDINATE ALL THIS TIME FOR OUR SAKE?

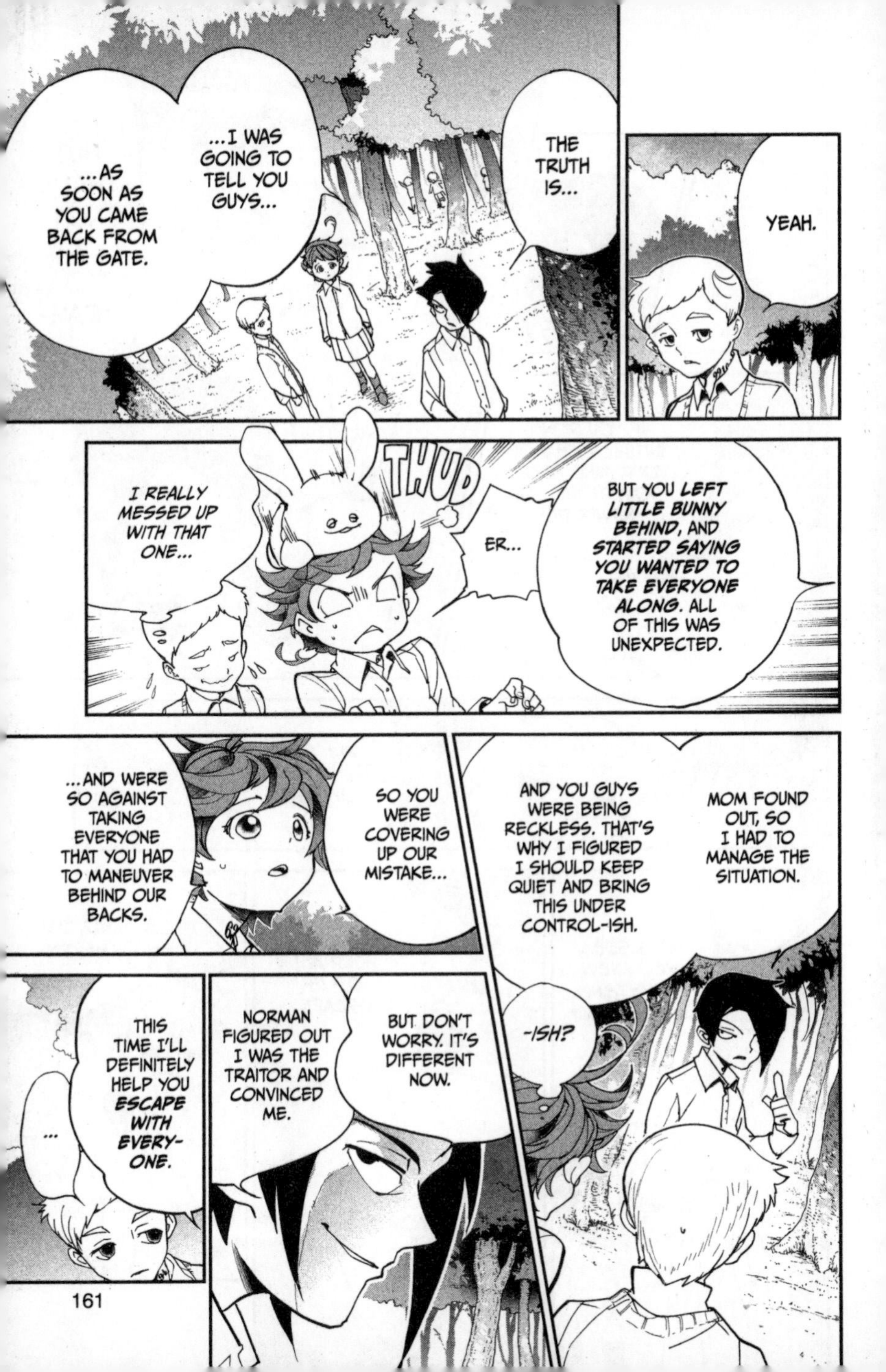
YEAH.
THE TRUTH IS...
...I WAS GOING TO TELL YOU GUYS...
...AS SOON AS YOU CAME BACK FROM THE GATE.
BUT YOU *LEFT LITTLE BUNNY BEHIND*, AND *STARTED SAYING YOU WANTED TO TAKE EVERYONE ALONG*. ALL OF THIS WAS UNEXPECTED.
ER...
THUD
I REALLY MESSED UP WITH THAT ONE...
MOM FOUND OUT, SO I HAD TO MANAGE THE SITUATION.
AND YOU GUYS WERE BEING RECKLESS. THAT'S WHY I FIGURED I SHOULD KEEP QUIET AND BRING THIS UNDER CONTROL-ISH.
-ISH?
SO YOU WERE COVERING UP OUR MISTAKE...
...AND WERE SO AGAINST TAKING EVERYONE THAT YOU HAD TO MANEUVER BEHIND OUR BACKS.
BUT DON'T WORRY. IT'S DIFFERENT NOW.
NORMAN FIGURED OUT I WAS THE TRAITOR AND CONVINCED ME.
THIS TIME I'LL DEFINITELY HELP YOU *ESCAPE WITH EVERY-ONE*.
...

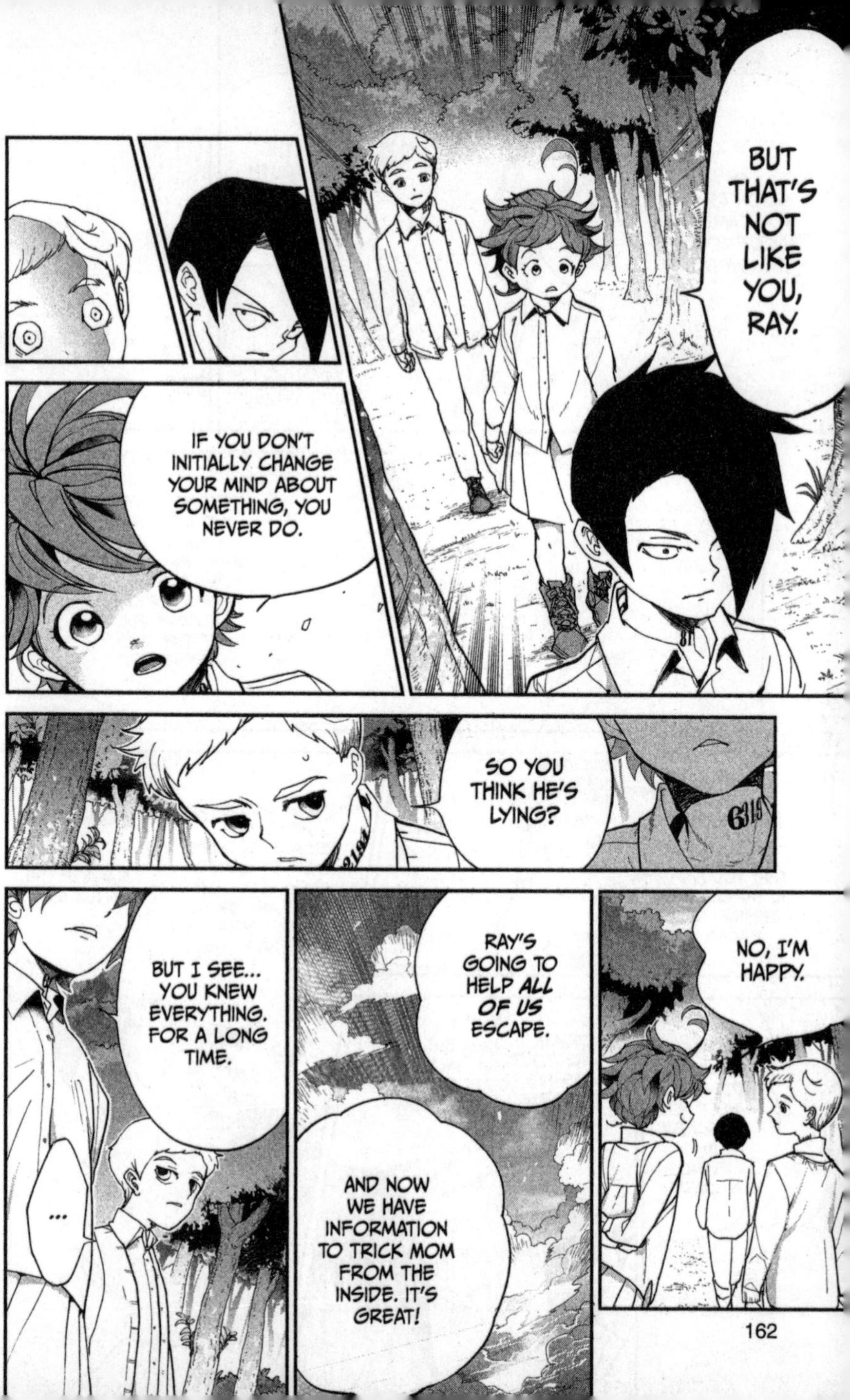
BUT THAT'S NOT LIKE YOU, RAY.
IF YOU DON'T INITIALLY CHANGE YOUR MIND ABOUT SOMETHING, YOU NEVER DO.
SO YOU THINK HE'S LYING?
NO, I'M HAPPY.
RAY'S GOING TO HELP ALL OF US ESCAPE.
AND NOW WE HAVE INFORMATION TO TRICK MOM FROM THE INSIDE. IT'S GREAT!
BUT I SEE... YOU KNEW EVERYTHING. FOR A LONG TIME.
...

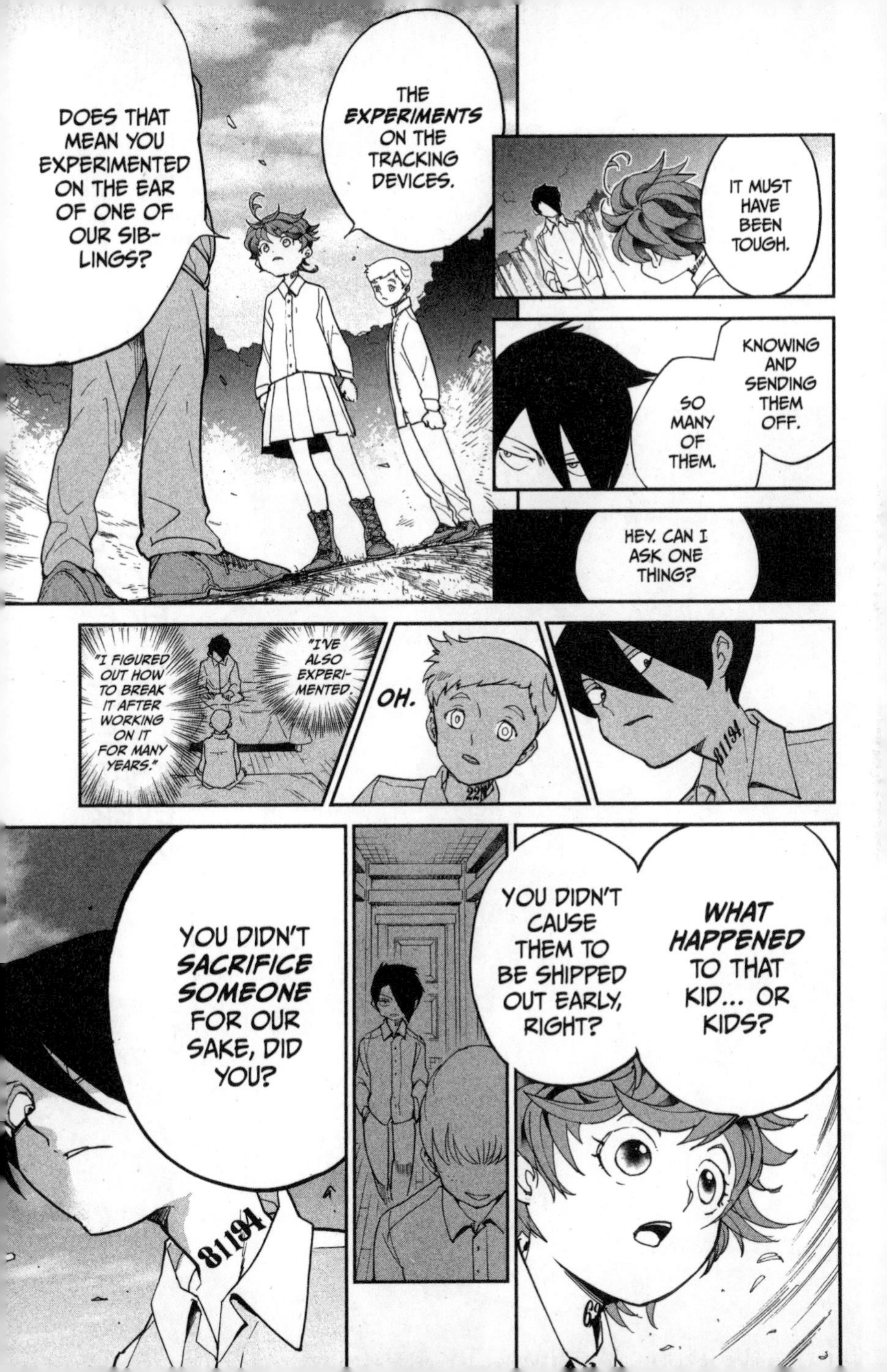
IT MUST HAVE BEEN TOUGH.
KNOWING AND SENDING THEM OFF.
SO MANY OF THEM.
HEY. CAN I ASK ONE THING?
THE *EXPERIMENTS* ON THE TRACKING DEVICES.
DOES THAT MEAN YOU EXPERIMENTED ON THE EAR OF ONE OF OUR SIB-LINGS?
81194
OH.
22
"I'VE ALSO EXPERI-MENTED.
"I FIGURED OUT HOW TO BREAK IT AFTER WORKING ON IT FOR MANY YEARS."
WHAT HAPPENED TO THAT KID... OR KIDS?
YOU DIDN'T CAUSE THEM TO BE SHIPPED OUT EARLY, RIGHT?
YOU DIDN'T *SACRIFICE SOMEONE* FOR OUR SAKE, DID YOU?
81194

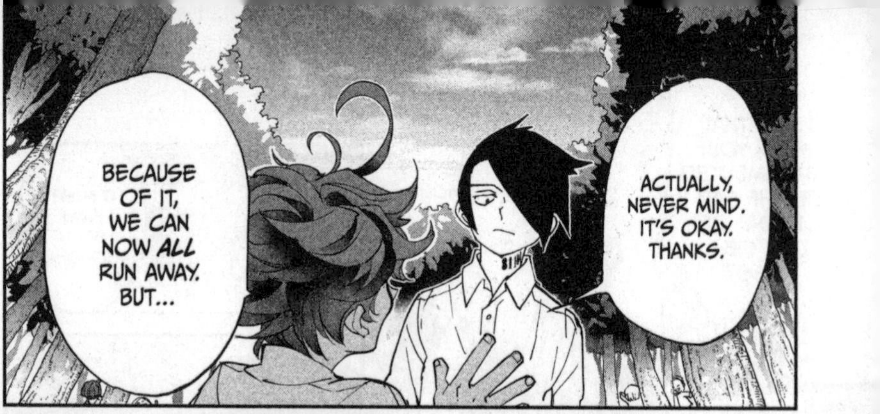
ACTUALLY, NEVER MIND. IT'S OKAY. THANKS.
BECAUSE OF IT, WE CAN NOW *ALL* RUN AWAY. BUT...
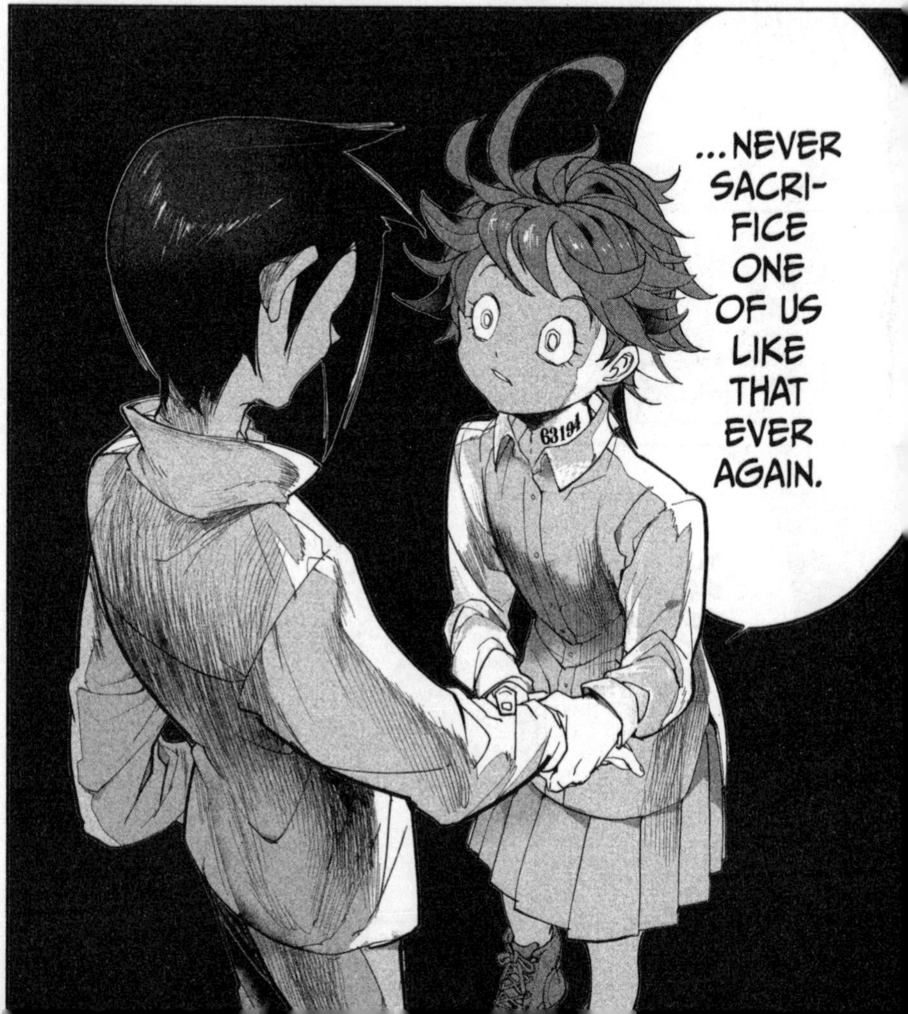
...NEVER SACRIFICE ONE OF US LIKE THAT EVER AGAIN.

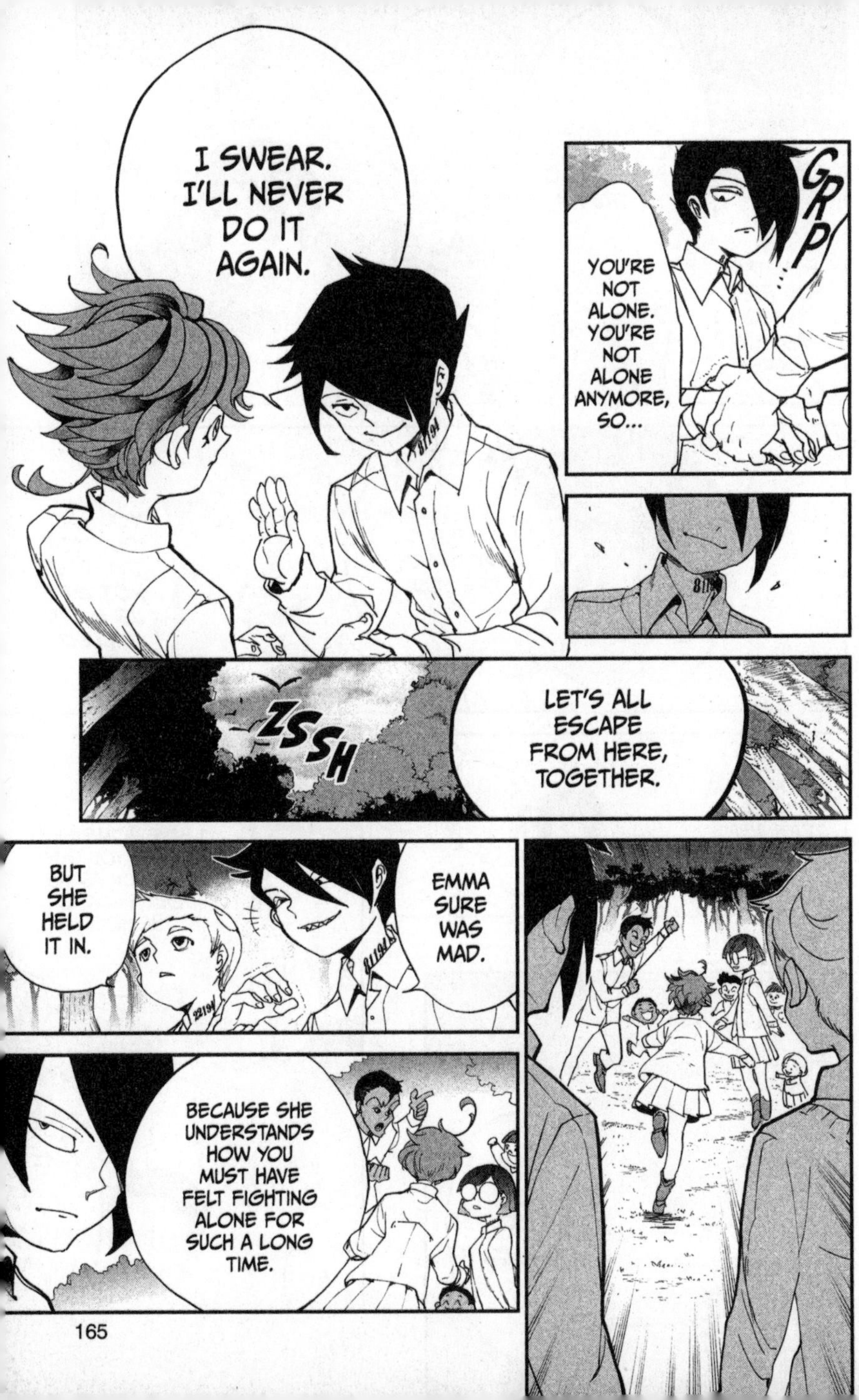
GRP
YOU'RE NOT ALONE. YOU'RE NOT ALONE ANYMORE, SO...
I SWEAR. I'LL NEVER DO IT AGAIN.
LET'S ALL ESCAPE FROM HERE, TOGETHER.
ZSSH
EMMA SURE WAS MAD.
BUT SHE HELD IT IN.
BECAUSE SHE UNDERSTANDS HOW YOU MUST HAVE FELT FIGHTING ALONE FOR SUCH A LONG TIME.

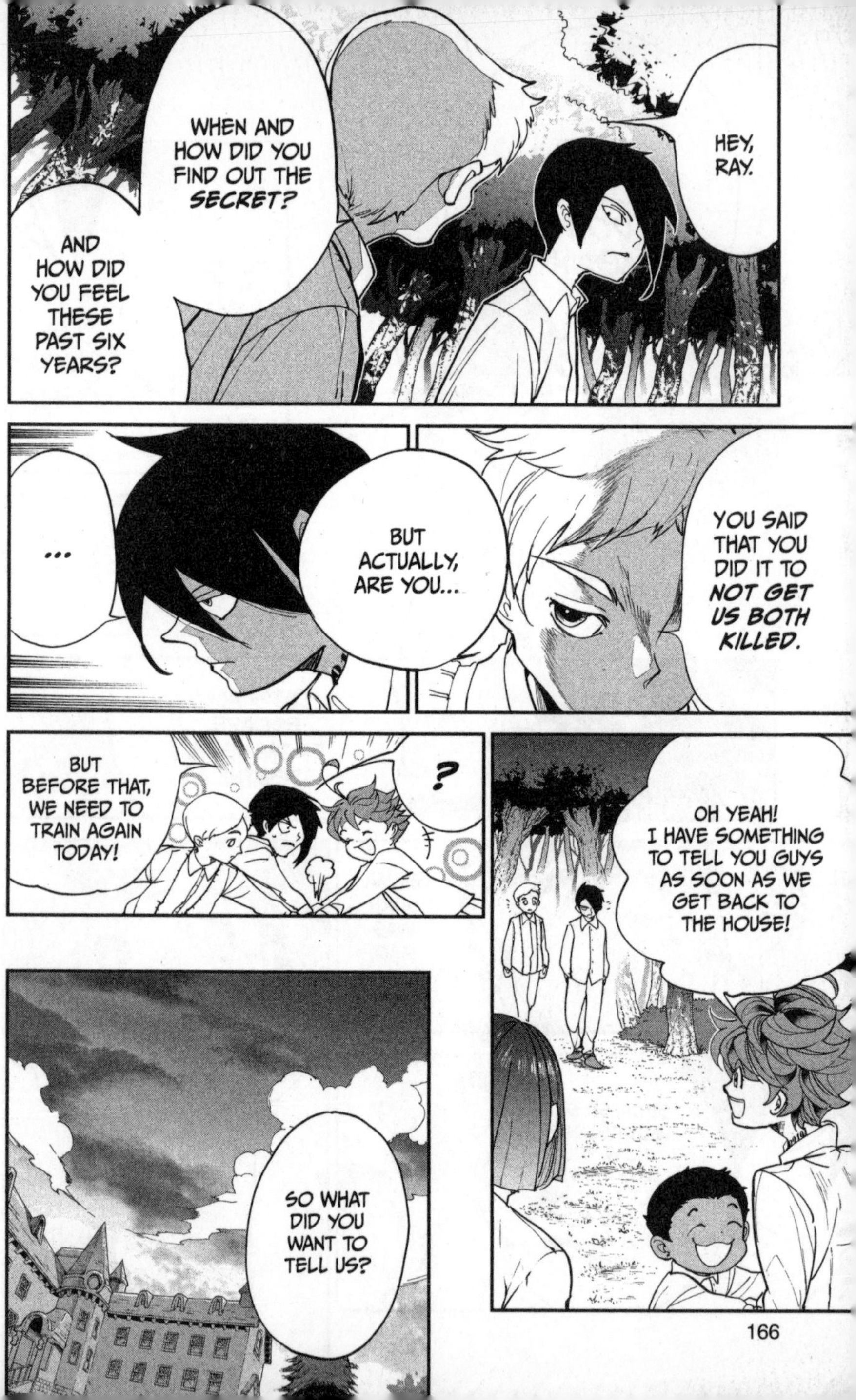
HEY, RAY.
WHEN AND HOW DID YOU FIND OUT THE *SECRET?*
AND HOW DID YOU FEEL THESE PAST SIX YEARS?
YOU SAID THAT YOU DID IT TO *NOT GET US BOTH KILLED.*
BUT ACTUALLY, ARE YOU...
...
OH YEAH! I HAVE SOMETHING TO TELL YOU GUYS AS SOON AS WE GET BACK TO THE HOUSE!
?
BUT BEFORE THAT, WE NEED TO TRAIN AGAIN TODAY!
SO WHAT DID YOU WANT TO TELL US?

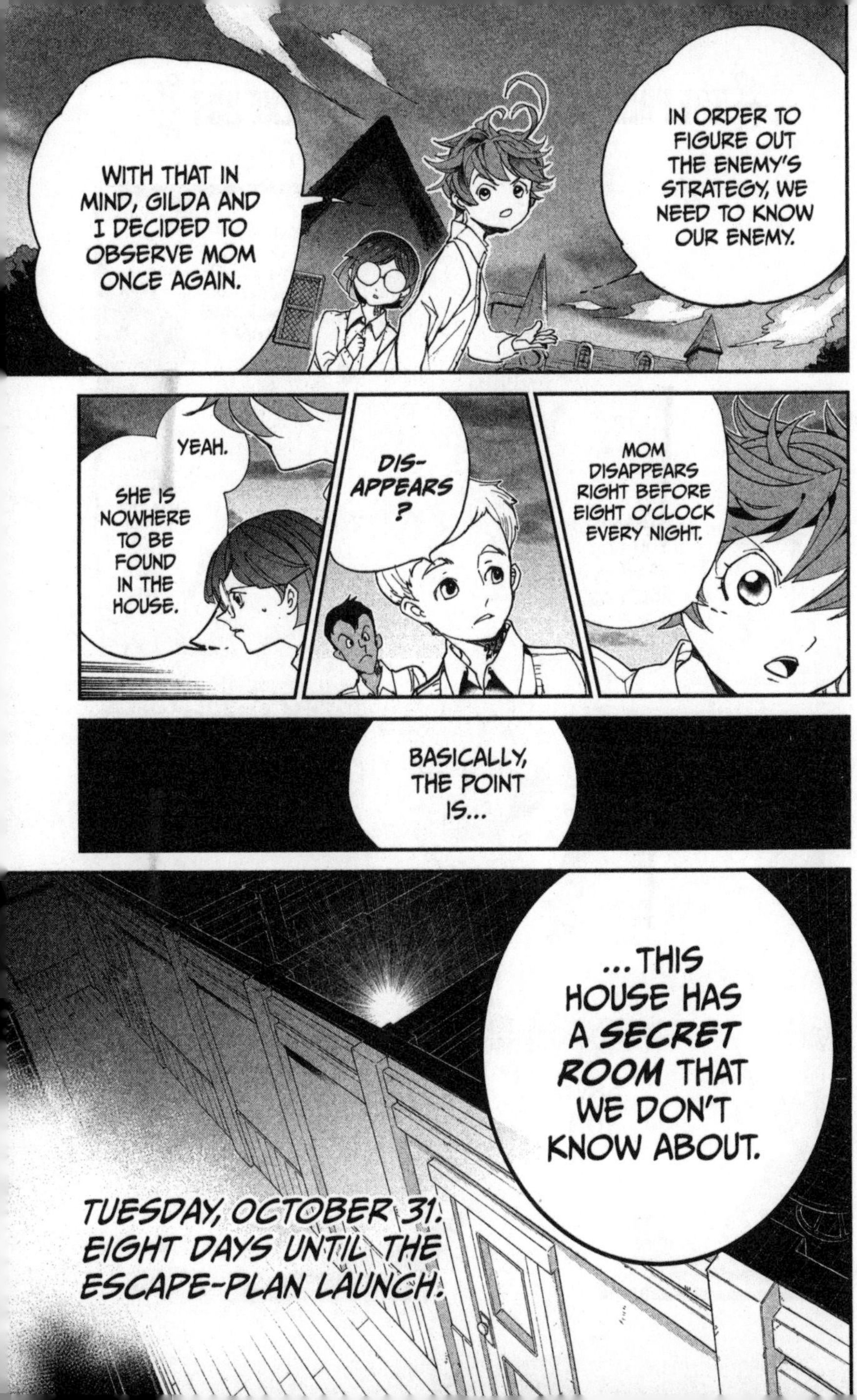
IN ORDER TO FIGURE OUT THE ENEMY'S STRATEGY, WE NEED TO KNOW OUR ENEMY.
WITH THAT IN MIND, GILDA AND I DECIDED TO OBSERVE MOM ONCE AGAIN.
MOM DISAPPEARS RIGHT BEFORE EIGHT O'CLOCK EVERY NIGHT.
DIS-APPEARS?
YEAH.
SHE IS NOWHERE TO BE FOUND IN THE HOUSE.
BASICALLY, THE POINT IS...
...THIS HOUSE HAS A SECRET ROOM THAT WE DON'T KNOW ABOUT.
TUESDAY, OCTOBER 31. EIGHT DAYS UNTIL THE ESCAPE-PLAN LAUNCH.

THE PROMISED NEVERLAND SIDE SCENE 003

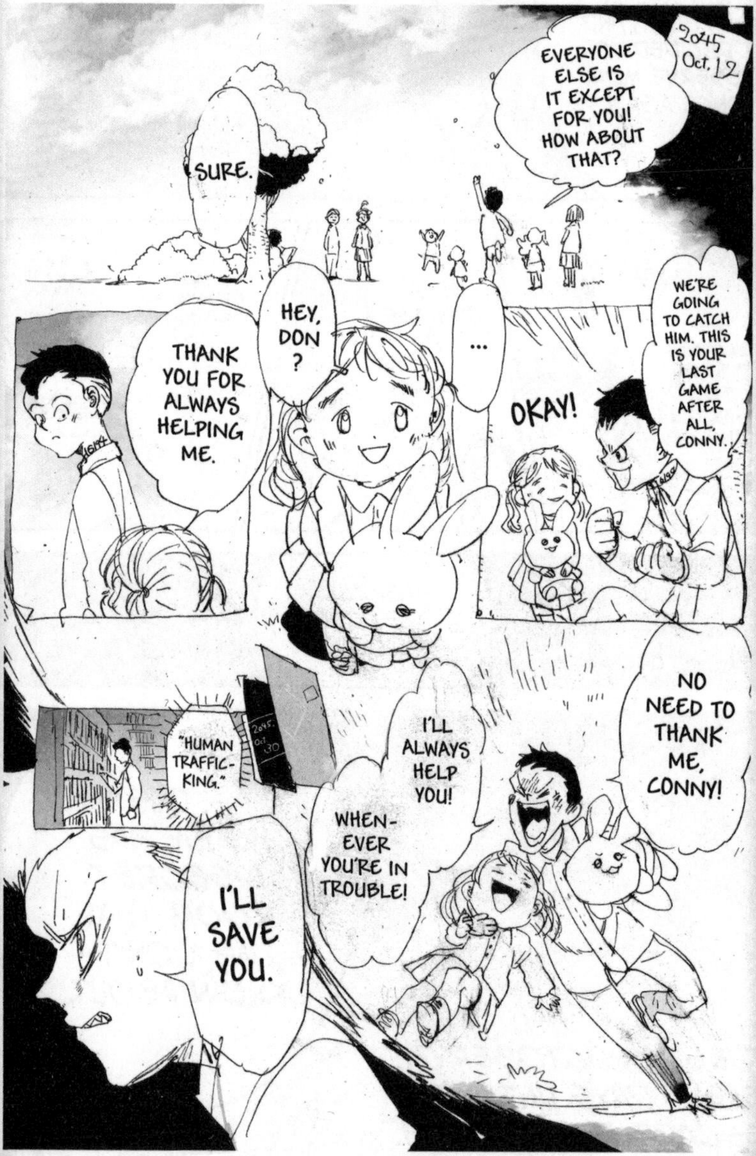
2045 Oct. 12
EVERYONE ELSE IS IT EXCEPT FOR YOU! HOW ABOUT THAT?
SURE.
WE'RE GOING TO CATCH HIM. THIS IS YOUR LAST GAME AFTER ALL, CONNY.
OKAY!
...
HEY, DON?
THANK YOU FOR ALWAYS HELPING ME.
NO NEED TO THANK ME, CONNY!
I'LL ALWAYS HELP YOU!
WHEN-EVER YOU'RE IN TROUBLE!
2045 Oct 30
"HUMAN TRAFFIC-KING."
I'LL SAVE YOU.

CHAPTER 16:
THE SECRET ROOM AND WILLIAM MINERVA, PART 1

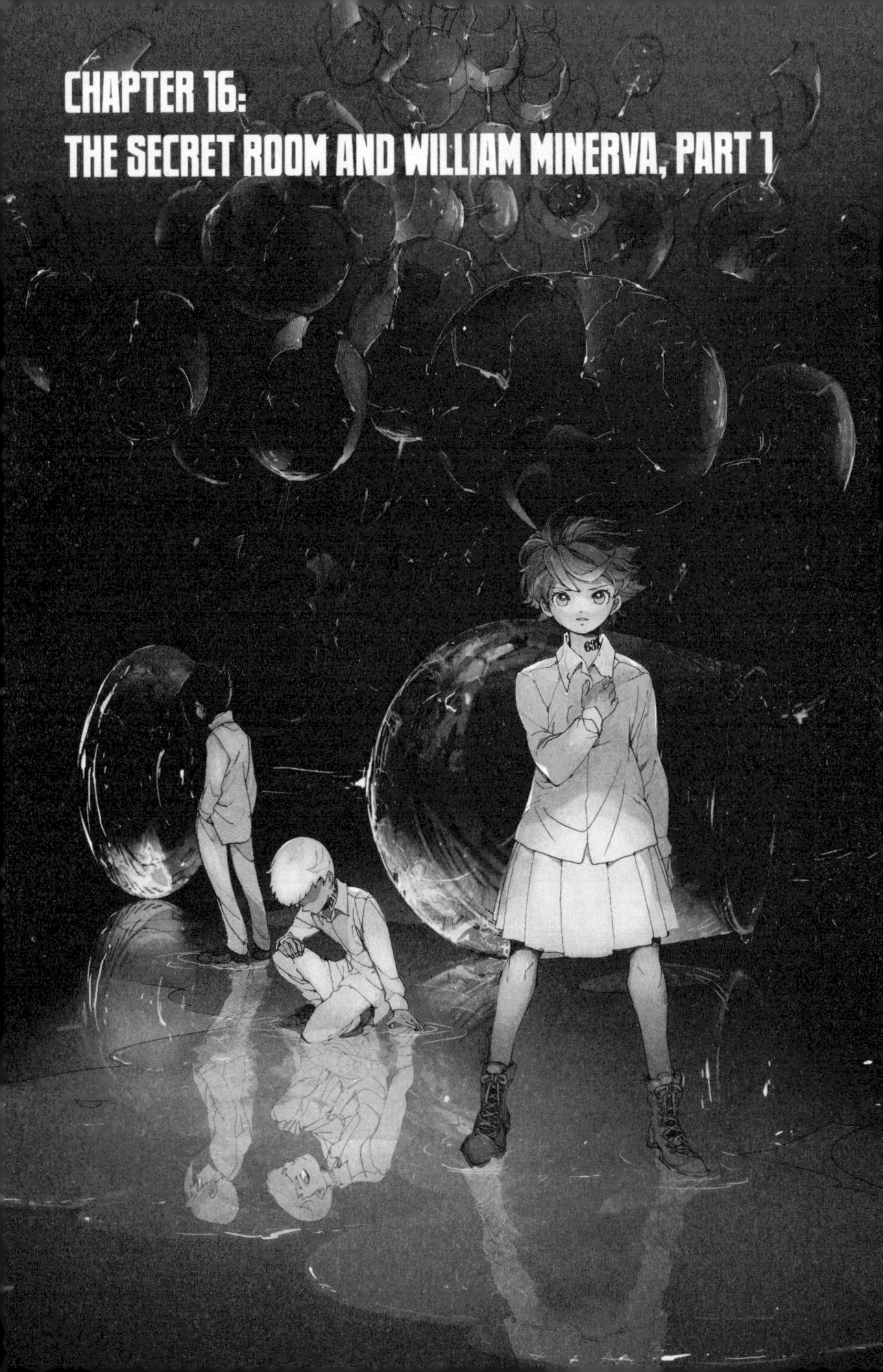

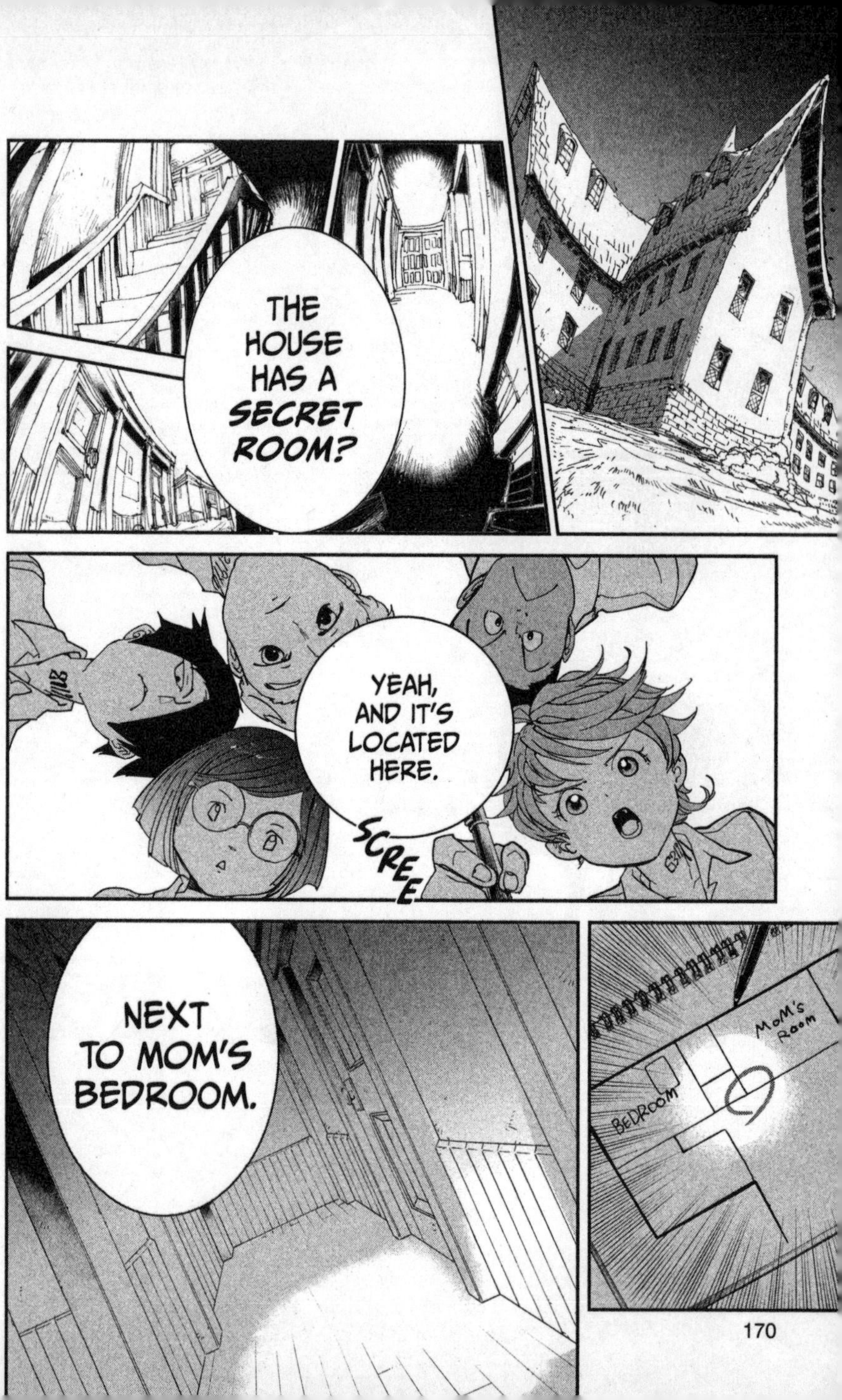
THE HOUSE HAS A SECRET ROOM?
YEAH, AND IT'S LOCATED HERE.
SCREE
MOM'S ROOM
BEDROOM
NEXT TO MOM'S BEDROOM.

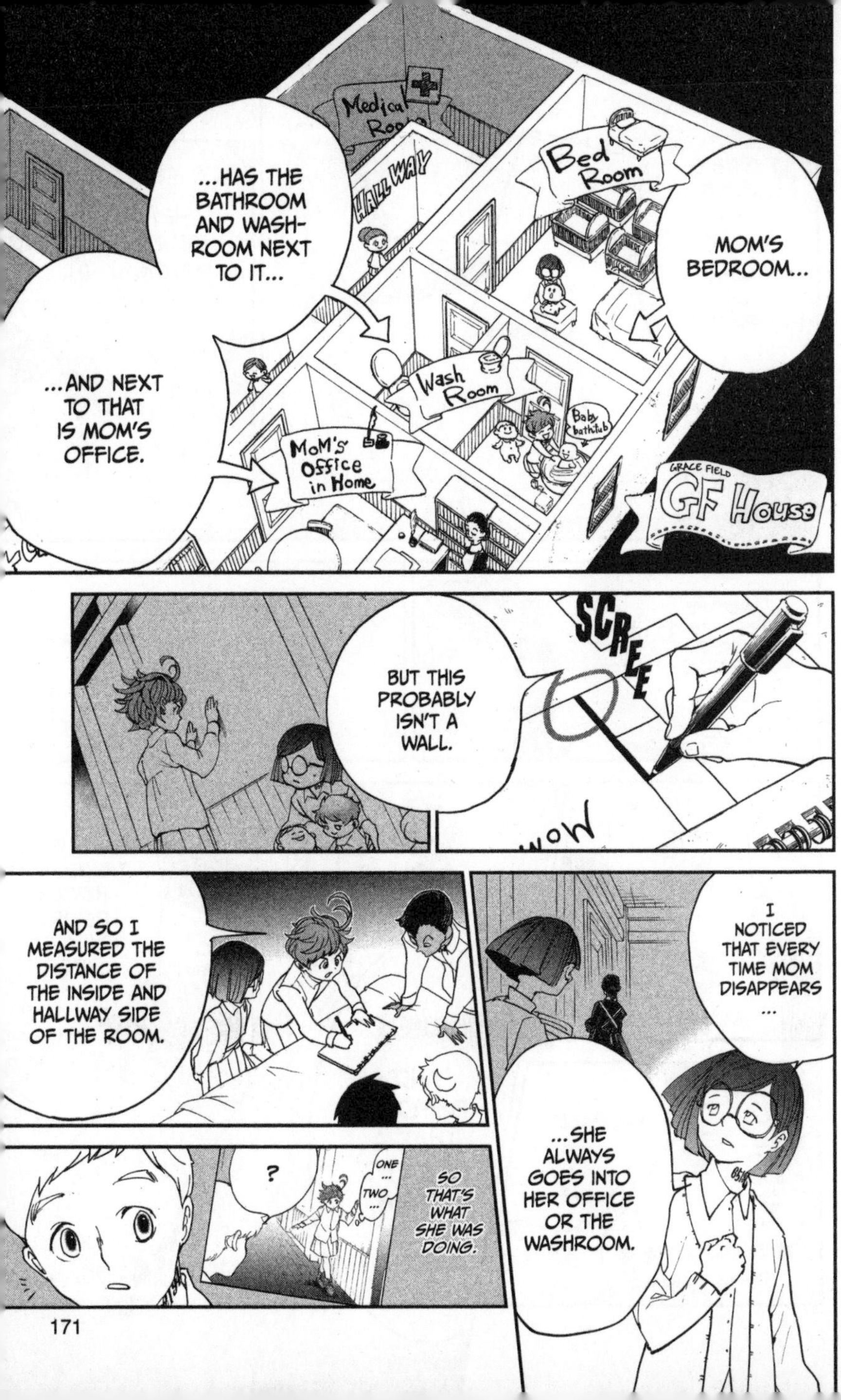
Medical Room
HALLWAY
Bed Room
MOM'S BEDROOM...
...HAS THE BATHROOM AND WASH-ROOM NEXT TO IT...
Wash Room
Baby bathtub
...AND NEXT TO THAT IS MOM'S OFFICE.
MoM's Office in Home
GRACE FIELD
GF House
SCREE
BUT THIS PROBABLY ISN'T A WALL.
WOW
I NOTICED THAT EVERY TIME MOM DISAPPEARS ...
...SHE ALWAYS GOES INTO HER OFFICE OR THE WASHROOM.
AND SO I MEASURED THE DISTANCE OF THE INSIDE AND HALLWAY SIDE OF THE ROOM.
SO THAT'S WHAT SHE WAS DOING.
ONE ...
TWO ...
?

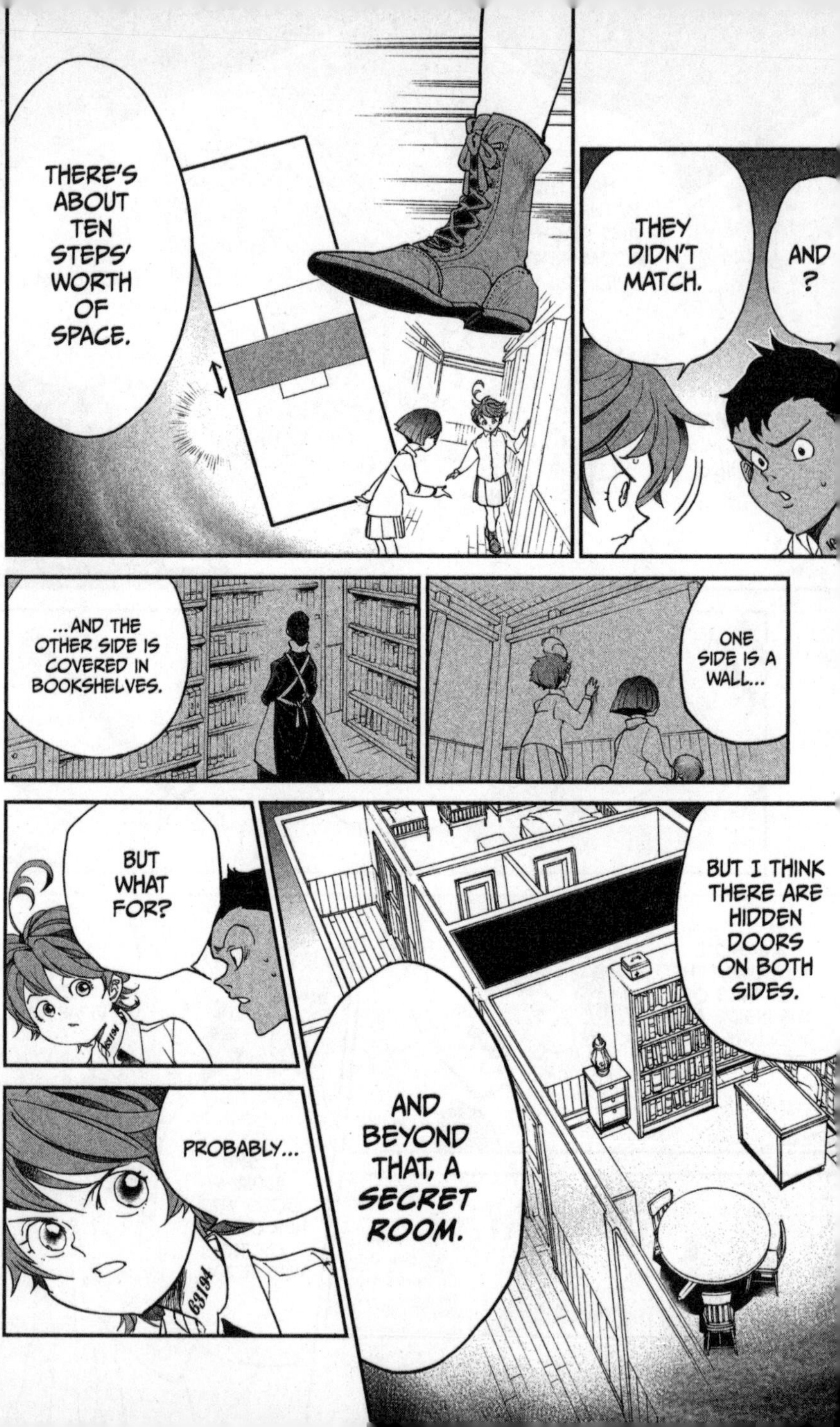
AND ?
THEY DIDN'T MATCH.
THERE'S ABOUT TEN STEPS' WORTH OF SPACE.
ONE SIDE IS A WALL...
...AND THE OTHER SIDE IS COVERED IN BOOKSHELVES.
BUT I THINK THERE ARE HIDDEN DOORS ON BOTH SIDES.
AND BEYOND THAT, A *SECRET ROOM.*
BUT WHAT FOR?
PROBABLY...
63194

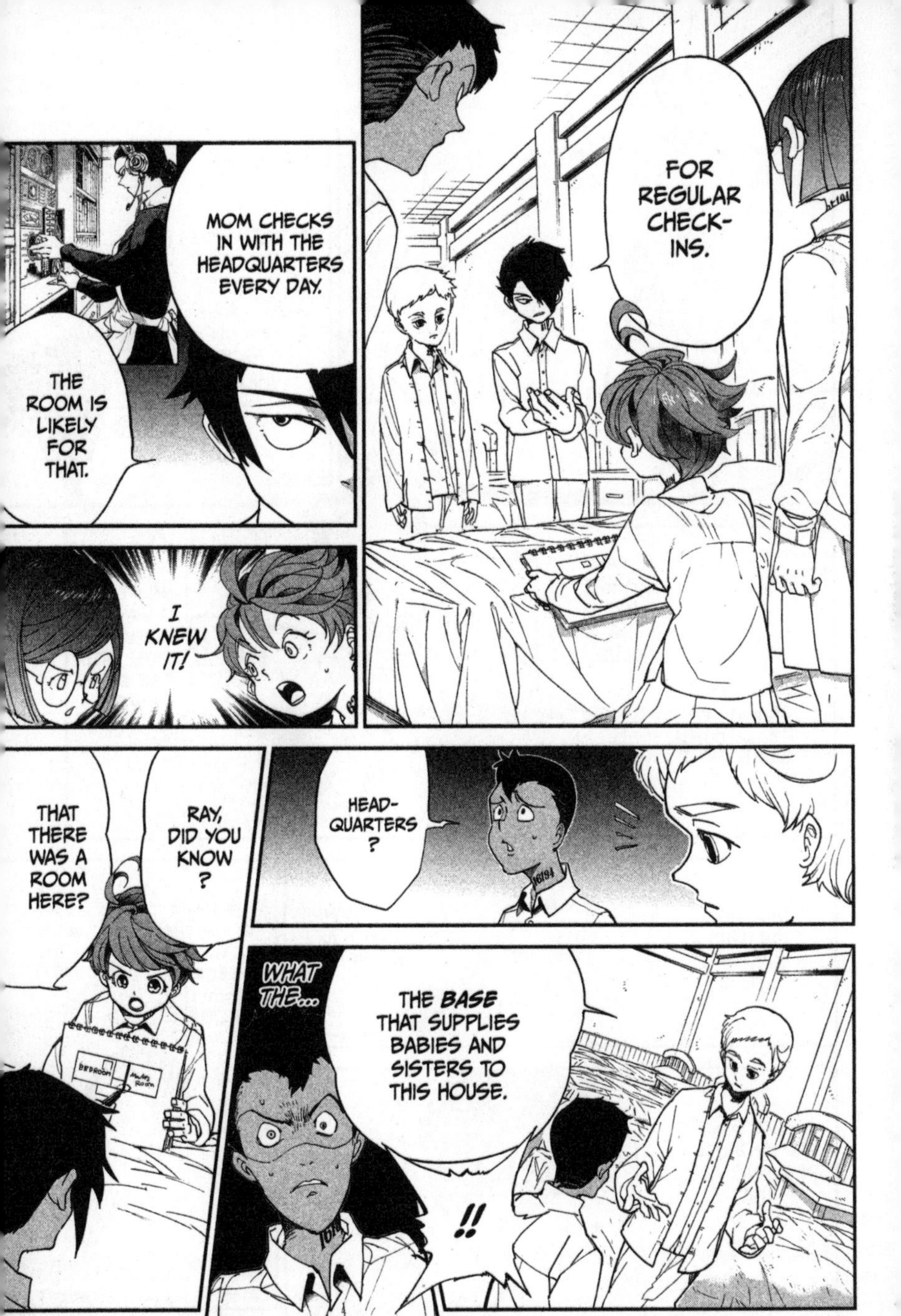
FOR REGULAR CHECK-INS.
MOM CHECKS IN WITH THE HEADQUARTERS EVERY DAY.
THE ROOM IS LIKELY FOR THAT.
I KNEW IT!
HEAD-QUARTERS?
WHAT THE...
THE BASE THAT SUPPLIES BABIES AND SISTERS TO THIS HOUSE.
!!
RAY, DID YOU KNOW?
THAT THERE WAS A ROOM HERE?

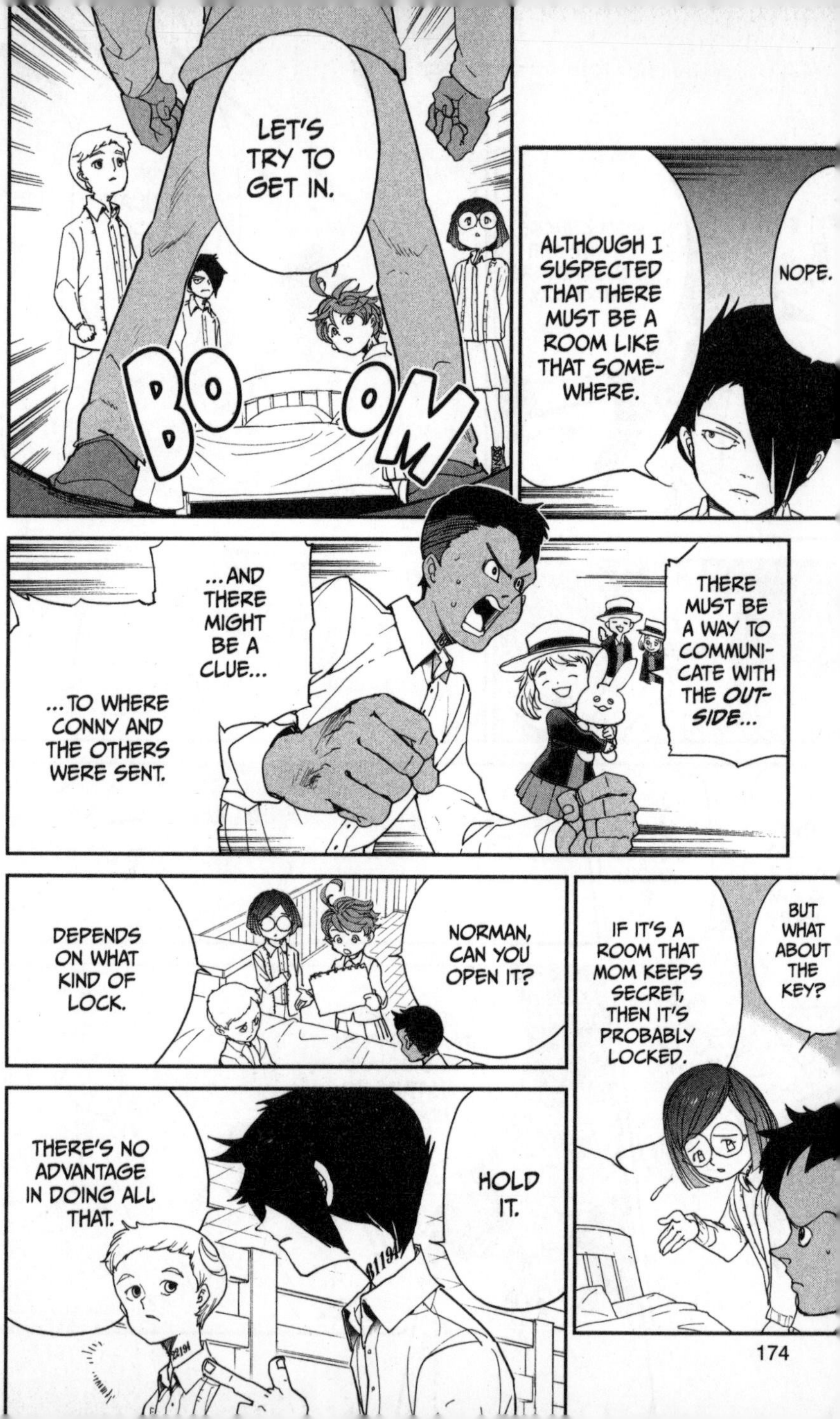
NOPE.
ALTHOUGH I SUSPECTED THAT THERE MUST BE A ROOM LIKE THAT SOME-WHERE.
LET'S TRY TO GET IN.
BOOM
THERE MUST BE A WAY TO COMMUNI-CATE WITH THE *OUT-SIDE*...
...AND THERE MIGHT BE A CLUE...
...TO WHERE CONNY AND THE OTHERS WERE SENT.
BUT WHAT ABOUT THE KEY?
IF IT'S A ROOM THAT MOM KEEPS SECRET, THEN IT'S PROBABLY LOCKED.
NORMAN, CAN YOU OPEN IT?
DEPENDS ON WHAT KIND OF LOCK.
HOLD IT.
THERE'S NO ADVANTAGE IN DOING ALL THAT.

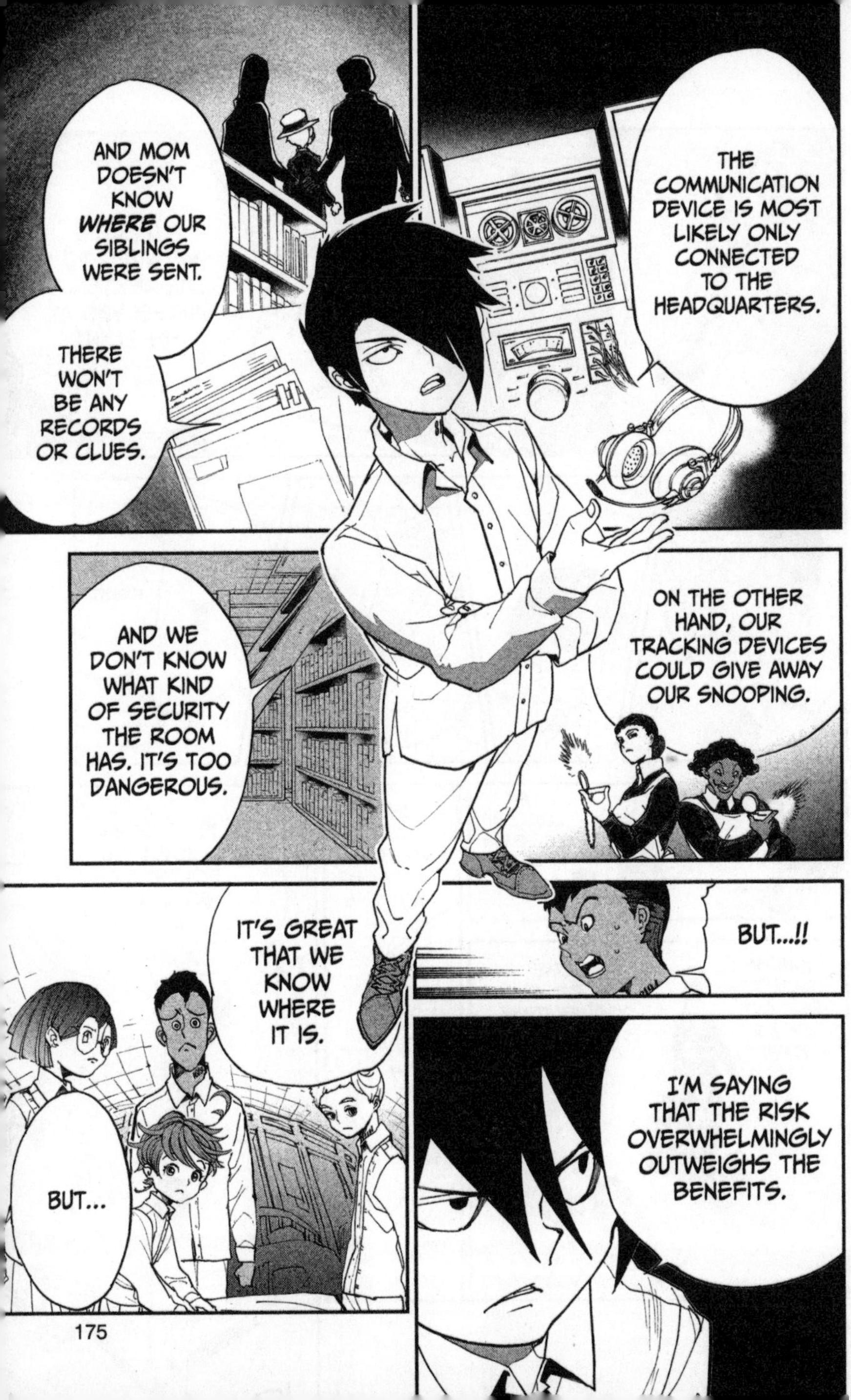
THE COMMUNICATION DEVICE IS MOST LIKELY ONLY CONNECTED TO THE HEADQUARTERS.
AND MOM DOESN'T KNOW *WHERE* OUR SIBLINGS WERE SENT.
THERE WON'T BE ANY RECORDS OR CLUES.
ON THE OTHER HAND, OUR TRACKING DEVICES COULD GIVE AWAY OUR SNOOPING.
AND WE DON'T KNOW WHAT KIND OF SECURITY THE ROOM HAS. IT'S TOO DANGEROUS.
BUT...!!
I'M SAYING THAT THE RISK OVERWHELMINGLY OUTWEIGHS THE BENEFITS.
IT'S GREAT THAT WE KNOW WHERE IT IS.
BUT...

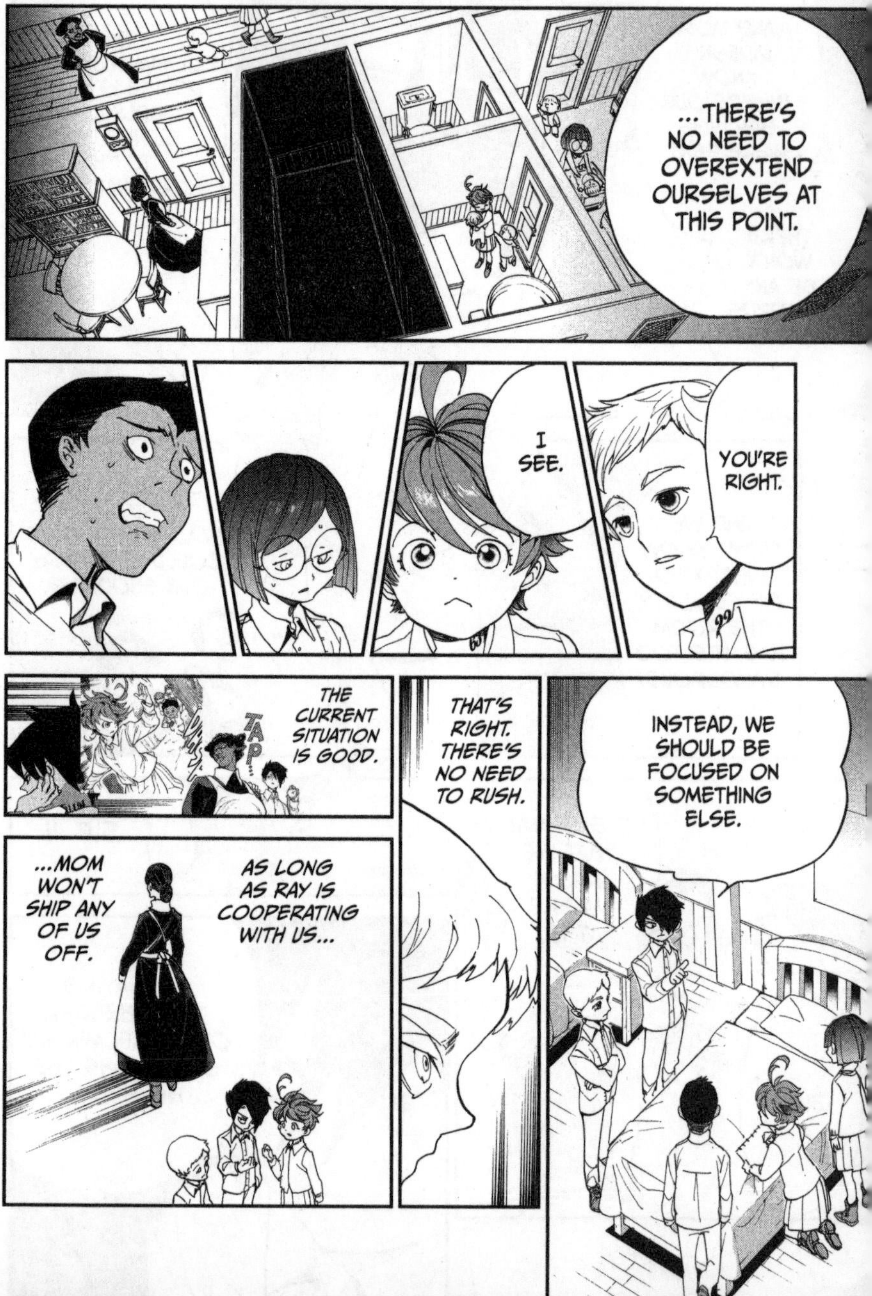
...THERE'S NO NEED TO OVEREXTEND OURSELVES AT THIS POINT.
YOU'RE RIGHT.
I SEE.
INSTEAD, WE SHOULD BE FOCUSED ON SOMETHING ELSE.
THAT'S RIGHT. THERE'S NO NEED TO RUSH.
THE CURRENT SITUATION IS GOOD.
AS LONG AS RAY IS COOPERATING WITH US...
...MOM WON'T SHIP ANY OF US OFF.

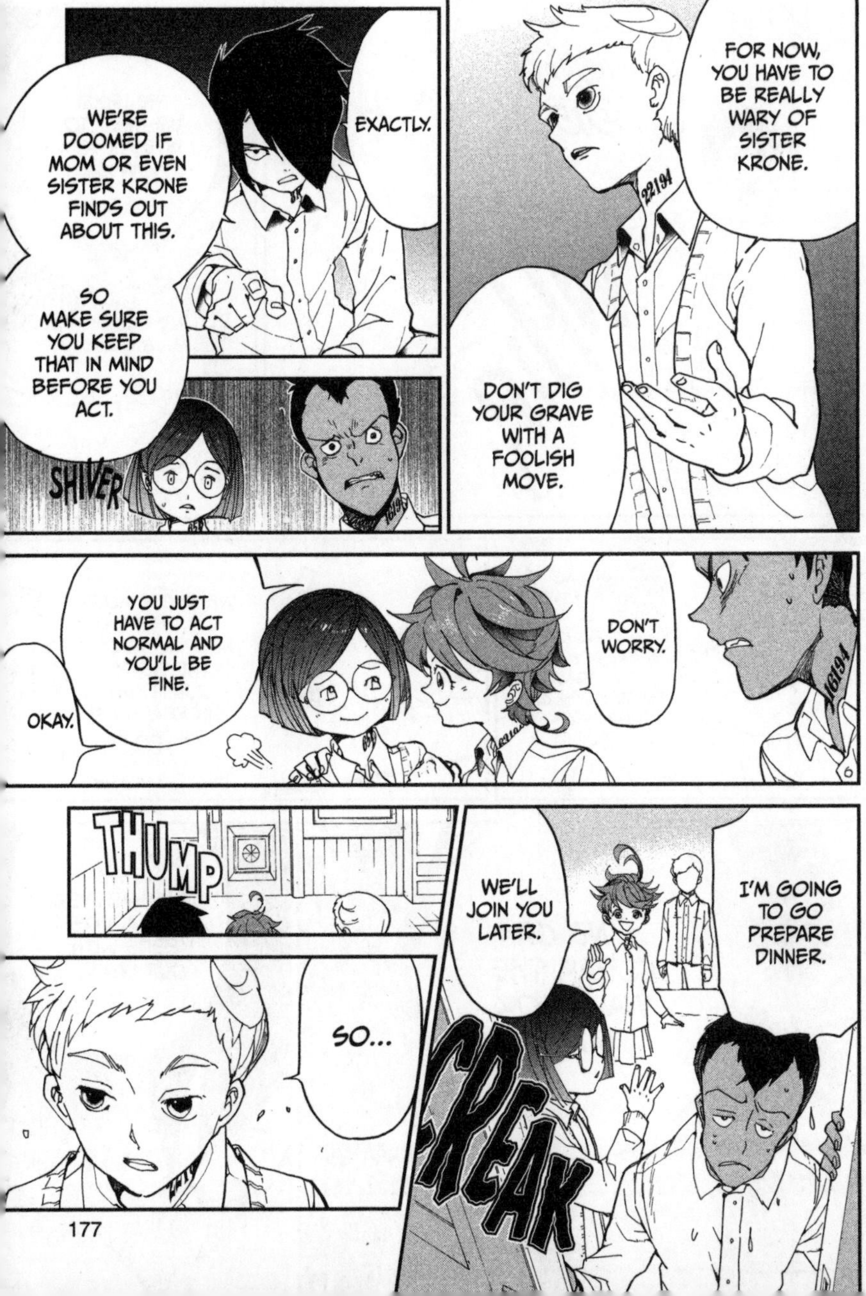
FOR NOW, YOU HAVE TO BE REALLY WARY OF SISTER KRONE.
DON'T DIG YOUR GRAVE WITH A FOOLISH MOVE.
EXACTLY.
WE'RE DOOMED IF MOM OR EVEN SISTER KRONE FINDS OUT ABOUT THIS.
SO MAKE SURE YOU KEEP THAT IN MIND BEFORE YOU ACT.
SHIVER
DON'T WORRY.
YOU JUST HAVE TO ACT NORMAL AND YOU'LL BE FINE.
OKAY.
I'M GOING TO GO PREPARE DINNER.
WE'LL JOIN YOU LATER.
CREAK
THUMP
SO...

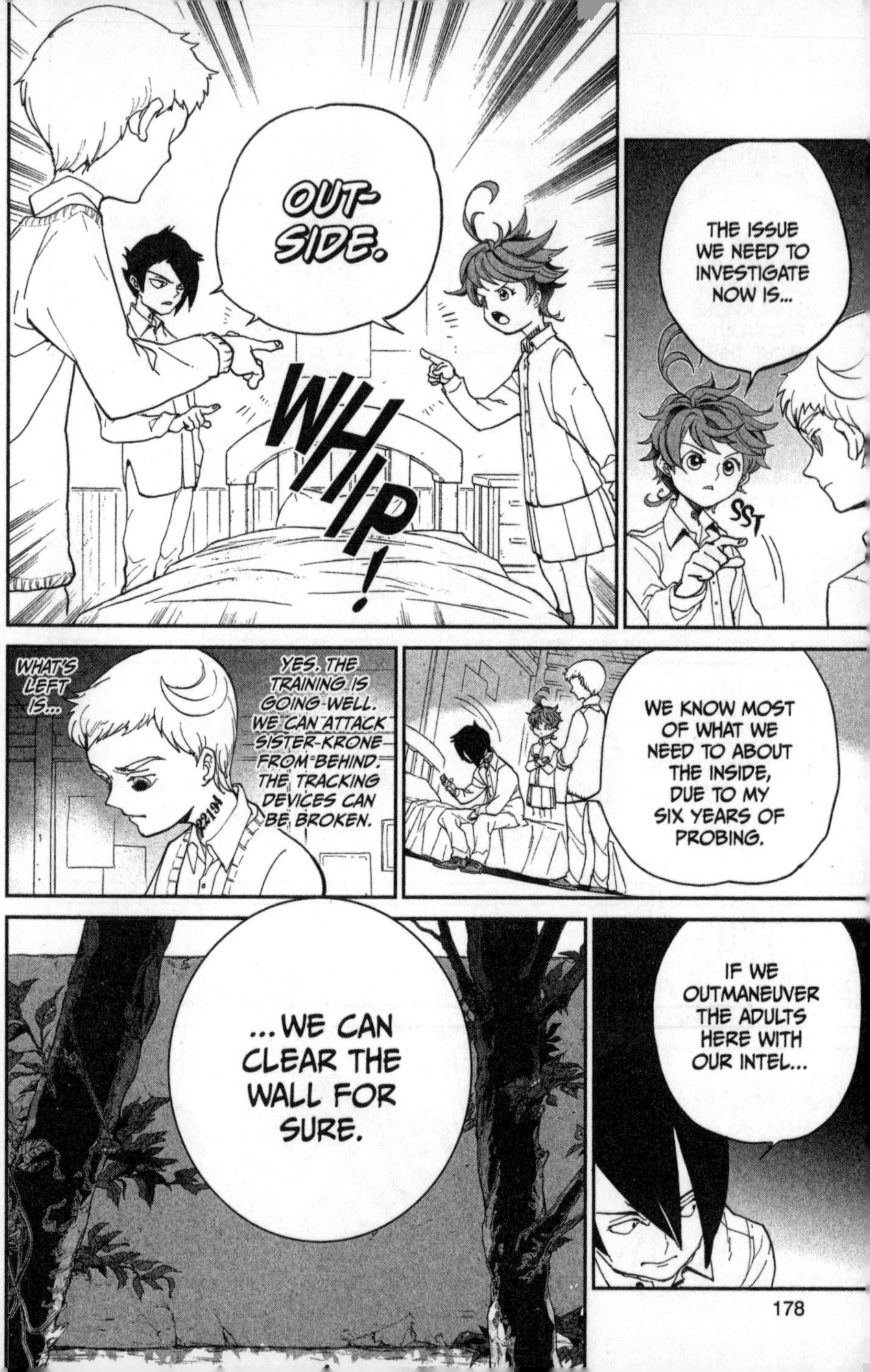
THE ISSUE WE NEED TO INVESTIGATE NOW IS...
SST
OUT-SIDE.
WHIP!
WE KNOW MOST OF WHAT WE NEED TO ABOUT THE INSIDE, DUE TO MY SIX YEARS OF PROBING.
YES. THE TRAINING IS GOING WELL. WE CAN ATTACK SISTER KRONE FROM BEHIND. THE TRACKING DEVICES CAN BE BROKEN.
WHAT'S LEFT IS...
IF WE OUTMANEUVER THE ADULTS HERE WITH OUR INTEL...
...WE CAN CLEAR THE WALL FOR SURE.

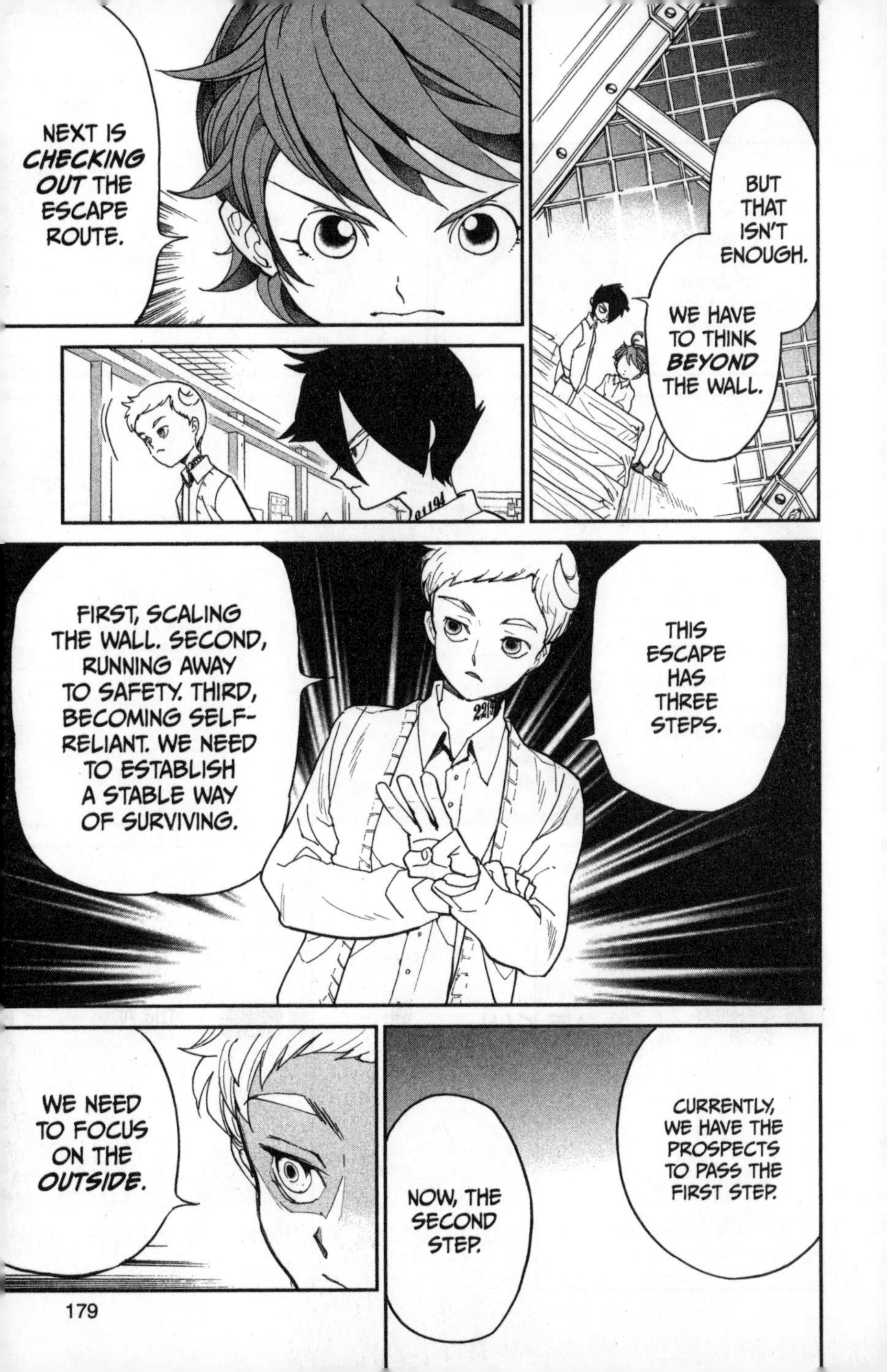
BUT THAT ISN'T ENOUGH.
WE HAVE TO THINK *BEYOND* THE WALL.
NEXT IS *CHECKING OUT* THE ESCAPE ROUTE.
THIS ESCAPE HAS THREE STEPS.
FIRST, SCALING THE WALL. SECOND, RUNNING AWAY TO SAFETY. THIRD, BECOMING SELF-RELIANT. WE NEED TO ESTABLISH A STABLE WAY OF SURVIVING.
CURRENTLY, WE HAVE THE PROSPECTS TO PASS THE FIRST STEP.
NOW, THE SECOND STEP.
WE NEED TO FOCUS ON THE *OUTSIDE*.

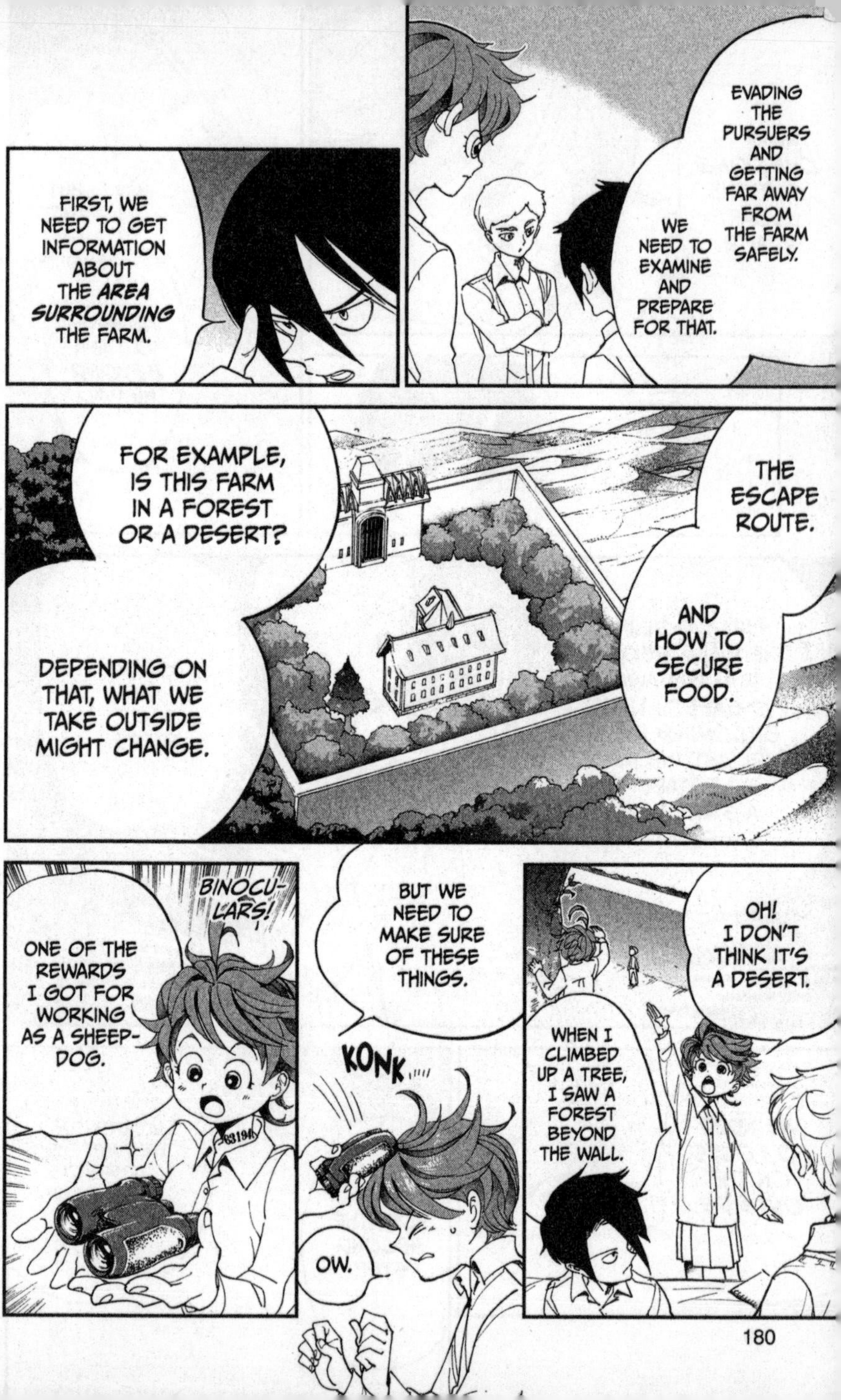
EVADING THE PURSUERS AND GETTING FAR AWAY FROM THE FARM SAFELY.
WE NEED TO EXAMINE AND PREPARE FOR THAT.
FIRST, WE NEED TO GET INFORMATION ABOUT THE *AREA SURROUNDING* THE FARM.
THE ESCAPE ROUTE.
AND HOW TO SECURE FOOD.
FOR EXAMPLE, IS THIS FARM IN A FOREST OR A DESERT?
DEPENDING ON THAT, WHAT WE TAKE OUTSIDE MIGHT CHANGE.
OH! I DON'T THINK IT'S A DESERT.
WHEN I CLIMBED UP A TREE, I SAW A FOREST BEYOND THE WALL.
BUT WE NEED TO MAKE SURE OF THESE THINGS.
KONK
OW.
BINOCU-LARS!
ONE OF THE REWARDS I GOT FOR WORKING AS A SHEEP-DOG.
63194

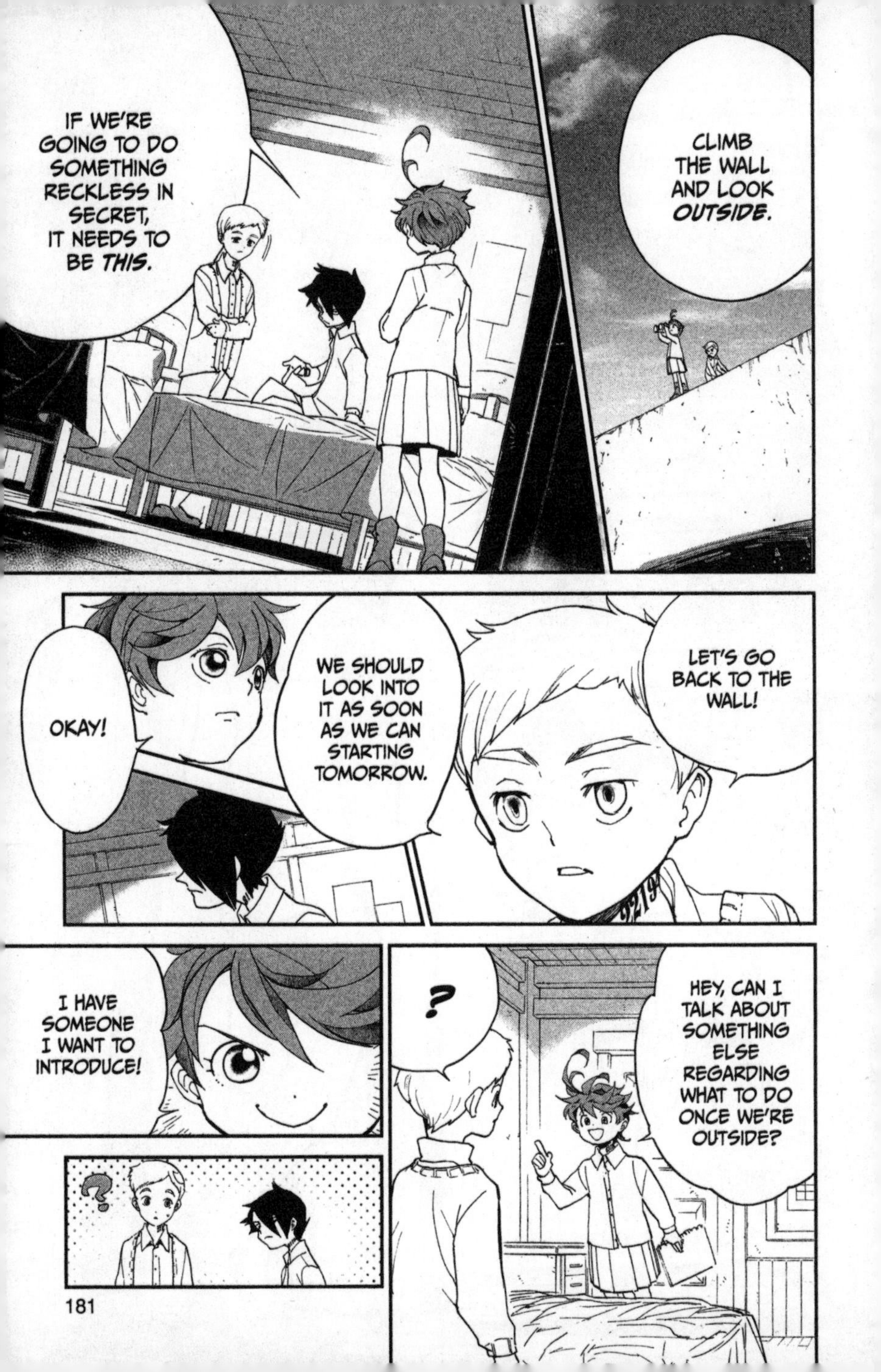
CLIMB THE WALL AND LOOK OUTSIDE.
IF WE'RE GOING TO DO SOMETHING RECKLESS IN SECRET, IT NEEDS TO BE THIS.
LET'S GO BACK TO THE WALL!
WE SHOULD LOOK INTO IT AS SOON AS WE CAN STARTING TOMORROW.
OKAY!
HEY, CAN I TALK ABOUT SOMETHING ELSE REGARDING WHAT TO DO ONCE WE'RE OUTSIDE?
?
I HAVE SOMEONE I WANT TO INTRODUCE!
?

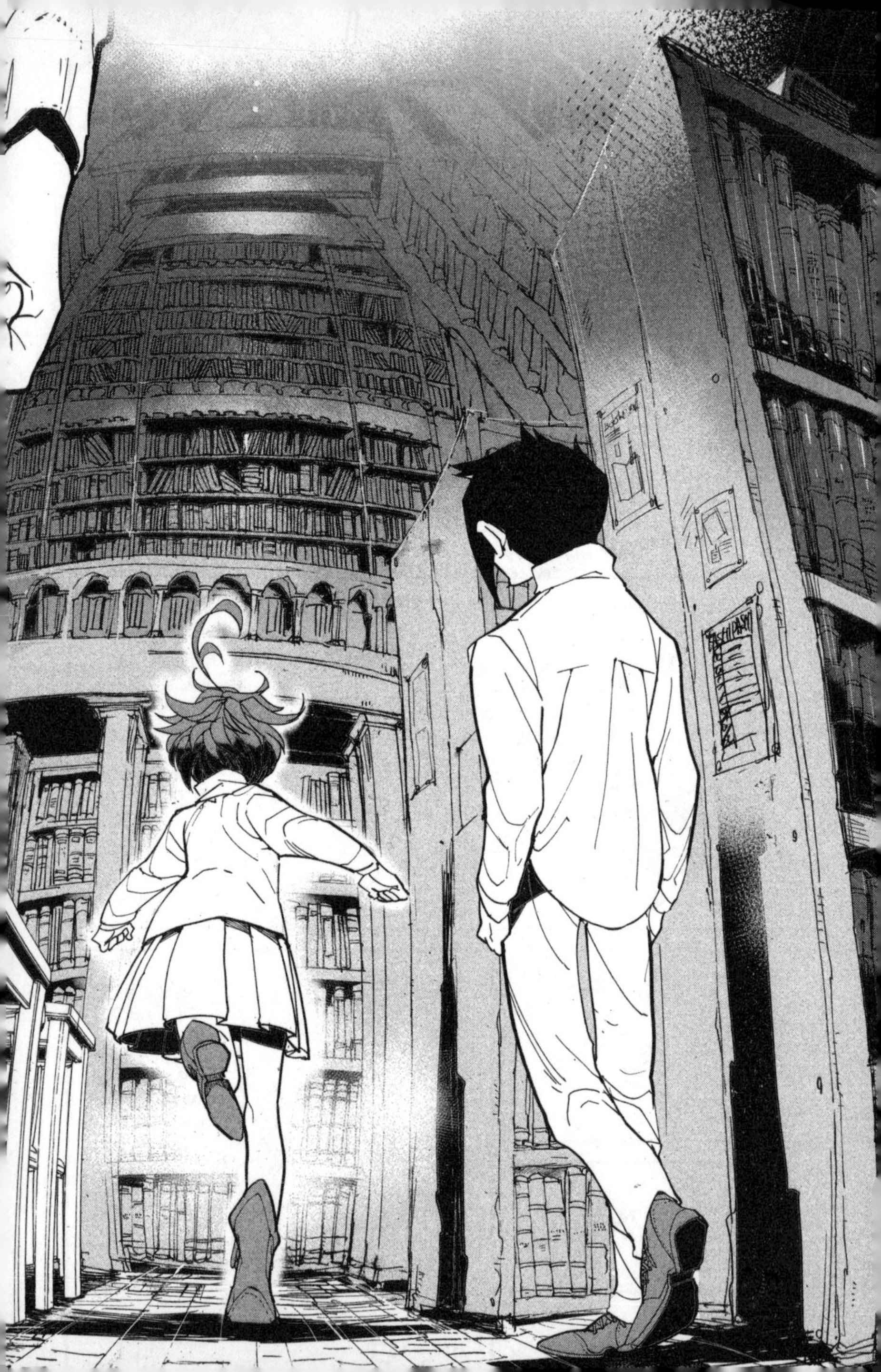